D
103
.R7

Rothrock, Geo:
Europe: a brie...

SCHOOLCRAFT COLLEGE LIBR...

3 30...   ...598

W9-CNE-047

BRADNER LIBRARY
SCHOOLCRAFT COLLEGE
LIVONIA, MICHIGAN 48152

EUROPE: A BRIEF HISTORY

EUROPE: A BRIEF HISTORY

George A. Rothrock
University of Alberta

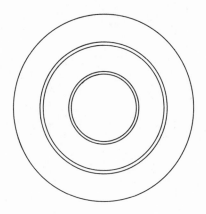

RAND MᶜNALLY & COMPANY • CHICAGO

D
103
,R7

RAND McNALLY HISTORY SERIES

Fred Harvey Harrington, *Advisory Editor*

940
R846c

Copyright © 1971 by Rand McNally & Company
All rights reserved
Printed in U.S.A. by Rand McNally & Company
Library of Congress Catalog Card Number 71–126836

For George Windell
with whom it all began

Preface

Confronted with the rich mosaic of national societies that comprise the world of the twentieth century, universities now are offering studies of the histories of many peoples and areas. Despite this wholly commendable trend, however, European history always must occupy a special place for the western student, for it is the background and foundation of his own past. It can claim consideration from non-western peoples, too, for many of the ideas and attitudes deeply affecting non-western societies in the modern world are products of western culture, from Christianity to communism. Thus, the broader range of historical studies now available may be expected to complement and enrich rather than displace European history.

There are several texts on the market that present the course of European history in one form or another, and it may be useful to suggest why the author was moved to write yet another. In general, the nature of introductory history courses has changed rather markedly in the last decade or two and textbooks have failed to keep pace with the change; perhaps a fondness for traditional patterns is the occupational hazard of the historian. I am persuaded that the courses now being presented to beginning students are much more sophisticated than was the case not very long ago. I think this development stems partly from the fact that our students are more sophisticated today and partly from two innovations: discussion groups and supplementary readings. In the recent past, reliance upon insufficient staff time resulted in courses depending almost wholly upon lectures, for few graduate students were available to cope with quantities of junior students in small groups; and supplementary readings usually entailed a chapter here and there from books placed on reserve shelves in the library, a system unsatisfactory to all concerned but unavoidable because of the cost of books. In recent years, however, the expansion of graduate study and the growth of the paperback book market have made both discussion groups and supplemental book purchase almost standard for introductory courses.

Despite these changes, textbooks today are little different in concept from those written long ago. There are undeniable improvements, such as broadened perspectives, which include social and economic history, and interpretive rather than purely factual approaches; but almost without exception texts still assume that a student's whole course must be subsumed between two covers, and that the instructor will lecture and examine from the text. This assumption and the attempt to bring a more sophisticated distillation of recent scholarly erudition to the beginning student result in rather formidable bulk and cost; a thousand to fifteen hundred pages and fifteen to twenty dollars is more or less typical to get from the fall of Rome to the middle of the twentieth century. A discouraging consequence is that an instructor must limit severely the number of paperback supplements that he can ask a student to buy and use if he has any regard for the limitations of the student's time and money.

In an attempt to avoid these frustrations, from time to time some of us have tried to run a course without a text, using a list of paperbacks instead, but the results have not been very satisfactory. The student emerges with several bits of fragmentary expertise and weak perspectives. There seems still to be a consensus among instructors of history that a summary text is highly desirable, and it was with this idea that the present book was conceived.

Another consideration that has influenced the writing of this book is my impression that the role as well as the level of sophistication of introductory history courses has changed rather radically since the Second World War. It once was fair to assume that most liberal arts students would take several history courses and that few other students would take any. Both of these assumptions now are open to serious challenge. On the one hand, the growth of new approaches to the study of human experience—in sociology, psychology and anthropology, for example—has provided meaningful competition to historical study, and working within systems of "options,"

ᐸ

many students now take only one or two history courses and sometimes none. On the other hand, more and more students from other
degree programs are turning up in history courses. In some rather
haphazard surveys made in several universities during recent years,
I have found that over half the enrollment in introductory history
courses came from outside the arts faculty. In part this trend is at-
tributable to the shift in emphasis from method to content study in
education faculties; in part it reflects a developing pattern of increased study of humanities and social sciences on the part of science
students. Whatever the reasons, many students will take only one
history course, and they will come from a variety of areas of study,
facts that should make us pause to reflect upon what the course
should accomplish.

In one way historians are singularly fortunate. A teaching department must provide its students with both scope and depth, broad
views and methodological precision. In contrast to the student in the
sciences, who must learn methodology and laboratory technique before proceeding, the history student can begin his study with either
aspect of his discipline, scope or depth, so long as he learns both
synthesis and criticism in the course of his total program. Future
history majors do not suffer by beginning with a broad view which
they will fill in with more intensive studies of particular periods and
societies, acquiring research methodology as they proceed.

An introductory history course can—and these days must—
serve many roles. For the history major it must provide a broad over-
view that will allow him to make meaningful choices of the areas in
which he wishes to concentrate and it must give perspective to his
later studies. For other students in the humanities and social sciences
it should offer a frame of reference that will add depth and understanding to studies of literature or economics or art. For the non-arts
student it should provide a background that can aid his comprehen-
sion of his own world and at the same time can challenge his ethno-
centrism by showing the validity of other societies based upon values
quite different from his own. And for the undecided student, who
might contemplate further historical studies, it should show how the
historian works, his tools and methods and materials, so the student
may judge realistically whether this is the sort of endeavor that he
would wish to pursue.

A course conscientiously structured achieves success in most of
these roles, however, if sufficient flexibility can be maintained, and

flexibility and variety are achieved best through the use of several different kinds of paperbacks. Paperback supplements can provide documentary collections to be analyzed, monographic studies to illustrate the complexity of the past, biographies to lend human perspective and "problems" books to show how interpretive theories vary. A prime goal of this book is to provide some perspectives on the European background in sufficiently small bulk and cost as to allow great flexibility in the assignment of paperbacks.

This approach offers several advantages. It should increase the utility of discussion groups, since assignments in the text will be sufficiently brief to permit the assignment of supplementary readings as the basis for group discussion. The use of several outside readings instead of just a few will make it possible to avoid overemphasizing the easy generalizations that are part of any text and to demonstrate how sharply historians disagree on the meaning of the past.

And such an approach should increase the instructor's freedom to determine the nature of the course, for the text presents only general perspectives, and areas of emphasis will depend upon the supplements selected. I envisage, for instance, that when a class comes to discuss Chapter V, which deals with the period of the Viking depredations, it might go in any of a number of directions. Instructors who consider the Vikings interesting only for their effects upon the more southerly regions of Europe may find the material presented here quite enough about the raiders themselves, but others might wish to assign a supplemental book on the Vikings. Those whose major interests lie in the British Isles may find the sketch of developments on the European continent sufficient and want to add a book on Anglo-Saxon England. Someone else may feel that western Europe is overemphasized and add readings on Kiev Rus, while yet another instructor might prefer a book on the Carolingian Empire. By the same token, in connection with Chapter IX, which concerns itself with tensions and conflicts in medieval society, choices might range widely over heresy, economic development, the apogee of the papacy or the court of Frederick II.

Thus, a course can be shaped around those elements of our European past that particular instructors find most interesting or most important, and the student can be exposed to the viewpoint of several authors. I hope this book provides the basic background while allowing whatever national or period or topical emphasis an instructor may wish to use. To this end, I have included some rather brief paperback "suggestions for further reading" which may prove convenient, but reference should be made to the full listings of *Paperbacks in Print* (dealing with the offerings of American publishers) and *Paperbound Books in Print* (British publishers) and to critical summary lists such as those in Lyon, Rowen and Hamerow, *A History of the Western World* (Rand McNally, 1969).

Obviously a book of this sort is indebted to a great many colleagues whose ideas and suggestions have helped to bring it to fruition and to the many historians on whose studies it relies. To all of these I should like to express my gratitude. I am grateful to Rand McNally's editors Larry Malley and Ted Tieken for their encouragement and help, and especially to my manuscript editor, Mrs. Laurette Hupman, whose infinite patience added so much. Particular thanks are due to L. C. DeLozier, who read and criticized the medieval chapters, and to Mrs. Elizabeth Barbour, who typed the entire manuscript. The usual bow to the author's wife is singularly appropriate in this instance, since in addition to loving patience she has contributed professional editing throughout. But most of all, I should like to thank my many undergraduate students whose questions and comments persuaded me that today's junior student is an adult who should be asked to read adult books, and that in consequence a far less massive text was needed.

GEORGE A. ROTHROCK

Edmonton, Alberta
December, 1970

Contents

Maps

Charts

Routes of the Barbarians

———	Huns	—·—·— Lombards
— — —	Visigoths	+ + + Ostrogoths
—··—··—	Vandals	+ + + Burgundians
—···—···—	Franks	+ + + Anglo-Saxons

375 —date people passed through region
200-375 —stop in region   507 —final occupation of region

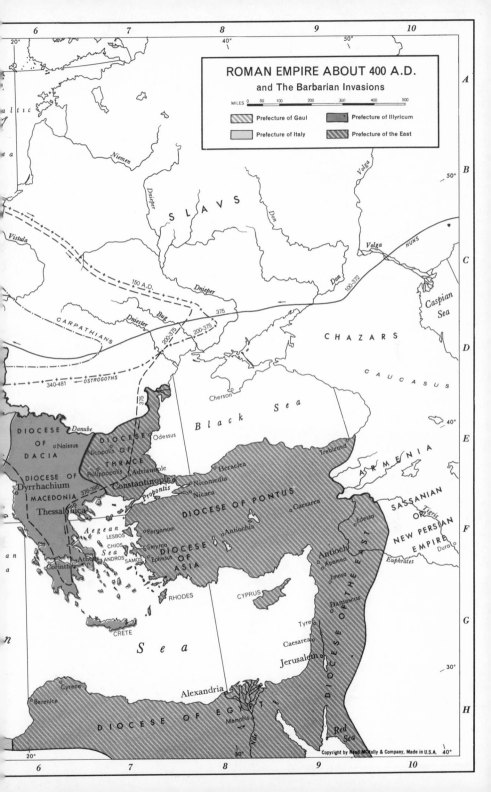

ROMAN EMPIRE ABOUT 400 A.D.
and The Barbarian Invasions

MILES 0 50 100 200 300 400 500

Prefecture of Gaul	Prefecture of Illyricum
Prefecture of Italy	Prefecture of the East

Baltic Sea

Niemen

Vistula

Dnieper

SLAVS

Don

Volga

Volga

HUNS

50°

Caspian Sea

150 A.D.

Dnieper

Bug

375

CHAZARS

100-372

CARPATHIANS

Dniester

200-375

200-375

375

CAUCASUS

340-481   OSTROGOTHS

Cherson

40°

Black Sea

DIOCESE OF DACIA

Danube

Naissus

Odessus

DIOCESE OF THRACE

Nicopolis

Philippopolis

Adrianople

Constantinople

Heraclea

Nicomedia

Nicaea

Probontis

Trebizond

ARMENIA

DIOCESE OF PONTUS

Caesarea

SASSANIAN

DIOCESE OF Dyrrhachium

376-395

MACEDONIA

Thessalonica

Pergamum

Smyrna

Ephesus

LESBOS

CHIOS

ANDROS

SAMOS

Aegean Sea

DIOCESE OF ASIA

Antiochia

Edessa

Antioch

Apamea

Emesa

NEW PERSIAN EMPIRE

OR Tigris

Dura

Athens

Corinth

RHODES

CYPRUS

Euphrates

DIOCESE OF THE EAST

Damascus

Tyre

Caesarea

Jerusalem

30°

Sea

CRETE

Cyrene

Berenice

Alexandria

Memphis

DIOCESE OF EGYPT

Nile

Red Sea

40°

Copyright by Rand McNally & Company, Made in U.S.A.

20°

30°

Chapter 1

Preliminary Considerations

The beginning student often is tempted to assume that history is a dead record of the past, and unfortunately a great deal of traditional instruction—emphasizing names and dates and battles and treaties—has tended to confirm that view. But new historical works continue to pour from the presses, and historians argue among themselves constantly. There is a dynamic, a process of continuous change in the understanding of the meaning of events.

No wholly satisfactory definition of history ever has been recorded. Descriptions have ranged all the way from Lord Acton's optimistic opinion that "history is the progress of liberty" to Henry Ford's observation that "history is bunk." Whatever else it might be, however, history is not a dead record but a living tradition, a collective memory offering some roots and a sense of continuity to men and women in any age, people who must confront the challenges and choices of their own times.

Several sorts of variables operate more or less constantly in historical scholarship. First, we continue to learn about what actually happened in the past, and new data often force changes of interpretation. For instance, the discovery and study of the famous Dead Sea Scrolls in the middle of this century has expanded greatly our understanding of life and customs and beliefs in early Palestine, with important consequences for Biblical history. The deciphering of an

1

early Minoan script some years ago added new perspectives to the study of early eastern Mediterranean societies. And recently the unearthing of an early map of Vinland has opened exciting new possibilities in the field of early Scandinavian voyages across the North Atlantic.

Moreover, other sources of knowledge have been added to the traditional basis of written records. The excavations undertaken by archeologists and the resultant analysis of physical artifacts—tools, weapons, ornaments and buildings—give us information about preliterate peoples for whom we have no written records and reinforce our studies of other peoples for whom the written record is meager. Related to these studies is the development of technical tools of great advantage; for instance, the carbon 14 dating process can be immeasurably valuable in helping to confirm estimates of dates on ancient sites. By no means do we know all that we would like to know about what happened in the past, and new knowledge may confirm or may invalidate what we long have thought we knew.

But more significant to the dynamics of historical interpretation is the transformation of our understanding of what events mean, changes that occur for a great variety of reasons. One obvious influence upon historical interpretation has been the development, during the last hundred years, of new techniques of analysis. In the late nineteenth century, Marxism, with its emphasis upon economic causation, produced more than political controversy; it forced historians to a more minute and more sophisticated analysis of the impact of economic factors upon social and political development. The psychological studies of Sigmund Freud early in this century have added enormous depth to our understanding of the complexities of personality and character, so that today one finds little of the "heroes and villains" interpretation that runs through a great deal of older work. New scholarly dimensions have been added by the work of anthropologists in comparative cultures and of sociologists in statistical analysis. So changes in historical interpretations sometimes are motivated by perspectives developed by scholars in related fields of study.

Perhaps the greatest stimulus to changing historical interpretation is the fact that we continually ask different questions of our past. It is remarked sometimes that every generation rewrites history for itself, and the remark carries a subtle implication that because history can be used to prove anything, it really proves nothing. Yet without the cynicism, the observation is valid. To a certain extent every generation *must* rewrite history, because every generation seeks perspective upon its own problems and, therefore, wants to know different things about its past. Certainly circumstances never repeat themselves sufficiently for one to be able to find in the past a definitive prescription for the ills of the present; but categories of problems recur, and at the lowest level of commonality all problems in history are problems of men in conflict with their environment and/or their fellow men. In the process of attempting to choose between competing courses of action—say between concession and repression in the face of political violence—the experience of our predecessors may aid us in making decisions.

The easiest illustration of this phenomenon is a theme that became extremely prominent in historical writing during the last two generations, the multi-national approach. It is no coincidence that many-volume integrated studies of European and world history were launched in three languages and in three different countries at roughly the same time—the years between the first and second world wars. Most histories written during the nineteenth and early twentieth centuries tended to have a distinctly national orientation, reflecting the great strength of nationalism in most European countries at that time. While conceding certain commonalities of a classical and Christian background and of modern alliances and trade, historians tended to stress the individuality and uniqueness of their own nations and to write histories of the development of national institutions and national cultures that helped to explain this individuality and uniqueness. Then the cataclysm of the Great War demonstrated irrefutably the close interconnection of the several national societies of Europe, showed clearly that whatever their differences of organization and aspiration their fates were interwoven inextricably. The need to understand better the development of Europe as a whole, the relationships among its various components, produced three new historical series: in France the *Peuples et Civilizations,* in Germany the *Propylaen Weltgeschichte* and in the United States *The Rise of Modern Europe.* All of these turned back to material often studied before, but they asked different questions of the material, and consequently they were able to offer new and different understandings of modern European history.

Another question that one must confront in any study of mankind, historical or contemporary, is the problem of free will and determinism. The problem is particularly acute when dealing with prominent or great men and women. Do individuals change the direction of their society and impose their will upon it, or are they but products of inexorable processes, puppets of economic, political and social forces? The ancients believed in the unreasoning vagaries of the gods and the fates, granting one man happiness and condemning another to tragedy quite haphazardly. Early Christians had to confront the problem too, for if they asserted the existence of an all-powerful God, how could they maintain that man had free will and, hence, the responsibility of choosing good instead of evil? (In general terms the rather complicated solution was to assert that God refrained from exercising his potentially all-determining power so as to leave mankind choice, offering the strength to choose goodness to all who sought it sincerely.) To the later medieval world the problem appeared in yet another guise. Astrology, a belief that the future could be read in the stars, was largely an import from the Moslem World and won wide support in Europe. The implications of determinism, and hence of lack of responsibility, were dangerous, but the church found a compromise, conceding that events in the physical world might be determined and their pattern revealed by God in the heavens, but asserting that man remained responsible for his moral and spiritual choices.

In more recent times determinist arguments have arisen most often from the development of the social sciences. A number of relatively recent approaches to the study of man have been quite disturbing to the supporters of free will. Psychology has demonstrated, for instance, that some human behavior is conditioned by sexual attitudes, parental relationships, and early experiences. And sociologists have been able to establish fairly accurate estimates of crowd behavior, suggesting that when a group of certain composition is confronted with a particular situation, given percentages will react in predictable ways. The proponents of free will reply, however, that psychology can predict only how an individual is likely to behave in certain categories of situations and cannot predict how a person will behave in every particular situation. By the same token, sociology can predict patterns of crowd behavior, but it cannot predict how particular individuals will behave.

Most modern students of human behavior tend to compromise between the extremes of absolute free will and complete determinism, asserting that man exercises free will within generally definable limits. In this context the social sciences may be regarded as helping to define the limits of the range of choice. Thus one might suggest that on the eve of the French Revolution the king could not have chosen to study and estimate popular discontent by holding a plebiscite and tabulating the results. This idea was wholly foreign to the structure of his society and the tools required to implement such an idea did not exist. On the other hand he did have to make significant choices—absolute repression, some combination of resistance and concession, sweeping reform. Or one may observe that in struggles for equal rights where prejudice operates against Negroes or Orientals or Jews or Catholics, only some men can choose consciously to reject their prejudices as a result of rational persuasion while others cannot make that choice because years of conditioning or deep-rooted psychological compulsions persuade them unshakably that the objects of their prejudice are inferior or evil or whatever.

* * *

Any historical study faces the serious problem of when to begin. History is an open-ended process, without a real beginning and—hopefully—without an end. There are no real openings or closings of ages or epochs, although we use these terms to indicate periods that are somewhat cohesive and somewhat distinct from what precedes and what comes after. It follows, then, that any decision to begin "here" is arbitrary and hence contestable. Such a decision turns largely on what the historian considers typical or major aspects of the period he wishes to describe.

How arbitrary and imprecise such periodization can be is illustrated well by the common division of our past into the Ancient

World, the Middle Ages and Modern Times. Presumably the ancient period endures until the fall of the Roman Empire (though as we shall see shortly even that attempt at periodization is rather vague); yet the differences between the ancient Near East of the Hittites and the Babylonians on the one hand and the Mediterranean world of the Romans on the other were enormous, and the phrase "the Ancient World" covers as much diversity as continuity. For that matter, the differences between the ancient Greeks of the city states and those of the Hellenistic world after the conquests of Alexander the Great are enough to render dubious a general designation. And the term "Middle Ages" is even more spurious. The first modern historians were enthusiastic classicists who read the literary heritage of Rome (and to a lesser extent of Greece), looked at remnants of old buildings, and decided it was all wonderful. They came to believe that modern times began with the revival and reinterpretation of the classics during the Italian renaissance. All that fell between the ancient glories and their own modern world was barbaric, degenerate, a long period of darkness which they dubbed the middle ages. The implications of an unchanging, static society, presumably little different in 1300 from what it was in 700, are quite misleading. Finally, the notion of modern encompasses a multitude of diversity, for it lumps together the sixteenth century and the twentieth century—from modified spears to atomic weapons, from manorial agriculture to industrial society, from Latin clerks to computers.

Yet there are conventions of usage, and little would be gained by discarding an accepted terminology and replacing it with a new jargon that might appear equally ill-conceived a few generations hence. Let it suffice to remember that when we speak of ages and epochs, we are not opening and closing doors upon separate compartments of our past, but only trying to impose order upon a chaotic mass of material that has its beginnings in the mists of a very distant past and continues into the future, and that all such decisions are rather arbitrary.

But we must begin somewhere. Our task is to delineate some major patterns in European history, so we must decide when the history of Europe began. And good arguments can be found for an assertion that the patterns of a distinctively European civilization began to emerge during the later Roman Empire, in the period of roughly the third to fifth centuries. A number of considerations support such an assertion. First, the Mediterranean Sea was the center of the Roman world, but it is only a border of Europe. Hence, the period during which the lands north of the Mediterranean basin were developing enough uniqueness to be considered apart from—though related to—Mediterranean civilization appears a reasonable time to begin. Secondly, the socioeconomic patterns of medieval Europe differed sharply from those of the Roman world; the breakdown of the urban and commercial patterns of classical civilization and the emergence of the rural and agrarian patterns of early medieval Europe reinforce the choice of the later imperial period. Thirdly, a cultural transformation entailing such diverse matters as the decline of classical philosophy, a growth of otherworldly religions, a transition from creative to imitative literature and the rise to social and governmental preeminence of people only semi-Romanized (in the sense of assimilation into the older classical culture)—this transformation further supports the impression of an age of transition. Undeniably classical civilization has had a marked effect upon Europe, and it may be argued that this book slights it unfairly, but the impact was largely the result of revival and reinterpretation during the Italian renaissance and the eighteenth century classical revival; the direct influence was slight, largely limited to the administrative and judicial patterns which survived much modified as part of the Christian church. And the development of the church itself, as it assumed the important role that it was to continue to play for centuries, further endorses the choice of the late imperial period. Finally, many other factors could be cited, for example, means of transportation and patterns of land tenure. The point is that all of these arguments are sound—and all of them face sound counter-arguments. This study begins in the third to fifth centuries because the author finds these arguments persuasive, not because they are definitive.

Even after choosing a starting point, another decision must be confronted: what threads from the past does one bring forward to weave the tapestry of historical narrative? Here all the problems considered in discussing interpretation become meaningful.

Most historians have looked to two great sources for the background of European history: the Greco-Roman and the Judeo-Christian traditions. There were many reasons for this, some of them excellent. First, it was for these traditions that the fullest record existed—the classical literary heritage on the one hand and Scripture and church records on the other. Secondly, most European historians have been Christians, and for many generations a modern education meant study of the classics: thus, by their faith and their early training they were prejudiced in favor of Christianity and classicism. These interests, however, have caused us to ignore almost wholly the Celtic and Germanic backgrounds of Europe. Nationalistic enthusiasms in the nineteenth century did evoke some assertions—often exaggerated—of the importance of Germanic traditions, but on the whole it is still true that the contributions of the northern European peoples have been ignored systematically. In all fairness it should be noted that before the Roman conquest both the Celts and the Germans were preliterate peoples, and archeology is a relatively young discipline (and the historian's interest in its results even younger). Until very recently it has been next to impossible for the historian, who normally relies upon written records, to glean more than vague impressions of these peoples from the few comments about them left by their Roman neighbors. Of earlier peoples absorbed by the Celts, only names remain to us, such as Ligurians and Iberians.

The only very extensive Roman description of the Celts is Caesar's *Commentaries on the Gallic Wars* in the middle of the first century B.C., and as a source this book presents serious problems. In the first place it presents Celtic society in the last years of its independence, but by that time many of the Celtic peoples had had long contact with the Romans and had been influenced by them considerably. The only Celts among whom Caesar moved very freely were allies of the Romans, those most likely to show Roman influence. Secondly, there were problems of bias. Caesar obviously liked the Celts as people, but he arrived as a conqueror, hardly a role best suited to objective analysis. And Caesar had his own interests to advance; he was politically ambitious, and his book was intended to serve that ambition. For his own political credit he wanted to emphasize the warlike qualities of the Celts to enhance his victories. And to magnify the value to Rome of his conquests, he was eager to stress the potential contribution of these people to the empire. Thus, he tended to portray them as noble savages—primitive and ferocious, but clever, brave and honorable. His work is very valuable for its uniqueness, but it must be used cautiously.

Two Roman sources exist for the early Germans, but again they present a problem. Once more Caesar is prominent; his *Commentaries* give brief descriptions of the Germans whom he met in battle, whom he captured, whose lands he visited on brief reconnaissance patrols. But his observations are sketchy, and again his bias is important. The German pressure on the Celts was one of the excuses for Roman intervention and Caesar's campaigns that ended in conquest. To both the Romans and the Celts Caesar wished to show himself as the protector. So the Germans were the enemy. He stressed their primitivism and savagery and exaggerated their differences from the peoples whom he wished to incorporate into the empire.

The other Roman source for the Germans is equally difficult to use, the *Germania* of Tacitus, written about a century after Caesar. First, Tacitus was not an observer; he compiled his account from information supplied by travelers back from the north. Second, he was a social critic of what he considered the degeneracy of the Romans, so he tended to idealize the bravery and the warriors' code of his Germans to heighten the contrast. Thus the written record offers no very reliable account of these early peoples.

The consequences of these historiographic patterns have been unfortunate. A general impression seems to exist that Europe was a land of extremely primitive barbarians called Celts, who were finally conquered and civilized by the Romans. Then more fierce primitives, Germans, swept in and destroyed this civilization, so that all reverted to barbarism until the influence of the church again produced a civilizing effect. Nothing could be farther from the truth.

We shall have a word to say later about the Germans and their relations with the Roman world, for they belong chiefly to our period of beginnings. And of course the mingling of classical and Judeo-Christian traditions will constitute a major element in our consideration of the later Roman Empire. But it is appropriate to say a few words here about the Celts, the peoples whose culture dominated Europe while the Greeks and Romans were building their civilizations in the Mediterranean basin. For though they lie farther back in time than most of the beginnings with which we will be concerned, they also contributed cultural patterns to the great matrix that was to become European tradition.

The usage by the Greeks and Romans of the word "barbarian" has had unfortunate effects for the modern student, for the connotations of the word have changed. To the Greeks and Romans the word simply designated the "they" in a pattern of "we and they," and the word certainly was no insult. Those who were not of the Greco-Roman cultural tradition were barbarians. But between the two civilizations, Celtic and classical, the differences were less significant than usually is assumed.

But for the single feature of a written language, and the important consequence of a surviving literature, the Mediterranean peoples enjoyed no great advantages over the Celts. The former excelled in their use of stone for building while the Celts built mostly of wood (often richly carved, one should note), but on the other hand Celtic metalwork clearly was superior and found a large Mediterranean market for products ranging from swords to bronze and gold jewelry. The Mediterranean peoples introduced the grape and wine to Europe, but it appears to have been Celtic carpenters who first built wooden barrels to store it, replacing the excessively fragile pottery amphoras of the Mediterranean. Celtic religion, a polytheistic cult, was presided over by Druid priests who were also educators and judges and seems no more primitive than that of the Greeks and Romans. And the Celts appear to have been as great travelers as their Mediterranean neighbors, trading tin and lead from the British Isles and metalwork, timber and smoked meats from Europe into the Mediterranean basin. Some hired out as mercenary soldiers, fighting in places as far from their northern forests as the Greek islands and Egypt. They never developed the effective military discipline of the Greeks and Romans, but as individual soldiers they had a high reputation, and their weapons were much admired. Celtic social structure greatly resembled that of the southern peoples, with an aristocracy of priests and warriors, a lesser class of free farmers and a social base of masses of slaves. Towns of considerable size existed, sited defensively and enclosed by strong walls that evoked even Caesar's admiration, though the Celtic nobility seems to have preferred living on country estates as did many Roman aristocrats.

That such a people, who settled most of Europe two to five thousand years before the Romans came into the area, should have left no significant influence is beyond belief, but their contribution is only beginning to be understood. After the Roman conquest of Gaul, in the middle of the first century B.C., the Celts on the European continent adapted quickly to Roman culture in government, language and religion—eventually adopting Christianity along with the rest of the Roman world. In England, Celtic civilization was little touched by the later rather superficial Roman occupation and endured until displaced by German (Anglo-Saxon) invaders, a process not completed until several centuries later, while Ireland continued as a Christian Celtic society into modern times.

As war, diplomacy, government and religion long have been the major interests of historians, the inattention to Celtic contributions to European culture is perhaps understandable, for it is in the folk culture that Celtic traditions seem to have survived, in such things as wearing trousers and boots rather than tunics and sandals, in the use of butter instead of olive oil for cooking, in love of country life. Simple festivals also seem to have old roots—as maypole dances, which appear to trace to some sort of phallic worship associated with spring fertility rites, and barbeques and beer. These things seem a minor counterpoint to such themes as war and religion, but until quite recently, at least, they influenced profoundly the way western peoples ate and drank and dressed and lived, and they should not be ignored.

In the period of about the third to fifth centuries, then, western Europe was populated by a mixture of Celts and Mediterranean peoples governed under the authority of the Roman Empire. Its civilization was a mixture of Celtic folkways and classical formal culture. It was reasonably prosperous, with an economy based upon flourishing agriculture, some manufactures and some exports. And in this society, a primitive Christian church was developing a channel through which a Judaic tradition would be added to the rich cultural mix. But troubles were developing which would rip apart the seemingly invincible empire, and western Europe as part of the empire was to experience its full share of those troubles. So before moving ahead into times of trial that were to shake Europe to its foundations and from which it would emerge as an independent society, we must consider briefly the Roman Empire.

Chapter 2

The Twilight of
the Roman Empire

The Roman Empire is difficult for the student to understand, both because it was very different from modern societies and because it has been idealized beyond recognition by classicists. Hence, to study its heritage and to make sense of the very complex process usually called "the fall of the Roman Empire," it is necessary to start with some quite elementary considerations of what the empire was and, just as important, what it was not.

First of all, it must be recognized that the empire never was united wholly, never was integrated into a socioeconomic entity. The only really unified aspects of the empire were military and, to a lesser extent, political. Roman armies had conquered a vast territory that centered on the Mediterranean Sea, but most of the time the Romans demanded only two things of subjected peoples: that they pay their taxes and keep the peace. One well-known example will serve for illustration. Roman troops were stationed in conquered Palestine, but the country was administered by the Jewish King Herod. When Jesus stirred controversy and was arrested, the Romans lent enforcement officers, but he was charged under Jewish law and tried in a Jewish court. Because the Jews were restive under Roman rule and prone to riot, the Romans reserved the right to review all capital sentences, so the prisoner was sent before Pontius Pilate. It is significant that even confronted with what he personally considered a gross miscarriage of justice, the Roman governor refused to interfere with local authorities and ceremonially washed his hands of the whole affair. Only a threat to Roman interests in policy or taxation would have justified intervention, for at that time the Roman Empire was an association of extremely diverse societies which maintained their own laws and customs.

Economic development never progressed very far either. The Mediterranean basin was largely homogenous, and consequently there was no great regional variation in products. Meats, grains, wines and olive oil were produced throughout the Roman world, so trade in these goods more or less was limited to a few large state enterprises that fed the armies and the large population of Rome. Conditions of transport also impeded trade, for despite fine road-building techniques and control of the Mediterranean, simple carts and small ships allowed little exploitation of these potential advantages. Hence, transportation of bulk goods required heavy capitalization by the state, as did trade in heavy building materials such as stone and marble. Under such conditions, private trade tended toward luxury goods of small bulk and high value, such as gems and fine cloth, with the consequence that the empire had only a very small middle class standing between its governing landed aristocracy and its mass of small proprietors, landless sharecroppers and slaves. These conditions should be kept in mind in any consideration of the Roman Empire, for such a consideration must recognize that Roman government sat atop enormous social diversity and that, given regional self-sufficiency, the government was not reinforced by any significant economic integration.

Basically, the Roman Empire was a military and political net flung across the Mediterranean, so consideration of the relationships between military and political authority offers a better understanding of it. The most important single fact about the later Roman Empire is that it had become a military despotism in which political authority depended upon military power, a state of affairs that had developed out of a series of crises.

The roots of the fusion of political and military power can be traced back into pre-imperial times, to the Roman Republic which ended in the last half-century before the birth of Jesus. Political power in the republic was vested in assemblies and officers responsible to the free Roman citizenry, with the preponderance of influence resting with an aristocracy. There was little that was democratic about this arrangement, for a large part of the populace was composed of slaves who had no political rights, and high office usually was a prerogative of the wealthy and well-born, but there was a certain responsiveness to the will of the free citizenry. All through Roman history, however, those who aspired to political success normally had to achieve some military reputation first, for many competing peoples lived around the shores of the Mediterranean, and Rome had to fight to survive. In the last century of the republic, political rivalry between Rome's common citizenry and her aristocracy erupted into civil war, and to reestablish stability the republic adopted the practice of granting extraordinary powers to a few prominent men, often popular generals who could depend upon the loyalty of their troops. Some Romans, recognizing the dangers of this practice, foresaw that some day the military dictators might refuse to obey the political authorities, but their voices went unheeded. And in the middle of the last century before the Christian era such a man emerged, Julius Caesar.

Caesar was a very able, very ambitious and very ruthless member of an old Roman family. By blatantly corrupt administration, he made a personal fortune as governor of part of conquered Spain and then used his wealth and connections to obtain the crucial military command of Roman Gaul, which became his stepping-stone to dictatorial power. When he assumed his command, Roman Gaul comprised only a bit of territory on the Italian side of the Alps and a sort of frontier colony at the mouth of the Rhone River around the port of Marseilles; but it was a very important command, for the fierce Celtic tribes whom the Romans called Gauls had to pass that way to attack the Roman homelands in Italy. Caesar, who proved to be a military genius, not only held this vulnerable position but went over to the offensive and conquered all of Gaul (in modern times France plus considerable parts of Belgium, Germany and Switzerland) and with a keen sense of public relations he immortalized his own campaigns in his *Commentaries on the Gallic Wars*. His conquest of Gaul made him a hero to his troops and to the Roman populace, and he used his popularity and power to subvert the republic.

In all fairness it should be noted that the republic may have been small loss. The senate had become an arena of bickering factions incapable of governing, incapable of controlling administrative corruption and incapable of maintaining the security of either the frontiers or the streets of Rome. Caesar already was a prominent political figure, and in 49 B.C. he simply marched into Italy with his loyal army from Gaul, drove out his rivals and took all the power into his own hands.

For the next four or five hundred years the pattern set by Caesar continued as the heart of the Roman political process. Emperors came to power because the army supported them, and though they often maintained the pretext of political institutions, these slowly were subordinated to a secretariat dependent upon the emperor's military might. But if the army could make emperors, it could also unmake them, or try to, and different units of the army might give their loyalty to different aspirants to the imperial throne. Thus the empire saw many civil wars, the most vicious of which occurred in the third century. It was attempts to solve the great crises of the third century that gave final form to the empire until its collapse in the west, and that form was a military despotism in which the whole populace and every political institution existed only to maintain the army, and the army had little purpose except to maintain itself.

The chaos of the third century was ominously far-reaching, for a military problem was developing on the frontiers that was quite as serious as the civil wars. The Roman armies had pushed south, west and north to the limits of practical and profitable conquest. South of the empire stretched the African desert; on the west the empire reached the Atlantic and the British Isles, excepting only the wild country of Cornwall, Wales, Ireland and Scotland; to the north the frontier rested rather solidly upon the Rhine and Danube Rivers. But to the east, a satisfactory military frontier never had been achieved, and in the third century Rome's eastern territories were threatened by the new and aggressive Persian Empire, while at the same time the German peoples of central Europe became more restive and pressed with greater frequency and determination upon the northern borders. The problem of trying to defend the terribly long frontiers of the Roman world was made even more difficult by the lack of any orderly process of succession to the imperial authority. Until the beginning of the reign of Diocletian in A.D. 284, no third century emperor ruled as long as twenty years; only two ruled more than ten years; fifteen ruled for periods of one to six years; and almost every succession was disputed. With government so confused, supply and pay of the army became chaotic; mutinies were not uncommon, and troops often intervened in politics to support the ambitions of a would-be emperor who promised to pay them. Taxation became increasingly heavy in the face of so many problems, but because of poor administration little was accomplished. Then an economic collapse set in, due in part at least to the combination of civil war and oppressive taxation.

Rome's changing military position aggravated all these conditions and generated still more problems. Campaigns under the late republic and early empire had resulted in conquests, which provided wealth in the form of booty, slaves and new tax resources to finance new campaigns. But by the third century, Rome was fighting on the defensive and had to meet the costs from her own resources. Moreover, the primacy of military concerns and the fundamentally military basis of imperial authority meant that usually the chief interest, and often the only talent, of even the more able emperors was military command. Hence, the economic situation worsened and political disintegration became marked under the government of heads of state who did not know how to grapple with these problems. Sometimes the emperors were good soldiers, but rarely were they competent statesmen.

At this low point in Rome's fortune the empire was reinvigorated and perhaps saved from extinction by two very able emperors, Diocletian (284–305) and Constantine (306–337). They achieved a total administrative reorganization which practically turned it into one great military camp. Recognizing that the empire was too large for effective management by one man, Diocletian divided it into eastern and western portions and chose a co-emperor; then he took up residence in the east while his co-emperor governed in the west. It should be emphasized, however, that the new arrangement was only a division of responsibility, not a partition. In theory the two emperors enjoyed equal authority throughout the empire, and edicts appeared over both names. In an attempt to ease the critical succession problem, both emperors chose assistants called Caesars who were to succeed them; this was appealing in theory, but it did not take into account those impatient Caesars who might try to hasten the succession or rivals who might not wish to share authority. Thus Con-

stantine, who was not a Caesar, came to the throne through hereditary claims and civil war and appointed no co-emperor. After
Constantine's death, Diocletian's system was practiced again from
time to time but with indifferent results, and Rome never found a
way to regularize the imperial succession.

To implement the imperial will, Diocletian and Constantine organized two great bureaucracies, one military and one civil, and to
meet the pressing necessities of frontier defense they increased the
military establishment by several expedients. It was not possible to
recruit or pay enough professional soldiers from the population of
the empire, so the old legions were supplemented by small permanent garrisons of soldier-farmers established along the frontiers;
these troops were backed up by mobile forces which could be
rushed to threatened points while the permanent garrisons tried to
blunt an attack and delay an invasion. In this context, heavily armed
cavalry became ever more important, and many bands of foreign
mercenaries were hired, a practice for which there were many precedents since traditionally the Roman forces were primarily heavy infantry. By these innovations Diocletian and Constantine succeeded
in raising Rome's armies to about half a million men, a considerable
increase over the three hundred thousand that they had averaged
before the third century civil wars, but Rome paid a heavy price for
increased numbers.

Although the empire long had welcomed foreign recruits in its
armies, usually they had come as individuals or in small groups, and
slowly they had been Romanized. The employment of large groups
of undisciplined tribesmen in separate units and of parttime soldiers,
Roman or foreign, lowered the overall standards of training in the
army and gave military importance, with implicit political influence,
to unassimilated mercenary chieftains. Contrary to popular impressions, it is unlikely that the new arrangements had a very great effect
upon the morale and the loyalty of the army, for the pattern of the
revolts and civil wars of the legionaries of the third century suggests
that like mercenaries they responded more to their paymasters than
to any patriotism or dedication to the Roman Empire. But there is
little doubt that the increased size of the army meant reduced military efficiency and discipline.

A fundamental reorganization, not only of civil administration
but of society itself, was required in order to pay for this large army,
in the declining economy of the time. Only high officials of the im-

perial government, who rapidly came to constitute a land-owning, tax-exempt aristocratic class, escaped crushing burdens. The rest of the society was organized along military lines and was governed by a civil administration whose chief purpose was to extract the taxes necessary to support the army. The currency had collapsed, so taxes were taken mostly in kind (goods) and were assessed upon both property and labor; small property owners and tradesmen bore most of the burden. Since municipal officials were most susceptible to legal processes, they were made responsible for collecting from their neighbors, and they had to make up deficits personally. As a result of unrealistic assessments and collective responsibility, small owners, tradesmen and town officials tried to abandon their farms, businesses and offices to flee, becoming soldiers or monks or bondsmen on aristocratic estates. Imperial response was swift and vigorous. Men were forbidden under heavy penalties to leave their crafts and trades and offices, and these obligations were made hereditary. The result was a rigid caste system supervised by an elaborate bureaucracy, all existing to support the army and the imperial government.

Constantine introduced another major innovation to the empire when he was converted to Christianity and gave imperial support to the spread of the new faith. Historical judgments of his policy have ranged from acceptance of his sincerity to cynical estimates of the advantages he may have anticipated, but probably his personal conversion was a matter of faith and his encouragement of Christianity proceeded from his convictions and from his hope that a dynamic and idealistic religion could help to bind the empire together. If this be true, it suggests that the emperor recognized that some moral force was necessary to undergird the governmental reorganization.

During the next century and a half the organization of the empire changed little. The more or less constant struggle with the Persians necessitated the concentration of the empire's best military forces on the eastern borders, while at the same time economic recovery progressed more rapidly in the area of the eastern Mediterranean than it did in the west. Thus, slowly the Greek-speaking eastern part of the empire became relatively more important, and when Germanic invaders began to cross the frontiers to plunder the northern and western Roman lands late in the fourth century, little help could be spared from the east. The only solution was to employ still more bands of tribesmen as mercenary allies. Thus barbarian chieftains with the titles of Roman generals came to fight other barbarian chieftains for control of Rome's western provinces, and while those provinces were pillaged the victors made and unmade emperors.

Perhaps the most salient feature of the new military expedients was that they were not very effective. Late in the fourth century a Germanic people called the Visigoths defeated a Roman army and ravaged the Balkans; early in the fifth century they crossed into Italy, where they sacked the city of Rome in 410, following which they wandered into southern Gaul. About the same time Gaul was overrun by other tribes, of whom the Vandals and the Burgundians were the most notable. Behind them, pressing westward, were the fierce Asiatic people known as the Huns, who fell upon the western empire in the middle of the fifth century. Rome's few successes in repulsing these raiders were won mostly by Germanic commanders in her service. Thus the empire's most successful defender at the end of the fourth and beginning of the fifth century was the Vandal Stilicho, and in the middle of the fifth century the Visigothic leader Theodoric played a major part in defeating the Huns. But despite occasional successes the western empire suffered grievously. Rome was sacked again in 455, this time by the Vandals, and all through the fifth century ill-disciplined armies wandered back and forth. By and large the population of the Roman empire met the invaders with indifference. Since the oppressive imperial government benefitted no one but the politico-military aristocracy, the mass of the populace had no motive to defend it.

Some of the Germanic tribes settled and established kingdoms within the old boundaries of the empire, and the emperors—helpless to do otherwise—legitimatized their rule by giving them imperial titles. Clearly the west was in serious trouble, but the deposition of Emperor Romulus Augustus in 476, traditionally considered the end of the Roman Empire, probably had no particular significance for contemporaries. Another emperor, Zeno, ruled in the east, and there was no reason to assume that the western title would not be restored. Such things had happened many times. Roman civilization did not so much "fall" as crumble away, and many historical arguments have turned around the questions of what it was that disappeared, and when, and why.

The first modern students to take very serious interest in the history of the ancient world were scholars of the Italian Renaissance, beginning in the fourteenth century, and their interest turned mostly to classical literature. The Renaissance scholars were rather hostile toward supernatural religion, so they tended to identify the waning of classical philosophy and literature with the rise of Christianity. Even though they had to admit a weak revival of classical literature under the restored empire of the fourth century, they tended at least implicitly to equate the decline of Rome with the growth of Christianity; and they saw in the later empire only an increasingly barbarized remnant of a once great classical civilization. In this context, the Germanic invasions and the deposition of Romulus Augustus only finished off a culture long on its deathbed.

By the eighteenth century, admiration of classical civilization had grown into adulation and, in addition, the eighteenth century witnessed the growth of an enormous interest in politics, producing Voltaire, Rousseau and Jefferson and the American and French revolutions. This different intellectual climate resulted in different evaluations of Rome. Most admired were her law, her government and her writers on duty and civic virtue. Hence, eighteenth century thinkers found tragic grandeur in the efforts of Diocletian and Constantine to revive the empire, wondered at the failure of the populace to rally to the defense of its government and identified disaster with the establishment of Germanic kingdoms in the place of the imperial government. By these standards, Germanic invasions brought about the fall, and the deposition of the last emperor in the west marked the final collapse of the empire.

The outstanding exponent of this view is Edward Gibbon in his *Decline and Fall of the Roman Empire,* based on a painstaking review of surviving Roman literature. Gibbon concluded that the cause of Rome's fall was a many-sided moral problem. He mustered evidence showing widespread corruption in both private and public life. He pointed to the use of mercenary troops as an indicator of the breakdown of any sense of patriotism and civic obligation. And he repeated the indictment of Christianity, both because the gentleness it taught undermined military ruthlessness and because the church attracted some of the later empire's best minds to its service, minds that otherwise might have served the state. Gibbon's arguments often are summed up superficially as a contention that all that interested later Romans was "bread and games," material support and daily distraction.

Gibbon's moral arguments have proved attractive both to his contemporaries and to later generations, for they express noble sentiments and they tend to equate virtue and success, but fundamentally they are rather simplistic. Most of Gibbon's charges against the Romans of the later empire are valid, but they would be valid also in earlier periods when Rome was at the height of her power, so they are not very persuasive as arguments accounting for her decline. Gibbon proved that not all Romans were models of virtue, but he did not prove that this fact had any particular effect upon the empire.

The experience of the late nineteenth and early twentieth centuries forced western intellectuals to recognize that there were factors other than culture and politics that had to be considered in evaluating social evolution. Industrialization, urbanization and global imperialism accentuated the enormous complexity of administrative problems that governments face when they rule over vast areas and large populations. And the contentions of new theorists, especially socialists with their arguments of economic determinism, forced historians to consider the possible influence of economic factors upon the development of historical societies. Applied to the decline of Rome, these modern considerations provide yet more arguments that must be weighed.

The most fully researched and carefully argued analysis of Roman administration was produced by a French scholar, Ferdinand Lot, in his *End of the Roman Empire and the Beginning of the Middle Ages*. Lot presents case after case in which orders were disobeyed, tax moneys misappropriated and problems allowed to become chronic because the imperial government learned of them too late, and he concludes that the Roman administration became "a worn-out machine that creaked slowly to a halt." In this context, of course, the end of the Roman Empire is to be found when the administrative machinery ceased to function adequately, which occurred at different times in various parts of the empire, and in some instances long after the coming of the Germans. Lot's arguments must be taken seriously, for he demonstrated that often the German kings did not attempt to destroy Roman administration but to make themselves its beneficiaries and that only over a long time did failures of administrative machinery become so common as to justify the judgment that it had broken down. But until someone can prove that there is something inherently biological or mechanical about government, the argument that "it grew old and wore out" is less than compelling. The question remains, why did a government that had functioned for centuries and had survived many crises finally break down?

Economic arguments were advanced most forcefully by the Belgian scholar, Henri Pirenne, whose thesis still is disputed hotly. To Pirenne, the "heart" of the Roman Empire was not a cultural product, not a political process and not an administrative structure but rather the economic organization of the lands lying around the Mediterranean Sea. He contended that the economic patterns established under Roman rule continued long after the cultural decline of the third century, long after the end of the western imperial title in the fifth century and even long after the administrative breakdown of about the sixth century. Pirenne asserted that the economic patterns survived so long as the Mediterranean remained a relatively open highway of communications and trade, until Islamic expansion turned the Mediterranean into a battleground between two hostile worlds, and he pushes the "end" of the Roman Empire forward into the seventh and eighth centuries. While most historians find this latter part of Pirenne's argument overextended, his insistence upon considering the economic organization of the later empire has proved a great contribution and has put analysis of the decline of Rome's domination of the western Mediterranean regions upon a much sounder basis.

The impossibility of definitive answers to the causes of Rome's decline does not impede an attempt to evaluate her contribution to medieval society. The Roman Empire provided a common classical background to much of southern and western Europe, and the recovery of the classical heritage over many centuries was a frequent stimulus to the intellectual vigor of medieval culture. The Latin language affected profoundly the speech of Germanic settlers and must be credited with much of the richness of expression of modern western languages. The Roman Empire provided a vague and idealized memory of peoples united under one government in peace and prosperity, a confused recollection of a sort of golden age in the past, and the desire to achieve again that happy condition—which in truth never existed—but which served as an inspiration to the growth of medieval civilization.

Above all else, by uniting the lands around the Mediterranean, the Roman Empire facilitated the spread of Christianity, despite persecutions, and the patronage of Constantine and most of his successors upon the imperial throne contributed enormously to the institutional growth of the church. And the Christian Church served as a channel through which some part of the classical heritage was transmitted to the future, while most was lost temporarily in the confusion of the early middle ages. The church was the major civilizing influence upon the newly settled and rather primitive Germanic peoples in the west; with some fragments and memories of classical civilization, the Christian-Germanic fusion gave birth to medieval European society.

Chapter 3

The Heirs of Rome

Thus far, both Christianity and the Germanic peoples who emigrated into the western Roman Empire have been mentioned only cursorily, but as important foundations of medieval European civilization they must be considered in more detail.

Unfortunately the origins of Christianity are obscure for a number of reasons. Jesus was born and reared in a province far from Rome, and neither his life nor his death attracted the serious attention of chroniclers in the imperial capital. Such local records as might have been useful largely were destroyed between A.D. 66 and A.D. 70 during Rome's suppression of a great Jewish revolt, when Jerusalem was levelled and the great Jewish temple destroyed. As a result, until rather recently it has been necessary to depend upon the accounts of Jesus' early followers, and these present serious problems: such accounts were written with the intention of inspiring and teaching early Christians rather than recording cold fact with strict accuracy, and in addition most were written many years after the events they purport to describe, depending upon recollection and word of mouth repetition. In consequence, they are less than wholly reliable as historical sources. In the twentieth century the discovery of the famous Dead Sea Scrolls, records carefully hidden away by the Jewish people during the Roman repression, have provided some alternatives to total reliance upon the Christian gospels for the history of the Jewish peoples in Jesus' time, and the origins of Christianity are understood somewhat better.

It is clear that Jesus was an inspired preacher and teacher, a humanitarian who preached compassion, tolerance and love in an environment little congenial to such thought. Certainly he offended and threatened the establishment in pointing out the hypocrisy in Jewish religious practice (for example, driving the money-changers from the temple) and in attacking the narrow exclusiveness of Jewish thought ("not all my sheep are of this fold"). Implicitly, too, he threatened the stability of Roman rule, for though he preached peace and said one should "render unto Caesar what is Caesar's," his followers accepted him as the messiah, the saviour long awaited by the Jews: while some saw this as an expectation of religious salvation, others—in the context of their times—thought it would mean deliverance from the Romans. Since he was viewed as a threat by both the Jewish and Roman establishments, it is not surprising that Jesus was seized and executed, but what is more important than the facts of his life and death is the interpretation that was put upon them afterwards. During his lifetime Jesus usually had been regarded as the leader of a dissenting Jewish sect, and such sects were not rare, but soon after his death the belief in his divine role spread to non-Jews and became a movement of considerable proportions.

In Jesus' time many otherworldly religions were widespread in the Roman Empire, particularly in the eastern Mediterranean, most of them derived from Egypt or the Near East which had long traditions of such belief. The nature of Roman society at the time encouraged the growth of such sects; while there was great luxury for those at the top of the social scale, life for most was hard and insecure, unending drudgery with no prospect for improvement. In such circumstances it is understandable that many turned to cults that promised another life in which goodness and simplicity would be rewarded rather than wealth and ruthlessness, a life in which "the first will be last and the last will be first."

The otherworldly religions, which Romans generally called mystery cults, shared a surprising number of characteristics, but despite this early Christianity enjoyed several advantages in competition with the others. Many included some "washing away" of sin, often in blood. This usually demanded the sacrifice of a valuable animal, as in the cult of Mithras wherein a bull was slaughtered on a sort of a trestle and everyone passed beneath to be drenched in the blood.

Such procedures required the participation of someone wealthy enough to provide the animal, but the Christian substitution of bread and wine as the body and blood made this symbolic cleansing available to the poor themselves. Almost all the cults were wracked by divisions and quarrels among their priests and by the disqualification of priests through immorality, but the Christians early agreed that the priest was only the channel or vessel of divine power and that the sacraments he had administered were valid despite human weaknesses. While certainly these factors were less important than the appeal of the central core of Christian teaching, they greatly strengthened early Christianity in the struggle with its competitors. No less important was the Christian belief that salvation was assured to those who died as martyrs for the faith; during the vicious persecutions that early Christians suffered at many hands, they faced death with a certain equanimity, confident of a heavenly reward.

But if early Christianity enjoyed certain advantages, it also confronted many problems. Perhaps foremost among these was the necessity to meet scornful criticism and attack from educated members of Roman society who brought Greek logic to bear upon the early faith and found it simply ridiculous. What was a Trinity, three in one? How could the Son be equal with the Father, since the latter presumably was necessary for the procreation of the former? How could God or a part of him be born of woman in human flesh? How could the crucifixion be considered a triumph if the Son of God were taken by his enemies and killed? In an attempt to meet these criticisms and to resolve the contradictions within their belief, the Christians turned to logic themselves and developed a group of theologians who, reasoning in the Greek manner, explained vague principles of the faith more fully and extrapolated rules of conduct from basic principles. St. Paul was one of the foremost of these early theologians. But Jesus had taught in nonspecific parables, and extrapolations could reach different conclusions, so the early church soon was torn by internal dissension while at the same time being persecuted sporadically by the civil authorities. In addition, as the new faith spread, rivalries developed among the larger Christian centers; in the west a certain limited supremacy had been conceded to Rome from the early fourth century, but in the east similar authority was claimed by Alexandria, Jerusalem and Antioch, and a bit later by Constantinople. Hence, in the spread of Christianity and in its development into an organized church there were many problems to be overcome.

The legalization of Christianity by Constantine at the end of the first quarter of the fourth century had an enormous impact upon the early church. The most positive result was that the church was freed from persecutions and was able to conduct its services publicly and to proselytize openly. But legal status and protection also meant that being a Christian was no longer a dangerous commitment requiring courage and deep conviction, and as the church became larger it attracted careerists who saw in it a road to security and power outside the army or the bureaucracy of the empire. Inevitably legality brought institutional growth and formalization, and the followers of Christianity were transformed slowly from small, persecuted communities into powerful congregations organized around their bishops. Paganism remained widespread, especially outside the cities, but during and after the fourth century the church grew rapidly into one of the important institutions of Roman society, patterning its organization and its law upon Roman governmental models.

Recognition and legality also brought to the fore the problem of the church's relations with the state. In legalizing Christianity, Constantine had no intention of creating an institution independent of his own authority, and indeed Roman tradition long had assumed some sort of fusion of civil and religious authority under the emperor. In the mid-320s an attempt to resolve a religious quarrel made this point quite clear. Once again the Greek love of hair-splitting argument precipitated a crisis. A priest named Arius taught that Jesus had to be of different substance than God the Father, thus undermining the whole structure of the Trinity; his views were called Arianism. The opponents of Arianism were called Athanasians, taking their name from one of their chief exponents, and taught that the Father and Son were of the same substance. As the quarrel rent the church, Constantine convened a council of bishops at Nicea over which he presided himself, and the Athanasian views were pronounced orthodox, or true, while Arianism was declared heretical, or false religious teaching. The quarrel was not resolved easily, however, especially since the Greek east and, even later, Roman emperors showed considerable sympathy for Arian views, and argument and violence continued for several decades. But the most important aspect of the quarrel may have been that in calling the council and presiding over it Constantine established in Christianity the basis for caesaropapism, the unity of civil and religious authority, which was to continue in the east and was to provide grounds for enormous conflict in the west.

Shortly after the legalization of Christianity, the Roman Empire began to experience serious difficulties with the Germanic peoples who lived beyond its northern frontiers. These were preliterate tribal peoples, but their primitivism ought not to be exaggerated simply because the Romans called them barbarians. They had a well-defined social structure comprising nobility, freemen and slaves, and a rather elaborate body of tribal law. Though ill-disciplined, their military prowess was to be respected, and they were also respected for their metalwork and, among some tribes, for their skill with horses. In addition, many of the tribes had been Christianized by missionaries, though unfortunately they were committed almost universally to Arian Christianity which had been declared heretical. They long had been neighbors of the Romans, traded with them, and served as volunteers in Roman armies. They certainly were not savages who suddenly erupted out of nowhere.

The Germanic tribes became exceptionally restive toward the late fourth century, and for the next two centuries their movements were a major influence upon European development. Fiercer and more primitive people from central Asia were moving into Europe, and their pressures upon the eastern Germans sent a ripple of unrest westward. Population growth made old German lands overcrowded, and tribal movements were at least partly a search for new land; in such a situation, the relative prosperity of Roman lands was a temptation too great to be ignored. A remarkable series of Germanic movements resulted, not so much military invasions as migrations in which whole peoples moved, including their women and children.

The first serious confrontation of Romans and Germans over the issue of German entry into Roman lands occurred in 378 with the Visigoths (West Goths). It should be recognized that in this and most ensuing struggles between Romans and Germans the question was not so much land as security and authority. Most parts of the Roman Empire were rather lightly populated, and there was much undeveloped land to be taken up; what mattered was whether the Germans could be integrated into Roman society and bound by imperial authority. In fact the Visigoths first entered the empire with Roman permission, but they soon protested that the Romans had not fulfilled their agreements (which included promises of some supplies) and they revolted. In the ensuing battle at Adrianople in 378 the Germanic cavalry proved its worth; the Roman armies were cut up, and Emperor Valens was killed. After that the sporadic fighting with the Germans became more frequent and more serious, and the Romans could not devote their best efforts to it because of the danger from the Persian Empire to the east. Despite retaliatory raids and such innovations as settling some bands as allies, called *foederati*, to keep out other bands, the frontiers were breached more and more frequently, and by the late fifth century many groups of Germanic peoples were wandering all over the western empire.

Shortly after the battle of Adrianople, the Visigoths were pacified temporarily and settled as *foederati* in the Balkans, but soon they were again hostile; they ravaged Greece, and when they were driven out of there they invaded Italy, sacking Rome in 410. About the same time an Asiatic people called Huns overran western Asia and parts of eastern Europe, setting other Germanic peoples in motion. Fleeing before the Hunnish onslaught, the Burgundians and the Vandals crossed the Rhine into Gaul; the former settled there, while the latter drifted toward Spain. Pressed by these attacks and still torn by civil strife, the Romans evacuated Britain in 407, and the undefended islands soon were subjected to invasions by Saxons and Angles. By about the middle of the fifth century Britain was gone from the Roman orbit and was being Germanized rapidly. After sacking Italy, the Visigoths wandered across southern Gaul and into Spain, driving the Vandals before them into Africa, and the empire recognized a Visigothic kingdom in southern Gaul and Spain in 419 and a Vandal kingdom in Africa in 435; these peoples were at least partially Romanized, and though they were quite uncontrollable, theoretically they became part of the Roman Empire, and their leaders were granted Roman titles and dignities. Italy seemed more stable, the Germans having passed on, and in the 430s imperial authority appeared secure when a Roman general of Germanic origin, Aëtius, succeeded in pacifying Gaul. Except for the loss of Britain, the empire seemed to be reviving.

The new stability was short-lived, however. In 450 the Huns, under their famous leader Attila, invaded Gaul. Repulsed there, they turned next to Italy but gave up the attack, probably because they were bought off and plague was spreading in their ranks. It was clear that imperial frontiers were still insecure, and when Aëtius fell vic-

tim to political assassination in 454 the military situation deteriorated rapidly. The following year Vandals crossed from Africa and
sacked Rome with a roughness that has made "vandalism" a permanent part of western languages. The next quarter century was very
confused with many military and political figures rising to brief
prominence, even to the imperial title in the west, and then falling
as quickly through deposition or murder. In 476 the deposition of
Romulus Augustus, last titular emperor of the west, was only one of
many incidents of this kind as Italy and Gaul fell into chaos once
again. Effective imperial authority was limited to a small area
around Ravenna on Italy's east coast, which had been made the capital because its communications with Constantinople could be assured easily, and in Ravenna imperial authority was wielded as often
as not by Romanized Germans. Only toward the end of the fifth century did it again appear that the situation was stabilizing. In the
480s the emperor recognized the power of the leader of yet another
Germanic tribe, the Ostrogoths (East Goths). With imperial military titles, this Germanic king, Theodoric, invaded Italy and took
Ravenna; he suppressed rival factions and ostensibly as the emperor's general established the Ostrogothic Kingdom of Italy, which
was recognized by Constantinople in 497.

About the same time, a stable state was being built in Gaul by
another Germanic people, the Franks. These were tribes settled
around the lower reaches of the Rhine, divided broadly into two
groups, the Salians who lived near the sea and the Ripuarians who
lived farther up-river. The Franks had served as allies of the Romans
on occasion, but they were more primitive and less Romanized than
the other Germanic peoples already considered; they differed from
them in another way, too, in that they did not abandon their old
homelands to migrate but rather spread southward into Gaul in a
steady expansion. In the 480s an extraordinary Salian king, Clovis,
crushed the last Roman military power in upper Gaul and united all
the Frankish people under his rule. In the 490s he defeated others
of his Germanic neighbors, and then shortly after 500 he conquered
both the Burgundians on the upper Rhone and the Visigoths in southern Gaul, creating an enormous kingdom. Like Theodoric the Ostro-
goth, Clovis was recognized by Constantinople and given Roman

titles, but despite these superficial similarities of military conquest and imperial acceptance, the Frankish and Ostrogothic kingdoms were very different from one another.

Though a Goth, Theodoric was quite Romanized, and he tried hard to fuse the vigor and military strength of his people with Roman culture and civilization. He kept close contacts with Constantinople, negotiated alliances with his Germanic neighbors and tried to keep the peace. He employed learned Italians in his government, and he based his edicts upon Roman law. He also was something of a patron of the arts. Clovis, on the other hand, was a simple barbarian chieftain, though very astute. He governed on the basis of tribal law and ruled through subchiefs, though the latter often were given Roman titles such as count or duke. He was a ruthless expansionist and was almost constantly at war.

But the most important difference among the late fifth and early sixth century kingdoms was in the matter of religion. Most of the Germanic peoples were Arian Christians, and this made serious problems in the Ostrogothic, Visigothic and Vandal kingdoms, for the populations and clergy upon whom these conquerors had imposed themselves were of Catholic (Athanasian) belief. At this time, theological quarrels were pursued with a ferocity almost incomprehensible to the modern student, for to the orthodox Christians the Arian was a heretic, a corrupter of religious truth, and the most detestable object on earth. By contrast, the Franks escaped this religious controversy.

The problem of heresy was particularly severe in Italy because of the growing power of the pope and of Rome as the western center of Catholic Christianity. It is clear that the bishop of Rome exercised no special authority in the very early church (in fact, the Latin *papa*, pope, was applied to bishops generally), but nonetheless Rome enjoyed considerable prestige. It was the old imperial capital, the site of the martyrdom of St. Peter and the keeper of the tombs of two apostles, Peter and Paul; and with the removal of the imperial capital to the east (330), the Bishop of Rome often found himself the only remaining political authority in Italy. All of these factors contributed to the growth of prestige and power, and early in the fifth century Roman primacy was set upon a scriptural basis by Pope

Celestine I who asserted the Petrine Doctrine drawn from St. Matthew's Gospel, that Christ had designated St. Peter the founder of the church and had conferred upon him "the power of the keys," which then had passed in succession to all the Roman bishops. A successor, Pope Innocent I, claimed universal jurisdiction over the church, and then in the mid-fifth century the first great pope, Leo I, brought all of these developments to a synthesis. He extracted from the emperor an edict declaring that papal decisions had the force of law; he proclaimed the mystical unity of St. Peter and his successors; he dictated a solution to another heretical quarrel; and he repudiated an attempt by a council of bishops to declare the patriarch of Constantinople supreme in the church. In addition, it was he who confronted Attila and his Huns (as an imperial representative) and turned them back; probably he pointed to spreading plague and the arrival of Roman reinforcements and negotiated a price for withdrawal, but as it was believed popularly that only a miracle spared Italy, he won tremendous prestige from the success. It was only some twenty years after Pope Leo's death that Theodoric and his Ostrogoths conquered Italy, and compromise between the aggressive and powerful leadership of the western church and the detested heretics proved impossible. Theodoric was a tolerant man, but he never was accepted by his Italian subjects and their Latin-Catholic clergy, and Pope Gelasius (492–496) even pronounced the formal independence of the church from civil authority (Gelasian Doctrine).

The Franks, on the other hand, enjoyed a much happier religious situation. When they began their conquest of Gaul they were still pagans, not having been reached by serious missionary efforts. As pagans they were much more acceptable to Catholics, for the church regarded pagans as untaught innocents and hoped for their conversion, while heretics were foul perverters of truth. Clovis became even more acceptable in 496 when he had himself and many of his warriors baptized as Catholic Christians. His motives can only be guessed at: he had married a Catholic girl; he had had several years' experience of the power and position of the Catholic clergy in Gaul; he claimed to have found strength in battle through prayer to the Christian God. Whatever his motive, his conversion was enormously important. Though a pretense of imperial authority endured, military and political power in the western empire was in the hands of Germanic kings, and of them all Clovis was the only one who was religiously acceptable to the indigenous population and its clergy. He was regarded as the sword of God, the deliverer from the heretic, and he enjoyed wide support.

Other circumstances also conspired to give stability to the Frankish kingdom while the apparently more civilized Ostrogothic kingdom proved short-lived. The emperors in the east had by no means abandoned hope of reasserting real authority in the west, and an imperial resurgence in the second quarter of the sixth century altered the balance of power drastically. The Emperor Justinian (527–565) dreamed of the reestablishment of a universal Christian empire under his authority, and after making peace with the Persians and crushing rival forces in the capital, he embarked upon the reconquest of the west. Because Justinian increased the bureaucratization of the government and the professionalism of the army, and because he gave definitive preference to Greek over Latin, the empire that he left to his successors was rather different from anything that preceded it, and his reign usually is considered to mark the transition from the Roman Empire in the east to the medieval Byzantine Empire. His interests were manifold, and he also lent his authority to the last great codification of Roman laws, known as the Justinian Code. But while Justinian is important historically for many reasons, his immediate significance to western development lies in the campaigns of conquest that he launched. In the 530s and 540s Byzantine armies landed in North Africa and crushed completely the Vandal kingdom there, bringing the whole area back under the rule of Constantinople. From the mid-530s to the mid-550s Byzantine armies fought over the length and breadth of Italy, finally destroying the Ostrogothic kingdom and reestablishing imperial rule. In the mid-550s the fighting was extended to Spain, of which the southeastern part was reconquered.

Thus patterns changed rapidly from the beginning to the middle of the sixth century. The Vandal and Ostrogothic kingdoms were destroyed by Justinian's armies; the Visigothic kingdom, reduced by the Franks in the early part of the century, was further weakened by Byzantine forces. Arian rule over Catholic Christians, which had caused so many problems, was abolished through Italy and Africa and a part of Spain (and in 587 conversion of the Visigoths from

Arianism to Catholicism completed the process). Except for the British Isles, Gaul and part of Spain, the lands of the old Roman Empire were again under imperial rule.

Justinian's great conquests did not long survive his death, however. In 568 another Germanic people, the Lombards, invaded Italy and conquered much of it while Constantinople was distracted by new political troubles and renewed war with the Persians. Thereafter Italy was a strange mosaic of jurisdictions with Byzantine rule (with its capital at Ravenna still) in parts of the east and south, papal rule (nominally under imperial authority) in Rome and adjacent territories, and Lombard rule (with its capital at Pavia) in most inland regions. Already torn by the Gothic and Byzantine wars and wracked with plague and famine, Italy largely was barbarized by the Lombard invasion. Though the Lombards gradually were absorbed to the extent of adopting the language and the religion of their subjects, they established governmental patterns resembling those of the Franks, personal rule of dukes and counts who usually were large land-holders and were responsible to the king. At the same time the grant of episcopal immunities (from government jurisdiction) made bishops practically the temporal rulers of the remaining towns, and the elevation of another strong pope, Gregory the Great, advanced the independence of the church from secular authority.

Yet one more important influence was to be felt before a new pattern in the west emerged fully. This was the rise and rapid expansion of Moslem power. Mohammed, the prophet of the new faith, came from the Arabian town of Mecca, which was an important center of trade and culture. Deeply interested in religion, he had studied Christian and Jewish religious ideas, and in 612, when he was in his early 40s, he began preaching, his chief themes being the oneness of God, the importance of charity and prayer, divine judgment, and submission to God's will (Islam). Ill received by the populace of Mecca, he fled with a handful of followers to Medina in 622 where he had great success with surrounding tribesmen. War with Mecca followed, but the Moslems, as the followers of Islam were called, eventually won, and by the time of Mohammed's death in 632 a great many Arab tribes had been won over or subjugated.

After Mohammed's death the direction of the faith was undertaken by a caliph, the vicegerent of the prophet, and rapid expansion continued, with the conquest of Persia, Syria and Egypt accomplished by the early 640s. In the latter half of the seventh century the pace of conquest was slowed by internal political and religious quarrels, but still the Moslem expansion pushed on, eastward to India and central Asia and westward along the north African coast where an alliance was made with the Berbers. Then, in 711 the armies spilled across into Spain where the Visigothic forces were defeated utterly, and by 715 all of Spain was taken, with resistance continuing only in the wild mountains of the north. Moslem armies moved into southern Gaul, taking Narbonne, and at the same time other forces advanced far enough in Asia Minor that in 717 and 718 they besieged Constantinople, though they failed to take the city.

In the next decade or two, however, a number of factors combined to halt the seemingly inexorable advance of Islam which was threatening to engulf Europe from both east and west. In the east, Byzantine defenses held; within the Islamic empire there erupted a great struggle for control of the caliphate, which ended by dividing Spain and the western parts of north Africa from the rest of the Moslem world; and in Gaul the Franks managed to defeat and contain the Islamic advance in a great battle at Tours in 732. While the struggle for Constantinople was to continue for centuries, the Frankish victory in the west proved decisive; a quarter century later the Moslems had been pushed back over the Pyrenees, and Frankish Gaul survived as a Germano-Christian synthesis on a Roman foundation.

Thus, by the early eighth century the destruction of the Roman Empire was complete, and in its place stood three distinct entities. Around the eastern, southern and western shores of the Mediterranean lay the Moslem world, strong, dynamic, and alien in religion and culture. East of Italy the northern parts of the Mediterranean basin belonged to the Byzantine Empire, the most direct heir of Rome perhaps, but by now Greek, bureaucratized and defensive. And in western Europe there stood the raw new Kingdom of the Franks, Germanic with a faint Roman tradition, still turbulent but with strength proved against the Moslems. Amidst these competing powers stood the Italy of the Lombards and the Pope and weak imperial pretensions, a power vacuum to which all looked hungrily. In the mid-eighth century a papal alliance with the Franks, provoked by the dangers of the Italian situation, proved a catalyst that completed the Germano-Christian fusion and launched medieval society in western Europe.

GERMANIC KINGDOMS AT DEATH OF THEODORIC (526)

ANGLO-SAXON KINGDOMS
London
Atlantic Ocean
KINGDOM OF THE BURGUNDIANS
Reims
Rhine R.
Meuse R.
Seine R.
Paris
Danube R.
Loire R.
Drave R.
Save R.
Tours
KINGDOM OF THE OSTROGOTHS
KINGDOM OF THE FRANKS
Lyon
Milan
45°
Bordeaux
Po R.
Garonne R.
Ravenna
CANTABRIANS
Arles
Adriatic Sea
KINGDOM OF THE SUEVI
Narbonne
Rhône R.
Ebro R.
CORSICA
Rome
Duero R.
Barcelona
Tagus R.
Toledo
SARDINIA
Tyrrhenian Sea
BALEARIC IS.
Mediterranean
Ionian Sea
KINGDOM OF THE VISIGOTHS
Palermo
Seville
SICILY
Sea
Str. of Gibraltar
KINGDOM OF THE VANDALS
5°
0 100 200 300
MILES

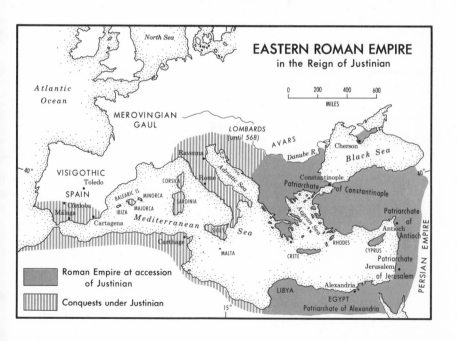

EASTERN ROMAN EMPIRE
in the Reign of Justinian

North Sea
Atlantic Ocean
0 200 400 600
MILES
MEROVINGIAN GAUL
LOMBARDS (until 568)
AVARS
Ravenna
Danube R.
Cherson
Black Sea
40°
VISIGOTHIC
Toledo
CORSICA
Rome
Adriatic Sea
Constantinople
Patriarchate of Constantinople
40°
SPAIN
BALEARIC IS. MINORCA
SARDINIA
Córdoba IBIZA MAJORCA
Patriarchate of Antioch
Málaga
Cartagena
Mediterranean Sea
Antioch
PERSIAN EMPIRE
Carthage
RHODES
CYPRUS
MALTA
CRETE
Patriarchate of Jerusalem
Jerusalem

Roman Empire at accession of Justinian

Conquests under Justinian

LIBYA
Alexandria
15°
EGYPT
Patriarchate of Alexandria

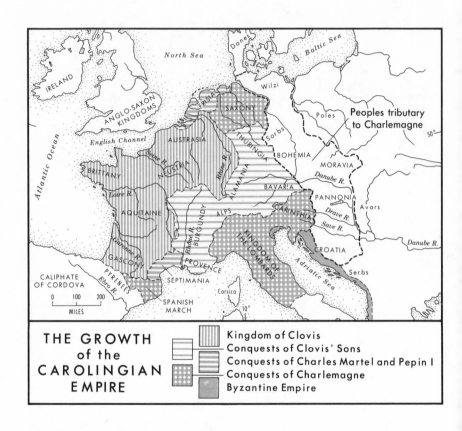

North Sea

IRELAND

Danes

Baltic Sea

Wilzi

Poles

Peoples tributary
to Charlemagne

ANGLO-SAXON
KINGDOMS

English Channel

FRISIA

SAXONY

Atlantic Ocean

BRITTANY

Seine R.

AUSTRASIA

THURINGIA

Sorbs

BOHEMIA

MORAVIA

50°

NEUSTRIA

Rhine R.

ALAMANIA

Danube R.

Loire R.

BAVARIA

PANNONIA

Avars

AQUITAINE

Rhone R.

BURGUNDY

ALPS

CARINTHIA

Drave R.

Danube R.

Save R.

Garonne R.

GASCONY

CALIPHATE
OF CORDOVA

PYRENEES

Ebro R.

PROVENCE

SEPTIMANIA

KINGDOM
OF
THE LOMBARDS

Adriatic Sea

CROATIA

Serbs

0   100   200

MILES

SPANISH
MARCH

Corsica

10°

THE GROWTH
of the
CAROLINGIAN
EMPIRE

Kingdom of Clovis
Conquests of Clovis' Sons
Conquests of Charles Martel and Pepin I
Conquests of Charlemagne
Byzantine Empire

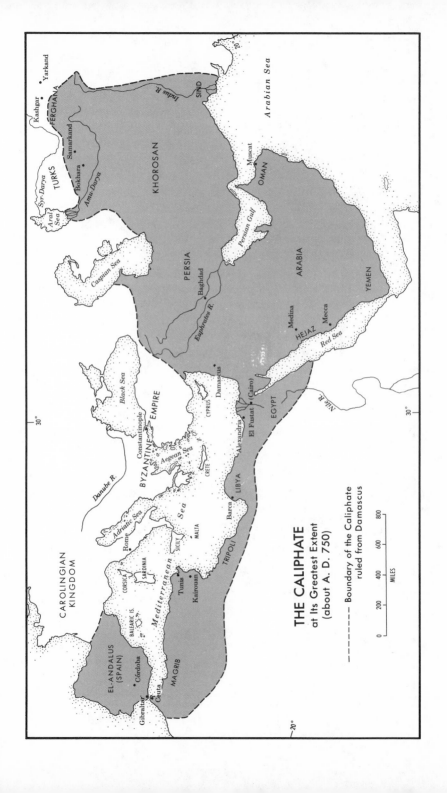

THE CALIPHATE
at Its Greatest Extent
(about A. D. 750)

– – – – – Boundary of the Caliphate
ruled from Damascus

MILES
0   200   400   600   800

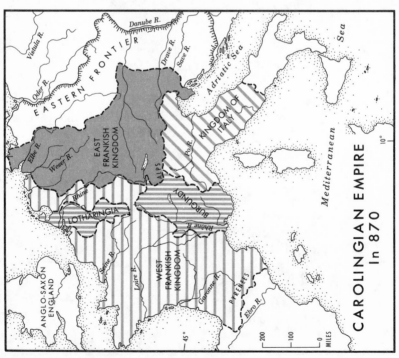

CAROLINGIAN EMPIRE
876-911

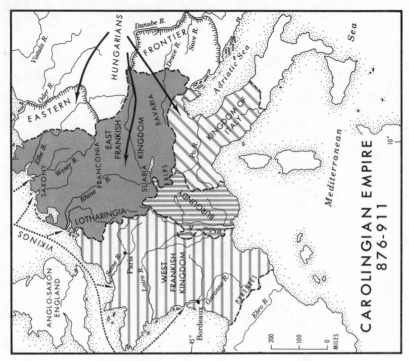

CAROLINGIAN EMPIRE
In 870

Chapter 4

Early Carolingian Europe

By the eighth century the focus of political and social development in western Europe was Frankish Gaul, but there had been no steady progress from the promising beginnings made by Clovis. Indeed, Clovis' family, called Merovingians after a semilegendary ancestor named Meroveg, produced singularly few competent kings. Except for the reign of Dagobert in the second quarter of the seventh century, Merovingian history is a sad tale of civil war and fratricide. In fact, royal authority deteriorated so far that after the mid-seventh century the Merovingian kings were no more than figureheads, and real power gravitated into the hands of great nobles, the dukes and counts. Merovingian power had been weakened further by territorial divisions to provide crowns for royal sons, and four more or less distinct kingdoms became generally recognizable: Austrasia, lying farthest to the east, was basically Frankish; Neustria, to the west, was essentially Gallo-Roman; Aquitania, in the south, was Gallo-Roman and Visigothic; and Burgundy, in the southeast, had a mixture of Burgundians, Franks, and lesser Germanic peoples. Had nothing happened to arrest this decline, it is likely that the Moslems would have overrun Gaul easily, but fortunately for the independence of Europe and of western Christianity, a revival of sorts took place in the early eighth century. The revival owed nothing to the Merovingians but turned rather on the ambitions and abilities of one of the great Frankish noble families, later called the Carolingians.

The growth of noble power that paralleled the degeneracy of the Merovingian kings had favored particularly the officials of the royal households who had access to the king's person and his treasury. In this situation the Mayors of the Palace, originally menials of the household, had grown to be important figures, representatives of the landed nobility controlling the reality if not the titles of royal power. To preserve their positions, the mayors developed the practice of proclaiming Merovingian infants as kings and then deposing them and locking them away in monasteries when they had grown to adolescence. With such practices it was the mayors, of course, who actually governed. Mayors occasionally tried to usurp the royal title, but until the eighth century they were unsuccessful, for the delicate balance of pretense and reality served the interests of the great landowners who had no desire to see governing power joined to legitimacy in a potent combination that might curb their personal ambitions. Early in the eighth century, however, an able and ambitious mayor of Austrasia found a way to consolidate his power without an overt attempt upon the Merovingian crowns. In the civil wars endemic in Gaul, Charles, called Martel "The Hammer," defeated his rivals and forced his acceptance as mayor in all four of the kingdoms. In the course of these struggles Charles Martel also developed an unusually competent military force, preferring a small band of well-armed heavy cavalry to the traditionally numerous but ill-equipped Frankish footmen. It was with this elite force that he led the Frankish armies that stopped the Moslems at Tours in 732, and after that victory, his prestige and the strength of his army assured his power. Still Martel did not attempt to usurp the royal titles, but contented himself with the title *dux francorum*, Duke of the Franks.

The revival of Frankish power under Charles Martel entailed far-reaching social and political developments, which are understood more easily if it is remembered that at the root of all of them was Martel's desire to improve his military force. Traditionally all Frankish freemen owed military service, but when the levies were called up, they often shuffled into camp with no equipment other than a spear. In place of this rabble Martel sought to develop a cavalry, well-mounted and equipped with spear, sword, shield and armor, but this was a costly program. In the eighth century, the major form of wealth was land, tenanted productive land, and it was this that would have to be "spent" to build the new army. Martel held considerable land, both his own family possessions and the royal estates he controlled as mayor, but he had no intention of impoverishing himself *vis-à-vis* the other great landowners of the kingdom, so he sought an alternative source, the church.

Through gifts and endowments the church had become a very large land-holder, and Martel determined to make use of church lands to support his army. This was a very delicate question, for churchmen always insisted that the holdings they "managed" were God's property and immune from governmental interference, and usually they had royal charters confirming this view. However, through a combination of persuasion and pressure, and the proposal of some very complicated arrangements, Martel finally got the church to agree to support his soldiers. Essentially, each of the new cavalrymen received the use of (but not the title to) some church land for his support; he held the land so long as he rendered the requisite service to Martel, but he also paid a token rent to the church, symbolic of his recognition of the church's continuing ownership. With this arrangement Martel stripped the church of vast tracts of land and built his army. (Fully cognizant of the potential advantages of the good will of the church and of the dangers of consolidated opposition, he tried hard to mollify the clergy, most notably by encouraging and supporting the work of the great missionary St. Boniface, who was trying to convert the German tribes beyond the Rhine.)

These innovations in land tenure were of great importance, for the creation of a class of propertied small nobility all over the kingdom who depended upon Martel strengthened his position with the great landowners. But even more significantly, Martel's practice of granting the use of land in return for military service, though not without precedents, was the first large-scale use of this arrangement; if on the one hand it symbolized the decline of a commercial monetized society in which it was possible to hire service, on the other it demonstrated a viable alternative that was to become the basis of medieval European feudalism.

Despite his many achievements, there was a real danger that Martel's work would not long survive his death in 741, for in keeping with Germanic tradition he considered his titles and powers personal property, and at the end of his life he divided them between his two sons, Pepin and Carloman. For a half-dozen years the two brothers shared power, but in 747 Carloman retired to a monastery (apparently voluntarily), and Pepin ruled alone until his death in 768. Though overshadowed by his son Charles, called Charlemagne, Pepin made great strides in the development of Frankish Gaul, and his achievements must not be passed over lightly.

Although Charles Martel tried to avoid any open quarrel with the church, despite his seizure of church lands, he seems never to have been moved by any deep personal convictions. By contrast, both Pepin and Carloman were influenced profoundly in their youth by the zeal of the missionary St. Boniface, and both appear to have been sincerely religious. In Carloman's case this sentiment resulted in his withdrawal into monastic life; Pepin, on the other hand, gave expression to his convictions through a total reform and revitalization of the church in Gaul and a close alliance with the papacy.

The condition of the church in Gaul and its relations with the Frankish government before Pepin's reforms defy the usual stereotypes of pious early Christians. Under the Merovingians the Franks had treated the church respectfully, almost as a tribal totem, had protected it and endowed it with lands, but had not taken its attempts to interfere in private life very seriously. Kings and nobles practiced polygamy, and in addition to several wives often kept concubines. Moreover, they murdered with equanimity, repudiated wives of whom they tired and generally treated Christian moral teachings casually. And the church was not much better. Bishops often were appointed through political influence before even being ordained as priests. Clerics often tried to steal church lands for their families, clerical marriage and concubinage were common and many instances were recorded of priests rebuked for drunkenness or brawling. Monasteries were ill-disciplined communities more noted for sloth and drunkenness than for religious practices. Hence, Pepin's ambitions for reform faced formidable problems.

Nonetheless, there were some bright spots in this generally gloomy picture. There were able and dedicated churchmen such as St. Boniface and those who followed him into the wilderness in Germany; and there was a reform movement within monasteries that sought to establish discipline and piety as the foundations of monastic life. By persuasion and command, through clerical appointments that he made and by convening councils of bishops, Pepin sought to strengthen these wholesome trends and to reduce abuses. To give the church a sound economic basis he restored some of the lands that his father had taken away, though not enough to undermine Martel's work, and he instituted tithing of the laity. To reestablish some sort of discipline within the clergy, he prescribed that priests must wear distinctive dress, setting them off from the populace at large, and he lent his support to the monastic reform movement and prescribed its practices for all the monasteries in Gaul.

The reformed monks who attracted Pepin's favorable attention were known as Benedictines, after their founder St. Benedict of Nursia, an early sixth century Italian. Monasticism in the early church usually meant hermits who dressed in tatters, begged food, engaged in long fasts and vigils and generally sought solitude in the wilderness. While this program offered the solace of years of contemplation to many in the eastern Mediterranean, in the harsher climate of western Europe it was simply a prescription for an early death. Consequently, European monks tended to gather in communities, but too often these were infamous for laxity and immorality. As an improvement over both earlier forms of monasticism, St. Benedict formed a community of monks and established a discipline for them that included a regular schedule of prayer, study and manual labor, so that they might remain sincere in their dedication, might become more learned in their faith and might feed themselves by their own efforts. With the motto "a sound mind in a sound body" St. Benedict prescribed normal rest and simple but adequate diet, and he forbade exaggerated fasting and excessively harsh physical disciplines. St. Benedict's own monastery of Monte Casino was a notable success, and his principles, or Rule, soon became the inspiration of other monastic communities. It was this Benedictine Rule that Pepin commanded be accepted by all the monasteries in Gaul, and not only did this command reform existing monasteries, it also stimulated considerable expansion of the monastic movement. Until the mid-eighth century Christianity was chiefly an urban faith, a congregation of townsmen governed by their bishop. Rural folk still were wedded to traditional primitive beliefs, a situation illustrated by the fact that the word for "countrymen" also meant "non-believers" (Latin *pagani*). As reformed monasteries sprang up all over Gaul, they carried the faith into the countryside and completed the internal missionary work that had been begun several centuries earlier.

The other great achievement of Pepin's rule was the establishment of a close alliance with the papacy. The papacy had sought such an alliance earlier, but Charles Martel had rejected it. By contrast, when the opportunity presented itself to Pepin early in the 750s, he welcomed it. In a sense, Pepin and the pope were both aiming at usurpations, and they needed each other; Pepin had ambitions for the Frankish crown, while the pope was seeking to wrest political control of Italy from the emperor at Constantinople. Pepin had the power to seize the crown from the enfeebled Merovingians, but he sought some legitimation, some religious sanction for taking what Germanic law regarded as property. When the pope asked for help against the Lombards and sought an alliance in 751, Pepin discreetly inquired "whether it would not be better that he who exercises the power of the kingdom wear its crown," and the pope answered in the affirmative; the last Merovingian promptly was packed off to a monastery, and Pepin was crowned and anointed by St. Boniface, who was acting as the pope's representative. Thus the crown of the Franks became more significantly Christian, dependent for its legitimacy less upon Germanic traditions than upon the religious sanctions of the church. Thereafter the ties that linked the Frankish monarchy and the papacy could not be broken easily, and the new relationship was strengthened three years later when the pope travelled to Gaul and anointed and blessed Pepin personally.

In fulfilment of his responsibilities under the new alliance, Pepin led his army into Italy in 754 and 756, defeating the Lombards and confirming the authority of the pope over disputed lands in a document called the Donation of Pepin; since technically these lands belonged to the emperor in Constantinople, Pepin's action amounted to recognition of claims that the pope was the heir of the Roman Empire in Italy and a major achievement for papal policy. The Donation founded the Papal States, lands governed directly by the pope, which were to endure until the late nineteenth century and which survive vestigially in the independent Vatican State.

In keeping with Frankish tradition, Pepin divided his lands and titles between his two sons, Charles and Carloman, before his death in 768, but again the state that the Carolingians were building survived intact; in 771 Carloman died, and Charles ruled alone until his death in 814. The astonishing achievements in many fields during

Charles's reign earned him the title "the great" in his own lifetime, and it is thus he is remembered—Charlemagne.

Most of Charlemagne's reign was filled with warfare, Frankish armies conquering in all directions. A series of campaigns southward pushed the frontier across the Pyrenees, establishing against the Moslems a buffer known as the Spanish March or March of Barcelona; it was during these campaigns that the mountain Basques annihilated the Frankish rear guard, an action commemorated in the famous "Song of Roland." War with the Saxons to the north and northeast lasted over thirty years, through eighteen separate campaigns, before they submitted to Charlemagne. The struggle with the Lombards was renewed, and Charlemagne destroyed their kingdom and pushed to the Adriatic coast and around the north end of that sea into Dalmatia, the coast of modern Yugoslavia. Campaigns eastward absorbed Germans and Slavs and finally defeated the Avars, an Asiatic people on the lower Danube. By the end of his life, Charlemagne ruled most of western and central Europe and considerable parts of eastern Europe.

Yet Charlemagne's fame rests on far more than conquest, for he developed complicated mechanisms to pacify and integrate new areas into his government. For instance, he defeated the Saxons several times, only to see them rise in rebellion again. He determined to force Christianity upon them as a civilizing influence that he hoped would develop moral bonds between them and his other peoples. To this end, he supported the establishment of churches and monasteries among the Saxons and insisted that they accept baptism; then if they were found gathering again in war bands and celebrating ancient pagan rites, they were guilty of heresy, which ecclesiastical crime Charlemagne made punishable by death. His ruthlessness extended even to large transfers of population, moving thousands of Saxons into Gaul for resettlement and displacing many Franks into Saxony, to break up the cohesiveness of Saxon resentment of the conqueror. After thirty years of struggle, these policies of forced conversion and deportations were successful.

In areas that were less troublesome, Charlemagne behaved less harshly. After defeating the Bavarians, he forced the Bavarian chieftain, Tassilo, to swear an oath of loyalty and obedience and then allowed him to retain his rule over his people, making him a Carolin-

gian duke; ultimately Tassilo violated his oath and revolted, whereupon Charlemagne deposed him, but he seemed willing to try moderate measures before resorting to extremes.

To govern his far-flung territories, Charlemagne developed an
administrative system of some sophistication. The land was divided
into districts ruled by counts, officers theoretically appointed for life
but often removed. Begun in old Frankish lands, this system gradually was extended into Italy, Saxony, and Bavaria, and the tribal
dukes largely were curbed. The counts had viscounts and vicars to
assist them, and they appointed landowners as judges, called *scabini*,
to oversee local justice. To limit the ambition of the tumultuous
noblemen upon whom his administration depended, Charlemagne
created two control systems. The first of these was his practice of establishing all through his domains loyal retainers whom he trusted;
these men, called *vassi dominici* (vassals of the lord), were given
land grants in return for oaths of loyalty and obedience to Charlemagne personally. The other control mechanism was a roving inspec-
torate of men called *missi dominici* (those sent by the lord). These
officers travelled in pairs, usually a count and a bishop; they held
their own courts, heard complaints and inspected financial, judicial
and clerical administration. When they found abuses or corruption,
they had wide discretionary powers for corrective and punitive action. They were the chief connection between central and local administration.

To provide for frontier defense, Charlemagne created special
border districts called *marches* or *marks*, governed by a margrave
(*mark graf*). These were highly autonomous counties whose administrators had wide military and financial powers so they could meet
emergencies quickly. Among the more famous marches protecting
Charlemagne's frontiers were the Spanish March against the Moslems and the Dane Mark against the Danes.

Charlemagne continued the good relations with the church established by his father, but like Constantine he expected the church
to serve him too, as in the pacification of the Saxons. In the same
way, he fought the Lombards to defend the papacy, and he confirmed the Donation of Pepin; but he expected the pope to crown
and bless Frankish kings, and he considered himself sovereign in

papal lands. Nor did Charlemagne limit his personal role in the church to worldly matters. When a new doctrinal quarrel arose, Charlemagne convened a council of bishops in 794, presided over it himself and dictated a solution. He was quite as much a caesaropapist as any Roman emperor.

Perhaps the most dramatic aspect of Charlemagne's relations with the church was the imperial coronation which took place on Christmas Day of the year 800. After further campaigns against the Lombards, the Frankish king went to Rome for the Christmas festivities, and after Christmas mass the pope set a crown upon his head and proclaimed him Roman Emperor, a title that offered Charlemagne many advantages. The German royal crowns were essentially tribal and ethnic, but Charlemagne ruled Lombards, Saxons, Bavarians and others in addition to his own Franks. By conquering and annexing royal crowns he could not bind these people to him, but the imperial title implied universality, and allowed him to stress the common Christianity of all his subject peoples, a tie that might hold them together. However, the imperial coronation raised serious problems. The Byzantine Empire resented it deeply, for it still considered itself the only empire and believed itself the legitimate claimant to all the western lands of the Roman Empire. To the Byzantines, Charlemagne was a German upstart and the pope a rebel for usurping the powers and functions of the empire. It required a dozen years before a compromise was achieved and Byzantium recognized Charlemagne's title as a sort of revival of the old Roman practice of eastern and western emperors.

An historical controversy long turned around the matter of the imperial coronation. Some years after the emperor's death, Charlemagne's biographer, Einhard, wrote that Charlemagne had regretted it. It has been suggested that he was unaware of the pope's intentions, but this is hardly credible, for the pope was in a weak position and utterly dependent upon the Frankish king; he could not have dared so important an act without Charlemagne's knowledge and consent, nor could the elaborate arrangements have been carried out in secret. Rather it would seem that Charlemagne had second thoughts on the matter. Considering the complications with the Byzantine Empire and reflecting upon the dangerous precedent implicit in having the imperial crown bestowed by the pope, he probably wondered later if it had been worth it.

Charlemagne also is remembered as a patron of learning, for he presided over a cultural reawakening usually called the Carolingian renaissance. Personally he could speak Latin in addition to his Frankish tongue, and he understood some Greek, but that was as far as his scholastic achievements went; he never learned to write. But he established a school in his palace and made himself a patron of scholars whom he brought from all over Europe. The foremost of them, Alcuin, came from York, in the north of England; Einhard, who wrote Charlemagne's biography, came from Fulda, deep in Germany; and Paul the Deacon and Peter of Pisa came from Italy.

The importance of the Carolingian renaissance is exaggerated easily, but it should not be underestimated either. The Palace School produced little that was original, though Einhard did his biography of the emperor and Paul the Deacon wrote a *History of the Lombards,* but it was a center for the recovery, copying and preservation of ancient writings culled largely from scattered monastic collections. But for the patient transcribing of ninth-century scholars, the surviving body of ancient literature would be much smaller than it is today. Also, the Palace School developed a smaller and much more legible handwriting, called Carolingian miniscule (upon which most modern typefaces are based), which replaced the older large cursive scrawl. Nor did the impact of Charlemagne's patronage of learning stop at the Palace School, for many who had been associated with it established schools of their own, and Tours, Rheims, Cologne and Fulda became famous centers of learning. So though its achievements were limited, the Carolingian renaissance was very significant. As it sometimes is expressed, "In the darkness of the ninth century the light of a single candle is important."

Under the rule of the early Carolingians, European society began to assume patterns, manorialism and feudalism, that were to be its foundation for many centuries. Manorialism was a socioeconomic pattern based upon self-sufficient estates which eventually included most people in Europe. There are precedents at least as early as the later Roman Empire, aristocratic estates called *latifundia,* but by the ninth-century towns nearly had disappeared and almost everyone was involved in manorialism in some capacity. Probably the reasons for this economic regression never will be explained to every historian's satisfaction, but the decline is indisputable and is attested to by a new silver coinage introduced by Charlemagne; gold was simply too expensive and could not serve as a medium of exchange for the petty transactions that survived. Hence, manorialism was a pattern of an essentially agrarian society.

Though there were many superficial differences from one manor to another, there were certain basic features that were common to all: a water source, fields for growing grain and vegetables, pasturage and some sort of fuel source—usually a wood lot though in some areas a peat bog. Dwellings clustered together in a village, often dominated by the castle of the lord of the manor; a powerful lord, however, would hold several manors, and of course he would not build a castle on each one. The distribution of manor lands was very complex. Usually the pasture and wood lot were "common," shared by everyone, but the arable lands were divided into a maze of strips worked by different farmers rather than into consolidated blocks of individual proprietorship. Division of lands among sons and multiple inheritance tended to make most manor lands a crazy quilt, and in addition, when new lands were cleared, it was common to distribute in strips so everyone shared equally in rich bottom lands, steep slopes and poor hilltops.

Since manors were largely self-sufficient, a wide variety of people lived on them: farmers, blacksmiths, carpenters, wheelwrights, etc. In early medieval Europe most of these people were serfs, neither slaves nor freemen. A serf was bound to his land, and certain of his actions were restricted; typically, the lord could not sell the land from under the man nor sell the man off the land (though he could sell land and man together), and the serf could not leave his land or marry without the lord's permission. It was a harsh existence, but many freemen entered into serfdom voluntarily to escape the crushing burdens of taxes and military obligations which they could not afford to meet.

The charges and obligations upon the tenants of a manor were heavy. Typically they would pay land rent, a share of the crop, for lands they worked for themselves, would have to work some days on the lord's own land, would have to render some personal service in the lord's stables or kitchens and would have to offer special "presents" at Christmas, Easter and other holidays. But the system did offer some security on both the personal and the collective level. It made the individual part of a closely interconnected community in times when war, famine and plague were more than a family could cope with alone, and it supported a professional military and governing class that could defend the whole society.

Feudalism concerned only the military and governing class of medieval society, ten or fifteen per cent of Europe's inhabitants. It was based upon a pattern of personal relationships in a society that had no concept of service to the state, and it provided a means of reimbursing for service in a nonmonetized society. The foundations of feudalism were the two institutions of benefice and vassalage, and these in turn depended upon the idea of granting not land but the products of it, in Latin *usufruct,* the right to the fruits of the land. Benefice was land granted in this way for service, with the grantor retaining title but the grantee enjoying the income. This was the way Charles Martel used church lands to support his soldiers, adding yet another complexity; the church retained title, Martel was given the right of disposition of usage, and the soldiers received the income of the land assigned them, rendering military service to Martel and token payment to the church. Vassalage was the practice of one man "commending" himself to another, swearing an oath of loyalty and promising service. There are precedents for benefice and vassalage in Roman and Germanic tradition, but in Carolingian times the two institutions came to be connected. The overlord would grant the *usufruct* of land to those who pronounced their oaths and became his vassals; in return they would promise to bear him military service with an agreed number of soldiers and to serve as advisors in his council when he required it. Often these vassals then would subdivide the lands granted to them so as to take vassals of their own, a process call subinfeudation. (One of the very delicate issues in medieval society was the question whether subinfeudated vassals owed primary allegiance to their lord or to his overlord if the two should quarrel.)

In a sense, every member of the feudal elite had a part in manorialism, for each was the lord of a manor or manors from which he drew his support, but that was the only point of contact between the two systems. Manorialism organized the great mass of commoners,

providing them some security in return for their support of the politico-military elite. Feudalism organized the elite within itself, providing some means of ranking and of remunerating service. Under the
early Carolingians, both of these patterns emerged rather clearly
and produced a society that was expansive, more secure than Europe
had seen for three or four centuries, and capable of sustaining a
modest cultural renaissance.

Chapter 5

A Time of Trial

By the time of Charlemagne, European society had developed rather elaborately, and it presented an appearance of considerable strength. In the south, the Islamic invasions had been stopped, and though raiding along the Mediterranean coast continued to inflict costly destruction, there was little threat of Europe's being overwhelmed. In the east and north, hordes of tribal peoples moved along the borders of the Carolingian Empire, and conflict with them was more or less constant, but the empire stood secure behind its shell of "marches." And most of the west enjoyed the security of a seacoast.

Within the Carolingian Empire it is possible to suggest a comparably optimistic picture of stability and progress. The cultural revival flourished. An administrative system focussed on the emperor was designed to enforce general peace, provide military forces in time of danger and offer justice through various levels of judgment. Men closely tied to the emperor were scattered throughout the land to guard against usurpation and rebellion while others roved, inspecting and checking the whole operation. Despite private quarrels, border raids, subsistence agriculture and massive illiteracy, European society in the early ninth century seemed to demonstrate stability and security and a modest intellectual rebirth.

In the islands off Europe's coast, the situation could be described with comparable optimism. Celtic kingdoms had grown up in Ireland, not without internecine warfare but with enough security to allow a flourishing monastic movement that made Ireland one of the centers of northern Christianity. Scotland and Wales still were peopled by wild tribesmen, but in England proper the Anglo-Saxon kingdoms seemed to be stabilizing somewhat as the larger absorbed the smaller and conquered most of the Celtic remnants in the west country. And the personal suzerainty of Offa of Mercia and Egbert of the West Saxons, roughly contemporaries of Charlemagne, suggested consolidation. In England, as on the continent, there existed cultural centers of note, especially in Northumbria. Churchmen from the British Isles had played no small part in Christianizing the continental peoples and in aiding the cultural revival in Europe. In the islands as on the continent, increased security, political consolidation and cultural revival appeared to be developing trends.

The reality behind the appearances was far less encouraging. Ireland still was divided, while in England the apparent political consolidation was but a personal bond with no institutional supports, and it masked bitter rivalries. No one man actually commanded in the islands, and no one was capable of raising really large military forces. Behind the appearance of growing consolidation lay the old anarchy of many petty rival kingdoms.

The reality on the continent was even more in contrast to appearances. Despite effective leadership and institutional development, there were appalling weaknesses. The military system was clumsy and inflexible. Under Charlemagne the Frankish army accomplished some quite remarkable feats of mobility and demonstrated a notable tenacity in campaign after campaign against the Saxons, but the whole structure depended utterly upon the capacity, the energy and the strength of the emperor—his ability to compel obedience and to lead to victory and glory. Equally the administration turned only upon its apex, the emperor. It was his capitularies that gave initiative, his authority that controlled the counts, his concern that directed the *missi* and the *scabini*. All depended upon him. And by the same token, even the cultural revival owed its main impetus to the rather remarkable Charles whom Europe called "the Great." His patronage of men of learning, the seminal influence of the Palace School, these were the real bases of the Carolingian renaissance.

Charlemagne had created an impressive edifice that rested wholly upon himself, like a new Atlas who upheld the world upon his shoulders. In that lay the seeds of disaster, for the structure of the empire provided no guarantee for the competence of Charlemagne's successors nor even for the stability of the succession. The succession, the problem that had plagued the Roman Empire so greatly, was not resolved clearly among the Carolingians. Pepin had ruled his father's kingdom in its entirety only because his brother preferred the monastic life. Charlemagne himself had acquired the whole Frankish kingdom only because of the fortuitous death of his brother. Even the transformation of a German tribal kingdom into a "universal" empire in the famous ceremony on Christmas Day of 800 had done nothing to modify the basically Germanic and personal conception of Carolingian rule. Charlemagne appears to have planned a partition of his lands, and only the accidents of human mortality preserved the empire intact; Louis the Pious was the only one of his sons to survive him. So behind the facade of Charlemagne's empire there loomed always the potential of division and fratricidal strife.

Nor should it be forgotten that Carolingian power depended upon wealth—the wealth to reward followers, to maintain impressive display and to underwrite innovation (such as Charles Martel's cavalry or Charlemagne's Palace School). But the increasingly agrarian foundations of the economy, reflected in the change from a gold to a silver coinage, meant there was only one real form of wealth in the society, land; and land is a decidedly inflexible sort of treasure. In the face of military necessity, Charles Martel had found an expedient in the expropriation of church lands, permitting large-scale expenditure without diminishing significantly the basis of his own power. But such an expedient could not be repeated very often, and land once granted, even with the technical limitation of granting only its fruits, was very difficult to reclaim. With declining monetary wealth, the successors of Charlemagne faced ever greater competition from the landed nobility.

To old dangers the Carolingians added some new ones. The closer alliance with the church—reflected in government support of St. Boniface's missionary efforts, in permission for tithing, in defense of the papacy—certainly produced advantages, such as help in pacifying the Saxons, a sanction for the exercise of power and an imperial crown. But at the same time this policy encouraged dependence upon clerics for governmental personnel, high military expenditures for expeditions into Italy and an implication of authority superior to the emperor's through papal coronation. So long as the church was

weak and threatened and the emperor a forceful person commanding military strength, the danger was only theoretical; but the potential for trouble was enormous.

Finally, one might note with some irony that the Carolingian
military establishment had very limited capacities, despite the great
conquests of Charlemagne. The weaknesses of organization were
many. Border defense pivoted upon local commanders who were
allowed enormous autonomy, who were controlled in fact only by
the dominant personality of the emperor. Hierarchical organization
meant considerable delay in response to a summons, and mustering
the entire host depended upon the cooperation and obedience of a
horde of lesser commanders. The weaknesses of integration and support are illustrated well by the famous Song of Roland, when the
rear guard of the army was wiped out in an ambush and its commander was left rather pathetically sounding his horn in a vain appeal for relief. But the greatest weakness of the Carolingian army
was its limited fighting capacity. It was definitely an offensive force.
Because of clumsy mobilization it had to fight at times of its own
choosing. Because of weak organization and indiscipline it was at
its best in a grand melée rather than in planned operations. The soldiers were brave, and by the standards of the day their equipment
was good; if the enemy chose to stand against them they could give
a good account of themselves, as they demonstrated against the
Moors and the Avars and the Lombards. But the Saxon wars demonstrated the army's weakness. Problems of supply and responsibilities
at home would not allow it to undertake a long-term occupation.
Discipline did not permit sending roving units to ferret the Saxons
out of their forests. The Saxon war was won by tenacity, and the fact
that it lasted thirty years is significant. The Carolingian army burned
villages and destroyed crops year after year, took hostages, deported
whole populations; and it defeated such Saxon forces as tried to
stand against it in open battle. Gradually it ground the Saxons down,
but so long as the will to resist endured, the Carolingian army was
unable to impose a solution, and it was unable to stop the raiding of
Frankish lands or the looting of churches. Only because the Saxons'
base areas were vulnerable were they finally worn out and defeated.

All of these problems became significant soon after Charlemagne's death early in the ninth century, and it is probably only a
slight exaggeration to suggest that the real strength of his empire was

his genius, his energy and his impressive qualities of leadership. His son Louis, a gentle man, followed a policy of subservience to the church that earned him the sobriquet "Louis the Pious"; one result was considerable loss of control over the church through the grant of immunities—freedom from governmental jurisdiction over church lands. And Louis proved quite unable to enforce obedience from the turbulent nobles or even from his own sons. His three sons quarreled and fought over the inheritance while their father still lived, and after his death the unity of the empire was broken as it was divided among them. To Charles (called "the Bald") went the western lands, known thereafter as the West Frankish Kingdom. To Louis went the eastern lands, which became the East Frankish Kingdom. The eldest brother, Lothar, received the title of emperor and a long narrow territory known as Lotharingia, which stretched from the mouth of the Rhine southward along the Rhine and Rhone valleys and into northern and central Italy. This last kingdom was destined to be the focal point of bitter conflicts. Geographically difficult to consolidate, it was also militarily indefensible; and in addition it offered great temptations to Lothar's brothers because it contained so much of the personal landed wealth of the Carolingian family, the royal fisc as it was called. Bloody fratricidal struggles ensued, and except for three years of peace in the late 880s, Charlemagne's successors almost constantly were involved in civil wars throughout the latter half of the ninth century.

But the weakness that was to rend most dramatically both the empire that Charlemagne had built and the Anglo-Saxon and Celtic kingdoms of the British Isles was their inability to cope with a new series of raids and invasions. The first of the new raiders arrived in Charlemagne's own lifetime. They came by sea from the north, so the Europeans called them Northmen, but they called themselves Vikings.

Scandinavia was populated by Germanic peoples of rather a primitive nature, peoples of whom little was heard until late in the eighth century when they began the great wave of raids and migrations that lasted through the ninth and tenth centuries. Viking long ships from Norway and Denmark swept the coasts of western Europe and the British Isles and probed deep inland along the river systems, while Vikings from Sweden, often called Varangians, sailed east through the Baltic and penetrated the river valleys of Russia, which they soon dominated.

The reasons for the sudden expansion of the Scandinavians still cannot be explained satisfactorily, but a number of contributing factors have been identified. At this period a process of political consolidation was under way, binding tribal groups into the kingdoms of Denmark, Norway and Sweden, and it has been suggested that some of the more turbulent elements of the Scandinavian population left rather than submit to this new authority. In addition the archeological record indicates that there was a considerable increase of population putting severe pressure upon the limited and relatively unproductive northern lands. Why this sudden population explosion should have taken place is unclear, but legends suggest that large families—and particularly many sons—constituted a status symbol, and the practice of polygamy and the maintenance of concubines as well as wives made possible very large families. Larger village sites imply an ample supply of young men, and primogeniture—total inheritance by the eldest son—meant many men were landless and eager to earn, through raids and plunder, the price of a farm or the bride price to buy a wife.

Trade also may have been a factor in the Scandinavian expansion. As the trade of the Mediterranean dwindled under the impact of the Moslems, a much more modest trade in the north seems to have benefitted. Charlemagne's Frisian subjects in the Rhine delta conducted a flourishing small trade with Scandinavia in such things as furs and walrus ivory, and there are grounds to believe that lucrative piracy and a desire to secure control of profitable legitimate trade were also factors in drawing the Scandinavians southward. In any event it is frequently the case in primitive commerce that when there is a parity of strength there is trade, and when there is a disparity the strong take from the weak.

A technological factor also seems to have been operative in the development of the Viking raids. Sails had been known in the Mediterranean for centuries, and in fact as far north as the west coast of Gaul some of the Celtic peoples were using sails in Caesar's time, but the Scandinavians appear to have built only rowboats until the sixth century. Then through the sixth to eighth centuries Scandinavian rowboats evolved into typical Viking longships with large sails and solid keels. They were built in various sizes but to a more or less standard configuration. Long and low, they were rather broad-beamed, which gave them stability in the rough North Sea and in the Atlantic. Their strength was increased further by the method of planking the hulls; boards were overlapped and then nailed or riveted together, rather than simply being butted and nailed to frames as was the case in the south. This technique allowed more solid caulking and produced a vessel more seaworthy in heavy weather. And their shallow draught allowed them to be brought close inshore or to ply quite shallow rivers.

On the other hand there were drawbacks to these ships too. They were open or only partially decked, offering little shelter for the crew. They were guided by a long sweep oar, they had a single square sail and they had a shallow though strong keel; all of this resulted in rather poor steering control. Running before the wind they were sleek and fast, but in a crosswind they drifted off course wildly. (At least part of the credit for the Norse discoveries of Greenland and North America would appear to be due to the inability to hold a course.) In consequence, the long voyages across the open sea must excite great admiration, for the ships really were ill-suited for such uses. But they were ideal as raiders, for they could slip along the coasts close inshore, looking for targets, and they could probe far up the rivers for the plunder of inland cities.

The men are as interesting as the ships. Noble chiefs often commanded while staunch peasant boys made up the crew, though in at least one famous instance some Vikings told the Franks that they were all equals. If the wind died they rowed. And when they happened upon a likely target, they disembarked and leaped to the attack with sword or battleaxe. Actually they seem not to have been particularly redoubtable fighters, as they had little success at first against Europe's professional military caste. Their complete indiscipline on early plundering raids and their relatively primitive weapons were quite surpassed by evolving European political organization and by the mounted knight. Charlemagne built a string of watch towers and beacons that largely protected the coasts of Gaul until well into the reign of his son, and late in the ninth century Alfred the Great organized generally successful campaigns against Scandinavians who had settled in England.

Though the large invading forces of the late Viking period appear to have learned something of planning and discipline, the private raiders seem to have been quite ill-organized. Sometimes they went into battle in a drunken stupor after an all-night drinking bout during which alcohol, songs and epics of great heroes were supposed to arouse their courage to its highest pitch. The seeming paradox of their primitivism and their devastating impact upon Europe and the British Isles is explained by their mobility and their choice of targets. Appearing suddenly, plundering and burning, and then withdrawing, the Viking raiders rarely fought pitched battles with European armies. Usually they were opposed only by the peasants or monks who were their victims, and by the time the noble knights could gather to resist them, they were completing their withdrawal to their ships, in which they sailed away safe from pursuit. If a selected target mounted a stiff resistance, they often abandoned it in favor of a different objective. One source of plunder was as good as another. So they hit the weakest aspect of Europe's military establishment—the slowness of mobilization. In contrast to the tactics that finally crushed the Saxons, it was not possible for European forces to retaliate with strikes at their base areas, destroying their homes and crops.

In the last years of the eighth century and the first half of the ninth century the raiders struck without warning against isolated monasteries and small villages, looted, and then returned to their homelands safely guarded by the sea. But about the middle of the ninth century the nature of the Viking incursions began to change. The men from the north had grown familiar with the lands they preyed upon, and a half-century of raiding had built a large reserve of experienced warriors. They grew bolder, and they learned to act together. Fleets as well as individual ships began to prowl, and they attempted more ambitious targets.

Early in the 840s a Viking fleet entered the Seine and plundered the city of Rouen, and another ascended the Loire and sacked Nantes. The latter force also set another precedent, establishing a winter camp on an island off the river's mouth instead of returning north. Early in the 880s England witnessed the same phenomenon as Danish raiders established a permanent base in the mouth of the Thames. And about the same period Swedish adventurers were founding permanent positions among the northern Slavic peoples of Russia, first at Novgorod—southeast of the Gulf of Finland—and then at Kiev—to the south on the middle reaches of the Dnieper. Thus both in the west and in the east the Vikings were settling.

From these new European bases they quickly extended the range of their depredations. Soon they had probed inland along the Loire and the Seine valleys as far as Orleans and Paris, had struck

the south through the Garonne and had rounded Gibraltar into the
Mediterranean and ascended the Rhone valley—raiding Spain, Morocco and the Balearic Islands along the way. England suffered as
severely, for there Danish raids turned into conquest in the last quarter of the ninth century, and before the situation was stabilized by
the Anglo-Saxon king of Wessex, the Danes held most of England
north of the Thames. In the east the Swedes who were settled in
Russia were developing contacts with the Byzantine Empire, sometimes raiding, sometimes trading, sometimes hiring out as mercenaries. So in all quarters the new peoples from the north were becoming ever more intimately associated with the older settlers in Europe.

It was only about the beginning of the tenth century that the
northmen began to be assimilated. By the middle of the century the
kings of Wessex had succeeded in subjugating the Danish invaders
to their rule and to Christianity, and they governed an England that
was jointly Anglo-Saxon and Danish. On the continent a sort of stability was achieved in 911 when the West Frankish king, Charles
the Simple, granted lands at the mouth of the Seine to the Viking
chief Rollo on the conditions that he defend the area and accept
Christianity. Thus the nucleus of a new principality was established,
which would develop—with later additions—into the powerful
duchy of Normandy. Thereafter Rollo's band protected the Seine
and Channel coast and helped to protect the Loire, so that during the
next two or three decades the Viking raids on the West Frankish
Kingdom died out.

In the latter half of the tenth century the Swedish state in western Russia was consolidated around Kiev, and through contacts with
Byzantium the prince of Kiev was converted to the Greek form of
Christianity just before the end of the century. Thus, by the end of
the tenth century large numbers of Scandinavians had been settled
and Christianized (at least nominally), but during the ninth and
tenth centuries they had spread destruction far and wide, and the
first bloom of cultural revival in England and the West Frankish
lands had been crushed.

The foregoing discussion would seem to suggest that the Eastern
Franks were fortunate. While the Anglo-Saxons, Celts and West
Franks were being ravaged by the Danes and the Norwegians, and
the northern Slavs were being conquered by the Swedes, the largely

land-locked East Frankish Kingdom was spared the Vikings except for some raiding along the Baltic coast. But the Eastern Franks did not escape the fire and sword. From the east—whence the Goths and the Huns and the Avars had descended upon Europe—appeared a new fierce Turkish people, the Magyars. The devastation of central Europe simply came a bit later than the sacking of the West.

When the Varangians penetrated Russia, the Magyars occupied the northwest coastal area of the Black Sea, and together with the Avars, whom Charlemagne had conquered and confined to the plains of Hungary, constituted a sort of wedge between the southern Slavs of the Balkans and the northern Slavs of Russia. At the end of the ninth century, under pressure from the Varangians, the Magyars migrated westward into Hungary where they joined the remaining Avars, to whom they were related. Then through the first half of the tenth century they raided into Germany, reaching as far west as the Rhine valley and on one occasion even probing deep into eastern France and sacking Rheims. Not until the middle of the century were they stopped, when the East Frankish king imposed a crushing defeat upon them, confining them—like their predecessors —to the Hungarian plains. In the year 1000 the Magyars were converted to Christianity by St. Stephen, and from then onward they, too, constituted a permanent element in the population of Christian Europe. Though the Magyar raids had lasted less than half as long as the Viking depredations, they had been terribly destructive.

Finally a word should be said about the southern borders of Europe at the end of the tenth century. In the east the Byzantine emperors had concentrated their attention upon their rich Asiatic provinces which were threatened first by the Persians and then by the Arabs. The European provinces had been left largely to their own devices, and during the seventh and eighth centuries there was a considerable alteration of population. It was during this period that Slavs and a Turkish people, the Bulgars, moved into the Balkans, and they and the Avars devastated the European provinces to the walls of Byzantium for the next two hundred years, until a Byzantine emperor crushed them and absorbed Bulgaria into the empire about A. D. 1000.

The rise of Mohammedanism and the rapid expansion of the Arabs from the second quarter of the seventh century onward had accomplished a major transformation of the balance of power in the Mediterranean. They held all of the eastern lands bordering that sea south of Asia Minor, and they had spread westward to occupy the whole of the North African coast and Spain, crushing the Visigothic Kingdom in the latter area in 711. In fact the expansion had halted only when the Moslems crossed the Pyrenees into Frankish lands and encountered Charles Martel's force, as was noted previously. Internal dissension sprang up during the attempts to consolidate these vast conquests, and the dynamic of expansion was never regained, but about the year 1000 the power of Islam remained the dominant force in the Mediterranean.

Italy was divided. Most of the peninsula was at least nominally under the control of the Holy Roman Emperor, but the Byzantines held several fortified positions from Venice in the northeast through coastal areas in the extreme south to Naples in the southwest, and the Moslems held Sicily. Fighting among these factions was endemic, and Italy—once the center of Western civilization—was torn and broken.

Chapter 6

The Birth of
Feudal Monarchy

During the ninth and tenth centuries, domestic quarrels and foreign invasions weakened Carolingian monarchical power to the advantage of the great nobility. Some noblemen succeeded in exacting concessions of land and authority from the kings as the price of their support in civil wars, while others achieved comparable gains as leaders of the defense against the Vikings and Magyars; by the late tenth century these trends had resulted in new ruling families and new patterns of government in both the western and eastern Frankish kingdoms. During the same period in England, the Saxons composed their differences in the face of the Viking threat, establishing a strong monarchy for a time, and then they collapsed completely before an invasion from Normandy in the middle of the eleventh century. Thus, England also developed new governmental patterns.

In the West Frankish Kingdom the decline of the Carolingians was related directly to the effects of the Viking raids. In the late ninth century a nobleman called Robert the Strong was sent by the Carolingian king to defend the Loire Valley against Viking incursions. Though he had only indifferent success in fulfilling this commission, he proved very successful in acquiring new lands for himself, several counties between the Loire and Seine Rivers, emerging as a powerful magnate of the kingdom. In 885 Robert's son Odo commanded the successful defense of Paris against a Viking attack, and a few years later the West Frankish nobility chose Odo as king instead of the Carolingian claimant. During the next century the throne alternated between the two families, four Carolingians and three of Odo's descendants holding it at one time or another, and then in 987 it passed definitively from Carolingian control with the accession of Hugh Capet, from whom the new ruling family derived its name, Capetian.

Hugh Capet (987–996) inaugurated policies so successful that his direct descendants ruled until 1328. Perhaps the most notable of these policies was his decision to associate his son with his rule during his own lifetime, with the consequence that the succession was not disputed. Continued by Hugh Capet's descendants, this practice negated the elective principle of Germanic monarchy so effectively that the French crown became hereditary. In addition, Capet began what usually is called the "domainal policy," concentration upon effective rule of his family's personal lands while avoiding interference with the great nobles who were legally his vassals but were actually his equals or superiors in power; thus he avoided antagonizing dangerous rivals while building a solid foundation for his dynasty.

In consequence of the domainal policy, the Capetian monarchy of the eleventh century was very different from that of Charlemagne. The kings ruled directly only in the Ile de France, their personal lands, contenting themselves in the rest of the kingdom with a vague suzerainty that produced prestige and a small revenue but no effective political control. They did not pretend to legislate for the whole kingdom, nor had they an administrative apparatus of controllable counts and *missi dominici.* Outside the Ile de France, great feudal lords governed their own domains as the king governed his, limited only by a few minor financial and legal obligations of their vassalage. On the other hand, the kings had a few advantages no other feudal lords could claim. They stood at the apex of the feudal pyramid, the only lords in the kingdom who had no overlord. They enjoyed the prestige of being the successors of Clovis and Charlemagne, anointed as God's lieutenants at their coronation. Finally, they benefitted directly from their special relationship to the church, both from the general support of the clergy, who saw the kings as the most viable alternative to the instability and the endemic violence of feudal rivalries, and from their regalian rights over two dozen bishoprics and three dozen monasteries all over the kingdom, rights which provided both revenue and control of appointments. These advantages were enough to maintain the Capetians for a century and a half, and only about the middle of the twelfth century did they embark on an effort to expand their effective political authority more widely in the kingdom.

Political development in the East Frankish Kingdom from the mid-tenth to mid-twelfth centuries followed a course rather different from that in the west, largely because conditions were quite different. Most of Germany never had been part of the Roman Empire, so civilization had come only with the missionary work of the church and with the conquests of Charlemagne. Thus, Germany had not developed so elaborate a pattern of hierarchical feudalism and had remained closer to its tribal origins, a sort of ethnic tradition exemplified by the survival of large regional subdivisions called "Stem Duchies"—Bavaria, Swabia, Saxony and Franconia. In the face of strong traditions and popular support of the Stem Dukes, Carolingian patterns of administration by controllable officials never had been established so strongly as in the west, and under the pressure of Viking and Magyar raids these patterns broke down altogether while the Stem Dukes grew stronger. One result was that the Carolingians were abandoned early in the tenth century, and weak kings were chosen or the throne was left vacant, which left the political power of the Stem Dukes uncontested.

In Germany as in France, however, churchmen favored the authority of a king rather than a number of dukes, and their arguments were accepted when it became evident that only unified leadership could curb the Magyar raids. In 919 the dukes reluctantly chose the strongest of their number, Henry the Fowler, duke of Saxony, as king, and he set to work immediately to rebuild the monarchy. Henry (919–936) tried to reestablish royal control of the counts, aided churchmen in the recovery of lands that had been usurped and gave them the power of counts in their lands, and led effective military campaigns against the Magyars. His son, Otto I (936–973) continued these policies with considerable success. He managed to acquire control of Franconia as well as his own Saxony, so that he held two of the four Stem Duchies; he continued to support bishops and abbots so that several became important secular as well as ecclesiastical lords and constituted an effective check upon the power of rural dukes; and he imposed a crushing defeat upon the Magyars in 955, which confined them to the Hungarian plain. In addition, Otto conquered Burgundy and Lombardy, thus adding important parts of the Frankish Middle Kingdom to his own domains, and as a logical conclusion to these successes he went to Rome and was crowned Holy Roman Emperor in 962. But though Otto I had reunited a vast territory and had revived the imperial title, his authority rested upon weak foundations. Only in Saxony did he have reliable local support; in south Germany the dukes of Bavaria and Swabia were more rivals than vassals, and in the rest of his domains he depended upon ecclesiatical fiefs and his army. His son and grandson proved unable to maintain the personal authority that he had created, and in the second quarter of the eleventh century the German monarchy underwent another transformation when the crown passed to the Franconian House, called Salians.

The first of the Salian emperors, Conrad (1024–1039), did little more than try to recover the authority lost in Germany while the late Ottonians were involved in Italy, but under his successors, Henry III (1039–1056) and Henry IV (1056–1106) the Salians inaugurated contentious new policies, the most controversial of which was the appointment of a class of untitled royal officials called *ministeriales.* These officials, completely dependent upon royal favor and wholly devoted to royal interests, were given command of castles all through the realm and were intended deliberately to undermine the power of the Stem Dukes and the powerful princes who had developed under the Ottonians; naturally they aroused great resentment. In addition Henry III encouraged the work of the monastic reformers known as the Cluniacs, who had support in the papal *curia;* he seems never to have realized that one of the chief aims of the reformers was to free ecclesiastical appointments from secular control, a goal which would undermine the foundations of the German monarchy since it depended so heavily upon the ecclesiastical princes whose powers the Ottonians had expanded. The harvest of these dangerous policies was reaped in the reign of Henry IV, princely revolt and a long-drawn quarrel with the papacy.

This great struggle, which broke the power of the Salian emperors, is called the Investiture Controversy, because the overt issue was the right to invest bishops with the symbols of their spiritual offices; the real issue, however, was the selection and appointment of high churchmen. As a consequence of policies begun by the Ottonians, the

German prelates were one of the most important bases of the imperial administration; the emperor considered this role their first obligation, and naturally he wished to control their appointments. By contrast, the religious reformers wished to free ecclesiastical appointments from secular control; to them, the prelate's first obligation was to the church, and his selection was a matter for the clergy of his diocese. The issue became a crisis with the election to the papacy of the fiery reformer Hildebrand, who took the papal title of Gregory VII (1073–1085).

Pope Gregory did not limit his claims to the empire, but he made his strongest effort there, for Henry IV was the most powerful prince in Europe, and if he surrendered, other princes would be likely to do the same. The quarrel became acrimonious; Gregory excommunicated Henry, while Henry called Gregory a false pope, improperly elected. Generally the German clergy, Henry's appointees, supported the emperor, while the German princes, who opposed Henry politically, supported the papacy. The outcome was a hollow victory for Gregory's successors and disaster for the empire. Compromise early in the twelfth century provided that diocesan clergy should elect bishops in the presence of the monarch or his representative; this provision made elections a farce and left effective control with the secular ruler. The only real gains were made by the German princes who managed to seize imperial lands and authority during the bitter struggle. For one more generation the Salians continued to hold the crown, but the reign of Henry IV's son was wracked by civil wars, and when he died without heirs in 1125, the Salian monarchy died with him.

The violence that marked the last quarter of the eleventh century and the first quarter of the twelfth century changed the whole political structure of Germany. During the turbulence freemen were forced into serfdom, and lesser nobles became the vassals of princes; at the same time the princes usurped royal offices and fiefs, making them hereditary, and built a multitude of castles to defend their recent gains. By the middle of the twelfth century manorialism and vassalage were established firmly in Germany, but they constituted a truncated feudalism, lacking an apex, for the hierarchy culminated in a number of princes, over whom the emperor reigned as no more than a figurehead.

England's political experience from the mid-tenth to mid-twelfth centuries was unique, chiefly because of invasion and conquest. The strong Saxon monarchy that had been built by Alfred the Great

(871–899) continued through the tenth century, and probably was the most effective government in western Europe. While an elective principle survived, the crown tended to remain with Alfred's descendants, the royal house of Wessex. Every able-bodied man owed military service at the king's summons, which provided the basis for an army. And the kings drew revenue from many scattered estates that formed the crown lands, from fines collected in criminal courts and, after 991, from a land tax called *danegeld* which originally was a levy imposed to pay tribute to Danish invaders. In addition the kings enjoyed extensive control of local officials called sheriffs and of prelates of the court.

In the middle of the eleventh century a succession dispute left this attractive kingdom vulnerable to invasion. Upon the death of the Saxon king, Edward the Confessor (1035–1066), the Witan conferred the crown upon Harold Godwin, a Wessex magnate, but there were two other powerful contenders: Duke William of Normandy, who had secured papal blessings for his claims, and Harold's brother Tostig, the latter allied with the king of Norway. In 1066 both launched independent attacks upon Harold, who succeeded in defeating the Norwegians but was defeated and killed by Duke William, who assumed the crown as William I (1066–1087).

Though the Norman conquest had profound consequences for the future of England, its immediate impact ought not to be exaggerated. Though scattered fighting continued for five years, the country did not suffer extensive military operations. As William considered himself Edward the Confessor's rightful successor, he promised to maintain ancient customs; moreover, Saxon landholders who had not opposed him openly retained their property, simply becoming his vassals, though the lands of others who had resisted were expropriated to reward his followers. Perhaps the greatest single impact of the conquest was the establishment of more fully developed continental feudalism and manorialism; both newly settled Normans and surviving Saxon landowners were compelled to accept the military obligations common to feudal relationships in Normandy, providing for an army of about 5,000 knights, and common farmers, most of whom had been freemen in Saxon England, were depressed into serfdom. To record the many obligations owed to him, William inaugurated a great survey of the value and tax assessment of English landholdings, called *Domesday Book*.

In the century following the conquest, the Normans introduced a number of innovations into England. One of the most notable was castle-building, begun by William I to tighten his hold on the country and to assure his route of retreat in case of a successful Saxon rising; his successors continued this construction program, and by 1150 England was defended by a network of about 1200 castles, which made another successful invasion very unlikely. Henry I (1100–1135) added improvements in the fiscal and judicial administration, permanent treasury officials in the exchequer and roving royal judges. After his death, quarrels over the succession plunged England into two decades of civil war during which the barons usurped great authority; by the middle of the twelfth century the English king appeared as helpless before his vassals as did the emperor in Germany, but thanks to the institutional growth encouraged by the early Norman kings, there remained in England the basis for a powerful royal revival.

Political developments between the middle of the twelfth century and the middle of the thirteenth century had enduring effects in the Holy Roman Empire. The crown passed to the House of Hohenstaufen, and a vigorous attempt to revive imperial power ensued. Emperor Frederick Barbarossa (1152–1190) did not attempt to govern Germany outside his own Duchy of Swabia. Instead, he concentrated upon establishing effective control of Burgundy and northern and central Italy. The new policy brought him into conflict with developing Italian towns and with the papacy, but after some military reverses he achieved considerable success through diplomacy. He granted autonomy to the towns in return for revenue, and he neutralized the papacy through a marriage alliance with the Kingdom of Sicily, which established Hohenstaufen positions flanking the Papal States both north and south. By the time of Barbarossa's death, the empire had been transformed totally; Germany had become a feudal monarchy in which the emperor was only the suzerain of the princes, but the House of Hohenstaufen enjoyed extensive revenues outside of Germany, and in Swabia and Italy it had solid political bases.

The short, troubled reign of Barbarossa's son, Henry VI (1190–1197), produced little that was remarkable except the integration of Sicily into Hohenstaufen possessions, but under Henry's son, Frederick II (1215–1250), the great struggle between pope and emperor for control of Italy was renewed. Fortuitously, Frederick's chief rival in Germany was defeated crushingly in a war with the king of France, and relieved of that concern Frederick practically abandoned Germany to its princes so he could concentrate his efforts on

Italy. Although his brilliant court in Sicily and his fascinating person-ality led his contemporaries to call him "the wonder of the world," Frederick achieved little politically, and after his death the House of Hohenstaufen declined rapidly. The German princes and the north Italian towns maintained their independence; papal fortunes revived in central Italy; and then the last Hohenstaufen lost Sicily to a brother of the king of France. After Frederick II the imperial crown was little more than an empty title, though one much fought over; there were no more revivals of imperial authority as a political force until the sixteenth century.

The period from the middle of the twelfth century to the end of the thirteenth century witnessed extraordinary and closely related developments in the two western monarchies. King Louis VII of France (1137–1180) had married Eleanor of Aquitaine, heiress to vast domains in the western and southwestern parts of the kingdom, but he had drawn little advantage from these lands as the local no-bility proved quite ungovernable. Thus, when Louis desired the an-nulment of his marriage, chiefly because Eleanor had given him no sons, the loss of Aquitaine did not seem very significant. However, no sooner was the annulment pronounced, in 1152, than Eleanor married again, and Aquitaine represented a very important addition to the domains of her new husband, Henry Plantagenet, count of Anjou, duke of Normandy, and two years later, king of England as Henry II (1154–1189). Thus Eleanor's remarriage brought together under a single rule the kingdom of England and most of western France from Normandy to the Pyrenees, creating what often is called the "Angevin Empire." Louis VII protested feebly because as feudal suzerain for Henry's continental lands he should have been con-sulted, but he could accomplish little against the vigorous Angevin monarch. Henry II and his son Richard the Lionhearted (1189–1199) pursued a policy of integration of their lands, and for the re-mainder of the twelfth century the French kings faced western vas-sals far stronger than themselves.

Louis VII did his best to maintain his dynasty, and a new mar-riage with the House of Blois and Champagne brought powerful sup-port to the French crown and produced the needed heir, Philip II, called Augustus (1180–1223). By his own marriage Philip later as-sured the alliance of the Count of Flanders and laid the foundations for a French recovery. But as both of the first two Angevins had real military talent, neither Louis VII nor Philip Augustus could accomplish much against them, and it was only when Richard the Lion-hearted died and was succeeded by his brother John (1199–1216) that fortune turned in favor of the French crown.

Philip Augustus understood the value of legal position in his struggle with John, and he exploited the possibilities of his role as feudal suzerain to the fullest. When John quarreled with one of his vassals and the latter appealed to Philip as John's overlord, Philip promptly escalated the issue into a major confrontation. He summoned John to appear before him, and when John refused, Philip's court declared him a disobedient vassal within the terms of his feudal contract and pronounced all his fiefs forfeit. Thus Philip acquired a clear legal right to take whatever he was strong enough to seize of John's continental possessions. By a combination of sieges and bribery of castle commanders, he secured one after another of the Angevin fortresses during the next few years, and by 1205 he had taken all of John's northern French lands and had won the support of many of the southern barons. The "Angevin Empire" survived only in the coastal regions of the southwest, Guienne and Gascony. John attempted to recover, attacking Anjou himself while his ally, Otto of Germany, Frederick II's rival, invaded France from the north. However, Philip Augustus smashed the German force at the Battle of Bouvines in 1214, one of the crucial military engagements of medieval Europe. As a result of this victory, John was forced to withdraw to England, the French crown's conquests in the west were secure, and Frederick II was free to embark upon his Italian adventures.

The great struggle between the Capetians and the Angevins stimulated important developments in royal government. Henry II increased the revenues of the English crown considerably by reviewing and raising the assessment of monies his vassals paid him in lieu of military service, by increasing his fees for royal consent on such occasions as the marriage of a vassal or the inheritance of a fief, and by expanding the operations of the royal courts which brought large sums to the treasury through fines. By-products of the last policy were a considerable expansion of the common law and the beginning of the extensive use of juries. Henry II's sons continued his practices, but the growing strength of the crown evoked a baronial reaction. King John, though a competent enough administrator, was never popular with his vassals, and after the humiliating loss of most of his continental possessions to Philip Augustus, his English barons revolted against him. Largely through the influence of the Arch-bishop of Canterbury, Stephen Langton, the barons pressed for general concessions instead of satisfaction of specific private grievances, and John was forced to agree. The document that embodied the agreements, *Magna Carta*, basically was a statement of the terms of feudal obligations and a definition of the powers of royal government in the early thirteenth century; most of its specific provisions were outdated quickly, but its limitation of the king's right to collect money and its requirement that arrests and punishments follow proper legal action amounted in fact to an admission that the king was bound by law, an admission from which has grown much English legal and constitutional tradition.

John died a year after his assent to the *Magna Carta*, and during the long reign of his weak-willed son, Henry III (1216–1272), the baronial reaction continued to erode the position of the crown. But at the end of the thirteenth century Henry's son, Edward I (1272–1307), again provided vigorous royal leadership, and feudal monarchy in England reached its fullest development. Under Edward I specialization of the royal administration continued, with further elaboration of the exchequer and the courts that had been created by Henry I and Henry II. But perhaps the most important political development of this reign was the growth of parliament in 1295. English kings long had consulted barons, prelates, knights and townsmen concerning various matters for which they felt the need of support; Edward I's innovation was to bring all of these elements together in one assembly, and by the end of his reign such a convocation of the whole realm—the king in parliament—generally was recognized as necessary to decisions regarding legal changes and tax levies.

A comparable governmental development took place in France during this same period. Philip Augustus' conquests increased enormously the revenues of the French crown, finally rendering it stronger than any of its vassals. This sudden increase in the lands governed directly by the king necessitated expansion and improvement of the crown's financial and judicial administration, and Philip created new salaried officials for this purpose, *baillis* and *senechals;* as numerous assistants to these officials were appointed, a rather large bureaucracy developed rapidly.

Philip's son reigned too briefly to be effective, but his grandson, Louis IX (1226–1270), called St. Louis, contributed importantly to the continued growth of the French crown, not so much through institutional developments as through the enormous respect for the royal personage inspired by his piety and his reputation for justice. It must not be assumed that these qualities implied weakness; though personally devout St. Louis staunchly defended the independence of the French church against papal pretensions, though famous for scrupulously honest judgments he vigorously enforced his jurisdictional rights when they were contested by his vassals, and throughout his reign he contended with considerable success against the private warfare that was endemic to feudal society.

Under St. Louis' son and grandson, Philip III (1270–1285) and Philip IV (1285–1314), these policies continued, though a baronial reaction forced Philip IV to grant charters resembling *Magna Carta* except that they were regional rather than national. The elaboration of the royal government, with specialized sections, also paralleled English developments. Philip Augustus had improved treasury procedures considerably, and under Philip IV this effort came to fruition with the establishment of the *chambre des comptes,* which resembled the exchequer. St. Louis had established his chief law court as a more or less permanent body called the *parlement* of Paris, and under Philip IV this court developed specialized sections. Like Edward I, King Philip IV recognized the advantage to the crown of support by a broadly representative body, and he fused several of the assemblies that the crown was in the habit of consulting, convening the first estates general in 1302.

There were, however, some important differences between English and French government. Most notably, France was larger and more populous than England, and the French king never was able to make decisions of the estates general binding in detail upon the whole realm as was the English king; in France, a multitude of regional assemblies continued and had to be dealt with even after general agreement in the estates general. This both reduced the estates general's value to the crown and impeded its capacity to present a unified opposition to the king. In addition, the French government used far more paid professional administrators than did the English government, which continued to rely heavily upon local landowners. Thus, the French bureaucracy developed more of a sense of separateness from the realm, a concept of being over the country rather than of it. This attitude was strengthened by the study of Roman law which contributed to the idea that the king was God's lieutenant on earth and that, consequently, while he had an obligation to rule with justice, he was not bound stringently by custom. Thus, lacking England's compactness, its common law and its dependence upon dedicated amateurism, French government—despite similar institutions—developed along more bureaucratic lines with a consequent alienation of the governing from the governed.

In addition to important governmental development, the thirteenth century also witnessed the growth of a practice in France that was to lead to serious problems for the crown, the designation of large areas as appanages to support younger royal children. That this practice did not lead earlier to considerable alienation of royal domain lands probably was due only to the fact that the royal family was small, for precedents for the establishment of appanages go back at least to Hugh Capet. But the thirteenth and fourteenth century Capetians, and after them the Valois, sired more sons, and providing for them led to the foundation of important new aristocratic houses related to the crown. In one way the creation of appanages probably helped the kings to control the country at last. After the conquests of Philip Augustus the area that owed obedience to the French crown was enormous, and both the state of communications and the rudimentary nature of thirteenth century government precluded direct administration of all of it from Paris. The kings had to trust others to act as their agents. In medieval society only someone of considerable personal stature could command even limited obedience from feudal lords; but most great nobles were more the kings' rivals than their trusted associates, so the use of close relatives probably was a reasonable expedient. The difficulty was that after a generation or two the appanages were held not by the sons or brothers of kings but by cousins, and family ties weakened accordingly. Thus, in late medieval France, while the crown was suppressing the independence of the great fiefs it was creating new princely houses that would prove just as troublesome in the late fourteenth and fifteenth centuries.

Despite the differences noted, certain generalizations are possible about the nature of feudal monarchy. Germany and Italy lie outside the consideration, of course, for in Germany the feudal structure was truncated, without an effective monarchy superior to the princes, and Italy was subdivided into a multitude of jurisdictions. But from the mid-twelfth century to the late thirteenth century feudal monarchy developed along similar lines in France and England, despite differences in detail between the two realms. As conquerors, the English monarchs started from a stronger position, while the foundation of the French monarchy was tribal tradition and election. But both depended originally upon the sanction of the church, and both drew their early revenues largely from the income of personal lands and from irregular fees, known as aids and reliefs, that derived of their positions as feudal overlords. In both realms the development of the monarchy as a dominant institution followed the same course: the exploitation of seigneurial and judicial rights for increased revenues, the specialization of administration for improved efficiency and, finally, the development of representative institutions for more effective consolidation. With the creation of the parliament and the estates general feudal monarchy reached its apogee.

Chapter 7

Merchants, Money, and Social Change

To some extent the political development of Europe between the early eleventh century and the late thirteenth century depended upon important economic and social transformations, of which the most significant were the revival of commerce and the renewal of urban life. These changes created new elements in the old agrarian-aristocratic society and introduced new forms of wealth in money and movable goods rather than in land and rights of *usufruct*.

It should be remembered that the decline of commerce, which began in the late Roman period and reached its nadir in the ninth century, never was absolute. Some universally necessary goods, such as salt and iron, were found only in limited regions, and people outside those regions had to barter to obtain them. Even a trickle of long-distance commerce survived; a few Jewish merchants moved between the Christian and Moslem worlds and carried on a small trade in luxury goods, and the Byzantine navy usually managed to protect the sea route between Constantinople and Venice, along which European grain and lumber were exchanged for the manufactures of eastern craftsmen. But the total commercial activity was of small volume, and it was on a basis of barter rather than money.

Though medieval European trade eventually included such exotic items as Chinese silk and Indonesian spices, the commercial revival began with more mundane goods, such as salt, grain, wine and textiles. The growth of monasticism contributed importantly to this trade, for the monasteries constituted large communities that had to be fed and clothed, and some of the earliest merchants of the European revival were monastic agents called *negotiatores* (negotiators), who offered the wine and wool of their monasteries for salt, iron and other commodities that could not be produced locally. This modest expansion of trade within Europe helped to create the accumulations of capital that made possible a revival of long-distance trade in more luxurious and consequently more costly goods.

In the tenth century, the surviving international trade through Venice had wide repercussions on the north Italian mainland, where the trickle of eastern goods stimulated local manufactures, particularly textiles. In north Italy towns had survived in a modest way, as civil and episcopal administrative centers, and in the tenth century they began manufacturing good cloth. Soon the existence of surplus products, which had little market to the east where it had to compete with the more developed industry of Constantinople, led north Italians to seek markets to the west. Despite the danger from Moslem raiders, ships from Genoa and Pisa began to sail along the coast of southern France in search of trade. When joint expeditions by the two towns succeeded in driving the Moslems from Sardinia and Corsica early in the eleventh century, and Norman knights conquered Sicily in the latter part of the century, the increased security for Christian shipping stimulated the western Mediterranean commerce, and it expanded rapidly.

While north Italy was developing as a focus of revived Mediterranean trade, a smaller but still important commercial center was growing in Flanders, the area that lay generally around the mouths of the Rhine and its tributaries. The region had been famous for its woolen cloth even before the Roman conquest of Gaul, and this industry had continued as one of the few bases of trade in Carolingian times. Though disrupted by the Viking raids, trade had revived as soon as the Counts of Flanders had succeeded in restoring order in the second half of the tenth century, and the area's communications—across the Channel to England, northward to Scandinavia and up the Rhine deep into Germany—soon stimulated a flourishing commerce. In the eleventh century business was so good that the Flemings began importing raw wool from England, and in the twelfth century England became Europe's chief wool producer, mostly for Flemish looms. England's commercial connections with the continent also were stimulated in another way after the conquest of 1066. England's Norman masters refused to abuse their palates with domestic ales, and a very active new trade developed around the importation of wine from France; until the middle of the twelfth century the Seine valley was the chief producer for this trade, shipping through Rouen, and then after the accession of Henry II the Loire valley and the Bordeaux region became important suppliers.

In the twelfth and thirteenth centuries Mediterranean commerce was stimulated considerably by the crusades, chiefly because they provided eastbound cargoes. Until the crusades north Italian merchants confronted the difficult problem that while demand for eastern goods was growing in Europe, there was little that Europeans could sell in the east, and sending ships out in ballast raised costs and reduced profits. The European military expeditions to the Holy Land offered cargoes of men and horses to be transported, and even when the crusaders went overland they expected to be supplied by sea; moreover, the soldiers were followed by hordes of religious pilgrims who wished to visit the Christian holy places, so the transport of passengers continued to be important for rather a long time; and upon returning home these people contributed to the growing demand for fine goods with which they had become familiar while in the East. The once popular notion that the crusades were the basic cause of the revival of commerce in Europe must be considered an exaggeration, for there was an important redevelopment of domestic trade before they began, but it is beyond dispute that the crusades contributed importantly to the expansion of Mediterranean shipping and, hence, to the diversification of the commercial revival throughout Europe.

The opening of a connection between the two trade centers of north Italy and Flanders established the framework for a fuller development of medieval European commerce. Storms, distance, and the threat of Moslem pirates around the Straits of Gibraltar precluded any extensive use of a sea route, so the connection was made overland along the French river valleys that the Romans had traveled long before. From north Italy, merchants sailed to Marseilles, then followed the Rhone and Saône into Champagne, where they could cross easily to rivers that flowed north and west—the Rhine, the Moselle, the Seine and the Loire. This route also presented serious problems in the form of poor roads, bandits and the exactions of feudal lords who charged tolls for the rights of passage across their lands, but nonetheless it was cheaper and more secure than the sea passage; in the twelfth century, merchants began moving silks, spices and Italian horses along this route to be exchanged for the furs, metals and hunting hawks of the north.

Inevitably, the revival of commerce affected the noble elite of European society, and the reactions of its members varied widely. Some noblemen saw merchants simply as focal points of mobile wealth which presented opportunities for pillage, and these robber barons had to be accepted as one of the hazards of trade, necessitating such precautions as armed guards for caravans. Other noblemen considered merchants a source of welcome cash income, for they would pay for the hire of some of the lord's men-at-arms as caravan guards, and their commerce provided tolls from charges on roads and bridges and market taxes from sales. Some few lords, the exceptions, studied the new developments, came to understand the economics involved and used their social position and resources to participate actively for enormous profit; the most notable examples of this latter group were the counts of Champagne.

Located at the junction of routes leading to the great areas of trade and manufacture in north Italy and Flanders, Champagne was situated ideally to develop as a center of exchange for all of Europe, and the counts of Champagne were astute enough to recognize and exploit this potential by sponsoring fairs. The counts established fair grounds at several points in their lands and made a fortune through the services they provided and through taxes on the trade. Probably their most famous fair was the one at Troyes, from which derive the Troy weights still used in the measurement of precious metals and gems. They built and rented out booths, set up police to keep order and judges to settle disputes, and provided money changers to handle the varied coinage that appeared at the fairs—all for a price. They collected tolls as goods were shipped in and out of Champagne and market taxes on sales. The fairs provided a veritable gold mine and the counts made every effort to encourage and protect them, using some of their large income in a new institution called the "money fief" to increase security for those coming to the fairs. Something like this had existed in Merovingian times, before the waning of a monetary economy had tended to equate benefices with grants of land; money fiefs were simply grants of cash rather than of land, and the counts of Champagne used them extensively to enlist barons along the main routes to Champagne as protectors of merchants coming to trade. Through the twelfth and thirteenth centuries the fairs of Champagne were among the greatest markets in Europe, but they waned in the fourteenth century; for one thing, the county came into the possession of the French crown which overcharged the merchants, and for another, effective competition was developed further east by a league of German towns called the Hansa and further west by sea-borne convoys of Venetian galleys sailing to England and Flanders.

Participation by nobles in the new commerce on the scale of the counts of Champagne was rare, but no great lord could escape entirely the impact of economic change. Undeniably life was becoming more comfortable—and more costly; the nobles' need for money grew and grew. Instead of rough cloth woven by local women, lords and ladies learned to desire the fine products of great textile centers. Instead of crude weapons made locally, the noble lord hungered for a fine blade from Damascus or Toledo. Instead of a long winter of smoked, salted or tainted meat, noble families desired the variety offered by spices from the distant east. The list was long, and the cost was great.

One of the more obvious results of the revival of trade was the redevelopment of towns as centers of production and commerce. As noted previously, some modest agglomerations of population had survived in Europe, usually around a noble's residence, an episcopal center, a great monastery or some combination of the three. Naturally such communities had resident craftsmen such as blacksmiths, carpenters, millers and weavers, and in some instances increased production projected these communities into the commercial revival, as has been observed in north Italy. In other cases, the location of such towns and the attitude of the local nobleman attracted merchants who settled there and established a base for their operations; generally this development required that the community be on a good route and that its overlord be willing to accept money payments in lieu of personal services and levies of goods. But whatever their origins, the new commercial communities required a degree of personal freedom and possessory rights that had no place in the older feudal and manorial social patterns.

A common arrangement was for a lord to issue a charter which, in effect, made the town a corporate person and made the townsmen collectively responsible for obligations calculated in money rather than goods and services. These charters delegated important powers of internal administration to the town, such as the right to establish a governing council, courts and law codes; such delegation allowed the development of commercial law, called law merchant, which dealt with problems of contracts and trade practices in contrast to older feudal law which concerned itself primarily with the rights and obligations of land tenure and inheritance. A common provision of such charters was that a runaway serf who came to the town and avoided recapture for a year and a day became free; lords granting charters often exempted their own serfs from this provision, but they were happy to receive serfs of other lords, and sometimes they chartered towns near the borders of their lands and deliberately encouraged this form of population growth. An active town could provide good income to its lord, despite his cession of arbitrary rights over persons and goods within it, for he collected fees for the issuance and periodic renewal of the charter, taxes on the trade that the town attracted, and sometimes a portion of fines levied in town courts. Though the initiative for early charters probably came from merchants, ambitious lords soon began issuing them of their own volition in hopes of atttracting commercial growth and its attendant income.

An early development in the new towns was the formation of guilds, associations to serve the common interest of merchants. The guilds had various functions, economic, social, and political; they maintained monopolies of local business, presented a common front to the overlord and looked after dependents of deceased members. Usually they dominated the council allowed by the charter, and commonly town officials were officers of their guilds. Normally a town began with a single guild, but conflicts of interest usually led to craftsmen forming their own guilds, for merchants sought to buy local products cheaply and sell imported goods dearly, while the craftsmen's interests dictated the opposite. Thus the early guilds tended to evolve into merchant guilds, while artisans formed craft guilds; by the thirteenth century the latter had proliferated with enormous variety as every craft organized itself separately. To the traditional functions of the merchant guilds the craft guilds usually added training programs (apprenticeships) and stringent regulation of quality, quantity and the price of products. The proliferation of guilds led to competition for political power in the towns, usually in the form of craft guilds disputing the traditional control of the merchant guild, and the resolution of this issue often was bloody, but by the fourteenth century it was common that representatives of all the guilds participated in town government.

Town charters usually established extensive economic rights and very limited political rights, essentially administrative autonomy within the town, but some towns obtained far greater political rights, amounting to independence, through armed rebellion. About the end of the eleventh century this phenomenon began to be seen in north Italy, where the towns joined nearby country noblemen in associations called communes, and in the twelfth century these communes fought successfully against the authority of bishops, pope and Holy Roman Emperor. Against the Hohenstaufen emperors they formed an alliance of towns called the Lombard League which defeated an imperial army. During the stalemate resulting from the quarrels between popes and emperors, these towns not only attained political independence but also established their authority over the surrounding countryside, re-creating a pattern reminiscent of the Greco-Roman city states. Competition among them was intense, and they hired armies of professional soldiers with which they tried to subject one another. As their commerce flourished, this competition spilled over into cultural matters, and by the late fourteenth century the north Italian towns were being embellished with new public buildings, magnificent private residences and a variety of art works.

Outside of north Italy the pattern of communes rarely developed so fully. From the late eleventh century onward armed uprisings did occur but in conditions so different as to make generalizations difficult. North of the Alps the communes tended to face political authorities that were stronger and more stable, and where such movements enjoyed success it often was more limited and was attained through the sympathy of some other political authority.

Thus, a king or feudal prince eager to see the power of bishops reduced might intervene in a dispute in the name of pacification and
render a decision generally favorable to the townsmen. In this manner many towns acquired full political rights—electing all of their
officials, exercising high justice, and excluding all other authority
from the town, but rarely did anything as independent as the Italian
city states appear in the north. More typical was the arrangement
in Paris, where local administration was handled by an elected
council headed by an official called the Provost of the Merchants,
but the king reserved to himself rights of high justice and maintained
strong points and soldiers both to defend and to control the town.
(High justice referred to serious crimes—as opposed to offenses
punishable by fines.)

The need for protection and the Christian character of medieval
society led to certain similarities of appearance in the new towns,
which were all huddled together on small sites and dominated by
their walls, castles and churches. The little communities that preceded the commercial revival were incredibly tiny. Gregory of
Tours described the Chateau of Dijon in the sixth century, observing
that as it had many towers and housed several hundred people it
really should have been called a town rather than a castle. In the
south of France, inhabitants of the Roman town of Nimes who survived the barbarian invasions refounded their community *inside*
the old Roman amphitheatre, blocking up the outer arches to make
a defensive wall; and there remained enough unused space for them
to pile earth on some of the spectator benches and make terraced
vineyards of them. Even at Paris both the royal and episcopal establishments fit nicely onto the Ile de la Cité, a small island in the Seine
River, though the monasteries that enjoyed royal patronage were on
the mainland.

The new mercantile settlements clustered around centers such
as these, forming little suburbs, and eventually, if they prospered,
a new wall would be built around the whole community. But walls
were expensive, so the space within them tended to be developed
intensively; tall, narrow houses, their upper floors projecting over
cramped streets, were typical. Such houses often had a shop or place
of business on the ground floor, with residential quarters above it,
storage space higher still, and a loft on top where apprentices and

household servants slept. Most were built of wood, though in the fourteenth and fifteenth centuries wealthy merchants began building fine stone residences in some quantity.

Most of the more important towns grew up around castles that could offer refuge in time of danger, and these castles long dominated them, as the Tower in London or the Louvre and the Bastille in Paris. In addition, the towns usually had a great many churches, and—with the castle—their towers dominated the skyline, as many old drawings show.

Conditions within the new towns cannot have been pleasant except for the very wealthy. The narrow streets overhung by the upper stories of houses were dank and dark by day and pitch black by night. Until the thirteenth century paved streets were a rarity, and most were dusty in summer and a sea of mud in winter. Garbage and sewage were thrown into a ditch in the middle of the street to be flushed away by rain. And water was drawn from rivers or open wells that must have been polluted most of the time. In these crowded, airless communities contagion spread like wildfire, and when an epidemic struck, as did the Black Death in the middle of the fourteenth century, mortality rates were astronomical. Yet the opportunities that existed in these settlements attracted large numbers of people, and despite all the shortcomings the towns became one of the most creative forces in medieval society.

The expansion of commerce was accompanied by the development of some international banking operations. At first the nature of these operations was dictated by two pressing problems: the need to evaluate and exchange enormous varieties of coins (for many feudal lords coined their own money) and the need to provide for the secure transfer of funds over very unsafe roads. There was profit to be made from both of these operations, and in the twelfth and thirteenth centuries much of this business was in the hands of two establishments of the church, the Knights Templar and the Knights Hospitaler. These were crusading orders of warrior monks who had been endowed heavily all over western Europe. Thus they were in an ideal position to accept deposits in one place and issue payment orders in another, charging for the service, of course; and when it was necessary to transfer funds physically, they could provide strong armed escorts. By the thirteenth century there also were merchant houses extensive enough to practice this business, and these forms of international banking expanded rapidly.

By contrast, lending operations developed slowly, largely because of restrictions imposed by the church. The church had shown itself suspicious of all business endeavor from the beginning of the commercial revival, for its ethics were as deeply rooted in the older agrarian-aristocratic society as were those of any feudal prince, but slowly it had come to admit that those who moved goods or money from one place to another performed a useful service deserving compensation. However, on the issue of lending money for interest, the church remained adamant, for such activity was interpreted as an attempt to profit from one's neighbor's need and hence contrary to the principle of Christian charity; the practice was called usury and was forbidden, with the result that until the thirteenth century money lending remained in the hands of Jews, who were not bound by church law. In most of Europe, Jewish communities of merchants and money-lenders were tolerated within but separate from Christian society; typically, a king or prince would protect Jews, at the price of frequent unrepaid loans, heavy inheritance taxes, and quite arbitrary special levies. The Jew in medieval Europe served a function basic to the revival of commerce and urban life, but he was totally vulnerable, pillaged by the princes who tolerated him and often victim of pogroms by a populace that detested him for his profession and his religion.

Even this tenuous position was undermined in the thirteenth century when Christians learned how to avoid the laws of their church and persuaded governments to eliminate competition by expelling Jews and confiscating their property. Many evasive practices developed, such as writing a long-term loan for a short period and then charging penalties for delayed payment or agreeing to repayment in goods at a predetermined rate below market prices. Thus, collusion between borrower and lender allowed the growth of Christian money-lending and permitted a fuller development of commercial society despite the conservatism of the church. By the fourteenth century a number of great merchant houses, of which the Medici of Florence probably is the most famous, were diversifying their interests into money-lending, credit operations and manufacturing, often with considerable political involvement.

The commercial revival had an enormous and multifaceted impact upon medieval Europe. The towns challenged many of the assumptions of the agrarian-aristocratic society. They possessed obvious and powerful wealth, but the wealth was not related to land. They housed people who were neither lords nor peasants, not only the wealthy new middle class but also the simple laborers who too often are overlooked. Towns and trade posed new problems in law—questions of interest rates and repayment schedules, of disputed ownership of movable and perishable goods, of rights of residence and participation in urban government, of charges and taxes upon commerce by governments. And leagues of towns were powerful political forces outside the old feudal patterns, as the Lombard League and the League of the Hansa demonstrated.

In one way or another most noblemen felt the impact of the commercial revival. The relations of a nobleman with his peasants on the one hand and his lord on the other were influenced massively by the availability of money. The presence of urban markets for foodstuffs meant that surplus agricultural products could be sold for cash. To the serf it could mean money to buy emancipation, to the lord money to buy out of the military obligations of vassalage.

The immediate effects upon the peasant should not be exaggerated, for freedom brought no sudden improvement in his economic condition. Emancipation meant the right to marry or move at will, but he bought the freedom, and usually he had to pay his lord a fee when he exercised his new rights. He might pay annual fees instead of labor services, but the fees were high. In the long run, however, the peasantry gained, for the charters of emancipation usually fixed obligations in perpetuity, and as the economy developed, inflation eroded the value of money. With rising market values the peasant's income increased while his obligations remained fixed. Thus the peasant benefited while his lord was caught with a largely fixed income in a time of rising prices.

The presence of money in the countryside also changed patterns of labor utilization on the land. Traditionally the serf had worked some time on his own land and some time on the lord's land, but with serfs freed and money available lords began to hire labor. In many instances it must have been his own former serfs whom the lord hired, for they constituted the only readily available labor force; many of them must have had plots too small to support their families and would have been eager for extra income.

The next step in the process, and it was common in the thirteenth century, was for the lord to abandon completely the role of agricultural producer and to rent out his land in blocks to individual farmers, so that the lord became simply a collector of rents. The sort of contract made had important long-term effects upon a noble family's economic position. If that contract, too, were drawn in perpetuity, the lord was completely vulnerable to inflation. But if shorter leases were adopted, and they were not uncommon, the lord had some protection since every renegotiation allowed a demand for higher rents and thus a share in the higher market value of the land's product. The feudal baron's world was growing much more complicated.

By the same token, money payments in lieu of personal service (so-called shield money) tended to change the traditional relationship between vassals and overlords, and this commutation of service to money payments had advantages for both sides. The lesser lord did not have to absent himself from his estates for the summer, and the overlord was able to hire soldiers who would fight so long as they were paid instead of a force that would quit at the end of forty days. Moreover, such new forces offered honorable employment to younger sons while leaving heads of families free to manage their estates. This new military pattern became quite significant in the fourteenth century when the Hundred Years War erupted between the kings of England and of France, for in that grinding struggle both kings had need of professional soldiers for long service.

In many ways the crusades reinforced the effects of the commercial revival, for they accentuated the lord's need to get money, making him more susceptible to bargains with his serfs and his vassals. Traditionally the lord who lived on his lands was provided with the substance of existence, but crusading was a different matter. Passages had to be purchased, men and horses outfitted, equipment and mounts transported, men and beasts fed and sheltered. It all took money, so the would-be crusader was the more inclined to sell his serfs their freedom and to commute his vassals' military service.

Even then only the more prosperous lords could go to a crusade independently. The lesser knights had to go in the service of a richer man. Thus the crusades introduced much more marked gradations of status within the nobility—those who went and those who did not, those who travelled independently and those who took service; other status symbols accentuated the differentiation—those who built fine stone castles and those who still lived in a wooden keep on top of a mound of earth, those who simply paid an overlord a fee and those who had to render personal service. And to complicate things further, townsmen were buying land and sometimes the noble titles that went with it. So the traditional notion of a homogeneous class differentiated only by administrative and military arrangements or by personal reputation was breaking down. The nobility became a heterogeneous body of petty knights and great lords, of old families and newly purchased titles, of crusaders and non-crusaders.

If a massive generalization may be risked, one might say that the emergent patterns resulted in advantage for the peasants and the great lords and a terrible squeeze upon the lesser lords, the simple knights. The transformation from labor services to money rents benefited the peasant when inflation depreciated money. Tied to a fixed income, the small lord suffered. On the other hand, great lords did well, for chartering fees and sales taxes from the towns on their lands increased with the development of the economy. At the root of all the turbulence and change lay the power of money.

GERMANY
under the Saxon
and Franconian Kings
Tenth to Twelfth Centuries

DENMARK

Baltic Sea

POMERANIA

POLAND

North Sea

FRIESLAND

Weser R.

Elbe R.

Oder R.

Vistula R.

Duchy of
SAXONY

EASTERN
MARCHES

0   100   200
MILES

Duchy of
LOWER LORRAINE

Rhine R.

THURINGIA

50°

Duchy of
FRANCONIA

Duchy of
BOHEMIA

CARPATHIANS

Duchy of
UPPER
LORRAINE

Meuse R.

Danube R.

AUSTRIA

FRANCE

Duchy of
SUABIA

Duchy of
BAVARIA

HUNGARY

Kingdom of
BURGUNDY

Saône R.

ALPS

Drave R.

Duchy of
CARINTHIA

Rhône R.

ITALY

CROATIA

Save R.

10°

Po R.

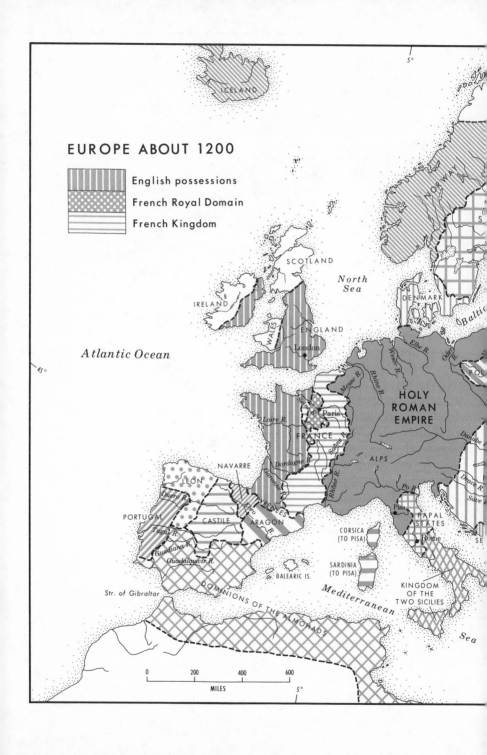

EUROPE ABOUT 1200

English possessions
French Royal Domain
French Kingdom

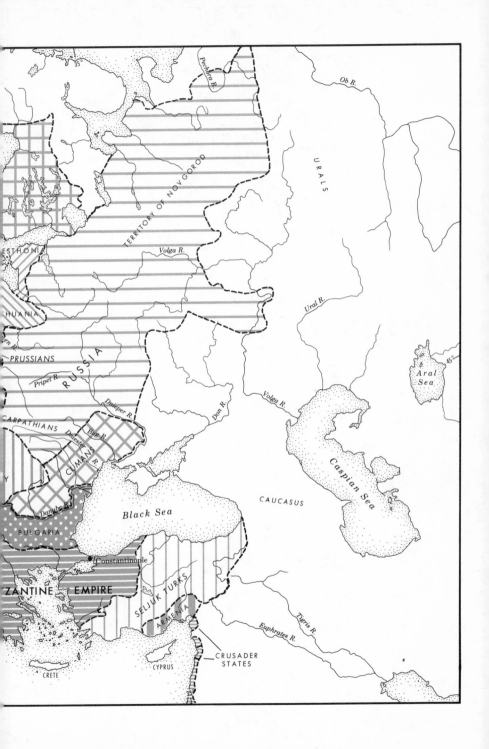

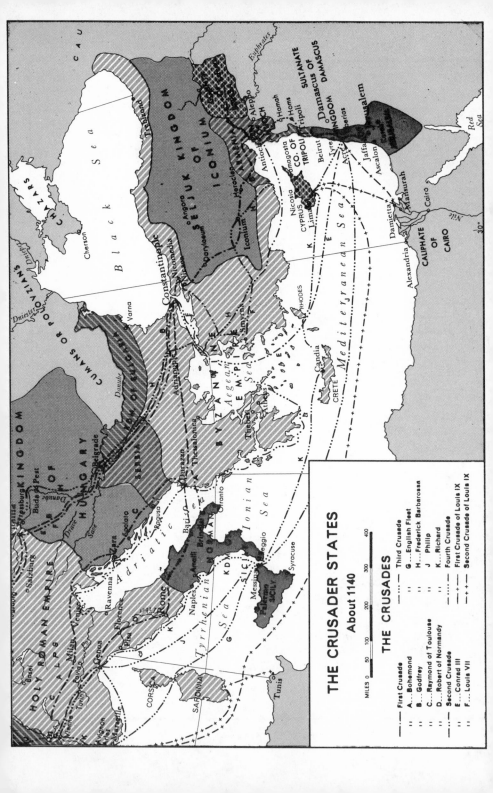

THE CRUSADER STATES
About 1140

MILES 0 50 100 200 300 400

THE CRUSADES

-----	First Crusade	.....	Third Crusade
" "	A...Bohemond	" "	G...English Fleet
" "	B...Godfrey	" "	H...Frederick Barbarossa
" "	C...Raymond of Toulouse	" "	J...Philip
" "	D...Robert of Normandy	" "	K...Richard
-----	Second Crusade	-----	Fourth Crusade
" "	E...Conrad III	+++	First Crusade of Louis IX
" "	F...Louis VII	+++	Second Crusade of Louis IX

CHAZARS

CUMANS OR POLOVZIANS

HOLY ROMAN EMPIRE

KINGDOM OF HUNGARY

SERVIA

NORMAN KD. OF SICILY

BYZANTINE EMPIRE

SELJUK KINGDOM OF ICONIUM

SULTANATE OF DAMASCUS

KINGDOM OF JERUSALEM

CO. OF TRIPOLI

CYPRUS

CALIPHATE OF CAIRO

Black Sea

Mediterranean Sea

Adriatic Sea

Ionian Sea

Tyrrhenian Sea

Aegean Sea

Red Sea

Constantinople

Rome

Jerusalem

Damascus

Aleppo

Antioch

Cairo

Alexandria

Tunis

Chapter 8

The Apogee of Medieval Christianity

During the ninth and tenth centuries, when Europe was being raided from every side, the church suffered severely. The raiders soon learned that cathedrals and monasteries often possessed treasure—gold and silver candlesticks, reliquaries, chalices, crosses and ornaments—and ecclesiastical buildings became favorite targets for pillage. Both in England and on the continent the destruction was frightful. In an endeavor to survive, the clergy was drawn ever more deeply into secular affairs, accepting feudal service and maintaining men-at-arms, so that by the mid-tenth century bishops and abbots differed little from other great feudal lords. The papacy was in an equally sad plight, beset by tumultuous mobs in Rome and attacked frequently by Moslem forces from Sicily. With libraries and schools burned, papal leadership distracted and most high clergy enmeshed in the military and administrative responsibilities of emerging feudal relationships, the church was fragmented, and its spiritual and moral leadership was at a low ebb. Its recovery and its enormous achievements between the eleventh and thirteenth centuries was one of the most dynamic developments of medieval society.

One of the most significant elements in the revival of the church lay in a new monastic movement called the Cluniac Reform. Early in the tenth century some churchmen, fearful of the direction in which the church was developing, prevailed upon the Duke of Aquitaine to establish a new monastery called Cluny in some rugged lands he held in Burgundy; the rules of the new foundation were designed to eliminate some of the dangers that threatened older establishments. Cluny was forbidden to accept gifts that required feudal service. Since most gifts of land included resident labor, the old Benedictine injunction that monks should work in the fields had proved impractical, so the monks of Cluny were required to spend far more time in religious services to avoid idleness. In order to prevent corruption of the intentions of the founders, it was provided that any new monasteries that accepted the Cluniac rules should be governed locally by a prior but should be under the general supervision of the Abbot of Cluny, who would make inspections. Through these provisions the reformers hoped to keep the new monasteries independent of secular entanglements, free of idleness and subject to effective discipline. Moreover, Cluny and its dependents were made directly responsible to the papacy, thus escaping potential corruption through local influences. The Cluniac Reform spread very rapidly in the tenth century both directly through the foundation of associated monasteries and indirectly through imitation by other houses that did not actually join the movement. As a result, the ideas of the Cluniac reformers were a powerful force in the eleventh century church, and they spilled over from the monastic to the secular clergy.

Obviously the reforms that were specifically a part of monastic discipline had little role in the improvement of the secular clergy, but the general principles of independence from feudal responsibility and appointments on the basis of religious qualifications inspired important developments. To free papal elections from the influence of both the Roman mob and the emperor, the College of Cardinals was created, providing for popes to be chosen by a clerical assembly. To extend papal influence across Europe, as a counterpoise to the influence of kings and princes, special agents called legates were created with either general or specific commissions to speak and act in the pope's name, and newly appointed archbishops were required to journey to Rome to confer with the pope before taking up their duties. Like the royal governments, the papacy expanded the scope and number of its courts in the late eleventh and early twelfth centuries, creating new appellate divisions, which increased both papal revenues and papal influence in the development of law. But the greatest effort came with the election of the reformer Hildebrand as Pope Gregory VII (1073–1085), for he initiated the great Investiture Controversy with the Holy Roman Emperors. Thus, the Cluniac reform had very wide repercussions in the church, and despite some failures it made real progress in improving the independence and the spiritual integrity of the clergy.

The eleventh century reformers also contributed importantly to strengthening the theoretical bases of the church by standardizing its practices and beliefs. Much of the standardization of practice was accomplished through the elaboration of canon law, the body of regulation that governed the church both internally and in its relations with the laity. This development was aided considerably by the fact that the zeal of the reformers was reinforced by the rediscovery and restudy of the great law codes of the sixth century emperor Justinian, which provided a model for new legislation. The standardization of belief, or doctrine, was advanced greatly from the early twelfth century onward by theologians who attempted to reconcile the contradictions of the Bible, the writings of the fathers of the church and the decrees of councils and popes, often taking some account, too, of the Greek philosophers. The first of the great theologians, Abelard, simply raised questions and indicated methods that might produce solutions, but successors, such as Gratian and Peter Lombard, wrote great summations that gathered together various ancient authorities and tried to resolve their differences through the application of faith and reason. In the thirteenth century these efforts reached their fruition in the work of St. Thomas Aquinas, whose great *Summa Theologica* embraced every aspect of faith and practice.

The enthusiasm sparked by the Cluniac movement and carried on by papal reformers continued to produce new offshoots within the church. In the late eleventh and early twelfth centuries severely ascetic hermits reappeared in Italy and France, seeking spiritual purification through stringent religious exercises; some of these formed communities famous for their dedication, most notably the Grande Chartreuse or Carthusian Order of France. There also were endeavors to improve the standards of parish priests by organizing them into communities and imposing a semimonastic rule upon them. These semimonastic priests were called canons, and through the twelfth century a number of groups of them developed, of whom the most famous were the Augustinians and the Premonstratensians.

Perhaps the most influential element in the twelfth century wave of monastic reform was the Cistercian Order, which took its name from the monastery of Citeaux. Founded at the very end of the eleventh century, Citeaux came under the influence of a fervent reformer, St. Bernard, in the early twelfth century. While St. Bernard was Abbot of Citeaux, from 1116 to 1153, the order expanded startlingly, from five to over 340 houses, and by the end of the thirteenth century this number had doubled. The rapid growth of the Cistercians is explicable only by the appeal that true religious devotion exercised upon medieval society, for the order enforced a very strict adherence to a narrow interpretation of the Benedictine Rule. The monks were allowed only the most utilitarian clothes and diet; the residences and churches of the order were furnished sparsely; no Cistercian monastery could hold populated lands, so the monks had to do their own labor. Moreover, the Cistercians provided for effective enforcement of this harsh discipline, for the new order adopted an hierarchical organization that resembled a sort of idealized feudalism. Having observed that the rapid growth of the Cluniacs made frequent inspection by the Abbot of Cluny impossible, the Cistercians provided for decentralized but effective control. Each monastery was permitted to found new monasteries, and the abbot of the parental establishment was responsible for overseeing them; when it had matured, the daughter house might colonize new monasteries in its turn, and its abbot was responsible for them. Thus regular and effective inspection was assured by limiting the responsibilities of each abbot to manageable proportions.

In addition to the high religious standard they set, the Cistercians also rendered another important service to medieval society; because the only endowments they could accept were uninhabited lands, and because their strict regulations insisted that they must support themselves, they were responsible for bringing much wasteland into production. Their most notable achievement was turning the wastes of northern England into sheep pastures, which became the foundation of England's great woollen exports, but on a smaller scale they made comparable contributions in several fields of agriculture all over western Europe.

The monastic movement contributed importantly to the growth of the church and of medieval society as a whole. Support by monasteries all over Europe was a major factor in the success of papal reforms. The maintenance of an example of an idealized Christian life helped to salvage the influence of the church at a time when many members of the clergy were enmeshed in secular politics, and such an example provided inspiration to new reforming efforts. To a large extent the development of canon law and theology depended upon monastic libraries and men who had been educated in monasteries. Monks acquired the habit of keeping detailed chronicles of events, and but for their efforts there would be little or no record of that part of the past. Finally, many innovations of medieval society derived from monastic communities—better tools, improved agricultural techniques, schools and the architectural style known as Romanesque.

Aside from the great expansion of monasticism, perhaps the most obvious expression of Christian zeal in medieval society was the crusades, but a great many other motives played a role in them, too. Europe had absorbed many peoples under the Roman Empire, the Germanic Kingdoms, and the Carolingian Empire, but there was little compromise between Christendom and Islam, two societies inspired by exclusive monotheistic faiths; fighting had been more or less continuous since the seventh and eighth centuries, and by the late eleventh century Europeans had made some important gains. In Spain, armies from the mountainous Christian principalities of Léon and Castile were driving the Moslems southward and had taken nearly half the country, as well as beginning the Christian reconquest of Portugal; during this struggle French influence became strong in Spain through the participation of French knights in search of fiefs, and, French monks, especially Cluniacs, who established new monasteries, and the Spanish wars became something of a European affair with ambition for lands and military fame thoroughly mixed with religious motivation. About the same time fleets from Genoa and Pisa had taken Corsica and Sardinia, and had begun raiding Moslem ports in North Africa, largely in the interest of their growing western Mediterranean commerce, and land hungry Norman knights were conquering Sicily. Thus, by the late eleventh century a number of precedents had been established for Christian campaigns against Moslem positions, but while religious zeal certainly was an important factor, other motives also were prominent. It was against this background that the first crusade was proclaimed.

In the third quarter of the eleventh century, a central Asian people called the Seljuk Turks seized control of the Caliphate in Bagdad and then intensified the old struggle with the Byzantine Empire. After suffering a serious defeat at the Battle of Manzikert in 1071, the Byzantine emperor appealed to Pope Gregory VII to send western troops to his aid, but Gregory was involved in the Investiture Controversy and could not help. However, the request was renewed in the 1090's, and this time it produced results, for papal problems had eased somewhat, and there were many reasons why the papacy was disposed to favor the appeal. After years of bitter quarreling, the eastern church had repudiated the authority of the pope in 1054, and there were grounds to hope that the breach might be healed if papal leadership played an important role in what could be construed as a religious war. The popes were trying to strengthen their position in Europe, and the successes of secular rulers against the Moslems of Spain and Sicily were achievements that the popes desired to equal. All over Europe, churchmen were quarreling with secular rulers and were trying to inhibit the destructive practice of private warfare; any project that might draw large numbers of the feudal class eastward would ease both of these problems. Finally, there were always many Europeans traveling as pilgrims to the Holy Land, and there were inevitable tales of ill-treatment by the Moslems of the area. Thus, for a variety of reasons Pope Urban II proclaimed a crusade at the Council of Clermont in 1095, and preachers all over Europe called upon nobles to set aside their private quarrels and turn their weapons upon the enemies of Christendom.

What the Byzantine Emperor Alexius Comnenus wanted was a body of European volunteers to be incorporated into the Byzantine armies; what Pope Urban II intended to send east was an army of heavily armed nobles under the command of a papal agent, the Bishop of Le Puy, to fight as allies of the Byzantines; the first European host to arrive at Constantinople was neither one nor the other but a motley rabble armed only with their zeal and their faith in God's support. Though Urban had intended raising an effective army of feudal barons, popular preachers had enlisted impoverished knights and peasants. When they arrived at Constantinople in 1096, a hungry mob after a hard overland march, Emperor Alexius promptly sent them to Asia Minor where the Turks annihilated them. Other such ill-organized groups never reached Constantinople; some bands so aroused the areas they passed through by plundering that the Hungarians destroyed them, and others dissipated their fervor in Europe in murderous attacks upon Jews, whom they called the Christ-killers. The whole of this early movement, called the peasant's crusade, was tragic.

The baronial crusade that left Europe toward the end of the summer of 1096 also started off with ill omens. Bitter rivalries divided the noble leaders, and some of them were mere adventurers hopeful of conquering new fiefs; they thought the Greeks soft and dissipated, while for their part the Greeks considered the western Europeans barbarians; Emperor Alexius wanted to reconquer the valuable provinces of Asia Monor, but the crusaders wanted to push on to the Holy Land. Under such circumstances relations between the allies were troubled; Alexius offered food and transport in return for oaths of allegiance and then left the crusaders to their own devices. Misunderstandings multiplied, and some of the crusaders plundered Byzantine lands and burned part of Constantinople. Finally Alexius got the troublesome army across the straits to Asia Minor, where it took Nicea from the Turks for him before marching off toward the Holy Land.

Political divisions among the Moslems had allowed the crusaders an easy victory at Nicea, but resistance stiffened as they moved on, and Turkish adoption of a scorched earth policy soon left them short of supplies. Moreover, however effective the individual European knight, he had never learned discipline and coordinated action; the army moved in two columns only vaguely in contact with each other, and one of the columns nearly was destroyed before the arrival of the other turned the Battle of Dorylaeum from defeat to victory. Next the crusaders succeeded in taking Antioch, and again they defeated a Turkish army. Their luck was incredible; the lightly armed Moslem bowmen had shown that they could keep away from

the heavier and slower European knights and cut them to pieces
from a distance, but both at Dorylaeum and at Antioch coincidence
and Turkish mismanagement had produced hand-to-hand battles in
confined spaces, a situation ideal for the crusaders. Leaving behind
some forces to consolidate the positions won, the rest of the host
moved on to Jerusalem, which it captured with frightful bloodshed
in the summer of 1099. Almost immediately the crusaders had to defend their gains against an army sent from Egypt, but this time the
Moslem force was light cavalry without bowmen, and it posed little
threat; it had to close with the European heavy cavalry, and the crusaders' victory at Ascalon was complete. The first crusade was over.

The successful crusaders quickly organized a Latin Kingdom
of Jerusalem, electing one of their number as king, and they divided
their conquests into fiefs in the European manner. Through the early
years of the twelfth century they expanded these positions, and with
the help of Italian naval forces they took the coastal towns, thus
gaining ports through which they had direct communications with
western Europe. By the middle of the twelfth century the Kingdom
of Jerusalem was a highly developed feudal state, differing from its
European counterparts, however, in that the king had only the carefully limited authority of a feudal suzerain. The three Christian
domains that the crusaders had carved out in Syria (Antioch, Tripoli
and Edessa) maintained only tenuous links with the Kingdom of
Jerusalem and with each other, developing into self-contained feudal
states themselves. Thus, in the absence of traditions such as those of
the Frankish or Anglo-Saxon crowns, the decentralization of authority always latent in feudal organization became dominant.

The Christian states in the east developed some local resources,
but a great deal of their support came from the west. Most especially, the great military-monastic orders—the Knights Templar, the
Knights Hospitaler and, a bit later, the Teutonic Knights—were endowed heavily all over Europe, and their hundreds of soldier-monks
formed one of the chief defenses of the crusaders' states. Replace-
ments for casualties were supplied by a constant stream of pilgrims
and soldiers from Europe, some of whom stayed only briefly while
others remained permanently. And the vital lines of communication
to the west were maintained by the fleets of the Italian commercial
cities.

Before the final destruction of the Kingdom of Jerusalem at the end of the thirteenth century, several other crusades set out from Europe to fight in the Holy Land. An expedition that started from Europe in 1101 achieved nothing and was cut to pieces by the Turks in Asia Minor. In the middle of the twelfth century, when Edessa fell to the Moslems again, the famous St. Bernard persuaded Europe to raise another crusade; this army was led by the king of France and the Holy Roman Emperor. After losing most of the German force and a large part of the French infantry, the princely leaders finally launched a fruitless attack upon Damascus and then returned home having accomplished nothing.

After the 1170's internal quarrels weakened the Kingdom of Jerusalem just when the great Turkish general, Saladin, was consolidating Moslem power in Egypt and Syria, and in 1187 Saladin destroyed the Christian army and reoccupied all of the crusaders' conquests except some coastal towns; again the crusade was preached in Europe, and the cause was taken up by the Holy Roman Emperor and the kings of France and England. Emperor Frederick I (1152–1190) was the first to go, in 1189, and he won some victories in Asia Minor, but before he could accomplish any permanent conquest, he drowned while bathing in a river, and most of his army went home. After many delays, Philip Augustus of France (1180–1223) and Richard the Lion-Hearted of England (1189–1199) set forth, sailing from Sicily in the spring of 1191, but Richard paused again to take the island of Cyprus, which he established as a kingdom and gave to a former king of Jerusalem; finally, in the summer of 1191 the armies of both Philip and Richard joined the remaining Christian forces in the east in besieging Acre. The two kings were too hostile to one another to organize a joint assault, but the garrison was starved into surrender. Then Philip went home, and Richard arranged a truce with Saladin that gave the Christians a few more coastal towns and guaranteed the rights of pilgrims in Jerusalem. Another crusade had ended with very small gains.

The crusades of the thirteenth century accomplished even less than those of the twelfth century. Pope Innocent III (1189–1216) launched an expedition, but as the price of transporting it the Venetians had the crusaders subject the Christian city of Zara (on the Adriatic) to Venetian rule in 1202; then in 1204 the crusaders attacked Constantinople instead of the Turks, setting up a Latin Empire which lasted about a half century until the Greeks took it back. Another crusade in 1218 tried to take Egypt, but after early successes it foundered in the confusion of the Nile delta and had to return to Acre without results. In 1227 Emperor Frederick II (1215–1250) led a long-promised crusade, and after more diplomacy than fighting he acquired Jerusalem and a corridor to it from the coast by signing a truce; a decade later two more crusading armies arrived, skirmished a little, and then confirmed and extended Frederick II's agreement. These were the greatest Christian achievements in the east since the first crusade, but in 1244 an Egyptian army wiped out these gains by recapturing all of Palestine except the coastal towns. A few years later Louis IX of France (1226–1270) made a last great effort to restore the Kingdom of Jerusalem, striking at Egypt once more, but his forces were defeated and its leaders captured; after paying a large ransom the king was freed and spent a few years in Palestine, but he returned home after no greater accomplishment than strengthening the fortifications of the remaining Christian towns. That some remnant of the crusaders' states survived another forty years largely was due to the fact that the Moslems were attacked in the east by the Mongols, an Asiatic people. When the sultan of Egypt had turned back these new raiders, he resumed the reconquest of the Christian positions, and the last one surrendered in 1291.

One of the most enduring achievements of medieval Christendom was the rise of the universities in the twelfth and thirteenth centuries. Most earlier medieval education was intensely practical and included little of a literary or scholarly nature. Young noblemen learned the skills of a knight while young noblewomen were prepared for marriage and the management of extensive baronial households. The guilds developed apprenticeship programs that taught crafts and trades. But education of an academic sort largely was limited to a few schools attached to cathedrals or monasteries, which taught reading and writing and some basic arithmetic, for it was desirable that clerics be able to read sacred works and calculate the dates of movable feasts such as Easter. An important exception to this general lack of academic schooling must be remarked in Italy, where schoolmasters continued to teach in the Roman tradition all through the medieval period; as noted previously, it was these centers of study that rediscovered the law codes of Justinian in the eleventh century.

The first universities appear to have grown naturally out of conflicts in places where schools became sufficiently famous to attract large numbers of students; fundamentally they were academic guilds that sought to deal with internal problems such as irresponsible masters and episcopal censorship and town and gown problems such as gouging landlords and student mischief. Hence, while later universities established under charters of princes or popes can be dated, no one knows exactly when the earliest were formed, though inference suggests the existence of universities at Bologna, Paris and Oxford in the late twelfth century, and others developed rapidly in the thirteenth and fourteenth centuries. In northern Europe it was usually the masters who formed the university, to contest the conservative control of bishops and their agents, but in Italy the students took the initiative, and they developed practices aimed at controlling the masters, too, requiring them to post bonds if they wished to leave town during term and fining them if they missed lectures. Despite these differences in particulars, however, all of the universities shared some general patterns of development. Secular and ecclesiastical authorities gradually granted more and more extensive powers of regulation and discipline to university officers, so that academic communities became largely self-governing. Masters and students slowly organized themselves around their particular interests and developed faculties of arts, law, medicine and theology, and conflicts between masters and university officers tended to reduce the power of the latter to awarding degrees to those presented by the faculties. Thus, the general form of modern universities took shape quite quickly.

The program of undergraduate studies in the early universities was not very rigorous. A student had to know Latin since all instruction was carried on in that language, but standards of proficiency appear to have been quite low; because books had to be produced by hand and were quite costly, most instruction involved listening to a master read a book aloud and comment on it, though a student might be required to read a few books himself. Degrees were granted when the masters affirmed that a student had heard and read the requisite books. Graduate work, on the other hand, especially in theology, was much more demanding. The method of instruction was largely the same, but a student might spend a dozen years at it, and in addition he was expected to engage in public debates, called disputations, before being awarded the title of doctor. In the late thirteenth century two developments worked an important change in the structure of some universities. On the one hand many requirements for degrees were waived by dispensation if a student paid special fees, and soon most students simply fulfilled the residency requirement and bought their undergraduate degrees, so that university lecturing dwindled; on the other hand, sympathetic benefactors founded student residences in the universities, such as Robert de Sorbon at Paris or Walter Merton and John Balliol at Oxford, and they usually provided endowments to support a master who lived with the students. Thus instructional responsibility for those who desired it passed slowly to these new collegial residences, with the university simply controlling general matters and awarding degrees.

Despite their shortcomings, the universities made important contributions to the development of medieval civilization. They supported most of the famous scholars of the society, and as their fame grew, they became authorities to which disputes could be referred, a function important to the growth and elaboration of medieval law and theology. They trained the clerks who served some of the great business houses and the officials who staffed royal bureaucracies and the papal administration. And their interest in the further development of the Latin language and of philosophical and legal studies led to reconsideration of ancient writers and the beginnings of the recovery of the classical heritage, developments that were to undergird the later renaissance.

However, one must not exaggerate the achievements of the medieval scholars, for the postulates of their society imposed limits upon their interests and investigations. The chief support of the universities was the church, and the primary interest of the society, in theory at least, was man's salvation in a Christian sense. Hence, theology was the queen of university studies, and all researches tended to be subordinated to the search for salvation. Ancient authors were revived, but Greek logic became servant to the proof of Christian doctrine, and Latin rhetoric was made a tool of theological exposition. Despite religious prejudice, some aspects of the far more sophisticated Moslem world were studied, and the Europeans borrowed from it the classical sources to which it had fallen heir and the mathematical and astronomical discoveries it had made, but always these borrowings were redefined within the framework of Christian conceptions of the universe. Sometimes these restrictions were formalities, and new concepts discovered in classical writings became extremely influential, but on other occasions the limitations were severe. For instance, new studies of Roman law suggested the concept of a ruler who could legislate with few restrictions, an idea quite different from the tribal king or feudal suzerain who was bound by custom and contract, and all over Europe this notion stimulated royal officers to seek an expansion of monarchical power through citation of Roman precedents. But at the same time the study of Greek philosophers stimulated a quarrel called the realist-nominalist controversy, which limited seriously the investigation of natural phenomena.

The realists, inspired by Plato, maintained that reality was a set of ideals of which individual manifestations were but accidental approximations, while nominalists, deriving from Aristotle, insisted that particulars were the reality and ideals were but generalized conceptions of common characteristics. Largely because of theological implications, the realists tended to dominate the argument, with the result that medieval studies concerned themselves primarily with the search for abstract types and ideals, and research into particular phenomena of the physical world was regarded as ephemeral and unproductive. Moreover, the environment of religious studies conditioned scholars to think in terms of authorities from the past, such as the Bible and the church fathers, and this attitude carried over into other subjects, so that writers such as Plato and Aristotle in philosophy or Galen in medicine tended to be read rather uncritically. Hence, while the medieval universities attained impressive results in the reintegration of the classical heritage and in the advancement of theological and legal studies, natural sciences languished and critical empirical methods did not develop.

Chapter 9

Challenge and Conflict
in Later Medieval Society

The thirteenth century often is considered the greatest of the medieval centuries, but if it was the apogee of a brilliant culture, it also saw the beginnings of processes that were to destroy medieval society. All the foundations of the medieval world were shaken badly. Relations between clergy and laity, between church and state, between peasants and lords and between lords and princes all changed considerably, and new military and administrative patterns emerged, still primitive but forerunners of modern forms.

Christianity was transformed massively in many ways. As one example, the church appears to have achieved considerable success in its long, slow battle to control public morality. No doubt it would be easy to exaggerate the church's influence; certainly the regulations of the canon law never were observed wholly, but it is interesting to note the wide range of moral matters that churchmen— even if overoptimistic—thought they could regulate.

Unable to keep the turbulent nobility from fighting, churchmen achieved considerable success in protecting noncombatants and directing the attention of the warriors to the enemies of Christendom. The crusades turned much of Europe's military effort to the service of Christianity (at least in theory), and tournaments introduced formal ritual to knightly combat, to the advantage of non-combatants who thus were spared. Moreover, the church seems to have influenced the warrior's code considerably during this period, and to the old virtues of courage and personal glory were added loyalty, the defense of women and children and the service of God. There were many influences leading to the development of the attitudes usually called chivalry, but the church's insistence that a soldier's efforts must serve some sort of higher purpose certainly was important.

During the early thirteenth century Pope Innocent III (1198–1216) achieved greater control over the church and greater political power in Europe than had been exercised by any of his predecessors. Under Innocent's rule, the papacy developed the most efficient administration in Europe, consolidated its hold on the Papal States and imposed its will upon secular rulers. Innocent was not an innovator, but he was a brilliant organizer, and under his rule the business transacted by the papacy increased greatly, and the machinery of papal government expanded rapidly to deal with it. The central institution of papal government, the curia, developed separate bureaus with rather clearly delineated responsibilities in correspondence, legal matters, finance and administration of ecclesiastical powers, which made papal authority far more effective. (One important consequence was that this rationalized administration soon was copied by several secular governments.) The use of armed force, or the threat of it, tightened the pope's authority over the Papal States. Considerable expansion of the use of legates, officers exercising delegated papal authority, extended enormously the influence of the papacy outside of Italy and facilitated a vast increase in appeals from local ecclesiastical courts to papal jurisdictions. And Innocent's argument that as the vicar of Christ it was his duty to judge any question that might involve sin, which included wars, treaties and royal marriages, justified papal intervention in almost any matter anywhere.

Perhaps the most dramatic demonstration of papal power over the whole church and of papal influence throughout Europe was the convocation of the Fourth Lateran Council in 1215. Attended by more than twelve hundred great prelates from all over Europe, as well as representatives of secular rulers, the council was controlled by Innocent, who guided it through considerations of the doctrine and discipline of the church, political affairs and the reform of morals. Heresies were condemned and the sacraments were clarified. The laity was enjoined to more Christian behavior, and the clergy was commanded to more responsible exercise of the spiritual office. Finally a new crusade was proclaimed, and pronouncements were issued on political quarrels all over Europe. The scope and vigor of papal activity during the pontificate of Innocent III made the papacy one of the most important of the influences that gave shape to medieval Europe.

The stronger authority of the papacy, as exemplified by Innocent III, achieved more efficient imposition of its will through the threat of various ecclesiastical penalties. Ecclesiastical courts could proceed against individuals on the basis of charges laid, assigning penances which had to be fulfilled or the sinner risked excommunication. Excommunication cut the individual off from the community of the faithful and denied him the comfort of the sacraments, falling hard even upon those who took their faith lightly; it cancelled all obligations to him who incurred it, voiding the service that vassals owed their lord and the monies that debtors owed their creditors. Some secular governments took a hand if the sinner did not make his peace with the church within a specified time, prescribing imprisonment in England, confiscation of property in France and death in Sweden.

A penalty that fell more broadly was the interdict, which forbade priests of a whole area to administer sacraments other than baptism and extreme unction. Thus a whole people could be deprived of the church's services until an heretical preacher had been expelled or a wayward king brought to obedience; the effectiveness of this grass roots pressure depended, of course, upon the willingness of the local clergy to obey the ban and upon the sensitivity of a ruler to the discontent of his subjects. With due regard for varying personalities and particular circumstances, however, it is safe to say that these threats were compelling.

For instance, marriage regulations came to be observed much more seriously in the thirteenth century. In earlier times the nobility had treated such regulations quite casually, putting aside wives and taking new ones with little regard for the fulminations of clerics, and the best the church had managed was to have one wife and her children designated legitimate so as to reduce fighting over inheritances. But by the twelfth century, the approval of a church court usually was sought for the termination of a marriage, though annulments were granted on quite thin excuses. Then in the thirteenth century there was a concentrated effort at enforcement of marriage bonds. Innocent III liberalized the calculation of relationships that would bar marriages because consanguinity (too close blood relationship) had become a facile excuse for annulments, and he insisted that a French king take back a wife whom apparently he loathed. The effects should not be exaggerated, but the regulations were clarified, and several attempts at enforcement achieved at least some success.

This period also saw the spread of new ideas concerning the very core of Christianity, the Holy Family. During the early medieval period, emphasis had been upon God the Father, a rather stern and harsh Old Testament concept often portrayed as a sort of omnipotent emperor. During the twelfth and thirteenth centuries emphasis shifted to the mercy of Christ and the compassion of Mary, His mother. The representations of the merciful saviour with arms outstretched, which still adorn many gothic cathedrals, illustrate this new view, and the spread of a new movement called the cult of the Virgin proliferated shrines and prayers for the intercession of the Mother of God. The religion of soldiers was being transformed into the faith of humbler and gentler people.

This adulation of Mary accompanied an improvement in the status of women that strikes another discordant note in the patterns of the old agrarian-aristocratic society. Female saints such as Mary Magdalene enjoyed growing popularity, another sign of a deepening respect for women. It became common practice during the thirteenth century to allow a woman to do homage for lands of her own inheritance, a marked departure from earlier practice in which she had to commit herself to the custody of a man. And noble ladies more and more often were entrusted with the management of estates while their husbands were off crusading. Finally, tightening marriage laws lent more security to a woman's position.

On the other hand the growing importance of women did not imply any weakening in the church's vehemently anti-sexual position. The virginity of Mary was emphasized and the concept of the immaculate conception much stressed. Nuns were upheld as the most holy of women. In consequence, the church's attitude toward women became quite ambivalent. On the one hand it defended their marriages, urged upon warriors an obligation for their protection and even glorified some women such as Mary and Mary Magdalene. On the other hand it failed to modify its obsessive concern with sex, and it continued to view women as the descendants of Eve, the temptress.

Virginity still was considered the ideal state, and marriage was more condoned than endorsed. Procreation remained the only legitimate reason for sexual relations, and many penitentials (guides for confessors) warned against even married couples taking pleasure from it. The church's regulations, if observed, allowed only limited sexual relations between married people and, of course, none outside of marriage. The church would not perform marriages during Lent or Advent; intercourse was prohibited from the discovery of pregnancy until forty days after the birth; it was prohibited on all Wednesdays, Fridays, Sundays and religious holidays; it was prohibited during a woman's period, during times of penance, and for three days before taking communion. It is probably safe to assume that the laity did not observe the rules without exception.

The changes taking place in the relations between clergy and laity in general were even more apparent in relations between popes and princes. The reinvigoration of the papacy begun by Gregory VII in the late eleventh century came to fruition later during the pontificate of Innocent III, and for over a hundred years the papacy undoubtedly was the strongest government in Europe. Innocent III persuaded Europe's strongest kings to suspend their quarrels with each other and to go crusading together in the service of the church. He made and broke an emperor of the Holy Roman Empire. He imposed his will upon a strong French king in marital matters. And he forced a humiliating (though not wholly disadvantageous) submission upon a king of England. The papacy's secular power over princes was never greater.

Such worldly power, however, invited too deep an involvement in worldly affairs. Whatever animosities they may have felt, contemporaries of Innocent III could never doubt his own deep convictions and his spirituality; the same was not true of his successors. About the middle of the thirteenth century Pope Innocent IV used all of the massive power of the papacy in a political quarrel with the Holy

Roman Emperor, Frederick II, and though this quarrel contributed in no small way to the collapse of the imperial office after Frederick's death, this cynical use of spiritual power diminished greatly the prestige of the papacy. Then Pope Boniface VIII (1294–1303) brought the medieval papacy to its final disaster.

It was the strong and consolidated monarchy of France that challenged the secular pretensions of the papacy. Boniface VIII was a determined and ambitious man who believed unshakably in the absolute power of the papacy. In the mid-1290s he attempted to forbid taxation of the clergy, but he was opposed by two very strong kings, Edward I of England and Philip IV of France; both impeded the flow of monies from their respective kingdoms to Rome, and as Boniface was involved in costly Italian quarrels, he was forced to back down. But he did not forgive, and in another quarrel in the first years of the fourteenth century he sought to humble the king of France.

In the course of the struggle Boniface made the boldest claims of papal power ever enunciated, but times had changed. The political involvements of the papacy had weakened its prestige, and the secular monarchies enjoyed wide support among their subjects. When Boniface attempted to use ecclesiastical weapons against Philip, he discovered that the French laity and much of the French clergy supported the king; then Philip counterattacked, sending agents to Italy in the autumn of 1303 to kidnap the pope, whom he proposed to try for his crimes. The kidnappers seized the pope, but his supporters rescued him before he could be spirited away. Boniface died shortly thereafter, however, and with him died the medieval papacy.

After the one year pontificate of Benedict XI and another year of haggling, French interest secured the election of Clement V, whose support depended upon the king of France. Clement moved from Rome to Avignon to wait for the turbulence in Italy to die down, and the papacy quickly became a pale shadow of the institution that Innocent III had ruled. It had broken the Holy Roman Empire, but it had collapsed in its struggle with France, and in western Europe the initiative passed to the national monarchies.

The troubles of Christianity went beyond changing social attitudes or church-state quarrels, however. The late twelfth and early thirteenth centuries saw the first great eruptions of popular protest against the hierarchy and doctrines of the church in the west, a movement that was to be more or less endemic in Europe until the Reformation of the sixteenth century finally destroyed even the much frayed theory of the unity of western Christendom.

The popular movements against the church were something rather new. The church had weathered challenges before: challenges to the legitimacy of authority had resulted in schisms, as when the eastern church rejected the authority of the papacy in the mid-eleventh century; and variant doctrines known as heresy had been proposed, such as those concerning the divinity of Christ or the equality of the members of the Trinity. But except for the early difficulties with Arian German settlers, these disputes had touched very few people in western Europe and had been confined largely within the clergy. By contrast the thirteenth century heresies were mass movements.

Never before had conditions in Europe been so favorable to popular religious movements, and a number of converging influences sparked an explosion. On the one hand, there was the contrast between increasing popular piety, as exemplified in the cult of the Virgin, and the wealth, power and worldly involvement of the church. Christians were disturbed by the abandonment of the apostolic poverty and disdain of material goods preached by Christ. The monastic orders had maintained the tradition more or less, but the secular hierarchy had not. Criticism of the seculars had come from the monasteries intermittently, and it was much more bitter in the aftermath of the Cluniac reform and the foundation of the stricter Cistercians and Carthusians. Moreover, it had much greater effect in the late twelfth and early thirteenth centuries as the new towns provided large audiences for troubled monks. Earlier, it had been impossible to reach many people, for the populace was scattered. The rise of the towns created concentrations of population that could be addressed by popular preachers, and such preachers—often monks—appeared in large numbers to exhort the faithful to love and serve God, to extol the Christian virtues of poverty and charity and to damn the worldliness of the bishops.

For many reasons townsmen were singularly susceptible to this preaching. In medieval Europe the church was much more central to life than is the case in modern times. Church buildings were usually the chief public structures of town or village, and they were social centers. There women met to gossip; there village and town meetings were held; there young lovers met in dark corners for a few whispered words. The church doors were bulletin boards where notices were posted, and it was in the church that public announcements were made after mass. A society that was largely poor and illiterate and lacked mass media communications turned to the church for news, for hope in hard times, for expressions of thanks in good times. Religious festivals meant holidays and celebrations, and sermons and religious plays and stories were important public amusements. The noble and ecclesiastical elite had some other interests, but most medieval Europeans poured their hopes and dreams and sorrows and frustrations into their religion.

The new towns brought large numbers of such people together, but the towns could be horrible places. Huddled within walls, the towns grew cramped and crowded. Without adequate water supply or sewage disposal or police systems or welfare programs they squeezed together masses of the poor in dark, disease-ridden slums, and they seethed with potential violence. Added to the frustrations implicit in such conditions was the fact that the lords of many towns were bishops, for it will be remembered that early townsmen often built around the fortified episcopal centers for protection. Thus the bishop was not uncommonly the focus of enormous local resentment for his exactions and his failure to relieve misery.

That the potential violence exploded in religious expression is not at all surprising. In the towns popular preachers, especially critical preachers, could always draw a crowd. When worried bishops refused permission to preach in the churches, they simply moved to the fields outside town and preached in the open air. The arrival of an itinerant preacher was an occasion, an excuse for a break from wearisome routine. His talk of God's love and God's wrath stirred popular piety; his fulminations against worldly clergy gave voice to deep-felt resentment. The labors of such men prepared the way for a harvest of violence, especially in the south of France.

In the town of Lyons a movement grew up in the 1170s around Peter Waldo, a merchant. Inspired by an itinerant minstrel's story of a saint, Waldo gave away his property and undertook a life of begging and preaching. He and his followers soon were reported to be preaching heresy, and first the archbishop of Lyons and then the pope forbade their activities, but they ignored the prohibitions; as

Waldensians, or The Poor Men of Lyons, they quickly became well known, and the penalties of the church began to fall upon them. Early in the 1180s the pope condemned them as heretics and excommunicated them, and the archbishop of Lyon expelled them from his archdioceses. Up to that point their only serious offenses were unlicensed preaching and refusal to obey church authority. Under persecution, however, they became more radical, declaring that Christ's teachings in the New Testament were sufficient for salvation and that the church and its sacraments were superfluous. With their explusion from Lyons they spread across the south of France, and their fate became entwined with that of an even larger heretical group, the Cathari or Albigensians.

The origins of the Cathari (the pure) probably go back to an eastern sect called Manichaeans during the Roman Empire. Direct survivals of this cult seem to have been limited to the east, but in the eleventh century small groups of its adherents were heard of again in the west, mostly in north Italy and southern France but with small congregations scattered all over France and Germany. The strongest western center of the Cathari developed around the French town of Albi, so that among the many names applied to these people Albigensians is the one best known.

Original Manichaeanism was a pagan alternative to Christianity, but after centuries of uneasy co-existence, competition and borrowing, the faith of the Cathari resembled a distorted Christianity sufficiently for its followers to be considered heretics in Europe. The actual doctrine is known only in outline, for most surviving materials concerning it come from its Christian enemies, whose revulsion colored their reporting. It would appear, though, that the core of the faith was a dualism: two powers, one good and one evil, the former the ruler of spiritual matters and the latter of material things. Thus complete asceticism was desirable, and Cathari were forbidden the possession of any material goods, again a challenge to the worldliness of the Christian church. The Cathari regarded the crucifixion as a triumph for the force of evil, and they called those who corrupted the tragedy into a tale of glory agents of the force of evil, thus condemning the pope and the whole Christian clergy. They believed man was tainted incurably, and their support of complete celibacy may have been rooted in a desire for voluntary genocide; only when corrupted humanity died out could good triumph.

The capacity of such a strict cult to win a large following, particularly in the highly cultured south of France, lay in the distinction it made between the perfects who practiced the hard discipline and the believers who simply endorsed it. The "believers" were quite free to live as they wished so long as they received the one sacrament of the cult, the *consolamentum*, before they died. Since the sacrament could be administered only once, a believer usually took it on his death bed, thereby wiping out all previous sins. The perfects, on the other hand, appear to have taken the *consolamentum* and then relied upon asceticism to preserve them from further sin. This distinction allowed most adherents a rather unfettered existence while encouraging great respect for the uncompromising austerity of the cult's leaders.

By the early thirteenth century the Albigensians and Waldensians had won such wide support that normal ecclesiastical weapons were impotent, and though Pope Innocent III was determined to crush them, his early efforts produced no result. Preachers sent in to attempt conversion by persuasion had no effect. An appeal to local lords was equally ineffectual, for the greatest of them—Count Raymond of Toulouse—though a practicing Catholic, was quite indifferent to religion, and another, the count of Foix, had Waldensians and Albigensians in his own family, though he professed Catholicism personally.

Innocent then turned to the king of France, Philip Augustus, and made a series of appeals for royal action. At first the king refused, for he was embroiled in a struggle with John of England, but in 1207—with his own affairs calmer—he agreed to allow northern knights to participate in a crusade in the south; for political reasons, however, he still declined personally to lead an expedition against his vassal. In the summer of 1209 the crusade began, and soon it left a swath of death and destruction in its wake. Under the able leadership of a baron with lands and titles in both France and England, Simon de Montfort, most of the south was conquered by 1213, with a large-scale slaughter of everyone suspected of heresy. Although the area remained restive for another generation, both the heresies and the power of the southern nobles who had protected them were broken, and later in the thirteenth century much of the area passed into the control of the French royal family. Courts of inquisition operating under special papal authority continued to seek out and persecute heresy, and such heretics as had survived the crusade went underground, so that the area again became nominally Catholic.

The force of popular piety which was largely responsible for the wide-spread heresies was not killed by the Albigensian crusade; rather, it found new channels of expression. Driven by the same religious fervor that had inspired the heretics, and moved by desire to restore confidence in the church's teachings, pious men formed new religious groups called the mendicant friars at the beginning of the thirteenth century; two of these groups became particularly significant, the Franciscan and Dominican Orders, dedicated not to monasticism but to service in the world—preaching and teaching. The activities of the mendicant friars were varied and important. Dominicans and Franciscans staffed the inquisition in southern France after the Albigensian crusade; they became leading scholars in the new universities; they undertook missionary work in lands as far distant as India and China; less dramatically, they preached, heard confessions and buried the dead all over Europe. Their effects were considerable: they provided an outlet for the religious enthusiasm that had fed the great heresies; they carried Christianity to the poor and the isolated; and as papal agents they flooded over Europe and increased the pope's power in the church at the expense of the bishops.

Inevitably, the spiritual fires that burned in the mendicants got some of them into difficulty with the hierarchy, for their enthusiasm encouraged extremism. Some of the followers of St. Francis emphasized his insistence upon apostolic poverty and, like the Waldensians, became very critical of the established clergy. This group, known as Spiritual Franciscans, eventually was condemned. Yet the movement of popular piety went on and on, producing new heretical movements in the fourteenth century, the Lollards and the Hussites, and culminating in the sixteenth century with the development of Protestantism.

About the middle of the fourteenth century Europe was struck by the terrible epidemic called the Black Death, bubonic plague, which seemed to contemporaries a visitation of the wrath of God. When the disease struck, it ran its course very quickly, with horrible symptoms, and it was usually fatal. Victims of the Black Death suffered sudden high fever, accompanied by splitting headaches, nausea and lethargy; then delirium set in, usually within twenty-four hours, followed by the appearance of buboes—large, hard swellings of black or purplish coloration in the armpits and groin—on the second or third day. Sometimes the buboes opened and drained, and the patient recovered, but most often he died less than a week after experiencing the first symptoms.

The Black Death seems to have originated in Central Asia in the 1330s and then spread along the trade routes, reaching the west about a decade later, where it washed back and forth across Europe for many years. Of course a society with almost no concept of sanitation was terribly vulnerable to epidemic; mortality was very high, while the agony of the sickness and the seeming inevitability of death aggravated popular terror. Fourteenth-century medicine was too primitive to isolate the source of the disease, which is carried by vermin from infected rats, but an Italian author, Boccaccio, in the introduction to his *Decameron,* indicates that it was recognized as a natural contagion spreading from place to place and that some attempts were made to control it by quarantine and isolation. In the crowded conditions of medieval towns, however, such efforts were fruitless, and the epidemic ran its course unchecked; Europe is estimated to have lost between a fifth and a third of its population in the latter half of the fourteenth century, a slaughter worse than the effects of any of the human invasions that medieval Europe had suffered.

The immediate effects of the Black Death were many and varied. Those who could afford to do so sought to escape areas where the plague was raging, and some regions were quite depopulated by death and flight; some squandered their resources in revelry, expecting they soon would die; many sought refuge in religion, often with wild devotional excesses such as flagellation—whipping one another viciously to mortify the flesh and free the spirit.

The long-term effects of the epidemic were even more serious. Extensive mortality caused labor shortages with a consequent rise of wages and prices, producing an apparent prosperity, but this was followed by a long and serious recession when the market felt the impact of reduced demand. Groups that exercised political power, aristocrats and wealthy bourgeois, tried to protect their position through governmental and guild regulation which shifted much of the burden of economic problems to the less organized and more vulnerable classes of society—peasants and lesser nobility in the countryside and the working force in the cities. The late fourteenth century saw a number of violent but generally fruitless revolts by these classes and even more violent repression by the dominant classes: the Peasants' Revolt in England, the *Jacquerie* in France and the Ciompi rising in Florence. The turmoil abated only about the middle of the fifteenth century, and even then serious problems remained. Western Europe experienced a widespread recovery, though the economy stabilized at levels of prosperity probably considerably lower than those of the twelfth and thirteenth centuries, and in Germany the economic recovery was limited to urban centers, leaving the peasantry in a very depressed condition.

Thus, chronic economic problems and extensive social change accompanied and probably intensified the religious restiveness of later medieval society. Nobles resented amply financed bourgeois who lived well, had money to lend and even were buying noble lands and titles. Urban populations resented lords who tried to squeeze ever more money from their towns and attempted to impede the growing independence of town life. Peasants resented the exactions of their overlords, which became more onerous as the lords felt the pressure of economic problems, and market controls in the towns, which tended to depress the prices that peasants received for their agricultural produce while maintaining the high prices that they had to pay for the towns' manufactures. The development of Europe certainly cannot be recounted as a steady progress, and there is no doubt that later medieval society witnessed a contraction of population, a shrinking of opportunity and an economic decline that were bewildering to those who experienced them. In such circumstances it ought not to be surprising that religious fanaticism, blind violence and brutal repression flourished.

Chapter 10

The Hundred Years War

From the middle of the fourteenth century to the middle of the fifteenth century, while Germany lay fragmented by aristocratic anarchy and Italy was torn by the rivalries of the city states, western Europe was dominated by a great conflict between the French and English crowns. Actually the struggle was a series of wars broken by treaties and truces, which lasted from 1337 to 1455, but usually it is called the Hundred Years War and is treated in its entirety, for issues changed little during its course.

It is difficult to isolate reasons for the outbreak of war in 1337, not because of any lack of causes for conflict but rather because several causes long had existed, and war might have broken out at any time. The French and English crowns had been hostile to one another ever since the Norman conquest of 1066 had made one of the French monarch's vassals a king in his own right; this issue had not been settled by Philip Augustus' conquests from John of England, for the kings of England continued to hold most of France's southwestern coastal region, an area called the duchy of Gascony. The Albigensian crusade, which strengthened the French king's control over much of the south, left the English position in Gascony rather tenuous, and this problem was aggravated further by the rapid development of the judicial authority of the French crown after the middle of the thirteenth century. Not only did the kings accept appeals from their vassals' courts to their own parlement of Paris, which had serious financial repercussions, but the administration of this appellate procedure often involved sending royal agents into the great fiefs. When these practices were applied to the duchy of Gascony, they often caused serious quarrels between the king of France and the king of England, and twice—at the end of the thirteenth century and at the beginning of the fourteenth century—the French crown seized the duchy, though in both instances the disputes were settled and it was restored. Nonetheless, by the second quarter of the fourteenth century precedents had been established for a major confrontation.

Exacerbating this quarrel, which was basically feudal in nature, were a number of lesser issues. By the early fourteenth century Flanders was a highly developed industrial area producing woolen cloth, but there was conflict between the wealthy merchants who controlled the trade in their own interest and the artisans of the craft guilds, who made the cloth. The artisans revolted, and when the count of Flanders proved unable to pacify the situation, the French crown intervened on the side of the merchants, who represented stability and traditional authority in the Flemish towns. But Flanders was the chief market for raw wool from England, that country's primary export, and any increase in the influence of the French monarch in this area posed the threat that he might control an important part of the English king's revenue. Consequently, while the king of France aided the merchants, the king of England aided the artisans.

Another disruptive issue was the problem of piracy in and around the Channel, where the transport of wine and wool and other lesser trade had led to the development of rather heavy shipping. Since English and French ships attacked one another on every occasion, both monarchs were deluged with requests for aid from their seamen; usually these requests were ignored, but the issue was readily at hand if an excuse were needed for military action. In the same category was French aid to the Scots who troubled England's northern borders; generally the matter was ignored, and occasional English protests met only bland excuses, but the issue always was susceptible to escalation.

Finally, another dangerous element was added to the rivalry between the two monarchies when the French succession came into question. In 1316 the tradition of passing the crown from father to son, a practice unbroken since Hugh Capet, ended when Louis X's death was followed within a year by the death of his posthumous son. After some dispute over the claims of Louis' daughter, the crown went first to his brother Philip V (1316–1322) and then to another brother Charles IV (1322–1328). The legal questions involved were complex, but the parlement of Paris appears to have unearthed an old provision of Frankish practice called the Salic Law, which forbade female inheritance and thus justified what had been done.

The matter became more serious in 1328 when Charles IV died without sons, for the senior male line of the Capetians died with him. If the Salic Law were observed, the heir to the throne was Philip, count of Valois, a nephew of Philip IV through the latter's younger brother. But there were no long traditions or strong precedents to support the exclusion of a female, and if a woman's rights could be upheld, Edward III of England (1327–1377) had a claim to the throne through his mother, who was a daughter of Philip IV. However, the issue did not become critical immediately. When the count of Valois was proclaimed Philip VI of France (1328–1350), Edward's mother registered a formal protest, but her son did homage for Gascony, and it appeared that the Valois succession would be accepted. Only a decade later was the arrangement challenged.

With so many contentious issues outstanding between them, it is not surprising that Edward III and Philip VI fought, but the reason for the war having begun in 1337 appears to turn on personal factors. Both monarchs were imbued thoroughly with the knightly desire to win glory through military achievements, and both considered their crowns and their resources personal property to be used as they saw fit. Hence, both were eager for a war and thought they could sustain its costs. As so many times before, Gascony provided the source of a new quarrel, one which Philip VI appears to have manufactured deliberately. The French crown declared that the homage performed for Gascony by Edward III had been faulty and demanded that he renew it as full liege homage; he refused, and Philip declared Gascony forfeit in 1337. Edward's response was to declare war on Philip, addressing him as "the so-called king of France," which implied clearly a revival of Edward's claims to the French throne, an implication later made explicit. In 1338 Edward crossed to the continent with an army, and the war that both kings desired so eagerly was begun.

Despite certain similarities of leadership (leadership which was generally vainglorious, often impractical and sometimes simply incompetent), there were striking differences between the English and French forces. The French army still depended primarily upon the armored knight, a small fraction of the realm's population, and its only infantry support consisted of pikemen from town militia and some hired crossbowmen. Such a force was reasonably effective in a heavy cavalry charge and the melée of hand-to-hand combat that followed, but as the crusades already had demonstrated, it was ill-disciplined and was vulnerable to attack from a distance with missile weapons. By contrast, the English army had developed some quite startling innovations; it was composed chiefly of infantry, commoners who served for pay, and it depended heavily upon an impressive new missile weapon, the longbow, supported by pikes. This new force had developed largely from Edward I's campaigns against the Welsh. In the rough country of Wales he had learned the value of infantry, and after feeling the power of the Welsh bow, his soldiers had copied it. The longbow was six feet in length and fired an arrow three feet long with sufficient velocity to pierce armor at short ranges. Its greatest advantage was its rate of fire, however; in random firing, such as into a densely packed mass of charging cavalry, the longbowman could get off about ten arrows per minute to the crossbowman's two, for the latter had a heavy and complex mechanism to rewind and reload. The pikes used by both sides were long wooden spears with iron points; when a group of pikemen set themselves, with the butts of their weapons braced against the ground, tips angled forward and upward, the resulting wall of points could stop a cavalry charge.

For eight years the war proceeded in a desultory manner, the two kings avoiding large-scale engagements and limiting their activities to skirmishes and sieges of castles. Then, in 1346 a major confrontation occurred, and the new English army proved its worth. Edward III had brought a force of about nine thousand men to Normandy, where he had plundered the city of Caen, but when Philip VI began gathering a large force at Paris, Edward decided to withdraw. Since his fleet had returned to England, leaving him stranded in France, Edward had no choice but to march northward to his allies in Flanders. A sort of race then developed, with the

English moving north by forced marches and the French trying to intersect their line of retreat and cut off their escape. By good luck Edward managed to get his troops across both the Seine and the Somme before the French caught up to him, but since the French cavalry could move faster than the English infantry, at that point he had to fight. On 26 August 1346 he took up a defensive position near the forest of Crécy and awaited the French attack; his position was well chosen, for his flanks were covered somewhat by the forest and a village, and he was at the top of a rise up which the French would have to charge to get at him. Organizing his force into three divisions, he dismounted his knights and set them with his pikemen between large bodies of archers. Then he waited.

What happened next is explicable only in terms of the ill-disciplined independence and vanity of the medieval knight. Philip VI could have moved around the English, and waited for Edward to attack or starve; or he could have concentrated his army and attempted an assault with the massed weight of his heavy cavalry. He did neither. Instead, he sent his crossbowmen forward to harass the English, but as the longbow outranged the crossbow, they could accomplish little. Then he allowed some cavalry to try to charge through the crossbowmen, which created a confused mob into which the English poured volleys of arrows. Finally, as the rest of the French army came up, he sent it forward piecemeal in over a dozen separate assaults, which lasted until midnight and only added to the slaughter wreaked by English arrows. The few who reached the English lines of dismounted knights and pikemen were killed or captured, and those who survived fled south. When morning came, the English realized that they had won a great victory, and instead of continuing his withdrawal to Flanders, Edward marched to the coast and besieged the port of Calais, which surrendered a year later. The English had acquired an invasion port which they were to hold until the middle of the sixteenth century.

Shortly after the capture of Calais, the Black Death swept across Europe and imposed a few years' lull in the fighting; major operations were not resumed until the middle 1350s, by which time Philip VI had been succeeded by his son John the Good (1350–1364), and Edward was being assisted by his son, the Black Prince. In 1355, while John and Edward III sparred inconclusively in and around Normandy, the Black Prince ravaged the south of France; by providing horses to transport his archers, he created a fast-moving column that swept through the countryside, avoiding strong-points while looting and burning everything else. In 1356 the Black Prince moved north with the same sort of expedition and plundered the rich Loire Valley, but this time King John set forth to meet him and tried to stop his withdrawal toward Bordeaux.

The Black Prince did not want to fight, for his army was tired and was burdened with a long wagon train loaded with booty, but in mid-September he was brought to bay near Poitiers and had to either fight or abandon his plunder. Sending the wagons on, the English took up a defensive position, as they had at Crécy a decade earlier. Their flanks were protected by a ravine on one side and thick woods on the other, and their front was covered better than at Crécy by rough ground and thickets unfavorable for a cavalry charge except along a narrow road that traversed it. In the face of this position, King John, who had even less military ability than his father, devised an incredible plan of attack that seems to have been influenced by the English victory a decade before. The vanity of the French nobles would not allow them to admit that Crécy had been won by commoners, whose arrows had cut to pieces the flower of French chivalry, so they concluded that the decisive factor must have been the dismounted knights. King John therefore ordered most of his knights to dismount and form three divisions to fight on foot, but there was a grave error in his calculations. In a defensive position a dismounted knight was simply an armored pikeman; on the offensive, as at Poitiers, a dismounted knight was a man in heavy armor who had to march a mile over rough country to get within striking distance of the enemy. The difference proved signifi-cant.

First, John sent a small body of cavalry charging up the road to smash a hole in the English line; confined to a narrow approach, it was cut up badly by the English archers. Then he sent forward his three divisions of dismounted knights, holding his crossbowmen in the rear where they would not interfere with the nobles and thus depriving his attack of any missile support. Some of the first division reached the English, and there was hard fighting, but the French knights—weary from the march and harassed by the archers—soon were killed or captured. Having observed this, the second division withdrew without attacking. The third division, led by King John himself, then repeated the first division's assault, with the same re-sults. When the Black Prince resumed his withdrawal to Bordeaux, he took along as prisoners the king of France, the king's youngest son, three dozen great nobles and a large number of lesser nobles, all of whom would command valuable ransons.

With the army destroyed and the king a prisoner, John's eldest son, the Dauphin Charles, had no choice but to negotiate, and in 1360 the Treaty of Brétigny-Calais ended the first phase of the Hundred Years War. England made great gains. France was to pay an enormous ransom for King John, and the king of England was to receive all of the old duchy of Aquitaine and a few other territories. Though most of the provisions of the Treaty of Brétigny-Calais never were carried out, the agreement brought a decade of peace marked by little of note except King John's death in 1364 and the succession of his capable son Charles V (1364–1380). The new king of France was determined to recover what his father had lost, but like his ancestor Philip Augustus he was conscious of the value of legal justifications. For a few years he continued paying instalments on the money owed to England and simply waited; then in 1369 the Black Prince, who was governing Aquitaine for his father, gave Charles the opportunity he sought.

Some Gascon nobles appealed from the Black Prince's harsh rule to the parlement of Paris, and Charles so maneuvered the case as to pronounce the whole duchy of Aquitaine forfeit to the French crown. The war was resumed, though the campaigns of the 1370s were curious in that the two forces pursued different objectives and never met in battle. The English continued their plundering expeditions across open country, but Charles V, who was more practical than chivalrous, simply harassed them from time to time and concentrated on retaking castles. His commanders, of whom the most famous was the Breton Bertran Duguesclin, were men capable of planning ambushes and midnight assaults and of using bribery. Though such practices scandalized contemporary concepts of knightly honor, they proved effective, and the English position was reduced to a coastal strip between the Garonne River and the Pyrenees, less than Edward III had held before the war began.

Unfortunately, this successful reconquest did not spare France from the depredations of soldiers. Both sides used hired troops, and when fighting slackened they simply dismissed them; many of these unemployed soldiers formed bands of brigands called free companies and continued to live off the land, plundering and killing wherever they went for the next century.

Changes of leadership and internal troubles in both kingdoms caused a stalemate in the war after the French recovery. Between 1376 and 1380 the Black Prince, Edward III and Charles V all died. The English crown passed to the Black Prince's son, Richard II (1377–1399), and then to his cousin, Henry IV (1399–1413), while Charles V of France was succeeded by his son, Charles VI (1380–1422). During most of this period England was occupied by baronial revolts, which precluded effective military action in France, but the French were in no better condition; after 1392 Charles VI suffered frequent fits of insanity, and France was divided as the government was disputed by two of his relatives, the duke of Orléans and the duke of Burgundy. Except for a truce signed in the mid-1390s, little happened in the war until 1413, when two important events caused it to take a new turn: in England Henry IV was succeeded by his son Henry V (1413–1422), who possessed real military talent, and in France the Armagnacs (as Orléans' supporters were called) succeeded in expelling the Burgundians from Paris, leaving the court seriously divided.

In the summer of 1415 Henry V led a new army to France, and while attempting to withdraw to Calais after some modest successes he had to face the French host at Agincourt. Again the English took up a defensive position with their flanks protected and their pikemen and dismounted knights set between formations of archers. Again the French ignored their crossbowmen and sent in a cavalry charge followed by three divisions of dismounted knights, just as at Poitiers. The results were even worse at Agincourt, for since the last confrontation French armor had been made much heavier in an attempt to find some defense against the longbow; by the time the French reached the English lines, across a muddy field, they were too weary to raise their weapons or to rise again if knocked down, and most of the first two divisions were taken prisoner. Unfortunately, at this point in the battle Henry V was told that the rear of his army was under serious attack, and he ordered the prisoners killed; by the time this was discovered to be a false alarm, many of the French nobles had been slaughtered, and the third French division had withdrawn, leaving the English once more masters of the battlefield. Agincourt destroyed the Orléanist party, and in the aftermath of the battle the Burgundians seized Paris again and allied with Henry V. They then imposed upon Charles VI's son, the dauphin, the Treaty of Troyes of 1420, which confirmed the English in Aquitaine and divided all of France north of the Loire between the English and the Burgundians; moreover, in one provision of the treaty the French queen declared that the dauphin was illegitimate, so when Henry V married Charles VI's daughter, English claims to the French throne were strengthened immeasurably. The Treaty of Troyes ended the second phase of the Hundred Years War with the English in an even more extensive position than they had enjoyed under the Treaty of Brétigny-Calais.

In 1422, only two years after the Treaty of Troyes, both Henry V and Charles VI died, and the infant Henry VI (1422–1461) was claimant to both crowns. However, the Dauphin Charles, resident in Bourges, was far from defeated, for most of the English aristocracy had no further interest in France, which had been picked clean of plunder, and the harsh rule of English and Burgundian officials drove many northern French nobles into his camp. What was needed by Charles, who was a colorless young man, was something to add excitement to his cause, and this was provided in 1429 by Joan of Arc. A peasant girl who had visions of saints, Joan managed an interview with the dauphin, and she impressed him by her complete confidence in his destiny to rule France. With his blessing, she went to Orléans, one of the cities being besieged by the English, and her inspiration began a new French recovery.

Joan of Arc's influence lay mostly in the factor of morale. Inspired by her unshakable faith, the French soldiery drove off the besiegers of Orléans, relieved other places threatened by the English and then defeated an English army in the field. Swept along by her confidence, the dauphin allowed himself to be persuaded into a mad dash across enemy territory to Rheims, the traditional site of coronations, where he was crowned King Charles VII (1422–1461) on July 17, 1429. However, Joan's zeal was not accepted as sanctity by her opponents; in 1430, when the Burgundians captured her and sold her to the English, she was treated as a witch, and the next year she was burned at the stake.

For several years the war continued in a desultory fashion, and then in 1435 the duke of Burgundy, whose ambition to control Flanders had resulted in a clash with his English allies, made peace

with Charles VII by the Treaty of Arras. After that the French recovery proceeded slowly but surely. Reverting to the strategy of
Charles V, the French captured castle after castle, and a last battle
in the north in 1450 and one in the south two years later left the
English only Calais. At that point the Hundred Years War simply
died out, but the strategic impact of the French victory was enormous. With her continental possessions wiped out, England found
her first line of defense forced back into the channel, and it is no
coincidence that the new Tudor dynasty, established in the late
fifteenth century, showed great interest in naval affairs from the
outset. With the threat from the west finally resolved, French armies
were freed for other ventures, and at the end of the fifteenth century
France's kings responded to the lure of Italy, as had the Carolingians several centuries before; in the mid-1490s Charles VIII led
across the Alps the first of those armies that were to involve France
in a new struggle and, incidentally, were to be so important in
bringing the Renaissance to France.

The last stages of the Hundred Years War witnessed some interesting military innovations, especially the development of French
artillery. Primitive cannon, called bombards, had been known since
the 1320s, but throughout the fourteenth century they remained
largely ineffective because they were too ponderous to move readily
and too inaccurate and slow to fire to cause much damage. By the
mid-fifteenth century there had been some improvements. Cannon
were still too clumsy to be much use in the field, and they threw too
light a round to have much effect on stone walls, but their concentrated fire could knock down the gates of castles or towns, and they
played no small part in the French successes. Also of note was the
redevelopment of a permanent professional army. About a decade
before the end of the war, Charles VII hired into his service on a
year around basis about six thousand of the mercenary soldiery who
long had plagued France, using them to fight both the English and
the infamous free companies; he also attempted to form a nationwide militia of archers, but nothing much came of this idea.

These mid-century forces differed markedly from those that had
fought at Agincourt, and the differences became more pronounced
through the second half of the century. Armor tended to grow
lighter again, since heavy plate made a soldier slow and clumsy

without providing adequate protection against arrows or pikes. Some officers still used full armor, and it was worn for tournaments, but most troopers began to wear only helmet, breastplate and back-plate in battle. Nobles still formed an important part of the army as they made up most of the cavalry and the officer corps of the in-fantry, but as paid soldiers they were more susceptible to discipline than the old feudal levy. And the growing importance of the pike, a cheap weapon capable of stopping cavalry, made infantry re-cruited from among commoners ever more significant. One far-reaching effect of these developments was that military power came to depend more upon financial resources than upon vast lands for the endowment of vassals. Thus, at the very end of the Hundred Years War some of the elements of modern armies began to appear.

During the century of war political as well as military changes took place, stimulated largely by the demands of the great struggle. In England, Edward III's preoccupation with the French wars had led him to allow certain powers to parliament that it likely would not have obtained otherwise, particularly the right to demand dis-missal of officers of the crown for improper acts; this power, which later came to be called impeachment, was an important step in the development of ministerial responsibility to the parliament. Ed-ward's reign also saw the House of Lords begin to take firmer form. The notion that the grand council, ancestor of the upper house, should be determined by feudal tenure as provided in *Magna Carta* clearly was obsolete by the late fourteenth century; Edward's pre-decessors had invited whomever they thought important, with small regard for the lands they held, and Edward tended to invite men whose fathers had sat. While the hereditary character of the House of Lords was not established definitely until the fifteenth century, it made great progress during Edward III's reign. And at the same time the king tended to meet prelates separately on church ques-tions, so far fewer bishops and abbots came to parliament; a sort of general principle developed that only those ecclesiastical lords attended who also held secular baronies, who were lords temporal as well as lords spiritual.

Finally, Edward summoned the knights and burgesses to par-liament with greater frequency and allowed some increase in the scope of their activities. During his reign it became habitual for these men, who were beginning to be called "the Commons," to draft petitions on matters they considered important and then to submit them to the grand council; if this second body endorsed the petition, it was sent on to the king, and petitions that he approved became statutes of the realm. Thus was born a form of parliamentary legislation in England. The king and the lords retained control, but it became customary for most legislation and all money bills to be initiated in the Commons. All of these developments owed something to Edward's involvement in the long and costly wars in France, but none more than parliamentary control of taxation. In order to get parliament to vote him money regularly, Edward promised to take no taxes without its consent and even agreed to allow parliamentary committees some right to audit royal expenditures. The results of all this were that during the reign of Edward III the outlines of the modern parliament became apparent, and parliament became an integral part of royal government, sufficiently important that later kings put considerable effort into manipulating its sessions and the election of its members.

Less a direct result of the war but perhaps influenced by Edward's desire that things run smoothly during his absences from England was the further development of royal justice. On the one hand, the king's chancellor developed a tribunal called chancery court with very wide powers in equity, to provide justice in the king's name in cases where there were no clear laws or precedents. On the other hand, a whole new group of judges was appointed all over the country, called justices of the peace; these men were drawn from that class of lesser nobility and untitled property owners called gentry, the same that provided the knights of the shires to parliament, and though officers of the king's government, they were unpaid. They soon became the chief power in local government.

In France, the unhappy course of the greater part of the war delayed further development of royal government except for the continuous increase in size of the royal bureaucracy. Though at the beginning of the fourteenth century Philip IV's administration was very similar to that of Edward I, by the end of the century the English government was much more sophisticated. The lack of development of the estates general, for reasons of provincialism already noted, made the raising of money by the French crown quite haphazard. A variety of levies was used: sales taxes, a tax on salt called the *gabelle*, a hearth tax, and in addition the crown very frequently debased the coinage so as to pay off its debts in cheap money.

All of these measures bore hard upon the bourgeoisie, and the annoyance of this class was aggravated by the magnificent incompetence demonstrated by the kings and the nobility, especially at Crécy and Poitiers. In the late 1350s, when the dauphin was in desperate straits to raise money for the ransom of King John, several of the towns of France, led by Paris, attempted to use the estates general to win some control of royal government, at least of its tax powers. The dauphin was in a weak position and was inclined to negotiate so long as the bourgeoisie remained moderate in its demands, but impatience led to violence, and the effort to attain political influence soon became a full-scale urban revolt. At the same time, the unrestrained ravages of English plundering expeditions and special war levies by noble lords resulted in a violent peasant rising in the north of France. The Parisian leader of the urban revolt, Etienne Marcel, tried to make common cause with the peasants, but this was their undoing. Troops repressed the peasant revolt savagely, and the conservative upper bourgeoisie, as disturbed as the nobles by the violence and the overtones of social revolution in the peasant movement, abandoned Marcel and the other urban leaders and opened the gates of Paris to the dauphin. The commoners' attempt to win a position of influence over royal policy had failed.

During the 1360s and 1370s the able and effective Charles V restored order and achieved an important gain for royal government; having persuaded the estates general to approve collection of taxes without putting a time limit on the approval, he collected them year after year, establishing a pattern of more or less regular taxation by the king's decision. But during the long reign of the insane Charles VI (1380–1422), the government again was disrupted seriously in the struggle between the Armagnacs and the Burgundians who fought to control the power and the patronage of the crown. Only in the reign of Charles VII (1422–1461), when France was recovering militarily, did governmental development make much progress, and then it was along lines very different from English development. Able ministers developed for the king not only the beginnings of a standing army, already referred to, but also complete independence from the estates general in matters of taxation, so that within the royal domain the king's authority was virtually unlimited. On the other hand, great princes such as the duke of Burgundy and the duke of Brittany were almost independent and many others enjoyed virtual autonomy. Thus, while Charles established in his domain patterns that were to lead to absolutism, at the end of his reign there were still large areas of France that lay outside his effective control, and the consolidation of most of France into an effective national monarchy came only in the latter half of the fifteenth century.

Chapter 11

The Disintegration
of Medieval Europe

In addition to the governmental and military changes that took place in the English and French monarchies during the course of the Hundred Years War, the fourteenth and fifteenth centuries also witnessed other significant transformations and innovations. Within these two centuries the medieval papacy collapsed, popular heresies flourished again, the European monarchies underwent important social consolidation and voyages of exploration discovered the New World and opened direct sea routes to the Far East.

When Clement V moved the papacy to the papally owned city of Avignon in the south of France in 1305, the transfer was intended to be temporary, but for seventy years the popes remained exiled from the spiritual capital of the west and dangerously susceptible to the influence of the French monarchy. Philip IV's high-handed treatment of Boniface VIII already had dealt a serious blow to papal prestige, and exile from Rome proved even more damaging. For all Europeans, Rome was a city with special connotations. It had been the capital of the Roman Empire, which continued to be remembered as a sort of golden age of the past; it was the site of the tombs of two Apostles, Peter and Paul; for centuries it had been the seat of the papacy. It was *the* Holy City of the west. The pronounce-

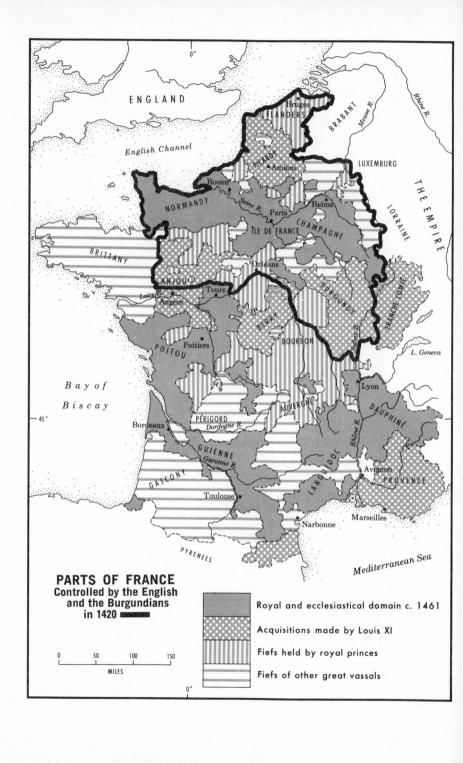

ENGLAND

English Channel

Bay of Biscay

ENGLAND

FLANDERS
Bruges

BRABANT

Meuse R.

Rhine R.

LUXEMBURG

THE EMPIRE

PICARDY
Amiens

Rouen

NORMANDY

Seine R.

Paris

Reims

CHAMPAGNE

LORRAINE

ÎLE DE FRANCE

BRITTANY

Orleans

Loire R.

ANJOU

Tours

Angers

BURGUNDY

Saône R.

FRANCHE-COMTÉ

L. Geneva

BERRY

BOURBON

POITOU

Poitiers

AUVERGNE

Lyon

DAUPHINÉ

45°

PÉRIGORD

Dordogne R.

Bordeaux

Rhône R.

GUIENNE

Garonne R.

LANGUEDOC

Avignon

PROVENCE

GASCONY

Toulouse

Marseilles

Narbonne

PYRENEES

Mediterranean Sea

PARTS OF FRANCE
Controlled by the English
and the Burgundians
in 1420

Royal and ecclesiastical domain c. 1461

Acquisitions made by Louis XI

Fiefs held by royal princes

Fiefs of other great vassals

0   50   100   150

MILES

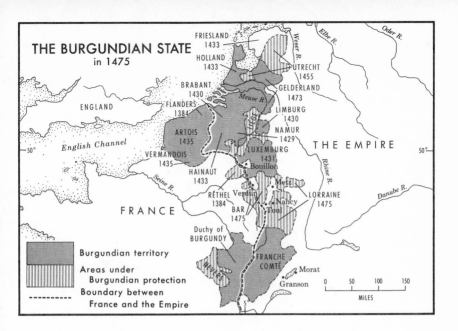

THE BURGUNDIAN STATE
in 1475

FRIESLAND
1433

HOLLAND
1433

UTRECHT
1455

GELDERLAND
1473

BRABANT
1430

LIMBURG
1430

FLANDERS
1384

NAMUR
1429

ARTOIS
1435

LUXEMBURG
1431

Bouillon

THE EMPIRE

ENGLAND

English Channel

VERMANDOIS
1435

HAINAUT
1433

Metz

LORRAINE
1475

RÉTHEL   Verdun
1384

Nancy

BAR   Toul
1475

FRANCE

Duchy of
BURGUNDY

FRANCHE
COMTÉ

Morat

Granson

Meuse R.

Weser R.

Elbe R.

Oder R.

Rhine R.

Danube R.

Seine R.

Burgundian territory

Areas under
Burgundian protection

Boundary between
France and the Empire

0   50   100   150
MILES

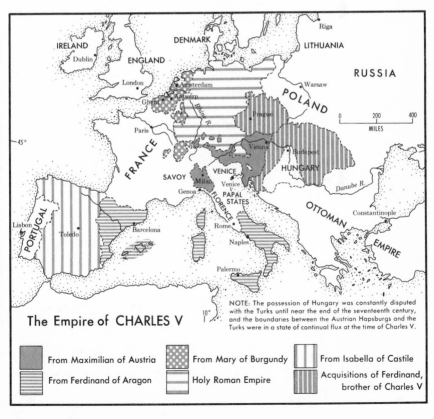

Riga

IRELAND

DENMARK

LITHUANIA

Dublin

ENGLAND

RUSSIA

London

Amsterdam

Warsaw

POLAND

Antwerp

Ghent

Prague

Paris

Vienna

FRANCE

Budapest

HUNGARY

SAVOY

VENICE

Milan

Venice

Danube R.

Genoa

PAPAL
STATES

FLORENCE

OTTOMAN

Constantinople

PORTUGAL

Lisbon

Toledo

Barcelona

Rome

EMPIRE

Naples

Palermo

The Empire of CHARLES V

Rhine R.

0   200   400
MILES

NOTE: The possession of Hungary was constantly disputed
with the Turks until near the end of the seventeenth century,
and the boundaries between the Austrian Hapsburgs and the
Turks were in a state of continual flux at the time of Charles V.

From Maximilian of Austria

From Mary of Burgundy

From Isabella of Castile

From Ferdinand of Aragon

Holy Roman Empire

Acquisitions of Ferdinand,
brother of Charles V

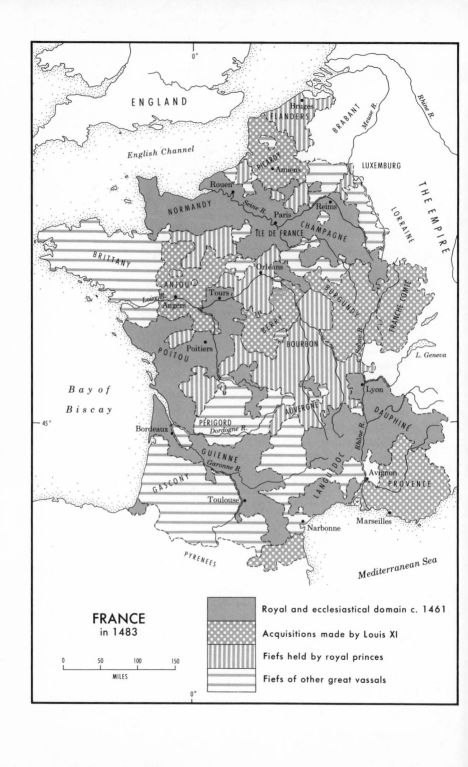

ENGLAND

English Channel

FLANDERS
Bruges

BRABANT

Meuse R.

Rhine R.

LUXEMBURG

PICARDY
Amiens

LORRAINE

THE EMPIRE

Rouen

Seine R.

Paris

Reims

NORMANDY

ÎLE DE FRANCE

CHAMPAGNE

BRITTANY

Orleans

BURGUNDY

FRANCHE COMTE

ANJOU

Tours

Loire R.

Angers

BERRY

BOURBON

Saône R.

L. Geneva

POITOU

Poitiers

AUVERGNE

Lyon

Bay of
Biscay

DAUPHINÉ

45°

PÉRIGORD

Dordogne R.

Rhône R.

Bordeaux

GUIENNE

Garonne R.

LANGUEDOC

Avignon

PROVENCE

GASCONY

Toulouse

Narbonne

Marseilles

PYRENEES

Mediterranean Sea

FRANCE
in 1483

0   50   100   150

MILES

0°

Royal and ecclesiastical domain c. 1461

Acquisitions made by Louis XI

Fiefs held by royal princes

Fiefs of other great vassals

0°

ITALY
in the
Late Fifteenth Century

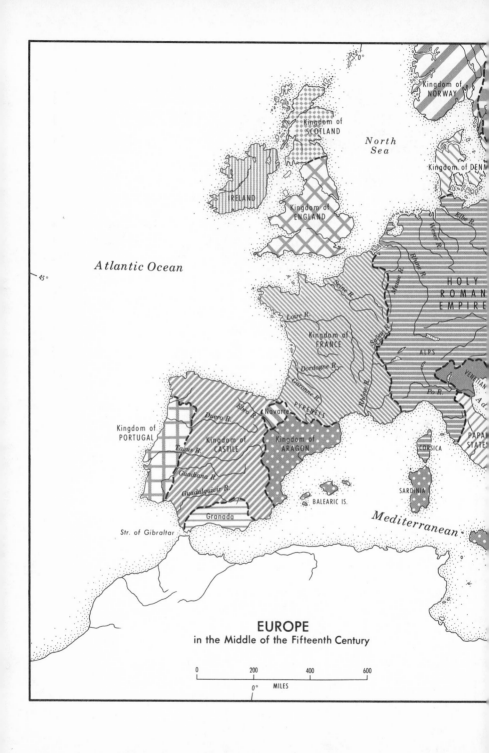

Kingdom of NORWAY

North
Sea

Kingdom of
SCOTLAND

Kingdom of DENM

IRELAND

Elbe R.

Kingdom of
ENGLAND

Weser R.

Atlantic Ocean

45°

HOLY
ROMAN
EMPIRE

Rhine R.

Meuse R.

Marne R.

Loire R.

Kingdom of
FRANCE

Seine R.

ALPS

Dordogne R.

Po R.

VENETIAN

Garonne R.

PYRENEES

Rhone R.

A d

Duero R.

Ebro R.

Navarre

Kingdom of
PORTUGAL

Kingdom of
CASTILE

Kingdom of
ARAGON

PAPA
STATE

CORSICA

Tagus R.

Guadiana R.

Guadalquivir R.

BALEARIC IS.

SARDINIA

Granada

Str. of Gibraltar

Mediterranean

EUROPE
in the Middle of the Fifteenth Century

0   200   400   600

0°   MILES

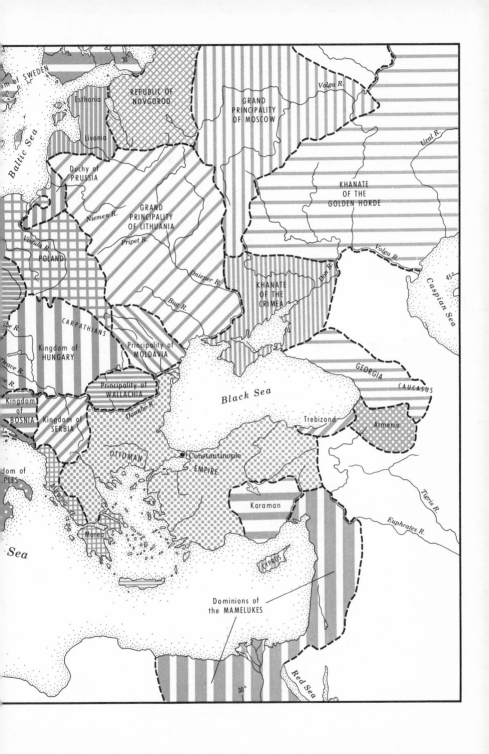

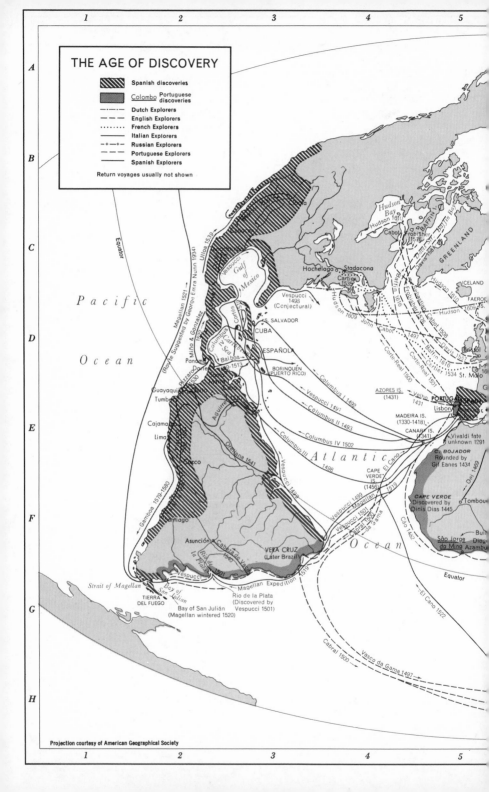

THE AGE OF DISCOVERY

Spanish discoveries
Colombo Portuguese discoveries
—·—·— Dutch Explorers
— — — English Explorers
·········· French Explorers
——— Italian Explorers
—+—+— Russian Explorers
— — — Portuguese Explorers
— — — Spanish Explorers

Return voyages usually not shown

Pacific

Ocean

Equator

Gulf
of
Mexico

Vespucci
1498
(Conjectural)

Ulloa 1539

Magellan 1521

(Route Suggested by George Emra Nunn 1934)

Niño & González 1509

Vespucci
1499

Cortés
1519

S. SALVADOR

CUBA

Columbus IV
Car. Sea
Balboa
Panamá
Darien
1509-1513

ESPAÑOLA

BORINQUÉN
(PUERTO RICO)

Pizarro
1530

Guayaquil
Tumbes

Cajamarca
Lima

Cuzco

Gamboa 1579-1580

Santiago

Aguirre

Orellana 1541

Asunción
Cabeza de Vaca
1541

Río de la Plata

Vespucci

Strait of Magellan

Bay of
San Julián

TIERRA
DEL FUEGO

Bay of San Julián
(Magellan wintered 1520)

Magellan Expedition

Río de la Plata
(Discovered by
Vespucci 1501)

VERA CRUZ
(Later Brazil)

Magellan 1519

Columbus I 1492

Vespucci 1497

Columbus II 1493

Columbus IV 1502

Columbus III
1498

Vespucci 1499

Vespucci 1501

Cabral 1500

da Gama

El Cano

El Cano 1522

Atlantic

Ocean

Equator

Hudson
Bay
Hudson 1611

BAFFIN

Cabot Frobisher
1576

GREENLAND

Hochelaga Stadacona
Cartier
1535

Cartier 1534 St. Malo

Hudson 1609 John Cabot

Davis 1585 Hudson
Frobisher 1576
Sebastian Cabot 1509
John Cabot 1497
Baffin 1616
Corte-Real 1500
Corte-Real 1501

ICELAND

FAEROE IS.
1609

Hudson 1610

Davis 1585

AZORES IS.
(1431)

Velho
1431

PORTUGAL
Lisbon

MADEIRA IS.
(1330-1418)

CANARY IS.
(1341)

Vivaldi fate
unknown 1291

C. BOJADOR
Rounded by
Gil Eanes 1434

CAPE
VERDE
IS.
(1456)

CAPE VERDE
Discovered by
Dinis Dias 1445

Tombou

São Jorge
da Mina

Diego
Azambu

Cão 1482

Bull
Bojador

Cabral 1500

Vasco da Gama 1497

Projection courtesy of American Geographical Society

6   7   8   9   10

A

Atlassov 1697

Nizhne

Okhotsk

Kolyma

Yakutsk Poyarkov

Lena

Amur

NOVAYA
ZEMLYA

JAPAN

B

LADRONES
(MARIANAS IS.)

GUAM

Equator

Magellan 1521

RYU KYU
IS.

Peking

Mota 1542

Pires 1517

L. Baikal
(Discovered
1643)

FORMOSA

Perhaps visited by
Europeans before Magellan.
Spanish conquest began
under Miguel Lopez
de Legaspi, 1565.

Vilalobos

1542

C

CHINA
(Ming Empire)

LUZON

Alvares

Canton
Macao

PHILIPPINE
IS.

MINDANAO

GILOLO

NEW
GUINEA
(PAPUA)

Moscow

Ob

After Magellan's death
his expedition wandered
aimlessly for months.

1513

TERNATE

TIDORE

MOLUCCAS

BANDA
IS.

D

Astrakhan Jenkinson

TIBET

Brahmaputra

Mandalay

SIAM

Pegu

Alvares

BORNEO

Serrao

AUSTRALIA
(Undiscovered)

Derbend

Caspian
Sea

Bokhara

Delhi

Goes

Agra

Ganges

Goes

Conti

Mota

Abreu 1511

Kaffa

Black Sea

Tiflis

Tabriz

PERSIA

Indus

INDIA
(Mogul Empire
after 1526)

Conti

Malacca

Conti

Ispahan

Baghdad

Basra

Ormuz

Damão

Diu

Bassein

Chaul

Goa

Canonor

Conti

Sequeira 1508

SUMATRA

JAVA

E

Damascus

Jerusalem

Cairo

Persian
Gulf

Muscat

Mailapur

Vijayanagar

Calicut

Cochin

CEYLON

Colombo

Alexandria

Red
Sea

Cabral

Covilha

Covilha

Vasco da Gama 1498

Indian

El Cano commanding Victoria (Magellan) Expedition

F

Aden

ABYSSINIA

Covilha 1487

Ocean

Malindi

Mombasa

Covilha

Covilha

Kilwa

Zaire and
Mani Congo
discovered by
Diogo Cão
1482-1483

MADAGASCAR
Discovered by Diogo Dias
(Cabral Expedition 1500)

G

Mozambique

Sofala

Vasco da Gama 1498

CROSS
covered by
go Cão 1485

Cabral

Discovered by
B. Dias 1488

H

Diogo Dias 1500

Dias
87

Copyright by Rand McNally & Company, Made in U.S.A.

6   7   8   9   10

ments of a pope at Avignon simply could not carry the same authority, the same sense of ecclesiastical majesty, as those issued from the
ancient See of St. Peter.

On the other hand, the period that the papacy spent at Avignon
was not without some notable achievements. Missionary work was
expanded considerably, especially in Persia and China. The papal
administration, the *curia,* was organized into highly specialized departments and became, probably, the most efficient government in
fourteenth century Europe; special sections staffed by experts dealt
with such matters as justice, finance, appointments and dogma. At
the same time, papal power over churches throughout Europe increased markedly as a consequence of determined efforts at centralization through more vigorous enforcement of papal rights in matters
of appointments and clerical discipline and of more efficient papal
taxation.

Unfortunately, some of these achievements were very unpopular throughout most of Europe. The expansion of papal control of
appointments often resulted in church positions being filled by unknown foreigners who were regarded with suspicion and hostility
by governments and populace alike, while papal taxation moved
money beyond the control of monarchs and reduced the resources
of the rest of the clergy. Normal resentment was aggravated by the
fact that the Avignon papacy was infamous for pomp and luxury,
expenditures that did not inspire willing contributions from all
Christians. As a result of financial issues the clergy became divided
against itself; there was no way to increase very substantially the
total amount of money that ecclesiastical taxation could extract
from the community of the faithful, so the usual result of new fiscal
mechanisms was redistribution. One churchman's gain became another's loss, and of course this was resented. When a bishop took
more of diocesan revenue, the parish clergy was left with less. When
the pope increased his levies upon the dioceses, the bishops lost.
Complicating the matter still further was the rivalry between regular
and secular clergy, that is, between monastic groups and the paro-
chial organization of priests and bishops; if monks or friars, who
often served as papal agents, increased their activities in preaching,
hearing confessions and administering sacraments, the offerings they
collected escaped from parish and diocesan coffers, for the regular
clergy usually answered only to their own superiors and to the pope

rather than to bishops. Thus, on the whole the Avignon period was quite damaging to the papacy. Despite positive achievements in administrative efficiency and the expansion of Christian missions, papal prestige declined and wide resentment of the papacy arose.

Some popes were aware that continued residence at Avignon was dangerous, and they made serious efforts to return to Rome. Pope Urban V (1362–1370) did return, but he found the city in such a shambles that he bowed to the pleas of the cardinals and went back to Avignon. Then Pope Gregory XI (1370–1378) visited Rome, possibly with some thought of re-establishing papal residency, and he died there; his death was a catalyst to much of the discontent that surrounded the Avignon papacy, and the consequences soon proved disastrous.

Not only had the papal government been the chief glory of Rome until the transfer to Avignon, it also had been the city's primary source of income through staff salaries, the household expenditures of popes and cardinals and the money spent by tourists and pilgrims. Thus, the Roman citizenry had many reasons to resent the transfer of the papacy to Avignon, and when Gregory XI died, there was a riot, and a mob threatened the cardinals with violence if they did not elect an Italian pope. Under this pressure the cardinals chose Urban VI, in 1378, but he quickly antagonized them by threatening to reduce the luxury in which they lived, and in any case many of them found Rome dismal and dilapidated. Regretting the splendor of Avignon, thirteen rebellious cardinals elected another pope, Clement VII, who returned to Avignon, and for the next four decades Europe was presented with the unedifying spectacle of rival popes in Rome and Avignon, who promptly excommunicated each other. The situation became still worse in 1409 when the pressure of public opinion, and especially the insistence of the king of France, forced the convocation of the Council of Pisa, attended by five hundred prelates. The Council deposed both the Roman and Avignese popes, successors of Urban VI and Clement VII, and recognized the election of Alexander V; however, the reform failed, for the first two refused to admit the council's authority to depose them, and Europe had three popes.

The Great Schism finally was healed a half dozen years later when another council met at Constance from 1414 to 1417. One pope was deposed and held prisoner to assure the effectiveness of the deposition; a second was induced to resign; the third was obstinate, but all of his supporters deserted him, so he could be ignored until his death in 1423. And the Council of Constance chose a new pope, Martin V (1417–1431), whom everyone recognized. The Great Schism was over.

Martin V reestablished a unified papacy in Rome, dissolved the Council of Constance and turned his attention to repossessing the Papal States, which had been usurped to a great extent during the century of troubles. Papal difficulties were not yet at an end, however, for the decline of papal prestige had led some Christians to assert the supremacy of councils over popes, the return to Rome necessitated an extensive and costly renovation of the papal buildings there, and the endeavor to reestablish effective control of the papal states committed the papacy to deep involvement in fifteenth century Italian politics.

The conciliar movement was the most immediate of these problems. The basic idea, that a council of prelates and representatives of the European governments held authority superior to a pope, was expressed by several fourteenth century writers, though there were differences of opinion concerning who could convene and dismiss councils and how they should function. When the papacy was dishonored and the religious affairs of Europe thrown into a turmoil by the schism, the conciliar idea won more support, including first the king of France and then the Holy Roman Emperor. One group at the Council of Pisa sought to impose limitations upon the papacy, but it was a minority, and in any case its proposals were lost in the general failure of the council. However, extreme conciliarists were stronger at Constance, and that council issued two decrees on the subject, one declaring councils superior to popes and the other providing for their frequent convocation.

Martin V took up the struggle against conciliarism as soon as the schism was ended, declaring it impious to appeal to a council against a pope and dissolving the Council of Constance. The conciliarists were not beaten, however, and Martin's successor, Eugenius IV (1431–1447), found that a council which he summoned at Basel was strongly antipapal; it refused to accept his commands, refused to dissolve when he so ordered, and even elected briefly another antipope. Happily for the papacy, the Council of Basel fell to quarreling over questions of heresy and reunion with the Greek

Church and proved ineffective; in 1449 it finally was persuaded to dissolve by Pope Nicholas V (1447–1455), but the questions remained to haunt successive popes for another century until it was buried by the Council of Trent in the 1540s.

Throughout the greater part of the fifteenth century and the early sixteenth century, much of the energy and the revenue of the papacy was absorbed by the struggle to rebuild the papal states, and the papacy became just one of several Italian governments vying for power in the peninsula at the expense of its spiritual responsibilities. At the turn of the century Italy was ravaged by armies paid for from the papal treasury and led by a pope's son, Caesar Borgia, while the same pope's daughter had become infamous through implication in murder by poison.

In addition, the papacy faced very high extraordinary costs in that the Vatican complex in Rome was in a state of ruin when the papacy returned from Avignon, and to maintain the prestige of the head of the Church rebuilding had to be done on a grand scale by the best artists. The major item was St. Peter's Church, the mother church of all of western Christendom. Architectural studies showed that the old church had deteriorated to a point where repairs and renovations were impractical, and it was decided to demolish the old structure and build a large domed church in the new renaissance style, the biggest and grandest church in Europe. Like involvement in Italian politics, the new construction work at Rome proved very expensive.

Financial strain all through the church and the long period of weakened papal leadership finally led to serious problems of clerical morality and blatant ecclesiastical corruption. Abuses of position by high clerics had become an open scandal. Bishops and popes kept mistresses and found careers in the church for their illegitimate offspring. There were many instances of laymen being forced to pay for the sacraments they received, of offices in the church being sold, of clerics holding church offices for their revenues but not fulfilling the duties of them. There was little conscientious preaching, few orthodox seminaries for the training of priests, too many instances of clergy who were ignorant and illiterate. Under such circumstances it is not surprising that the church failed to command any great loyalty among the laity.

There was another problem, too, that in the long run proved even more serious. The church had become a formal, highly-structured organization. It offered the possibility of salvation to all who accepted the faith as the church taught it, participated in the rituals that the church presented and took the sacraments that the church provided. In such a pattern there was little room for devotion, for love, for personal religious experience. Rather, the individual Christian was to follow a carefully marked path and trust the church to assure his salvation. But through the late fourteenth and fifteenth centuries, deep-rooted popular piety was growing into a fervent evangelical movement, a Christian revival. In the forefront of the new movement were the Lollards in England and the Hussites in Bohemia, both popular heresies potentially as dangerous as thirteenth century Albigensianism.

The Lollards were led by John Wycliffe, a royal chaplain and Oxford don, who in the 1370s preached and published such ideas as a church without property and a laity in direct communication with God without the intervention of the clergy; he also was a major participant in the first English translation of the Bible. Wycliffe's efforts were so successful that it was said that every fourth man in England was a Lollard by the end of the fourteenth century. The movement declined after Wycliffe's death, though in the sixteenth century it seems still to have had a few adherents who were absorbed into Anglicanism. Wycliffe's doctrines spread to eastern Europe through Lollards in the suite of an English princess who was married to the king of Bohemia, and there they stimulated John Hus, a professor at the university in Prague. Until his death in 1415, Hus preached and wrote tirelessly, demanding reform of the church and asserting the supremacy of the Scriptures. The Hussites soon became involved with Bohemian resentment of German influences, which were strong in the clergy and in the university, and when the Council of Constance burned Hus as a heretic in 1415, in violation of a safe-conduct that had been given him, the identification of religious reform and Bohemian national feeling was complete. Despite a decade and a half of religious wars, including papal proclamation of a Bohemian crusade in imitation of the earlier Albigensian crusade, the Hussites remained unconquered, and in the mid-1430s the Council of Basel finally worked out a compromise that ended the fighting. The Hussite movement remained an important element of Bohemian society and formed a basis for the rapid spread of Calvinism in Bohemia in the sixteenth century.

In sum, the fourteenth and fifteenth centuries saw developments dangerous to the unity of western Christendom. Even after the end of the schism, papal prestige was at a low ebb, and papal leadership of the church was practically non-existent. Clerical morality was an open scandal, and the whole church was wracked by financial abuses. And popular piety was generating evangelical movements with strong anti-clerical overtones. To make matters worse, princely governments were growing ever stronger and ever more aggressive, and the policies they were attempting were growing more expensive. As an international institution of considerable wealth and influence, the church often had been regarded by princes as an obstacle, but by the early sixteenth century the problem had become even more serious. All over Europe ambitious princes eyed the wealth of the church greedily and resented the church's support of the *status quo*.

In the second half of the fifteenth century the European monarchies underwent further important development. Shortly after the end of the Hundred Years War, Charles VII of France died and was succeeded by his son Louis XI (1461–1483). A thoroughly unlikeable person—homely, coarse and overbearing—Louis had a keen mind and relentless determination to rebuild the power of the French crown. Only a few years after his accession he faced a great alliance of nobles called the League of the Public Weal, and he immediately set the pattern that he was to follow throughout his reign in dealing with the princes. First he appeared to concede all they asked; then he bribed away their support; then he set them to quarreling with one another so that they were no longer any threat to him and slowly rescinded what he had granted earlier. This notably unchivalrous conduct was politically successful, and it avoided fighting. Partly through calculated efforts and partly through good fortune Louis added immense territory to the possessions of the royal family. Anjou and Provence came to the crown by testament of their last ruler, a tribute to Louis' diplomacy and bribery; Berry and Gascony were acquired by inheritance, simple good fortune.

But Louis XI's most important success in his struggle to reduce the great princes to obedience to the crown was his victory over the duke of Burgundy. One of the most interesting political phenomena of fourteenth and fifteenth century Europe was the brief prominence of the collection of territories between France and Germany usually called the Burgundian inheritance. In 1361 the duchy of Burgundy came into the possession of the French crown, and King John "the Good" gave it to his younger son, Philip. Duke Philip married the daughter and heiress of the last count of Flanders, and upon the count's death in 1384, he added to his possessions the extremely wealthy county of Flanders with its textile industry, the imperial fief called the Franche-Comté and numerous lesser territories. Then he pushed his possessions into the Dutch Netherlands through the marriages that he arranged for his children. Thus the duke of Burgundy became one of the greatest princes of France, and during the minority and then the madness of King Charles VI, he disputed control of the whole realm with the House of Orléans. John "the Fearless," who succeeded to the Burgundian titles in 1404, fought the Armagnac (Orléans) faction, allied with the English in the Hundred Years War and saw the French crown humbled before he was assassinated in 1419. Thereafter the Burgundians, under John's son Philip "the Good," supported the English until 1435 when the French king recognized most of the duke's claims in the Treaty of Arras.

By about the middle of the fifteenth century, the Burgundian inheritance had grown to include much of the old Carolingian Kingdom of Lotharingia except Alsace and Lorraine, a great sweep of territories from the Franche-Comté, on the Swiss border, through the duchy of Burgundy in eastern France and down the Rhine to the Dutch Netherlands. It appeared that the end of the Hundred Years War might see the English threat to France from the west replaced by a Burgundian threat from the northeast, but Duke Philip "the Good" was a gentle man and a patron of the arts, not an expansionist. So long as he lived, Burgundy was more notable for its cultural vigor, especially the painting of the Van Eycks, than for any danger it might pose to the French crown. However, in 1467 Duke Philip died and was succeeded by his ambitious son, Charles "the Rash"; it was he whom Louis XI had to confront.

Charles "the Rash" hoped to build his lands into a kingdom between France and Germany, and he constituted a real danger to the French monarchy's recovery from the Hundred Years War. To check him, Louis XI stirred up revolt in his lands and subsidized his enemies, but nonetheless Charles made progress, for in 1473 he managed to seize Alsace and Lorraine. Then three years later Louis XI enjoyed success when a Swiss force in the service of the duke of Lorraine (but paid by Louis) defeated the Burgundians and killed Duke Charles, leaving the whole Burgundian inheritance in the hands of Charles' daughter Mary. Louis XI would have liked to obtain the whole inheritance for the French crown, but Mary refused marriage with his son (who was still a child), and the king had to content himself with seizing the duchy of Burgundy, for which there were legal pretexts. The rest of the inheritance went to the rulers of the Holy Roman Empire when Mary married Maximillian von Habsburg, and once again the old "middle kingdom" became a matter of contention between French and German rulers.

When Louis XI died in 1483, the only French prince who remained largely independent of the king was the duke of Brittany, and Louis' daughter Anne de Beaujeu, acting as regent for her young brother Charles VIII, soon assured that Brittany, too, would come into the possession of the crown. She arranged for young Charles to marry the daughter and heiress of the duke, so that by the close of the fifteenth century French territorial consolidation had made great progress. Except for the large eastern areas of Alsace, Lorraine, Franche-Comté and Savoy, only small border territories would be added in the shaping of the modern French nation.

Social consolidation also progressed considerably in France in the fifteenth century. Resentment against English depradations and the inspiration of leaders like Bertrand Du Guesclin and Joan of Arc had built a strong national feeling, though in a realm the size of France regionalism remained strong, and divisions between classes still were to loom large in France's future. The fifteenth century is too early to speak of nationalism, for "isms" imply deep commitment to abstract concepts, and at this time national feeling still was identified with the king. Nonetheless, the French had developed a sense of their own uniqueness and a pride in their culture that might be called national consciousness; as a result of this territorial and social consolidation the government of Louis XI and his successors usually is referred to as national monarchy in contrast to earlier feudal monarchy.

England, too, underwent important political development in the late fifteenth century. After the death of Henry V in 1422, England's affairs deteriorated rapidly as military reverses in France were paralleled by aristocratic rivalries at home. Henry VI (1422–1461) was first a minor, then a weak young man, and then insane, and civil war soon broke out between his Lancastrian relatives and the house of York; the struggle is known as the Wars of the Roses because of the devices adopted by the contenders—a red rose for Lancaster and a white rose for York. After Henry's death two Yorkists wore the crown, Edward IV (1461–1483) and his brother Richard III (1483–1485), but the civil wars continued unabated. Not until 1485 was stability restored with the victory of a somewhat distant Lancastrian claimant, Henry Tudor, who took the crown as Henry VII (1485–1509) and married the heiress of the house of York, uniting the competing claims.

Henry VII rebuilt the strength of the English crown rapidly, and in the process he both encouraged and drew support from the growing merchant class. Establishing an administrative court called Star Chamber, he levied heavy fines upon many of the great noble families which maintained private military forces in defiance of old statutes; this policy reduced somewhat the political importance of the great families and abolished large feudal armies and private warfare, two results very popular with the business classes that sought stability for peaceful trade and greater political influence for themselves. Henry's most successful effort to strengthen the alliance between the crown and the middle class was his negotiation of a commercial agreement with the Habsburg government of the Netherlands in 1496, the *intercursus magnus,* which regularized the position of English woolen merchants and fixed customs duties. Henry VII's consistent encouragement of the middle classes won their firm support, and when he died, his son Henry VIII (1509–1547) inherited a crown that was both strong and popular.

Taken together, the administrative developments of the late fourteenth century and the popular policies of Henry VII in the late fifteenth century resulted in a growing integration of the various classes of English society. There is no doubt that by the fifteenth century most Englishmen of all social classes thought of themselves as a distinct people, and when they went to Flanders to trade or to France in war, they were conscious of an alien environment in more than language. Given the compactness of England and its insularity, national consciousness had developed even more strongly than in France, and the Tudors quickly built a consolidated national monarchy.

Two other monarchies developed importantly in the late fifteenth century, and a marriage alliance joined them together into a vast new political complex. Maximillian von Habsburg, who married the Burgundian heiress, was the son of Frederick III of the Holy Roman Empire, and though that crown was elective rather than hereditary, the Habsburgs managed the election so that at Frederick's death, his son succeeded him as Maximillian I (1493–1519). Since the middle of the fifteenth century, the Habsburgs had held, in addition to the imperial crown, family lands in southeastern Germany—Austria, Styria, Carinthia and the Tyrol—and the crown of Bohemia. Maximillian's marriage added to these holdings the wealthy and strategically located Burgundian lands of western Germany and the Netherlands. Thus, for the first time in three centuries there appeared the possibility of a Holy Roman Emperor having sufficient resources to control the German princes and to undertake effective monarchical development.

At roughly the same time a territorial consolidation took place that unified all of the Iberian peninsula except Portugal. In 1469 Ferdinand, heir to Aragon, married Isabella, heiress to Castile, and when they ascended their respective thrones in the 1470s, they combined the resources of the two kingdoms to complete the Christian reconquest of Spain; the Moorish kingdom of Grenada in the south fell to their armies in 1492. Forced Christian conversions were instituted immediately, thousands of Moors and Jews were expelled from Spain in the decade following the victory, and the Spanish Inquisition (founded in 1478) was expanded greatly. By modern standards these policies are reprehensible on humane grounds, and they had adverse economic effects very quickly, but given the Spanish tradition of seven hundred years of crusade, Catholic uniformity was an important and effective aspect of national consolidation.

Joanna, a daughter of Ferdinand and Isabella, was heiress to all of Spain, and when she married Maximillian I's son, Philip, an enormous collection of territories was brought together. The son of this marriage of Joanna and Philip was named Charles. In 1516 he became king of Spain; in 1519 he became Holy Roman Emperor as Charles V, the title by which he is known most commonly; he held the family lands of the Habsburgs in southeastern Germany and all of the Burgundian inheritance except ducal Burgundy; Spanish armies and Spanish rights of inheritance brought him Naples and Milan, assuring him control of both ends of the Italian peninsula; and rapid Spanish expansion in the New World made him lord of the Indies and master of the booty of conquered Indian empires. Jealous contemporaries were prone to remark: "Oh happy Austria; while other powers fight, Austria marries," and certainly marriage alliances had resulted in unprecedented expansion of Habsburg rule. But Charles V was not spared the necessity of fighting, for his reign witnessed renewed Turkish expansion in the Danube valley and the Mediterranean, intensification of French efforts in Italy and the Lutheran Reformation in Germany.

One of the most far-reaching European achievements at the end of the Middle Ages was the great development of seafaring that resulted in the opening of new routes to the fabulous east and the discovery of new continents to the west. Europeans had traveled and traded fairly extensively in both the Near and Far East in the thirteenth and early fourteenth centuries when the great Mongol Empire maintained stability and security all the way from the China coast to the eastern frontiers of Europe; Marco Polo is only the most famous of many travelers of this period. Then in the middle of the fourteenth century the Mongol Empire collapsed and was succeeded by a number of smaller states. In western Asia this political convulsion was accompanied by a Moslem resurgence which inspired the capture of Constantinople by the Turks in 1455 and much confusion and fighting everywhere; as a result, security of travel declined and the cost of trade increased, which provided increased incentive to seek new routes to the sources of spices and silk. The commercial motive was also reinforced by a religious motive, for the Moslem revival intensified the hostility between Christendom and Islam, and the fall of Constantinople frightened Christians everywhere. A widely believed medieval myth held that there was a Christian kingdom in east Africa, and there was considerable enthusiasm, especially on the part of the papacy and the Iberian governments, for finding this kingdom and establishing an alliance against the Moslems.

Probably this crusading ideal was the chief motivation of the most organized exploratory work, the expeditions sent out by the Portuguese Prince Henry the Navigator in the last years of the fourteenth century and the first half of the fifteenth century. Prince Henry's captains explored the Madeira Islands and the Azores and pushed down the west coast of Africa. By the 1440s they had passed the barren northern reaches of the coast, rounded Cape Verde and established a flourishing trade with west Africa. Though Prince Henry died in 1460, the exploratory work went on; in 1487 Bartolomeu Dias rounded the Cape of Good Hope, the southern tip of Africa, before returning to Portugal, and a decade later Vasco da Gama followed his route and continued on to India. Thus, the Portuguese were the first to develop a direct all-water route to the east.

Voyages westward were much more haphazard affairs. Vikings settled Greenland late in the tenth century and visited the North American coast early in the eleventh century; records of their activities are sparse and inconclusive, but it would appear that the Greenland colony lasted until the mid-fifteenth century with at least sporadic ventures to the mainland. There also is some inferential evidence that European fishermen fished the Grand Banks in the fifteenth century and probably saw the mainland, though this cannot be proved. However, none of these early voyages, known or assumed, had permanent effects or influenced later attempts.

Little is known of the early life of Christopher Columbus save that he was a Genoese who spent several years in Portugal and made some voyages under the Portuguese flag. Since Ptolemy's *Geography* had been translated into Latin in 1410, the ideas that the earth was round and that the east could be reached by sailing west had gained ever wider acceptance. Columbus wished to try this idea, but he needed financing. Turned down by the king of Portugal, he approached the Spanish rulers, Ferdinand and Isabella, and though he had to await the successful conclusion of the war against Granada, Queen Isabella financed him in 1492. It is not altogether clear just what Columbus' voyage was supposed to achieve, but it would appear that he and his patroness hoped for both the discovery of new lands and the opening of a direct route to China. In any case, Columbus' four voyages in the last decade of the fifteenth century and the first years of the sixteenth century established the Spanish flag firmly in the Caribbean Islands and Central America.

The successes of Da Gama and Columbus sparked a whole series of voyages. In the late 1490s John Cabot, an Italian resident in England, explored some of the North American coast, but since he found neither gold nor spices, the effort was abandoned after two voyages. At the turn of the century, Alonso di Ojeda and Amerigo Vespucci explored some of the South American coast for Spain, discovering the Amazon River, and in 1501–1502 Vespucci returned, this time in the Portuguese service. It was largely in consequence of his account of this second voyage and his insistence that this was a new land, not part of Asia, that geographers began calling the New World America. And after these first voyages, exploration proceeded rapidly. In a three year voyage (1519–1522) only a quarter century after the successes of Da Gama and Columbus, Ferdinand Magellan's expedition circumnavigated the earth.

At the end of the fifteenth century some important elements of medieval society, such as the papacy, clearly had declined in importance, while others, such as the towns, had become more significant; monarchical government was more elaborate than it had been a century or two earlier, and it rested upon different bases; explorations and discoveries had opened wider horizons, but no one about 1500 could have predicted the great growth of colonial empires that was to follow. With hindsight it is relatively easy to indicate that medieval society was dying and that Europe stood upon the threshold of the modern world, but it is doubtful that in most of Europe there was any sense of entering a new era. An exception might be made for Italy, where a very self-conscious cultural revolution had been developing for a century and a half; but since the Italians drew their inspiration from classical sources, they did not call their achievements innovation but rather a rebirth, the Renaissance.

Chapter 12

The Renaissance

Throughout this survey of the early development of Europe, a number of cultural changes have been noted, and it should be obvious that to a large extent the nature of the cultural product of any given period was determined by the interests of the social elite that controlled the society's resources. Thus, Greco-Roman culture, in which the social elite was a leisured class of worldly aristocrats, consisted largely of philosophy which tried to explain man's place in the natural and social world and of plastic arts which idealized the human form and embellished daily life; this culture disintegrated before the impact of economic decline, civil war and barbarian invasions.

The society that emerged after the decline of Rome had to struggle at first for bare subsistence, and the new elite consisted largely of illiterate soldiers. Artistic product seems to have been limited to a few articles of daily life, such as ornaments for clothing and tableware of precious metals, and to finely worked hafts for weapons and accouterments for horses; items of this sort, which survive today as museum pieces, suggest highly skilled craftsmanship, but the scope of such artistry was very limited, and of course it was accompanied by almost no literary product in a primarily illiterate society. Some of the more Romanized Germanic kings supported a weak revival of Latin pagan literature, but with few exceptions it was the church that could provide literate and reflective individuals and only the church that had the resources and willingness to support them. Thus, it is not surprising that Europe's outstanding writers between about A.D. 400 and A.D. 800 were two bishops and a monk: St. Augustine (*Confessions* and *The City of God*), Gregory of Tours (*The History of the Franks*) and Bede (*The Ecclesiastical History of the English People*). This sort of cultural development reached a peak in the Carolingian renaissance and then suffered another decline under the impact of the Magyar and Viking invasions.

During the rapid development of medieval society between the eleventh and thirteenth centuries, a period that produced the monastic and cathedral schools and then the universities, there was a corresponding cultural revival, but again it was largely in the service of the church. One must not ignore the impressive military architecture of medieval castles, the beautifully carved furniture and finely woven tapestry that embellished later medieval households or the intricately developed epics and poems recited and sung for the entertainment of the nobility; but the finest products of medieval culture were the great cathedrals with their rich decoration and the scholastic works of theology and Christian philosophy, all produced under the patronage of the church. Despite contact with highly sophisticated Islamic thought and the recovery of important parts of the classical heritage, medieval culture subsumed all to the Christian interests of its patrons. Thus, though the idea may be repugnant to modern artists and intellectuals, the direction of European cultural development depended upon the interests of the elite that commanded sufficient wealth to support that culture; in medieval Europe the elite meant primarily churchmen, though noble patronage produced a minor counterpoint to the dominant religious culture.

While the Hundred Years War was being fought in western Europe, a cultural revolution was developing in Italy that was to inspire a whole series of transformations of European society. This movement, called the Italian renaissance, began in the fourteenth century, and in the fifteenth century it swept through northern and central Italy. The culture that grew out of the Renaissance differed from medieval culture in that its chief interests were in political and social life, with stress upon the human individual, rather than in religion and eternity with stress upon God. This secular emphasis reflected a new sort of patronage, town governments and wealthy businessmen instead of the church and wealthy ecclesiastics.

Ever since they had attained virtual independence under the Hohenstaufen emperors in the twelfth and thirteenth centuries, the towns of northern and north central Italy had been developing rapidly, both economically and politically, and rivalries among them were fierce. One of the most prominent was Florence, in Tuscany; its industry and commerce grew so successfully that in the mid-thirteenth century it reestablished gold coinage, the florin, and its money quickly was accepted all over Europe. Florence fought wars with its neighbors, especially Pisa and Siena, and its internal politics hardly were less violent, with twenty-one guilds struggling for control of the city government, but despite these vicissitudes the city continued to increase in wealth and strength, and in the fourteenth century it became the cradle of the Italian renaissance.

The Renaissance appeared first as a new human element within the general Christian context of medieval Italian culture. This new interest showed itself in two ways, a greater concern with man and the world he lived in and a growth of a literature in the vernacular, the language of the people, instead of Latin. In the arts it appeared in the form of more realism, especially in the treatment of human subjects. In the birth of this new literature and painting, two Florentines were prominent, Dante (1265–1321) and Giotto (1276–1337).

Dante worked with a Christian subject, but he treated his material in ways that differed from his predecessors. His *Divine Comedy*, still one of the great works of European literature, illustrates well the tentative beginnings of Italian humanism. Presented as a journey through Hell, Purgatory and Paradise, the *Divine Comedy* is fundamentally a synthesis of medieval Christian thought, but in a series of imaginary conversations with and about great historical figures, Dante makes it clear that his judgments are based less on what people believed in hair-splitting theological arguments than on how they behaved toward their fellow man and what they contributed to humanity. Thus, though religious in content, its goals were ethical rather than theological, and the author showed great sympathy for pre-Christian pagans who had contributed humane philosophical ideas to the world. Finally, Dante composed his work, in verse, in the Tuscan vernacular rather than in Latin, making it accessible to educated laymen. In summation, through its concern with human behavior, its sympathetic interest in classical authors and its appeal to a lay audience, the *Divine Comedy* showed in primitive form the most important of the humanist elements that were to dominate early renaissance literature.

In painting Giotto illustrated the same sort of early humanist tendencies shown by Dante in literature. Probably his most famous work is the series of allegorical panels honoring St. Francis, which he painted in the late thirteenth century for the church of the Franciscan Order at Assisi. Again the theme was totally Christian, the life of a simple and pious saint, but Giotto's treatment of it made his work a new departure in painting. Early Christians had turned away from Greco-Roman realism in art in favor of a slightly abstract primitivism which allowed the treatment of spiritual subjects without the appearance of glorification of the flesh; this style had continued to dominate medieval Christian art, offering little differentiation of human figures, so individuals had come to be identified by spiritual symbols associated with them—keys for St. Peter (the keeper of the keys), a gridiron for St. Lawrence and arrow wounds for St. Sebastian (the instruments of their martyrdoms), etc. By contrast, Giotto painted St. Francis as a real person and portrayed incidents in his life which illustrated his piety, his humility and his simple faith; he made his subject a man with whom anyone could identify and explained his life pictorially so that all could understand. Then, in the first years of the fourteenth century, he gave even fuller scope to his new humanist treatment in a beautiful series of frescoes he painted for the arena chapel in Padua, which turned around scenes from the life of Christ.

Another development in early fourteenth-century Florence that was to prove important to the development of the Renaissance was the beginning of large-scale public works. To a considerable extent this reflected another aspect of the competition among Italian towns; the city fathers determined to beautify Florence beyond anything that neighboring towns could rival, and for a first project they decided to build a new cathedral. Again the theme was Christian, but the treatment was new. That the cathedral of Florence would be an episcopal center and a house of worship were secondary considerations; primarily it was to be a monument to the wealth and glory of the city. Moreover, the construction of the cathedral and its ancillary structures, a bell tower and a baptistry, lasted all through the fourteenth century and well into the fifteenth century and provided commissions for many important Renaissance artists.

The enthusiastic reception of vernacular literature and artistic realism and the undertaking of public works all reflected the growth of the Florentine bourgeoisie, worldly men of wealth who had leisure and wished to fill it with interesting and beautiful things. They were Christians, but they were businessmen, not churchmen, and they did not find theological debates or edifying accounts of saints either entertaining or interesting. They were building large comfortable houses, and medieval Christian art did not provide the warmth, the gaiety or the sense of luxury that they sought in the decoration of their new homes. Urban politics, business rivalries and warfare with other towns posed problems for which they found no guides in medieval literature. And their wealth, leisure and local power gave them an enjoyment of daily life for which there was little justification in medieval tradition. This class comprised potential patrons of enormous resources, and scholars and artists soon began producing for it in quantity.

Classical authors had concerned themselves with many of the interests reborn in the Italian cities, and through the fourteenth and fifteenth centuries masses of manuscripts—mostly Roman and some Greek—were unearthed in old libraries, recopied and circulated widely. Here were poems and essays extolling the intrinsic value of man and the joy of life, treatises expounding the purposes and methods of government, speeches and letters on the subject of patriotism, scandalous biographies and racy stories simply for entertainment, a whole literature concerned with man and his place in the world. In addition, the physical remains of classical civilization—triumphal arches, amphitheaters, aqueducts, temples, villas and public baths—provided models of monumental construction for city councils seeking to embellish their towns and for wealthy merchants and princes desirous of building impressive palaces; the larger remains were excavated, measured and studied, while smaller artifacts such as statuary were sought eagerly for private collections.

So vast and exciting was the human content of the classical heritage, that soon *studia humanitatis* came to refer to the study and imitation of classical culture, and both the literary and the artistic remains of classical civilization soon were being emulated.

A generation after Dante and Giotto, Florence produced two more eminent writers important to the development of the Renaissance, Petrarch (1304–1374) and Boccaccio (1313–1375). The revival of interest in Roman literature led to the study of classical Latin, which differed considerably from the Latin commonly used in the fourteenth century, and Petrarch became famous as an outstanding classical Latinist. He also wrote beautiful lyric poetry which contributed to the growing appreciation of man and nature. His friend Boccaccio was a many-faceted scholar and writer, one of the first Italians to read ancient Greek fluently, a collector of classical manuscripts, a lecturer on Dante and the author of the first prose work in Italian, the *Decameron*. In the *Decameron* Boccaccio took as his setting a group of wealthy young men and women who had shut themselves away in a country house to escape the Black Death which was raging in Florence; to pass the time they told one another stories, a schema which allowed the author scope for the use of different styles and for the presentation of themes ranging from social criticism to sexual satire. Not only does the gentle humor of the *Decameron* still make delightful reading, but subsequently its literary device of isolating a group of people and having them recount stories was used frequently; probably the most famous example is the work of Boccaccio's near contemporary, Geoffrey Chaucer, whose *Canterbury Tales* is one of the seminal works in English literature, but the device is timeless and still is used.

During the fifteenth and early sixteenth centuries the Italian renaissance developed rapidly, and Florence remained its center. Under the patronage of the Medici family, especially Cosimo and Lorenzo the Great, the city produced distinguished artists in every field: the painters Fra Angelico and Botticelli, the architects Brunelleschi and Alberti, the sculptors Ghiberti and Donatello, and those two universal artists who defy categories, Leonardo da Vinci and Michelangelo. Humanist scholarship also flourished as Cosimo di Medici founded the Library of San Marco, the Medici

Library and the Platonic Academy for Greek studies, and in the early sixteenth century Florence produced the brilliant and controversial historian and political theorist, Machiavelli.

In the middle of the fifteenth century the Renaissance spread to Rome, Milan and several other Italian cities. Pope Nicolas V (1447–1455) had been a librarian for Cosimo di Medici before his election to the papal throne, and as pope he continued his interest in humanism and the collection of manuscripts by founding the Vatican Library and supporting scholars and artists. His immediate successor opposed the new culture; but most of the late fifteenth century popes supported the Renaissance with varying degrees of enthusiasm. In the early sixteenth century popes of the Borgia, della Rovere and Medici families made the papacy famous for artistic patronage, political intrigue and immorality at the price of religious leadership. In Milan the Renaissance was associated chiefly with the rule of the Sforza family and reached its peak under the patronage of Ludivico "the Moor" (1479–1500). The Sforzas undertook large public works in the city, bringing in Florentine architects and painters, including Leonardo da Vinci, until Milan was established as a cultural center in its own right. Though the Milanese renaissance was short-lived, the city was beautified greatly. By contrast, Venice with her strong eastern orientation toward Constantinople, long remained outside the mainstream of the Renaissance, and older Byzantine and Gothic influences continued dominant. Ironically, the high quality of Venice's printing industry from the late fifteenth century onwards resulted in much of the Renaissance literature of other Italian cities being generalized through the Venetian presses, but except for the painting of the Bellini family in the second half of the fifteenth century, there was little sign of a Venetian renaissance until after 1500. Then the city suddenly exploded into prominence by producing two of Italy's best Renaissance painters, Tintoretto and Titian.

In the course of the fifteenth and early sixteenth centuries the Italian renaissance developed a philosophical basis that moved far beyond the simple humanism of its early writers and artists. Christian thematic material was used less and less, and admiration of the classical Greeks and Romans grew into adulation, so that the Renaissance became a pagan cultural movement. The Italians conceived a new ideal to replace the medieval Christian, the *uomo universale*, the universal man who did everything well with no apparent effort. This Renaissance individualism was only for the elite, of course, for it assumed wealth and leisure, but it became the goal of many wealthy fifteenth- and sixteenth-century Italians. They not only patronized artists and scholars but also painted and composed Latin songs and verses themselves, designed new palaces and public buildings, laid out gardens and developed elegant and witty society. This adulation of man was reflected in the art works of the period. Portraiture became a major subject in painting as merchants and princes sought a secular immortality; palaces, city halls and gardens replaced cathedrals as the chief subjects of architects; and authors concerned themselves primarily with man and his works as exemplified in Castiglione's *Book of the Courtier* (a handbook of elegant behavior in everything from table manners to seductions), Guicciardini's *History of Italy* and Ariosto's epic poetry.

Perhaps the work that best sums up the purely secular, pragmatic and somewhat cynical intellectual climate of Italy toward the end of the Renaissance, however, is *The Prince*, published in 1514 by Niccolo di Machiavelli. Not only was this book one of the last great literary works of the Italian renaissance, it was also one of the most controversial books ever written and may be considered the first step in the establishment of political science as an empirical study rather than as an exercise in moral philosophy. Almost without exception, classical and medieval writers on government had concerned themselves with political theory, reflecting upon the goals that government should seek to attain, the forms of political organization that would assure the fullest social development, the governing apparatus that best would provide justice, or the underlying principles that could legitimatize some men's power over others. Machiavelli cast all of this aside. He had been involved personally in the political life of Florence, and when his party was ousted he was forced to retire to a country house, where he passed his time reflecting upon and writing about politics. All around him he saw strong states swallowing weaker ones, *condottiere* captains of mercenary bands of soldiers seizing control of states they were supposed to serve, political rivals using torture and assassination to defeat each other. He had seen Caesar Borgia, a pope's son, subject most of central Italy to papal rule, using every means no matter how unscrupulous. Thus, the major influence upon Machiavelli's thought was experience of turbulent Renaissance politics. Abandoning moral judgments and philosophical commitments, he attempted in *The Prince* to present a rational and dispassionate analysis of the political process that he had observed. It was largely this amoral position that his critics found scandalous.

In Machiavelli's analysis, politics is the means whereby some men acquire and attempt to retain authority over others. Thus, it has no goal, no moral purpose; it is a mechanism for the exercise of power. Starting from such a postulate, Machiavelli necessarily concluded that the important questions for anyone interested in politics are: what succeeds? what fails? The observations he presented in trying to answer these questions revealed a view of man and society that moralists found as shocking as his basic amorality. He stated that a prince could sustain himself and command respect through fear; if laws were enforced harshly and consistently most people would prefer to avoid trouble and would render obedience. He stated that a prince ought not to be impeded by the moral precepts of religion or philosophy where his self-interest was concerned; if it were advantageous to break his word or violate a treaty, he ought to do so. Implicitly he justified the use of bribery, torture and assassination if they would strengthen a prince against his enemies. Perhaps the most cynical aspect of *The Prince* is the author's judgment of public opinion: however moral and just a ruler might be, he observed, if he be overthrown he soon will be despised and forgotten by the public; but a ruler who succeeds in maintaining himself securely, even if cruel and unjust, will be acclaimed, and his worst deeds will be forgiven, for the public admires nothing so much as success and will judge that the ends have justified the means.

About the beginning of the sixteenth century the influence of the Renaissance began to spread significantly, northward to France and England and westward to Spain, largely as a result of foreign military involvement in Italy. There were five major states in the peninsula at this time: Milan, Venice, Florence, the Papal States, and the kingdom of Naples; they competed viciously with one another in a web of shifting alliances, and at the end of the fifteenth century they began invoking foreign aid. Both the French and the Spanish crowns had some claims in Italy, and the Holy Roman Emperor still possessed at least theoretical rights, so there was no lack of pretext for intervention. The French came first, in 1494, at the invitation of the Sforza ruler of Milan, and by 1500 German and Spanish forces were involved. For the next three and a half centuries Italy was to be a battleground for Europe's great powers, but the most important immediate effects were to expose large numbers of influential foreigners to the culture of the Renaissance and then, through the devastation consequent upon the wars, largely to put an end to the growth of that culture in Italy.

The cultural ferment of the Renaissance already had had some effect outside Italy even before 1500, chiefly in the field of scholarship. News of the study of ancient languages and the recovery of classical manuscripts had attracted students from other countries to northern Italy, and by the middle of the fifteenth century they were there in some numbers. Through their efforts, northern scholars developed a considerable acquaintance with the classics, and studies in Latin, Greek and Hebrew were established firmly, but prior to the great invasions of Italy the impact of the Renaissance upon the north was limited almost wholly to literary activity carried on in scholarly circles. The invasions exposed princes and wealthy noblemen to the opulence of Italian art and architecture and to the elegance of Italian social life, opening the way for the expansion of the Renaissance on a much broader basis.

As it spread outside Italy, Renaissance culture changed considerably, adapting to very different social and political circumstances. In France, Spain and England, for instance, the existence of strong royal governments tended to make Renaissance artists depend primarily upon monarchical patronage, and the courts of the kings became the focal points of the new culture. Moreover, Gothic traditions in art and architecture were much stronger beyond the Alps than in Italy, where the Gothic style never had displaced Byzantine and Romanesque forms; one result was that Renaissance styles were used at first simply as decorative motifs in the north, producing unlikely combinations of columned porticoes, arcaded facades and sweeping staircases on basically Gothic buildings.

Perhaps the most notable adaptation consequent upon the expansion of the Renaissance was the transformation of humanist thought. Lacking the strong pagan backgrounds of Italy, French and English intellectuals tended to be more religious than their Italian counterparts, and the universities with which they often were associated generally were more conservative, more closely linked with church and monarchy. Consequently, while they adopted with enthusiasm the Italian passion for collecting old manuscripts and studying ancient languages, they balanced classical interests with studies of early Christian sources; and while they concerned themselves with man in his world, it was primarily Christian man in a Christian world that they considered. In Spain seven hundred years of war against the Moslems had produced a fervent Christianity that had no tolerance for the pagan elements of Italian humanism, and in consequence the Renaissance was more influential in changing artistic styles than in effecting any basic intellectual re-orientations. Thus, though northern and western Renaissance writers produced secular and satirical literature, as exemplified by the works of Shakespeare, Rabelais and Cervantes, the intellectual climate generally remained less frankly pagan, and Christianity retained a far more important role in scholarly endeavor.

The German experience of the early sixteenth century differed so greatly from that of the rest of Europe that there is a real question whether there are grounds to justify speaking of a German renaissance, though on a scholarly level the impact of humanism was felt strongly. About the middle of the fifteenth century the new learning, particularly ancient languages, began to take root in the universities, largely through the influence of German scholars who had studied in Italy, and these studies evoked enough enthusiasm that some of the German princes founded new universities. In the sixteenth century some Italian art was imported and even copied to a limited extent. But the new learning and the new styles failed to arouse deep interest throughout German society, and the best artists and most able scholars of the Holy Roman Empire tended to come from Flanders, the Netherlands and the Rhineland, where the flourishing culture of the late medieval Burgundian court had established a solid foundation. German intellectual interests remained more religiously oriented than those of either Italy or other northern areas.

No doubt the deep-rooted pietism for which German Christianity was known had some effect; and perhaps some influence may be attributed to the fact that the beginnings of German civilization east of the Rhine went back to Christian missionary work rather than to Roman experience, with the result that a search for origins led through the medieval church to early Christianity rather than through a Roman conquest to classical culture. In any case, though German humanist scholars were no less able or less learned than the Italians, their interests were very different and their religious commitments far more profound, while Renaissance influence upon German art and architecture remained slight until the seventeenth century, when it penetrated Germany from France.

Outside of Italy the Renaissance made its strongest impact in France. Direct contact between France and Italy was frequent and profound for a quarter of a century after the first Italian expedition of Charles VIII in the mid-1490s, and it continued on a reduced scale throughout the sixteenth century. Generous patronage by Kings Francis I (1515–1547) and Henry II (1547–1559) established Renaissance artistic influence firmly, first as decoration added to older French forms and then as a vigorous new French style, exemplified by the sixteenth century portions of the Louvre in Paris and by the splendid chateaux of the Loire Valley. Secular humanism found expression in the works of Rabelais, Ronsard and Montaigne, while distinguished religious scholarship developed in a Paris group, of which the most famous members were Lefebvre d'Etaples and John Calvin.

In sum, the Renaissance, which was born in and first flourished in Italy, stimulated a comparable movement in France and to a lesser degree in Spain and England, and while it may be debated whether one can speak of a German renaissance, there is no doubt that there were important specific influences in Germany. Everywhere it spread, the movement released great creative energies, resulting in impressive scholarly achievements and vigorous artistic development which changed profoundly both the content and the style of European culture. The classical and early Christian heritage of Europe was reestablished. Princely residences were transformed from gloomy uncomfortable fortresses into graceful pleasure houses. The entourages of kings developed from bands of crude soldiers into royal courts with highly formalized etiquette, peopled with courtiers who sought to practice elegance and wit.

The creative impulse of the Renaissance continued much modified on into the seventeenth century, when far-reaching religious and political developments demanded symbolic expression. One result of the Reformation was to accentuate the dramatic elements of Christian conceptions of the power of God and of the struggle between good and evil, while at the same time the kings of France developed power undreamed of by their predecessors and indulged in policies that threw all of Europe into turmoil. In an attempt to give expression to these dramatic new developments, Europe's architects and artists combined elements of Renaissance styles in new ways, abandoning earlier commitments to static forms and introducing instead a new plasticity and dynamic line. Drawing upon tentative experiments of Palladio and Michelangelo in mid-sixteenth century Italy, they began designing buildings so that the play of light and shadow upon colonnades and windows would give a sense of movement, and they began incorporating spatial masses in their designs, tying courtyards and gardens to facades by paths and balustrades. Sculptors moved away from figures in repose to subjects in tension, caught in the midst of action, and painters oriented entire canvasses around a single dramatic focal point. The new style, which was called baroque, was well adapted to express the evangelical vigor of seventeenth century Christianity and the aggressive ambition of seventeenth century monarchy, and it flourished, further illustrating the impressive adaptability of the artistic creativity unleashed by the Renaissance.

The considerable cultural development consequent upon the Renaissance ought not to be allowed to obscure the movement's negative aspects, however, for a number of adverse effects upon European society can be identified. The Renaissance certainly was not consciously progressive. In a famous letter to a friend Petrarch damned the printing press because he feared it would cheapen knowledge and open the scholar's preserve to a large literate public. The enthusiasm for the classics led to an attempt to purify Latin by reestablishing the language of Cicero and Livy, deleting all the changes of vocabulary and grammar that had developed through fifteen hundred years; the result was that Latin was destroyed as a vibrant living tongue and became a dead language, more and more restricted to the formalities of legal and governmental usage as time passed, and Europe slowly lost the linguistic unity that had characterized its cultural development since the Roman Empire. The adulation of classical authors also had an adverse effect upon natural studies. While the medieval intellectual climate was not conducive to any considerable scientific advances, there had been some progress in the later Middle Ages, exemplified most notably by Friar Roger Bacon, but the great admiration of Greek scientific writers, such as Aristotle and Ptolemy, largely destroyed confidence in modern data and set European science back to the level of the ancient Greeks; for instance, European maps continued for years to show features derived from Ptolemy despite the fact that modern voyages showed some of them to be erroneous, and medical schools continued to teach Greek anatomy although it was contradicted by modern dissections.

Finally, it seems likely that the amorality, the ostentatious luxury and the hostility to religion that were intrinsic to so much of Renaissance culture aggravated the social and political problems that already were assuming serious proportions in fifteenth and sixteenth century Europe, further alienating an elite that accepted these values from a population still largely committed to the medieval ideals of piety, charity and stability. In its negative as well as its positive influences, the Renaissance had far-reaching effects upon Europe.

Chapter 13

Religious Reaction and Reform

The medieval church had experienced many movements of reform, and in fact its history almost could be written in terms of cycles of deformation and reformation. Anticlericalism, heresy and schism had been confronted many times, and national churches were clearly identifiable within the broad framework of medieval European Catholicism. Thus, the real problem in attempting an estimate of the reformation of the sixteenth century is to try to determine what was different in the mixture of problems so that the church was unable to contain the movement within itself.

The woeful condition of the early sixteenth century church inspired frequent criticism of two sorts. There were those who sought to reform and purify the church by improving those who served it, accepting its doctrines and structure; and there were those who believed that not only the clergy but also the doctrine of the church had become corrupt and had to be reformed. The two positions were exemplified best by Erasmus and Luther.

Erasmus has been accused of lacking courage, by comparison with Luther, but such a judgment is unfair, for his purposes were different. As a Christian humanist he was scandalized by the condition of the clergy and wrote biting satires designed to shame the corrupt and provoke a reform of morals, but he never doubted the fundamental truth of the church's doctrines. Confident that God's love and mercy, aided by the sacraments, would bring salvation, his concern was with the Christian life—how laymen might live in greater love and charity and clerics might fulfil their offices in God's church more worthily. If Erasmus' criticisms contributed to Luther's movement, the contribution certainly was inadvertent; he never would have agreed that the corruption of men justified the destruction of the unity of God's church.

By contrast Luther's major concerns were very different. While he certainly shared the horror of clerical abuses and was deeply concerned that the clergy should fulfil a pastoral role in guiding their flocks to a better Christian life, these things were for him secondary considerations. What mattered above all else, the heart and essential core of Christianity, was the fulfilment of Christ's promise of salvation, and it was in this fundamental matter that Luther lost confidence in the church. Like many Christians he found several grounds on which to base criticism, but his intransigence, his refusal of all compromise, is explicable only on the issue of salvation. To imagine that Luther was willing to overturn the traditional church because of the human frailties of some of its clergy is to underestimate him. Rather, he became convinced that the church's teachings regarding the means to salvation were wrong and that, in consequence, many laymen risked damnation. As a responsible priest and theologian he could not compromise on that issue.

Probably too much has been made of the matter of indulgences, but because they are widely supposed to have been at the root of Luther's protest, they must be considered. In fact, they were more a catalyst than a cause. The concept of indulgences is rooted in rather complex doctrines developed by medieval theologians, doctrines which made a clear distinction between the guilt of sin and the penalties of sin. No one ever claimed that any man could forgive sin, wipe away its guilt, for that power belonged only to God, Who presumably would grant forgiveness to those who prayed for it with sincerity and true repentence. God's forgiveness would assure ultimate salvation, but only after the penalties had been paid. Since most men were assumed to accumulate more penalties than could be expiated by good works during a lifetime, the theologians posited the existence of purgatory, a condition between the heaven of the saved and the hell of the damned. In purgatory the soul continued its expiation through suffering, until the penalties had been fulfilled and it was released to heaven. On the basis of the power of the keys, the power of loosing and binding, the pope was asserted to have control over these penalties for sin in the same way that modern civil authorities can grant pardons, which do not eradicate the guilt of an act but do excuse the offender from the fulfilment of the usual penalties. An indulgence was this alleviation of penalties, granted for good cause.

In the medieval period indulgences first were granted for extraordinary personal effort, such as going crusading, which involved enormous cost and risk in the service of the faith. Then they were granted for money payments so that those who were old or crippled could participate in the good work and the benefits of it even if they could not serve personally. Given the financial strains of the early sixteenth century and the corruption of the clergy, probably it was inevitable that indulgences were exploited as a source of revenue, sold at varying prices for different periods of alleviated penalties. The papal agents who handled transactions in indulgences often added poor taste to what was already poor practice and became, in effect, hucksters. One of the worst of these was the monk Tetzel, who was operating in Germany in the early sixteenth century. An evangelistic preacher who painted horrifying word pictures of the torments of purgatory, Tetzel was notably successful as a salesman, but his crass merchandizing of ecclesiastical benefits offended many, including Luther, to whom the whole process was simply blatant extortion and financial exploitation of the faith of simple Christians. It was the indulgence issue that persuaded Luther to pose his first overt challenge to papal authority, but the challenge was the result of years of patient reflection and meditation upon the problem of salvation.

In essence, Luther had become convinced that salvation was attainable only through faith, through a personal commitment of love and belief in man's worthlessness and God's mercy. Holding this conviction he could not believe in the efficacy of priests or saints as intermediaries between the individual and God, he could not accept the role of the sacraments as steps to salvation, and he could not accept the formalized role of papal powers in distributing God's mercies to men. In many ways Luther was the revivalist voice of medieval pietism hurled against worldliness and formality, the voice of St. Bernard reborn, protesting both the pagan corruption of the clergy and the genial tolerance of Erasmus' Christian humanism. If in any way Luther represented the Renaissance spirit in religion as often is asserted, it was in the individualism of his belief, his conviction that a man must stand naked and alone before his God, without intermediaries and with nothing but his faith to justify him.

Moved to action by Tetzel's scandalous behavior, Luther offered his first overt challenge in October of 1517 by posting his Ninety-five Theses on the doors of the church in Wittenburg, where he was professor of theology. It was a very modest revolt; the theses were simply theological positions relative to indulgences which he wished to debate, and traditionally the churches were the centers of their towns and their doors the bulletin boards. The posting of the theses was simply an attempt to stimulate interest among other theologians in the hope that ripples would spread with beneficial effect. The rapid and explosive effects of the theses must have astonished their author.

The church's reaction to Luther's challenge followed normal practice, for he was simply another dissenting priest. In 1518 he was summoned before Cardinal Cajetan, the papal legate in Germany, and ordered to retract his statements, but he refused. Then in 1519 a theologian of some eminence, Dr. Eck, undertook to debate with him, and almost immediately the situation took a more serious turn. An experienced debater, Eck maneuvered Luther into extremist positions—denial of the divine right of the papacy, assertion of the supremacy of Scripture, doubt of the authority of councils and defense of some Hussite propositions that had been condemned as heresy. Luther's excommunication followed naturally, in 1520, and in an act of defiance he publicly burned the papal document of excommunication (called a bull from the Latin *bullus,* for the great seal on it). Since heresy was considered a serious offense by civil as well as religious authorities, carrying the penalty of outlawry, the case was reviewed by the emperor at the Diet of Worms in 1521; there Luther maintained the positions he had adopted and consequently the emperor outlawed him. At this point Luther might have been executed, as had happened to Hus, but the emperor honored his safe-conduct and allowed him to go in peace. As he had become a controversial figure, his life was in real danger, and one of the German princes, the elector of Saxony, soon took him into protective custody, and his movement continued to grow.

Thus far Luther's protest had revealed nothing that the European church had not experienced many times, and the question as to why it succeeded while earlier efforts failed becomes more and more complicated. One new factor which probably was important was the recent invention of reasonably cheap printing. This fifteenth century invention, usually attributed to Johannes Gutenburg, made possible the wide distribution of Luther's statements, first his theses and later the eloquent pamphlets in which he explained and developed his positions. The printing press made available to him a larger audience than earlier preachers of reform had been able to reach, and while recognizing the limitations posed by widespread illiteracy, one must regard the press as important in the rapid and extensive communication of Luther's ideas.

In the successful establishment and expansion of the Lutheran movement, however, as distinct from its origins in Luther's own agony of conscience, the most important factor was its relationship to the secular power structure. In the early 1520s the political and social situation in north Germany was singularly receptive to the sort of movement that Luther launched. Agrarian depression, the decline of the once-prosperous Hanseatic league of trading towns, increased exactions by manorial lords to meet their own rising costs—all of these factors brought hardship to those who were economically vulnerable; among commoners this meant chiefly peasants and urban workmen, while among the nobility it meant that turbulent group known as the free imperial knights, a group of petty lords who were for all practical purposes independent of any higher authority. Luther's teaching that all men were equal before God appealed greatly to these groups, and they extended this spiritual equality to speculation upon social and economic equality. Moreover, Luther's ideas were capable of stimulating greed, for he said that the church was too much drawn into worldly affairs because it was a great landowner; his church, he said, would be maintained by the contributions of believers. The prospect of large tracts of church land available for seizure was attractive even to great princes of the empire.

Luther's movement was launched at a time when many of the German princes were resisting seriously the authority of the church and of the emperor. Many of them were attempting to consolidate territorial states based on Roman and Renaissance concepts of the sovereignty of the prince, and the loose medieval suzerainty claimed by the emperor and supported by the church was international in character and obstructive to this development. Emperor Charles V's position was vulnerable, for not only was he Holy Roman Emperor; he also was king of Spain and its growing colonial dominions and ruler of various Italian and Netherlands territories, and in the Danube valley he was beset by ferocious Turkish attacks which broke the kingdom of Hungary in 1529 and besieged Vienna. In these circumstances the princes sought to increase their power at the emperor's expense, and support of Lutheranism would help finance the effort with confiscated church lands, would eliminate the generally pro-imperial influence of Catholic clergy, and would offer a religious issue on which to rally the populace. German princes began to convert rapidly and to encourage Lutheran preachers. By the mid-1520s most of north Germany down to the Main River was Lutheran.

The spread of German Lutheranism stopped almost as suddenly as it began, however. In 1522 there was a revolt of imperial knights, and in 1524–25 there was a costly and destructive peasant revolt. Both groups claimed inspiration from Lutheranism, and though Luther disclaimed them, the revolts intimidated the princes by suggesting that Lutheranism carried the seeds of social revolution. Princely conversions stopped, and a few princes who had declared for Lutheranism even returned to Catholicism. The revolts were crushed, but Germany was left with a religious division, a Lutheran north and a Catholic south, each group eager to destroy the other in the name of the true faith.

The emperor, who was a dedicated Catholic, sincerely sought compromise. He recognized the validity of much of the criticism levied against the Catholic Church and wanted the pope to convene a council to reform the church and heal the rift, but the pope feared the anti-papal conciliar movement which had survived from the previous century, and he refused. Within the empire, Charles V convened a diet at Speyer in 1526 to try to find a compromise. When this produced no result, a second was called in 1529. The second Diet of Speyer was dominated by Catholics and it resolved that the empire's laws against heresy should be enforced. This meant civil war.

The Lutherans withdrew to Augsburg, where they drew up a confession (basic creed) of their faith and a protest, whence the term Protestant. In their own defense they also formed a military alliance known as the Schmalkaldic League, while their opponents formed a Catholic Union. The Lutherans soon got aid from France, which was willing to help any enemy of the emperor, while Catholic forces were supported by the emperor's Spanish resources. For the next quarter century Germany was torn by religious war that ended only in 1555 with the Peace of Augsburg. Religiously the wars changed little; for the north remained Lutheran and the south Catholic. Politically they had important results, however, for the Peace of Augsburg allowed every prince to choose between Lutheranism and Catholicism for his state, although the ecclesiastical reservation forbade further secularization of church lands; this meant legality for Lutheranism where the prince supported it, and also it meant the transfer of an important area of decision from the emperor to the princes.

Implicit in the German religious wars and the Peace of Augsburg was a general principle: religious protest movements could succeed where they had the support of important elements of the political establishment, but without that support they failed. This general principle also was supported by the experience of Lutheranism outside of Germany. Henry VIII of England opposed religious innovation and wrote a pamphlet attacking the Lutherans (which, ironically, won the papal title "Defender of the Faith" for the man who later was to launch the Reformation in England), while the king of France actually persecuted and burned any Lutherans he caught; in neither England nor France did Lutheranism make significant progress. In fact, after the mid-1520s the only area of notable Lutheran expansion was Scandinavia, and there the religious reformers had political support; in Sweden a new monarchy in revolt against Danish domination supported Lutheranism as an element of national consolidation, and a bit later the Danish crown did the same thing to rally the populace against the Catholic nobility.

Another dissident religious movement of wide influence was launched by John Calvin. At the same time that Luther was taking the first steps toward founding his church in Germany, there was emerging in Paris a reformist group of which the most prominent member was LeFebvre d'Etaples. Calvin, a brilliant young man educated in both theology and law, was influenced strongly by this group and undertook extensive study of early Christian writing, particularly the work of St. Augustine; in 1536, at the age of twenty-nine, he published the first edition of his *Institutes of the Christian Religion.* This highly sophisticated theological tract, which Calvin continued to develop and expand through subsequent editions, became the foundation of a new church. Calvin's doctrines differed radically from both Catholicism and Lutheranism, for Calvin believed that there was nothing an individual could do that would help him to achieve salvation. Both Lutheranism and Catholicism maintained that though man was too degraded by sin to merit salvation through his own efforts, if the efforts were sincere, God's mercy would extend the necessary grace. Calvin argued that if God were all-knowing and all-powerful, as was necessary by definition of God, then He must have known from the day of creation who would be saved and who would be damned, and, moreover, men were saved or damned because God willed it. This doctrine, known as predestination, divided humanity into two groups: those whom God intended to save, called the Elect, and those whom God intended to damn. Instead of evoking fatalism and resignation, as might seem likely, this doctrine proved very dynamic. Though a man could do nothing to improve his chances of salvation, he could seek signs that he was chosen for the Elect. He could never really *know*, but since everything in the world happened by God's will, the individual might hope that if his affairs prospered, it was a sign of God's blessing upon one of His chosen. Thus the followers of Calvin were motivated to live frugally and work hard, not for their own prosperity or comfort but to demonstrate through their activities the power of God's blessing and to find in their success some encouragement for their hopes of salvation.

King Francis I enjoyed good relations with the Catholic Church, and by agreement with the papacy (the Concordat of Boulogne, 1516) he had important patronage powers controlling most high appointments in the French church. Consequently he was hostile to religious innovation, particularly after seeing and encouraging the division and violence it brought to Germany. He launched persecutions which broke up the Paris group and forced Calvin to flee abroad. The brilliant eighteenth century writer Voltaire later observed cynically that Francis I was a good king, burning heretics at home while subsidizing them in Germany, both for the greater glory of France.

After some wanderings, Calvin went to Geneva, in Switzerland, where he had been invited by a group that was attempting a two-fold change in the city: religious reform and overthrow of the authority of the bishop who was the city's overlord. Calvin soon was accepted as the leader of this group, and it was in Geneva that he established the theocratic government that became the model Calvinist community. The city and the church were run by the same people, the laws of the civil government enforced the rules of the church, and church and state together supported an extremely puritanical moral code that sought to force Genevans to be godly.

Because Calvinism was dynamic and sympathetic to worldly success, it appealed strongly, though not exclusively, to middle-class people. Its spread from Geneva can be traced along the trade routes: down the Rhine to the Netherlands, down the Rhone and thence along the great highways of southern France. In neither France nor the Netherlands did it become an important social force, however, until the latter half of the sixteenth century when political circumstances became favorable. In France King Henry II was killed in a sporting accident in 1559, leaving a minor heir, and confronting a weakened royal government Calvinism spread rapidly; in the Netherlands a great revolt broke out in the 1560s against the king of Spain who ruled the area, and Calvinism soon became the unifying force of the revolutionaries. Both of these processes will be considered in more detail later.

Generally it was in the towns that the new church found support at first, though it soon began to recruit noblemen. In fact, one of its greatest successes—Scotland—depended upon the support of nobles. The Reformation in Scotland was enmeshed so deeply with political revolution that it is difficult to separate religious and political motivation. In the middle of the sixteenth century the Scottish crown was held by Mary, Queen of Scots, a woman reared in France and very French in outlook. A Scot, John Knox, was Calvin's most dedicated disciple in Geneva, and when Knox returned to Scotland the new faith he brought soon became the rallying issue for a consolidated aristocratic opposition to the crown which, in 1568, drove Queen Mary to seek refuge in England. The uncompromising new faith found wide support among the Scots, and Scotland soon was predominately Calvinist except for the highlands, which remained Catholic until the mid-eighteenth century.

Luther and Calvin were not alone in launching religious dissidence, however, for there were other important movements. In

Switzerland an independent protest movement was started in 1518 by a priest named Zwingli; though differing from Luther on important doctrinal points, the Zwinglians also insisted upon the unique importance of personal faith and the inefficacy of the clergy as intermediaries. Their movement spread importantly through some of the northern Swiss cantons, but after Zwingli's death it was absorbed by Lutheranism and Calvinism. And much more radical than Lutherans, Calvinists, or Zwinglians were the Anabaptists. These were people who sought to re-create primitive communal Christianity. It is difficult to generalize about them, for they never established any formalized organization. Though their name implies opposition to baptism, what they were against was infant baptism, maintaining that such an initiation into the Christian community should be an adult decision. Some were pacifists who "turned the other cheek" while others had the reputation of fighting like lions. What they shared was a primitive and simple faith in Christ the Redeemer and in the Bible as God's word. They were persecuted by both Catholics and Lutherans and never became a very influential movement, surviving in modern times as Mennonite and Amish communities.

A unique reformation occurred in England, where the movement was directed by the crown and in its origins was clearly political. Henry VIII was only one generation removed from the devastating Wars of the Roses, which had been based chiefly on the lack of a clear line of succession to the throne. Thus the king was terribly aware of the succession issue and was disturbed deeply that in twenty years of marriage the queen had produced only one child, a girl, Mary. Henry desperately desired a male heir to ensure his family's succession, and in 1527 he sought a papal annulment of his first marriage so that he might remarry. There were grounds, and such annulments often were granted to royal families, but in this case the pope was reluctant. In 1527 Rome had been occupied and sacked by the armies of Emperor Charles V; Queen Catherine, whom Henry was seeking to divorce, was Charles' aunt, and the pope feared to give offense in that family. He tried to procrastinate, hoping to find a solution, but Henry became impatient, for his mistress was pregnant and he wanted to marry her before the birth so the child would be legitimate. He used his considerable power over the English church to confiscate church lands, cut papal revenues from England and intimidate the English clergy, and when these attempts at pressure proved unavailing, he had his annulment pronounced by the archbishop of Canterbury. Undaunted by papal excommunication in 1534, the king passed an Act of Supremacy through the English Parliament, cutting off the English Church from Rome and making himself "Supreme Head of the Church of England." Additional benefits of these actions were increased control over the church and increased support for his government from those to whom he had distributed the confiscated church lands.

Henry VIII was a religious conservative, however; in his lifetime few doctrinal changes were made in the English Church, and he resisted the efforts of reformers of Lutheran or Calvinist inclinations, maintaining a sort of Catholic Church that denied the authority of the pope. Henry's bold action had secured him greatly increased political and economic power as well as matrimonial freedom, but England was to suffer religious struggles despite his efforts to control religious change.

Despite several marriages, at his death Henry left only three children: Mary, Elizabeth and Edward. The male took precedence over his older half-sisters and succeeded to the throne as Edward V (1547–1553), a sickly boy. His government was run by a regency council sympathetic to religious reform, and a number of changes were made in the English Church, moving it far in the direction of Calvinism. But after only six years, young Edward died and was succeeded by his half-sister Mary (1553–1558), an ardent Catholic who was married to Philip II of Spain, the European champion of Catholicism. Persecutions and violence followed as Mary attempted to return England to Roman obedience, and then she too died and was succeeded by her half-sister Elizabeth.

It was during the reign of Queen Elizabeth I (1558–1603) that the English Church was stabilized as a moderate and national reformed church. The queen had no sympathy for extreme Calvinism, and she could not support Catholicism for Catholics considered her illegitimate and hence ineligible for the crown. She chose a middle course, continuing to deny papal authority in England but otherwise adopting deliberately vague positions and avoiding enforcement of laws that required membership in the Church of England, so as to give offense to as few people as possible. The enormous personal prestige she developed in defending England against Spanish aggression combined with her moderation to create a situation most unusual in late sixteenth century Europe—a strong and popular monarchy supported by a stable church.

Finally, the mid-sixteenth century witnessed another important reform movement, the Catholic reformation. Pious and responsible popes rebuilt the dignity and spiritual responsibility of papal government and then led a reform movement within the church along rather Erasmian lines. The chief instrument of this reform was the Council of Trent, which met in three sessions in the middle 1540s, the early 1550s and the early 1560s. The church made no doctrinal compromises with Protestantism, to the great disappointment of the emperor, who long had pressed for this solution, but it achieved a considerable reform program for morals and practices. After confirming the authority of the pope and traditional Catholic doctrine, it forbade financial abuses, plurality of offices and non-residence of clergy; and it provided for the foundation of new seminaries to produce better-educated priests. It took a long time for some of the council's proposals to be effective, and some never were, but the council marked the beginning of an important rejuvenation of the Catholic clergy.

As well as internal reform, the reinvigorated papacy also began a counter-attack upon Protestantism, for which two new instruments were the Roman Inquisition (not to be confused with the corrupt Spanish Inquisition) and the Index of Banned Books. The Roman Inquisition was a special court with jurisdiction over the whole church; it heard questions of faith and tried to establish a little clarity in the sixteenth century confusion of argument and counter-argument. Unfortunately it proved a very conservative body, and in the early seventeenth century, in the Galileo case, it put itself in the ludicrous position of condemning as heresy a scientific hypothesis. The famous Index was an attempt to limit the spread of Protestantism by establishing a list of persuasive but heretical books forbidden to Catholics. In the long run neither of these efforts was very effective.

Without a doubt, the most successful Catholic response to the challenge of Protestantism was the foundation of the Society of Jesus or Jesuits. Authorized by the pope in 1543 the society was the creation of a former Spanish soldier, St. Ignatius Loyola. Setting a very high educational standard for its members, the society dedicated itself especially to preaching, teaching and instructing the conscience in the confessional. By the end of the sixteenth century Jesuit colleges, such as the University of Ingolstadt on the Danube, had won the reputation of being among the best and most progressive schools in Europe. Jesuit scholars had achieved considerable fame as controversialists defending the validity of Catholicism, and the society was developing rapidly the missionary work that with expanding European colonialism was to carry its priests as far as China and the Philippines.

By about the middle of the sixteenth century the first phase of the Reformation had ended. New churches had been founded and the old unity of western Christendom, often more apparent than real, had disappeared. Lutheranism had run its course and dominated Scandinavia and north Germany. The Church of England had left the Roman fold, and though it was still incompletely developed at Elizabeth's accession, it was established solidly as another variety of Protestantism. Calvinism, the dynamic new force in the mid-sixteenth century, had a secure base in Geneva and was reaching out to the south of France, the Netherlands and Scotland. And a reform movement had been launched within Catholicism. The latter half of the sixteenth century witnessed another phase in which the lines of controversy were drawn more sharply as Protestant Europe was put on the defensive by the ambitions and might of King Philip II of Spain.

THE EARLY CAROLINGIANS

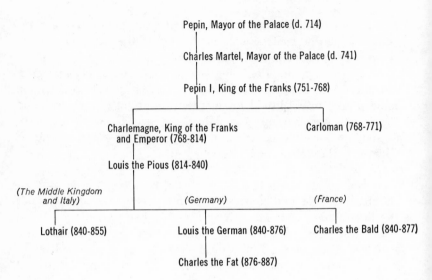

Pepin, Mayor of the Palace (d. 714)

Charles Martel, Mayor of the Palace (d. 741)

Pepin I, King of the Franks (751-768)

Charlemagne, King of the Franks and Emperor (768-814)   Carloman (768-771)

Louis the Pious (814-840)

(The Middle Kingdom and Italy)   *(Germany)*   *(France)*

Lothair (840-855)   Louis the German (840-876)   Charles the Bald (840-877)

Charles the Fat (876-887)

THE SAXON AND FRANCONIAN KINGS

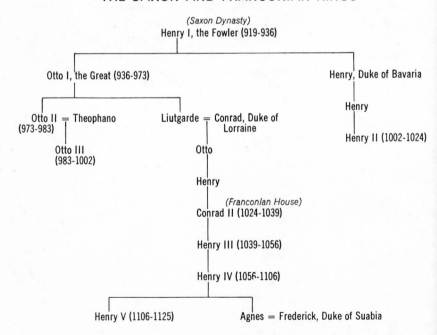

(Saxon Dynasty)
Henry I, the Fowler (919-936)

Otto I, the Great (936-973)   Henry, Duke of Bavaria

Otto II = Theophano   Liutgarde = Conrad, Duke of   Henry
(973-983)   Lorraine

Otto III   Otto   Henry II (1002-1024)
(983-1002)

Henry

(Franconian House)
Conrad II (1024-1039)

Henry III (1039-1056)

Henry IV (1056-1106)

Henry V (1106-1125)   Agnes = Frederick, Duke of Suabia

THE NORMAN AND ANGEVIN KINGS

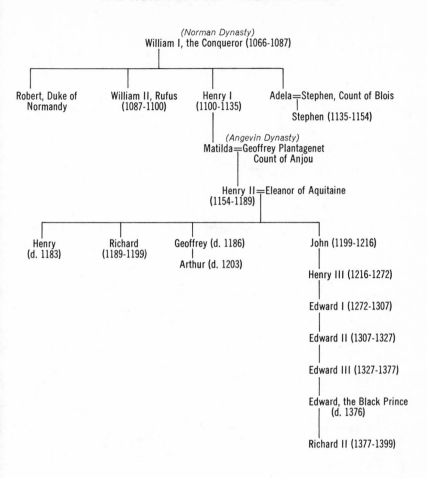

THE CAPETIAN KINGS

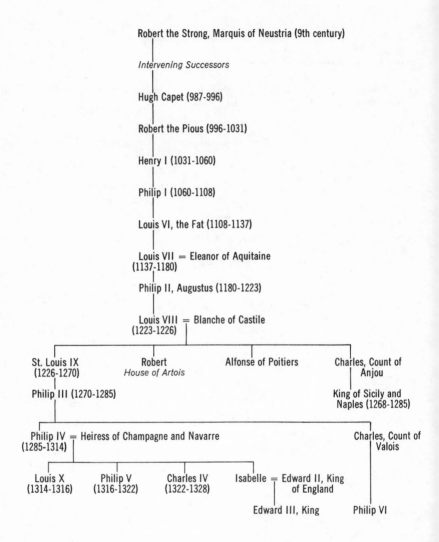

Robert the Strong, Marquis of Neustria (9th century)

Intervening Successors

Hugh Capet (987-996)

Robert the Pious (996-1031)

Henry I (1031-1060)

Philip I (1060-1108)

Louis VI, the Fat (1108-1137)

Louis VII = Eleanor of Aquitaine
(1137-1180)

Philip II, Augustus (1180-1223)

Louis VIII = Blanche of Castile
(1223-1226)

St. Louis IX   Robert   Alfonse of Poitiers   Charles, Count of
(1226-1270)   *House of Artois*   Anjou

Philip III (1270-1285)   King of Sicily and
                                              Naples (1268-1285)

Philip IV = Heiress of Champagne and Navarre   Charles, Count of
(1285-1314)   Valois

Louis X   Philip V   Charles IV   Isabelle = Edward II, King
(1314-1316)   (1316-1322)   (1322-1328)   of England

                                      Edward III, King   Philip VI

THE HOHENSTAUFEN KINGS

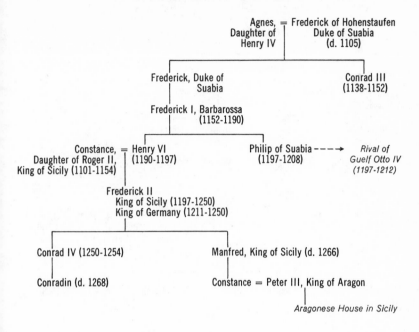

Agnes, = Frederick of Hohenstaufen
Daughter of | Duke of Suabia
Henry IV | (d. 1105)

Frederick, Duke of Suabia — Conrad III (1138-1152)

Frederick I, Barbarossa (1152-1190)

Constance, = Henry VI (1190-1197) — Philip of Suabia (1197-1208) - - - → *Rival of Guelf Otto IV (1197-1212)*
Daughter of Roger II, King of Sicily (1101-1154)

Frederick II
King of Sicily (1197-1250)
King of Germany (1211-1250)

Conrad IV (1250-1254) — Manfred, King of Sicily (d. 1266)

Conradin (d. 1268) — Constance = Peter III, King of Aragon

Aragonese House in Sicily

THE VALOIS KINGS

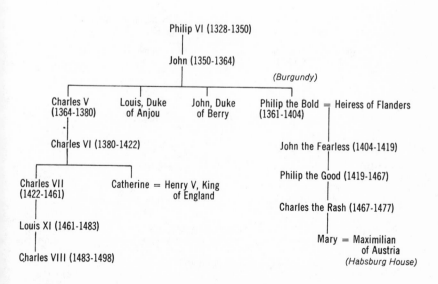

Philip VI (1328-1350)

John (1350-1364)

(Burgundy)

Charles V (1364-1380) — Louis, Duke of Anjou — John, Duke of Berry — Philip the Bold (1361-1404) = Heiress of Flanders

Charles VI (1380-1422) — John the Fearless (1404-1419)

Charles VII (1422-1461) — Catherine = Henry V, King of England — Philip the Good (1419-1467)

Louis XI (1461-1483) — Charles the Rash (1467-1477)

Charles VIII (1483-1498) — Mary = Maximilian of Austria
(Habsburg House)

THE LANCASTRIAN AND YORKIST KINGS

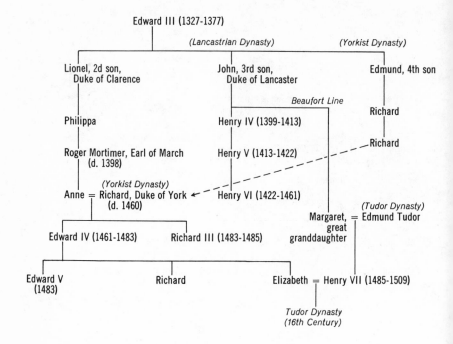

THE LUXEMBURG AND HABSBURG DYNASTIES

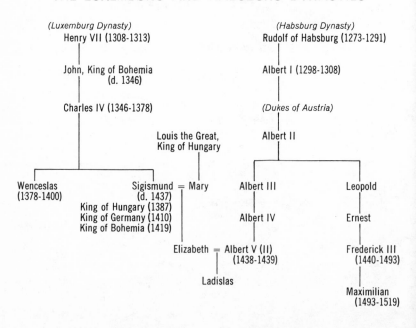

THE HOUSE OF HABSBURG

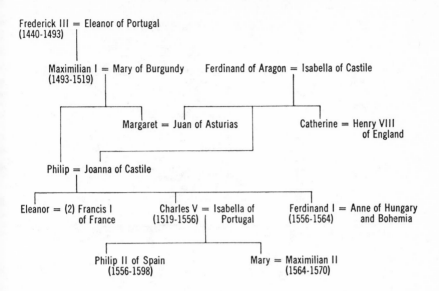

THE HOUSE OF VALOIS

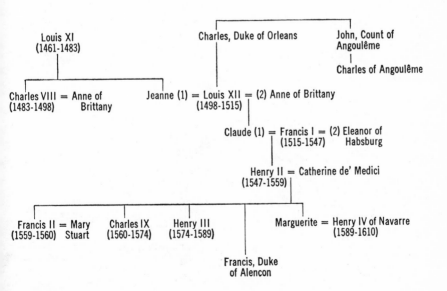

THE HOUSE OF TUDOR

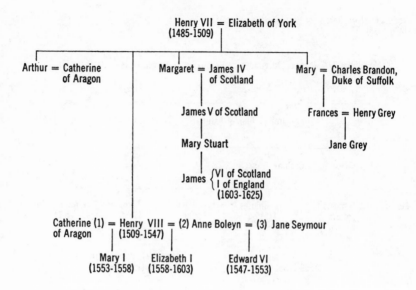

Henry VII = Elizabeth of York
(1485-1509)

Arthur = Catherine of Aragon

Margaret = James IV of Scotland

James V of Scotland

Mary Stuart

James { VI of Scotland
I of England
(1603-1625)

Mary = Charles Brandon, Duke of Suffolk

Frances = Henry Grey

Jane Grey

Catherine (1) = Henry VIII = (2) Anne Boleyn = (3) Jane Seymour
of Aragon (1509-1547)

Mary I (1553-1558)   Elizabeth I (1558-1603)   Edward VI (1547-1553)

THE HOUSE OF BOURBON

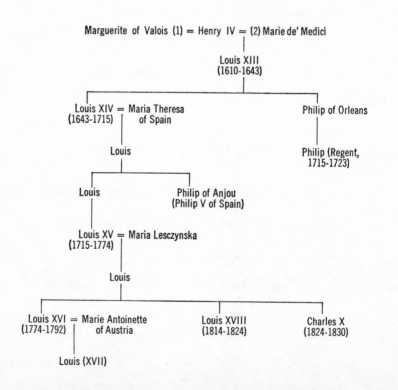

Marguerite of Valois (1) = Henry IV = (2) Marie de' Medici

Louis XIII
(1610-1643)

Louis XIV = Maria Theresa
(1643-1715) of Spain

Louis

Louis

Philip of Anjou
(Philip V of Spain)

Louis XV = Maria Lesczynska
(1715-1774)

Louis

Philip of Orleans

Philip (Regent, 1715-1723)

Louis XVI = Marie Antoinette
(1774-1792) of Austria

Louis (XVII)

Louis XVIII
(1814-1824)

Charles X
(1824-1830)

THE HOUSE OF STUART

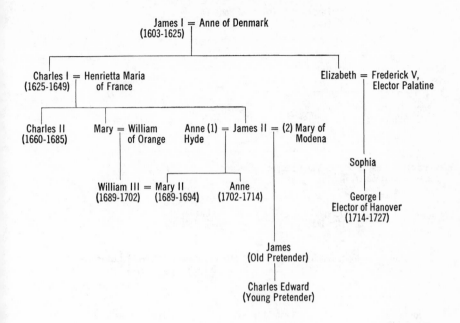

James I = Anne of Denmark
(1603-1625)

Charles I = Henrietta Maria
(1625-1649)   of France

Elizabeth = Frederick V,
              Elector Palatine

Charles II
(1660-1685)

Mary = William
        of Orange

Anne (1) = James II = (2) Mary of
Hyde   Modena

Sophia

William III = Mary II
(1689-1702) (1689-1694)

Anne
(1702-1714)

George I
Elector of Hanover
(1714-1727)

James
(Old Pretender)

Charles Edward
(Young Pretender)

THE HOUSE OF ROMANOV

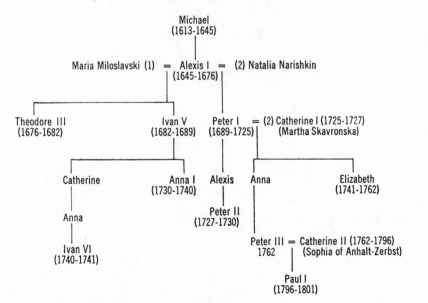

Michael
(1613-1645)

Maria Miloslavski (1) = Alexis I = (2) Natalia Narishkin
                        (1645-1676)

Theodore III
(1676-1682)

Ivan V
(1682-1689)

Peter I = (2) Catherine I (1725-1727)
(1689-1725)   (Martha Skavronska)

Catherine

Anna I
(1730-1740)

Alexis

Anna

Elizabeth
(1741-1762)

Anna

Peter II
(1727-1730)

Ivan VI
(1740-1741)

Peter III = Catherine II (1762-1796)
1762   (Sophia of Anhalt-Zerbst)

Paul I
(1796-1801)

THE AUSTRIAN HABSBURGS

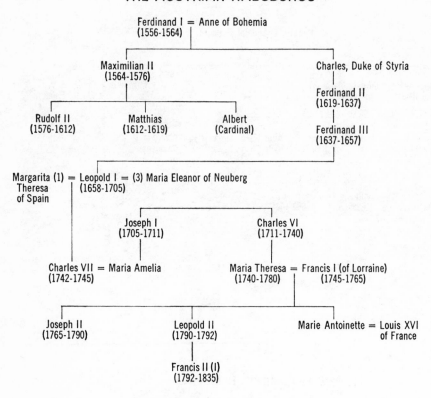

Ferdinand I = Anne of Bohemia
(1556-1564)

Maximilian II
(1564-1576)

Charles, Duke of Styria

Ferdinand II
(1619-1637)

Rudolf II   Matthias   Albert
(1576-1612)   (1612-1619)   (Cardinal)

Ferdinand III
(1637-1657)

Margarita (1) = Leopold I = (3) Maria Eleanor of Neuberg
Theresa   (1658-1705)
of Spain

Joseph I   Charles VI
(1705-1711)   (1711-1740)

Charles VII = Maria Amelia   Maria Theresa = Francis I (of Lorraine)
(1742-1745)   (1740-1780)   (1745-1765)

Joseph II   Leopold II   Marie Antoinette = Louis XVI
(1765-1790)   (1790-1792)   of France

Francis II (I)
(1792-1835)

THE SPANISH HABSBURGS

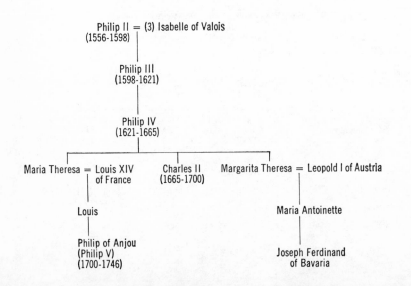

Philip II = (3) Isabelle of Valois
(1556-1598)

Philip III
(1598-1621)

Philip IV
(1621-1665)

Maria Theresa = Louis XIV   Charles II   Margarita Theresa = Leopold I of Austria
of France   (1665-1700)

Louis   Maria Antoinette

Philip of Anjou   Joseph Ferdinand
(Philip V)   of Bavaria
(1700-1746)

Rulers and Regimes of the Leading States
of Europe since 1815

AUSTRIA

Francis I, 1792–1835
Ferdinand I, 1835–1848
Francis Joseph, 1848–1916
Charles I, 1916–1918
Republican Regime, 1918–1938
Union with Germany, 1938–1945
Republican Regime, since 1945

ENGLAND

George III, 1760–1820
George IV, 1820–1830
William IV, 1830–1837
Victoria, 1837–1901
Edward VII, 1901–1910
George V, 1910–1936
Edward VIII, 1936
George VI, 1936–1952
Elizabeth II, since 1952

FRANCE

Louis XVIII, 1814–1824
Charles X, 1824–1830
Louis Philippe, 1830–1848
(Orléanist Monarchy)
The Second Republic, 1848–1852
Napoleon III, 1852–1870
(the Second Empire)
The Third Republic, 1870–1940
Pétain Regime, 1940–1944
Provisional Government, 1944–1946
The Fourth Republic, 1946–1958
The Fifth Republic, since 1958

GERMANY

William I, 1871–1888
Frederick III, 1888
William II, 1888–1918
The Weimar Republic, 1918–1933
The Third Reich, 1933–1945
Military Government, 1945–1949
The Federal Republic (West) and the
Democratic Republic (East),
since 1949

ITALY

Victor Emmanuel II, 1861–1878
Humbert I, 1878–1900
Victor Emmanuel III, 1900–1946
(Mussolini Regime, 1922–1943)
Humbert II, 1946
Republican Regime, since 1946

PRUSSIA

Frederick William III, 1797–1840
Frederick William IV, 1840–1861
William I, 1861–1888
Part of United Germany, since 1871

RUSSIA

Alexander I, 1801–1825
Nicholas I, 1825–1855
Alexander II, 1855–1881
Alexander III, 1881–1894
Nicholas II, 1894–1917
Provisional Government, 1917
Communist Regime, since 1917

SARDINIA

Victor Emmanuel I, 1802–1821
Charles Felix, 1821–1831
Charles Albert, 1831–1849
Victor Emmanuel II, 1849–1878
Part of United Italy, since 1861

Chapter 14

Habsburg Hegemony

When Charles V abdicated his many titles in the mid-1550s, he divided his vast holdings between his brother and his son. To his brother, Ferdinand, who already was king of Bohemia and Hungary, he left his central European domains; to his son, Philip II, he left the Spanish crown with its New World dependencies, the Netherlands, the Franche-Comté and the Italian territories of Naples and Milan. Thus the old emperor tried to rationalize somewhat the crushing burdens of governing the far-flung Habsburg lands.

The troubles in Germany had abated after the Peace of Augsburg; if its recognition of Lutheranism was distasteful to the pious emperor and its transfer of religious decisions to the German princes marked some further diminution of imperial authority, at least the settlement brought an end to much of the exhausting military conflict and weakened the excuse for French intervention. In the Danube Valley the Turkish wars had settled to a series of sieges and sporadic peace treaties. Internally and on both the eastern and western borders, German conflicts were dying down, while Spain, with a rapidly expanding colonial empire, seemed to be developing rapidly.

The new Habsburg rulers appeared to be men of great promise. Ferdinand was a central European in his attitudes; his experiences in Bohemia and Hungary involved him in a point of view wholly congenial to the Holy Roman Empire, and as Charles V's deputy for German affairs since 1522 he appeared to have won wide respect among the German princes. Young Philip had been reared mostly in Spain, spoke the tongue naturally, and had the piety and austerity of the Castilian; his obvious intelligence, his capacity for hard work and his serious demeanor all promised well for a man who was by birth one of Christendom's most important princes. Both branches of the house of Habsburg seemed to be in good hands, and at the same time there were possibilities for a further growth of Habsburg influence. In England, there appeared hope for a stronger Spanish alliance and perhaps even for England's return to Catholicism, for Mary Tudor—Catherine of Aragon's daughter—married Philip of Spain in 1554, and England was drawn into Spain's war with France in 1557; even after Mary's death in 1558 the situation was far from irretrievable, for her half-sister and heir, Elizabeth, held forth hope of Catholic conversion and Spanish marriage.

But behind this optimistic facade stirred many troubles. The religious peace in Germany reflected exhaustion more than agreement. The settlement merely extended to Lutherans (if their prince so decided) the position formerly enjoyed only by Catholics; it made no provision for the various groups of Anabaptists nor for the aggressive new Calvinist cult. It accepted things as they were, but it sought to impede further change, and the religious protest movements had not exhausted their dynamics yet. Despite the ecclesiastical reservation of the Peace of Augsburg, church lands continued to be secularized, and Calvinism—quite without legal recognition—became the established faith of the Rhineland state of the Palatinate.

The Spanish branch of the family also ruled over undercurrents of potential trouble. Castile and Aragon were staunchly particularistic, and amalgamation had made little progress under Charles V. The Moorish south was still restive under Spanish Catholic rule, breaking into revolt in 1569. The New World provided some treasure, but its importunities were many, and the sea routes were dangerous. The Netherlands were prosperous but also very particularistic, and the Spanish Philip, so very different from his cosmopolitan father, soon was to fan fires of rebellion with an attempt to impose outside authority. Italy seemed firmly in the Habsburg grip, but the Republic of Venice was hostile, and the papacy never had countenanced quietly a dominating secular power. The Turks, relatively quiet on the Danube, still controlled the Mediterranean and threatened Christian shipping. And no one could guess how long France would be willing to accept a secondary role, ringed in by Habsburg power. The potential of conflict lay on all sides.

Philip II of Spain (1556–1598) long has been the subject of characterizations ranging from fanaticism and bureaucratic rigidity to saintly devotion and impractical idealism. During the nineteenth century he was portrayed often as a king who had sacrificed the national resources of Spain to a religious crusade, much to the disgust of nationalist historians. But modern study has delineated a man of much more persuasive character—pious, austere and unbending but intelligent and hard-working and quite as devoted to the secular ambitions of his dynasty as to religious goals. It was easy for generations of historians still fascinated by the internal divisions of the Christian faith and still reacting to the universal pretensions of Roman Catholicism to portray King Philip as a Catholic crusader; yet, while such an interpretation can be defended, modern research has added broader perspectives, and historians now believe that the king's religious goal should be considered as one among many motivations of his policy. Certainly Philip II saw himself as the champion of the counter-reformation; as the strongest Catholic king in Europe, he felt God had laid upon him a special obligation to defend the church. But this aspect of his character should not be allowed to obscure his other important motives.

Moslem naval power constituted an old threat to European shipping on the Mediterranean, and in fact Moslem raiding of the south coasts of Europe continued into the seventeenth century, but Spain's vigorous efforts under King Philip made European commerce a bit more secure. In 1571, with support from the papacy and Venice, Spain mounted a strong naval expedition led by the king's half-brother, Don Juan, and struck at the main Turkish flotilla. The two fleets, totalling nearly four hundred and fifty galleys, came together off the coast of Greece, and the ensuing engagement took its name from the nearby town of Lepanto. The fighting was bloody, and both sides sustained heavy losses, but in the end the Turkish fleet was destroyed, and though the Turks rebuilt, they remained somewhat weakened in waters west of Sicily. It would be an exaggeration to suggest that the western Mediterranean became safe, for piracy was rife, and expeditions from north Africa still descended upon the European coast to carry off plunder and slaves; but there was a difference between such irregular activity and the constant threat of regular battle squadrons.

King Philip had a long-standing interest in England, and although religion undeniably was a motive, there were important commercial and political considerations, too. He and Mary Tudor had tried to restore English Catholicism, and as the champion of the counter-reformation, Philip hoped to see his task completed. But there also was the fact that England's seamen proved an expensive nuisance and a potential danger to Spain's colonial empire; the great days of the Elizabethan sea-dogs were just beginning, but there was enough harassment to make the Spanish government eager to control English activity at sea. And finally, there were political issues. After 1567 King Philip faced insurrection in the Netherlands, armed resistance to what he believed to be his just authority; England was aiding the rebels, and Philip felt that if he could neutralize England he would be able more easily to pacify the Netherlands. Thus, an important element of Spanish policy all through Philip II's reign was an attempt to dominate England.

Philip began peacefully enough with proposals for a marriage alliance with Elizabeth, but when these efforts met no result he sought alternatives. It was an age when some men still took their religion more seriously than their country, so of course the king of Spain had supporters among English Catholics; intercepted correspondence and often-exaggerated rumors of plots and conspiracies escalated the tension between the two governments, and growing popular animosities resulted from increased English raiding of Spanish colonial interests—activities at which Queen Elizabeth connived, often providing part of the capitalization of such expeditions. A crisis developed only in the 1580s, and by that time religious, commercial and political interests were intertwined thoroughly. The focus of the crisis was the exiled queen of Scotland, Mary Stuart.

In the third quarter of the sixteenth century Scotland underwent a violent religious and political transformation. It was the misfortune of the house of Stuart that the crown became the object of religious and political opposition at the same time. Mary Stuart had succeeded her father while still an infant, had been reared in France and when grown was married to the French King Francis II (1559–1560). During her minority and her absence abroad, her mother, a French princess, ruled as regent of Scotland, and French influence was strong at the Scottish court. But French governmental concepts of monarchs who ruled as well as reigned grated hard upon the stubborn independence of the Scots nobility, and there was trouble even before the frivolous and head-strong Mary Stuart returned from France in 1561 to begin her personal reign; her autocratic views worsened the situation. At this inopportune time John Knox returned to his native Scotland to preach the Calvinist gospel; his detestation of the Stuarts and their French adherents was exceeded only by his hatred for the Church of Rome. Knox's preaching won wide support, and soon the religious and political protests fused. Queen Mary antagonized the nobility by her autocratic behavior and all of her Calvinist subjects by her frivolity, her lovers and her gay court. Knox's fiery attacks upon the queen rallied popular support to the aristocratic opposition, and civil war broke out. Mary was forced to abdicate in favor of her son James in 1567, and the next year she fled to England to seek refuge, despite the fact that Elizabeth had been helping the Scots rebels.

In England Mary Stuart constituted a political danger to Elizabeth. Anne Boleyn's daughter had been born while Henry VIII's first wife, Catherine of Aragon, still lived; she was considered illegitimate by English Catholics who did not recognize Henry's divorce, and they denied her right to the throne. By an unhappy coincidence, if Elizabeth's claims were disallowed, the next heir to the crown of England was Mary Stuart. She was, therefore, the natural rallying point for Catholic opposition in England.

Mary did nothing to make Elizabeth's problems easier, for she intrigued constantly to usurp the throne of her protectress. Legend to the contrary, Elizabeth's treatment of Mary was not ungenerous. She was provided with a residence, and though her movements were restricted, close confinement came only when her subversive activities made it a political necessity. Still she dabbled at conspiracy, attempting to bribe one of the servants whom Elizabeth had assigned to her; but that individual delivered her secret correspondence straight to a member of the royal council. Despite massive provocation, Elizabeth tolerated this sort of behavior for more than

eighteen years. If not moved by sympathy, at least she had no desire
to continue the unhappy precedent of shedding royal blood.

Meanwhile, Philip of Spain had grown weary of the cat and
mouse game that Elizabeth had been playing with him. In 1577
she had made an alliance with the rebels in the Netherlands, and
in 1585 she sent troops to their aid; English depredations upon
Spanish shipping had grown worse; England was a bastion of heresy
and a haven of pirates. Philip conceived a grand plan to make an
end to England. In 1580 he had added Portugal to his domains by
a combination of inheritance and military force, and in the port
of Lisbon, one of the finest in Europe, he began to assemble a great
fleet, the proud Armada. It was to sail north, embark the Spanish
troops in the Netherlands, then cross the Channel and invade England. Simultaneously, English Catholics were to rise in rebellion,
rally to Mary Stuart, and overthrow Elizabeth. The joint operation
was to culminate in a Spanish marriage for Mary and reimposition
of Spanish influence and Catholicism in England. Probably the
English government, which was informed of all these projects,
exaggerated the danger of a great Catholic rising, but undeniably
Mary had become a serious political threat. Reluctantly, Elizabeth
ordered her execution in February of 1587.

In the summer of 1587 Sir Francis Drake struck another damaging blow against Philip's plans. Off the south coast of Spain he
caught and burned ships carrying hardwood to make the Armada's
water casks; replacement was difficult, and England gained a year.
More bad news came; Philip's brilliant commander in the Netherlands, the duke of Parma, insisted that the rebels were so strong in
the shallow coastal waters off the Low Countries that the Armada
would be unable to embark the troops. Philip prayed, hoped and
decided to gamble. The Armada sailed anyway; somehow it would
have to manage. Then disasters succeeded one another.

England did not flame with rebellion. English ships harried
the Armada, rearming and reprovisioning from English ports while
the Spanish ships were far from a friendly base. The Armada was
forced into the lee of the European coast, and incompetent command and unfavorable winds wrecked many ships. A storm drove
the rest of the fleet north; there was no hope of embarking troops,
and the Spanish were without charts for these waters. They tried
to round the British Isles to return to Spain, but bad weather con-

tinued, supplies ran low, and wrecks multiplied. Only a third of them got home, and England was saved.

Philip took the disaster bravely and decided that God was punishing him for his sins. Begging God not to punish all of Spain for her king's misdeeds, he sent other fleets to comparable fates during the remaining decade of his life, but the defeat of the Great Armada of 1588 had ruined his English policy. England preyed more vigorously upon Spain's shipping, continued to help the Netherlands and opposed Spanish interests in France. It should be obvious from this that a second important pivot of Philip II's policy was his quarrel with his subjects in the Netherlands. The civil war which resulted was carried on by his successors and lasted but for one brief interlude until the middle of the seventeenth century. Religion was only one of many issues, and at the outset it was not even the most important. Rather, the roots of the revolt in the Netherlands lay in the traditions and complex organization of that area.

The Netherlands were part of the old Burgundian inheritance, a loose association of seventeen separate provinces with many differences among them. Particularist traditions were strong, for the fishing and farming population of the north long had been secure behind the marshy barriers of what was almost a wasteland, and the wealth of the great textile cities of the south had made them proudly independent. When the area passed to the Habsburgs, both Maximillian I and Charles V humored local particularism. They used deputy governors in the Netherlands, maintaining a sort of autonomy from other Habsburg holdings, and they recognized the traditional right of local estates to determine grants of taxes and troops, thus allowing a large role to aristocratic and bourgeois interests. Not until 1548 did Charles V formally annex the Netherlands to the empire, and even then he created a Burgundian Circle (military district) which preserved much of the old autonomy. On the whole Charles and the Netherlanders got on well.

Within a decade of Philip II's accession, however, trouble broke out. At first two issues were involved, political authority and religion, but soon an economic consideration complicated matters further. Philip had introduced a Spanish garrison and Spanish clerics to the Netherlands, and religion became a sensitive issue as

Calvinism spread through the poor and restive lower classes of the southern cities, resulting in desecration of some Catholic churches and occasional riots. The government's heavy-handed endeavors to enforce religious uniformity no doubt reflected Philip's sincere convictions, but harsh penal edicts against heretics, the threat of the use of Spanish troops and a rumor that the dreaded Spanish Inquisition would be introduced seemed to violate the Netherlands' jealously guarded autonomy. There were sporadic outbreaks of popular violence, but the first organized resistance came not from a popular religious movement but from a league of three hundred nobles who protested the imposition of foreign authority.

Philip reacted with even harsher repression, sending from Spain the duke of Alva with twenty thousand troops. Alva created a special tribunal, soon called the Council of Blood for the many executions it prescribed, and prominent local aristocrats as well as many humbler folk were sent to their deaths.

Thus far the resistance to Philip had come chiefly from two sources: popular religious protest and aristocratic political protest. The persecutions gave rise to a much more general resentment, however, and Alva added a third force to his opposition, the urban oligarchies, those proud merchants and manufacturers who formed the wealthy backbone of the Netherlands' economy. The policies that Alva was attempting to implement were both unpopular and costly, and, certain that the estates would not support him, he sought financial independence by imposing a sales tax of ten percent on all transactions. Such an imposition would have ended all local restraint upon government and probably would have meant ruin to the area's important commerce. There was a new revolt. Alva had drawn into alliance against himself and his master the most disparate elements—urban magnates and their workmen, who usually detested one another, and the old nobility, who generally scorned both. Religious, political and economic issues melted together, inflaming the entire population to armed resistance. His policy a failure, Alva was recalled in 1573 at his own request.

Thereafter command changed rapidly: Requesnes from 1573 to his death in 1576; Don Juan of Austria (the victor of Lepanto) from 1576 to his death in 1578. Neither could suppress the revolt, but the ferocity of the Spanish armies led in 1576 to the short-lived Pacification of Ghent, a compact wherein the seventeen provinces agreed to overlook their own rivalries and to unite to drive out the Spaniards. Philip II had achieved the greatest unity the Netherlands had ever known, but it was unity in opposition to him rather than in the service of his crown.

At the end of the 1570s the war settled into the patterns that were to mark its course until 1648, with the seven northern provinces in revolt and the ten southern provinces loyal to Spain. The catalyst of this change was the appointment of a new Spanish commander, Alexander Farnese, duke of Parma. A man as able in negotiations as he was brilliant in command of armies, Parma quickly exploited the conflicting interests that divided his opponents. The great bourgeoisie of the southern cities was Catholic in faith and conservative in politics; the merchants and manufacturers found the Calvinism and social radicalism of the urban lower classes frightening, and they resisted Philip chiefly in defense of traditional privileges and through fear of the sort of taxation that Alva had attempted. Parma persuaded King Philip to allow him to compromise. He confirmed ancient privileges, especially with regard to taxation, and he had the troops to guarantee social stability; the southern oligarchies agreed to return to obedience, to enforce religious conformity and to provide financial support for Parma's forces. At the price of some sacrifice of his personal political authority, Philip achieved his religious goals in half of the Netherlands and secured for his forces a base of operations against those who remained rebellious.

The seven northern provinces were a different matter. In contrast to the urbanized and industrialized south, this was a land of small towns, farms and fishing villages, a population of stubborn peasant stock. At first Calvinism had grown slowly in this conservative peasant society, but once it became the rallying standard of the revolt, it had spread rapidly. The northern provinces had offered refuge and men to aristocratic resistance leaders such as William of Nassau-Orange, called the Silent, and their men had gained some of the first victories over the Spaniards when their light fishing craft were armed to harass Spanish ships and raid Spanish positions. In the course of the war some of the northern towns, especially Amsterdam, grew in importance and wealth as they became centers of rebel shipping and the bases from which the Dutch raided Spanish commerce. After 1580, when Portugal became part of Philip's domains and hence fair game, Portuguese shipping began to suffer, and at the end of the sixteenth century a Dutch fleet sailed to the East Indies and cracked the Portuguese monopoly of the affluent eastern trade.

These stubborn northerners did not abate their resistance in the slightest when the southerners made their peace with Spain. In 1579 they bound themselves into the Union of Utrecht, and in 1581 they declared their total independence. It seemed a futile if brave gesture, for Parma appeared unbeatable, and in 1584 he captured the port of Antwerp, the last of the great cities that had not made terms with Philip. But the English sent aid in 1585, and Philip's attempt to bring the war to a quick conclusion ended with the disastrous loss of the Armada in 1588. Then in 1592 Parma died from an infected wound, and thereafter the fighting was intermittent and inconclusive. To the year of his death in 1598, Philip never abandoned hope of crushing the rebels, and his successor Philip III was equally determined to make no peace recognizing independence. Sheer exhaustion finally produced a twelve years' truce in 1609, and when hostilities were resumed early in the 1620s the Dutch war was subsumed in the larger struggle known as the Thirty Years War. Peace did not come to the Netherlands until 1648.

In all fairness to Philip II it should be noted that he attempted little that was not being done by his contemporaries. Toleration was foreign to the thought and spirit of the sixteenth century, and most governments sought religious uniformity; most governments also were trying to increase taxation sharply, for rising prices and increasing military costs made more money essential. But it is particularly ironic that Philip should be damned for his efforts to suppress particularism in the Netherlands, for similar efforts in the next century by the French government of Louis XIII and Richelieu, by the Prussian Hohenzollerns and by the Swedish Vasas are praised, and nationalist historians long have lamented the failure of Germany to achieve such a result until the late nineteenth century. Much of Philip II's policy in the Netherlands was a failure, but there was nothing unique or particularly wicked about his efforts, and in the south he managed to hold a strategically and economically important area for his crown and his church.

One other great effort was important to Philip II's reign, his attempt to establish dominant Spanish influence in France and perhaps even to secure the French crown for his family after disaster struck France in the middle of the sixteenth century. The Peace of Cateau-Cambrésis, which brought peace between the Valois and the Habsburgs in 1559, was the occasion of celebrations. One of the events was the old noble sport of jousting, and through a freak accident King Henry II was killed when a lance broke, and a splinter passed through his visor and penetrated his eye. Henry's oldest son, the sickly young Francis II (husband of Mary, queen of Scots), succeeded to the throne until his death in 1560; then he was succeeded by Henry's second son, Charles IX (1560–1574), who was only ten years old. The deaths of two kings and the succession of a minor removed the stabilizing influence of royal authority, and France was thrown into turmoil.

France had escaped serious religious trouble during the first half of the sixteenth century, for the French Church was largely in the king's hands, and no strong secular power was ready to offer the sort of support that the princes had given Lutheranism in Germany. But Calvinism won some adherents toward the middle of the century, and by then the political climate was more congenial to religious dissent. The long wars which France fought against Charles V largely had pauperized the lesser nobles, and they had tended to seek the support and patronage of a few wealthy aristocratic houses, creating a client system often called bastard feudalism. By the middle of the century, four great cliques existed: the royal house of Valois; the house of Bourbon, related by blood to the Valois; the house of Guise, a French branch of the important imperial house of Lorraine, related by marriage to the Valois; and the house of Montmorency, a proud old family with vast lands and great wealth. Until Henry II's death the Valois had maintained control, and the conservative Montmorencys usually had supported the crown, while the Guises and Bourbons had fought and quarreled for offices and patronage. But upon the death of Henry II the fortunes of the royal family passed into the hands of his widow, Catherine de Medici, and though clever and unscrupulous, she faced a difficult task in the scramble for power that marked the last half of the sixteenth century.

The succession of Francis II gave great influence to his uncles by marriage, the Guises. The Bourbons opposed this favor, and soon the Montmorencys also went into opposition. Younger members of both houses espoused Calvinism, and religious dissent took on strong political overtones. Under persecution French Calvinists took up arms and formed a political organization, and soon the cult had grown to impressive proportions. Called Huguenots (probably from a German word meaning "covenanters"), the French Calvinists at their peak claimed something near to half of the French nobility as well as many townsmen in the south and west, Montmorency and Bourbon territory; few peasants were attracted to the movement, however, and generally the north and northeast were little penetrated by the new doctrines. For both religious and political reasons the government tried to suppress the Huguenots, and fighting broke out which was to continue sporadically until the mid-1590s. Generally the Huguenot cavalry (drawn from the ranks of the nobility) was the best on the field, while royal armies fielded better infantry (peasants) and had the financial resources to support more artillery. The wars were savage.

In 1574 Charles IX was succeeded by his brother Henry III (1574–1589), a well-meaning but weak and vacillating man who sought peace with the Huguenots. To oppose Henry III's attempt at compromise, the fanatical Guises formed a Catholic League in 1576 and sought help from Philip of Spain, who thus was drawn into the French civil wars. Then France's troubles were aggravated further as a succession crisis loomed. Two of Henry II's sons had sat upon the throne and died childless. The third, who then reigned, was childless and was expected to remain so as he appears to have been homosexual. A fourth brother, known as the duke of Anjou, was the dynasty's last hope, but he died—also childless—in 1584. Under the old Salic Law, which governed the French succession according to male blood lines only, the next heir to the throne was Henry of Bourbon; but he was a heretic, the leader of the Huguenots and unacceptable to French Catholics. The Guises hoped to set aside the Salic Law and probably aspired to the throne themselves, arguing with some justice that the religious requirement of Catholicism went back to Clovis and was as old as the principle of heredity by male blood lines. Philip II of Spain hoped to have the Salic Law set aside in favor of his daughter, who was a granddaughter of Henry II.

When Henry III was murdered in 1589, the fighting became even more intense, and the pattern of the struggle clarified. Bourbon claimed the crown with the support of his Huguenots and of some Catholics called *politiques*, who set civil peace above religious uniformity; he was opposed by the Catholic League, which had the support of Philip of Spain. In the early 1590s, Bourbon managed to conquer most of France, but Paris was too strong for him to take, and after long negotiations he was persuaded that most of France would accept him if he were Catholic while Paris would accept him on no other terms. With many reassurances to his Huguenot supporters, he converted to Catholicism in 1593 and reunited the country as King Henry IV (by royalist tradition reigning from Henry III's death in 1589 until his own assassination in 1610). Everywhere opposition collapsed, and another of Philip II's policies was bankrupt.

In 1598 Henry IV fulfilled his pledges to his former coreligionists with the proclamation of the Edict of Nantes. By this edict he guaranteed freedom of conscience to all Frenchmen, extensive freedom of public and private worship to the Calvinist minority, equal access to governmental offices to people of both faiths and special mixed courts to avoid religious prejudice in judicial processes. In addition, he granted the Huguenots the right to fortify a number of cities for protection against the Catholic majority, and he agreed to help defray the costs of their fortifications and their garrisons. Thus France achieved internal peace again, and during the remainder of Henry's reign the country recuperated rapidly from the ravages of the civil wars. Despite Philip II's efforts, France—like the Dutch Netherlands—survived to become a major opponent of the Habsburgs in the seventeenth century.

Chapter 15

The Scientific Revolution

About the middle of the sixteenth century western man's traditional assumptions about his physical environment were challenged seriously by the growth of a critical movement usually called the scientific revolution. In the course of approximately two hundred years, from the mid-sixteenth century to the mid-eighteenth century, basically modern conceptions of astronomy, mechanics and anatomy were established, and perhaps most important of all this period saw the development of that critical and quantitative approach to natural studies which is called the scientific method.

To understand the problems and the achievements of the scientific revolution, it is necessary first to consider the broad framework of scientific theories that constituted earlier accepted opinion. These theories were outlined under the title of natural philosophy by the Greek thinker Aristotle in the fourth century B.C., for which reason this older body of thought is termed Aristotelianism. Though modern science has discredited most of Aristotle's ideas, he should not be underestimated. His brilliant mind conceived theories that integrated all branches of natural studies into a coherent whole, explaining persuasively the varied natural phenomena of man's environment.

Though Aristotelian natural philosophy was extremely complex, it rested upon a few relatively simple assumptions. Aristotle assumed, with many of his contemporaries, that there were four basic elements in the universe—earth, air, fire and water—and that each of these elements had inherent properties such as warmth or coldness, wetness or dryness. Since all material objects comprised some combination of these elements, physical differences could be explained.

The four elements also had natural positions in the universe, places where they would come to rest were they not prevented from doing so by mixture with other elements. Freed from constraint, the elements had a natural motion toward their places of rest. The natural position of earth, the heaviest of the elements, was at the center of the universe; water, the next heaviest element, found its place around the earth; and two successive layers formed the blankets of air and fire. Thus Aristotelians conceived of the terrestrial environment as a series of concentric spheres and believed that only a fortunate imbalance allowed some earth to stand above the level of the waters, forming a home for mankind. (One interesting result of this idea was the theory almost two thousand years before Columbus' voyage that another continent must exist on the other side of the world, the antipodes or counterbalance of the Eurasian land mass.)

The concept of natural position and its related theory of natural motion permitted a whole system of mechanics. An object was heavy, and fell when dropped, because its major element was earth, which sought to move to the center of the universe. Flames leaped upward because burning something released the fire that was entrapped, and, freed from restraint, the fire sought its position farthest from the center of the universe. Unnatural motion could be imparted to an object, but it required the application of an outside force, and such motion stopped when the force wore out. Hence an arrow, with a large proportion of earth in it, could be made to fly perpendicular to the direction of its natural motion by the force the bow imparted to it; but as the external force was used up, natural motion would reassert itself, and the arrow would fall.

A theory of astronomy was made possible by the addition of the assumption that natural motion could be inherent to form as well as to matter, particularly that it was a natural motion for a sphere to rotate. Aristotle theorized that beyond the terrestrial environment lay concentric spheres of heavenly crystal—a substance that was colorless, weightless and frictionless by definition. These spheres rotated because it was natural for them to do so, and planets imbedded in their walls were carried around with them. Separately these notions might appear superficial and even amusing to the modern student, but if one remembers that Aristotle was forced to depend only upon naked eye observation and his power of reason, his achievement is impressive. His system could explain coherently the appearance and behavior of the everyday phenomena of life.

Over years and centuries fundamental Aristotelian ideas were elaborated in detail. A basically physical theory of the human body developed in which health was dependent upon a happy balance of four humors—blood, phlegm, yellow bile and black bile; these humors were various combinations of the four basic elements. For instance, blood was the hot humor because it contained a large proportion of the element fire. Hence, fever was diagnosed as an excess of blood, and the standard remedy was bleeding. (It should be recognized that this theory appeared sound; bleeding lowers blood pressure and temporarily reduces fever. This was, of course, treatment of symptoms rather than of causes, but it had some temporary effectiveness.)

The growth of Christianity reinforced Aristotelian thought. Aristotle's science placed the earth in the center of the universe. Christians assumed that the universe existed only as a stage-set for the drama of the struggle for man's salvation, and naturally they expected to find the drama set center-stage. Moreover, popular preachers could derive many useful analogies from the Aristotelian universe. The outer sphere, nearest to the purity of God's heaven, held the fixed stars, which sparkled with the white of purity; the planets, closer to the corruption of earth, shone in softer colors; and of course poor dross earth, corrupted by man's sin, did not shine at all. Thus, on both theoretical and practical levels Christianity found Aristotelianism congenial, and with appropriate modifications to make room for God's creation and God's will as a motive force the medieval church adopted the Aristotelian world view. In consequence of this adoption, Aristotelianism remained the basis of "establishment" opinion for over fourteen hundred years.

One of the fascinating questions posed by the scientific revolution of the early modern period is why it succeeded with relative rapidity after so many centuries of Aristotelian predominance. An attempt to answer this question must consider several different subjects: the accumulation of challenges, the development of better mathematical tools, the invention of instruments and the growth of improved communications. The combination of these developments rather than any one of them ultimately overturned Aristotle.

Challenges to Aristotelian science had existed from the beginning—some sound and some foolish. There were some who maintained that the world was flat, not round. (This idea has been exaggerated greatly in popular lore; anyone who lived by the sea saw the curve of the horizon, and those who watched a ship disappear into the distance—hull down, then sail down, then masthead down—could not doubt the curvature of the earth.) Others asserted that the sun, not the earth, was the center of the universe. But generally these challenges posed too many problems. For instance, if one displaced the earth from the center of the universe, the whole structure of physics would collapse. Why would heavy objects fall if the element earth were not seeking its natural position at the center of the universe? Why would flames leap if the element fire were not seeking to move to the outer ring? An old Greek experiment had attempted to determine whether the earth moved by measuring angles to fixed stars at different times. The experiment was well-conceived, but it failed to produce valid results, for the Greeks vastly underestimated the distance to the stars, and their instruments were too primitive to detect the differentials of angle that such a measurement produces. They concluded that the earth did not move.

Yet by the later middle ages serious criticisms had accumulated, particularly in the areas of astronomy and medicine. The great vogue for astrology which entered Europe from the Arab world stimulated astronomical observation considerably. The scientific studies of the Franciscans, of whom Roger Bacon probably was the most notable, raised problems. And Renaissance experiments in medicine, clandestine dissections and attempts to treat illnesses with herbs and minerals, refuted some traditional medical views.

The greatest interpreter of Aristotelian astronomy was the Alexandrian geographer Ptolemy. In the second century A.D. he had translated complex Aristotelian natural philosophy into astronomical charts on plane surfaces, showing planets revolving around the earth in concentric orbits. Even Aristotle had recognized, however, that planetary orbits were not perfect circles around the earth, and he had theorized that the spheres which carried the planets around turned on eccentric centers (that is, that they did not share the same focus), which made their revolutions appear irregular to an observer on earth. As a device to transfer this conception to plane surfaces,

Ptolemy had devised the epicycle; a planet followed an orbit around an imaginary point, which point revolved in an orbit around the earth. Accumulating astronomical data made Ptolemy's device more and more necessary, for astronomers were attempting the impossible task of describing elliptical movement around the sun in terms of complex circular movements around the earth.

By the sixteenth century, accepted charts of the solar system included one hundred and forty epicycles, a complexity that raised serious doubts in the minds of some astronomers. Copernicus, a Polish astronomer-mathematician, saw the problem in its starkest terms. He came to believe that such complexity defied reason and that he must assume either that the observational work of his predecessors over several centuries was sloppy and inaccurate or that the theory was wrong. He chose the latter assumption and tried to fit the observations to a theory that the sun rather than the earth was the center, resolutely ignoring the problems this would create in physics and mechanics. The results were promising but inconclusive. Because Copernicus continued to assume that planetary orbits were circular, he could not achieve total harmony of data and theory, but he was able to cut the number of epicycles by about half. His conclusions were published in 1543, after his death, in a work titled, *The Revolutions of Heavenly Objects,* and aroused violent controversy.

In the same year, 1543, another book challenged Aristotelian conceptions in the medical field. A young Italian, Vesalius, produced a book called *The Structure of the Human Body.* In this work the challenge lay not so much in any theory in the text but rather in the illustrations. For centuries the great medical authority had been Galen, a Greco-Roman doctor of the third century A.D., who had codified medical knowledge on an Aristotelian basis. However, Galenic medicine faced even more serious problems than Ptolemaic astronomy. Many early societies have strong taboos against desecration of the human body, and Greco-Roman society was no exception. Consequently, most of Galen's dissections seem to have been practiced upon apes and pigs, whose anatomy differs importantly from that of humanity. Moreover, Galen's treatises survived into the middle ages only in condensations, with many of his explanations drastically cut or abbreviated, and the Christian church of medieval Europe reaffirmed the traditional opposition to dissections, so his descriptions rarely were checked or criticized. In consequence, for centuries the teaching of basic anatomy was derived from animal analogies.

In the later middle ages, however, human dissection began to be practiced again, especially in Italy. It was mostly clandestine, depending upon grave robbers and sympathetic rulers who would give medical schools the bodies of condemned criminals, but it was sufficient to cause serious unease among anatomists who found results at variance with those described by Galen. Vesalius' book exemplifies the conflict well. His text is conservative, repeating a lot of Galenic error, but his illustrations showed what he actually saw, and new techniques of reproduction—engravings and woodcuts—quickly spread his sharply detailed illustrations throughout European medical circles, encouraging those who otherwise might have faulted their own methodology rather than Galen's theories.

Thus, in the mid-sixteenth century two important challenges were posed to traditional science. Yet this simple fact does not explain why these challenges launched a successful scientific revolution while other challenges had been discounted. The greater body of conflicting evidence that the new challengers could muster represents a difference of degree rather than of kind. And vague statements about a Renaissance spirit of inquiry are not satisfactory either, for the Renaissance was not an unmixed blessing to scientific investigation. The adulation of classical writers—very much a part of any definition of Renaissance spirit—tended to make challenges to Ptolemy and Galen and especially to Aristotle all the more scandalous. Recognition of the very real achievements of these men, especially Aristotle's logic and Ptolemy's geography, tended by analogy to lend authority to all of their theories, many of which simply were erroneous, such as Ptolemy's astronomy. In fact, the intellectual establishment offered enormous opposition to the new challenges. Classicists damned those who dared to criticize the ancient Greeks and Romans. Universities, which have a tendency to structure and formalize knowledge, opposed the radicals who would overturn traditional teaching. The church condemned the desecration of the human body and damned those who would assert that the divine drama of good and evil was played upon a stage that was but a speck of dirt spinning at dizzying speed through the universe.

Luther, who often is taken to represent the Renaissance spirit in religion, characterized Copernicus as a damned fool who would turn the universe upside down.

Nor can the traditionalists be faulted seriously for failing to adopt the new theories with enthusiasm. Copernicus could not offer an integrated and unified astronomy, only some simplification. Vesalius could not explain the mysteries of disease and death, only some structural errors of Galen. And to have accepted the theories of these men would have meant discarding all that was known of astronomy, physics, mechanics and medicine, to begin again fumbling into the vast unknown.

Nonetheless, the challenge was established successfully, and it did prove revolutionary. The printing press was one important factor, for it allowed dissemination of the new ideas not as ill-copied manuscripts with multiplying errors but as consistent treatises with careful illustrations. And the printing press was but one of several new tools, both physical and intellectual, that were developed about this time.

The ancient Greeks had not progressed beyond geometry, no mean achievement but only a first step in the development of mathematics, and they had instruments no more sophisticated than the astrolabe, a primitive device for measuring elevations above the horizon. The medieval period saw important additions to the mathematical tools known in Europe as well as some improvement in physical aids to research. From the Arab world had come arabic numerals (the advantage of which will be recognized readily by anyone who ever has tried to multiply or divide with Roman numerals) as well as the mathematics known as algebra. In addition, the Arab world had transmitted to Europe the Indian concept of zero, a concept terribly important to the continued development of mathematics. The most important new instrument to appear in medieval Europe was the compass, probably an import from China, and this was accompanied by a slow but steady increase in the availability of research data, such as compendia of astronomical observations. The early modern period saw both of these kinds of tools, intellectual and mechanical, proliferated further. By the end of the seventeenth century, mathematics had progressed to calculus, and laboratories and observatories were equipped with lens systems and all sorts of devices for measuring time, temperature and pressure.

Finally, the early modern period inaugurated a much fuller communication among experimenters. Sir Isaac Newton, originator of the hypothesis of universal gravitation, was to remark that he felt like a pygmy standing on the shoulders of giants, and although perhaps overmodest, the comment illustrates another important achievement. In Paris and London, in Naples and Salerno and as far away as Philadelphia and Warsaw, scientific investigators of the seventeenth and eighteenth centuries formed societies that began to publish papers and proceedings. No longer did the investigator work in a vacuum or from the basis of bits of other peoples' results that came to him by chance, but rather he could read of earlier experiments and could submit his own results for learned criticism.

In consequence of all these developments, the revolution launched by Copernicus and Vesalius progressed relatively rapidly despite opposition. There were those who tried to absorb the new theories into older ideas, such as the Danish astronomer Tycho Brahe (1546–1601), who postulated a universe in which the earth circled the sun while all of the other planets circled the earth. (Of greater long-range significance were the vastly improved astronomical instruments that he designed.) But there also were a few men who struck out boldly to substantiate the new ideas. In the late sixteenth and early seventeenth centuries, two men in particular contributed to the Copernican hypothesis, Galileo Galilei (1564–1642) and Johannes Kepler (1571–1630).

Galileo really was more important to mechanics than to astronomy, his experiments such as those with projectiles and with falling bodies providing some viable alternatives to Aristotelian notions. But probably he is most famous for his demonstrations with telescopes. It appears that he learned of experiments with lens systems that had been carried out in the Netherlands and that he undertook to duplicate them. In any case, he built telescopes, and with them he succeeded in giving visual refutation of the old astronomy. From observation of the phases of the inner planets, Venus and Mercury, he could show that they circled the sun, not the earth. With telescopic magnification he also could show that other planets, particularly Jupiter, had satellites, a serious blow to the defenders of Aristotelian astronomy. Over the course of a long life, he built hundreds of telescopes, progressing from early three-power models to something over thirty-power before his death. His dramatic descriptions of the universe revealed to him by his telescopes and his defense of the new astronomy attracted much attention and made him one of the foremost popularizers of the new astronomy.

Kepler, on the other hand, worked out the mathematics that established the sun-centered hypothesis beyond dispute. Discarding the Copernican theory of circular orbits, he tried and rejected other regular forms such as the oval, and he discovered ultimately that if orbits were assumed to be elliptical, the observational data could be fitted to the sun-centered theory without need for epicycles to explain discrepancies. A further problem remained in that planets moved at varying speeds along their elliptical orbits, and Kepler sought a regular and calculable basis for the variation. He found this basis in a relationship that linked the variations in a planet's speed with its distance from the sun. The results of these successes were Kepler's laws.

The latter seventeenth century saw continued scientific progress. Mathematics was advanced by the French philosopher René Descartes (1596–1650), who invented analytical geometry, a mathematical system that made it possible to express curves in algebraic equations and conversely to translate formulae back into curves on graphs, and by Blaise Pascal (1623–1662), whose work in combinations and permutations opened the whole field of number theory. A bit later, in independent but contemporary developments, the Englishman Sir Isaac Newton (1642–1727) and the German Baron Gottfried von Leibniz (1646–1716) invented calculus, a shorthand system of calculation and annotation to handle varying speeds and curves of movement.

In astronomy, these developments came to a sort of fruition in other works of Sir Isaac Newton, whose world view remained fundamental to science until whole new areas of consideration were opened up by Albert Einstein early in the twentieth century. That the sun-centered hypothesis was valid was obvious after Kepler, but Newton was intrigued to discover how it worked. The results of his investigations were the hypothesis of universal gravitation, which stated that all matter exercised an attractive force upon all other matter, and Newton's laws, which expressed the force of attraction between two bodies in terms of relationships between their masses and the square of the distance between their centers.

About the same time, the challenges posed by Vesalius were producing fruitful results. William Harvey (1578–1657), an English doctor who had studied in Italy, denied the old theory of two separate blood systems, venous and arterial, and propounded the circulation of the blood. He could advance his theory only inferentially, however, for he could not show the connection between the two systems; it remained for an Italian, Marcello Malpighi (1628–1694), using a microscope, to show the capillaries that passed the blood from the arteries to the veins for return to the heart.

By the early eighteenth century, Aristotelian science clearly was dying. Its greatest strength, overall unity, also was its greatest weakness. A challenge to part of it opened enormous problems, but if the challenge to part of it could be substantiated, then the whole structure had to be doubted. Vestiges of Aristotelianism lingered long. Aristotle's dictum that nature abhors a vacuum resulted in all sorts of imaginary substances filling outer space long after his crystalline spheres had been abandoned; Descartes spoke of celestial fluids, and as late as the early twentieth century many people found some sort of ether a notion more congenial than vacuum. Popular parlance still carries echoes of Aristotle in such phrases as "the sun is trying to shine." But by and large the scientific revolution was an established fact by the eighteenth century. Copernicus and Vesalius had posed challenges which men such as Galileo, Kepler and Newton, Harvey and Malpighi had substantiated. Not surprisingly, the new and radical scientific thought spilled over into other fields.

The late seventeenth century saw new speculation stimulated by patterns of stratification, such as those exhibited by the famous cliffs of Dover, by fossils unearthed in the Netherlands and by what appeared to be sharks' teeth found on mountain tops in Italy. These phenomena had disturbing implications; it appeared the earth was older than the Bible suggested and, moreover, that life forms had disappeared and new ones had appeared in ways not accounted for in Biblical accounts of Genesis and the Flood. Already in the eighteenth century, concepts of evolution were being suggested, though no one could advance any very persuasive arguments of how evolution might have worked until the mid-nineteenth century when Charles Darwin (1809–1882) published his *Origin of the Species* (1859), which suggested that natural selection by environment could transform species over the course of many generations. And the eighteenth century saw a variety of advances in a whole range of scientific studies: electricity (Galvani and Volta), chemistry (Lavoisier), botany (Buffon and Linnaeus), geology and paleontology (Hutton and Lamarck) and composition and behavior of gases (Boyle and Cavendish). Obviously a new and very productive approach to natural studies had evolved.

Inevitably there were those who tried to sum up and explain the new approach that had proved so fruitful, the discipline eventually called the scientific method. Most prominent among the explainers were the English Francis Bacon (1561–1626) and the French René Descartes. Neither described the whole of the scientific method, but each described a part of it in a way probably important to the continued progress of early modern science. Bacon stressed observation and careful recording of observed data, though it may be said in criticism that he seems to have assumed that explanations would pop into the head of the observer and that he probably was convinced that there existed a relatively limited set of general principles that would explain all scientific phenomena. Descartes, on the other hand, stressed the subdivision of problems into component parts that could be subjected to individual study and the casting of hypotheses susceptible to testing; he may be criticized for giving too little weight to careful and critical observation, for seeming to assume that once a part of the natural world had been studied, a great deal more could be explored by pure reason. Yet taken together, these two men caught the essence of the new science: an attempt at detachment from *a priori* assumptions, careful observation of quantitative data, construction of hypotheses to explain data, and exhaustive testing of the hypotheses to substantiate or refute them.

It is almost impossible to overestimate the impact of the new science, and especially of the scientific method, upon the mentality of early modern Europe's intellectual elite; for the new science destroyed age-old beliefs and set intellectuals to speculating in wholly new directions about the nature of the universe. In accord with Descartes's and Newton's basically mechanical conceptions, the European intellectual came to view his world—socially, politically, and physically—as a great machine in which understanding depended upon mathematics and quantitative data rather than upon theology and speculation. Descartes's method of analysis, blocking out separate problems within larger ones and using the solutions of these as building-blocks of a larger understanding, grew to be the dominant methodology of European thought. This geometric spirit, as it was called, was believed to hold the key to all fields of knowledge, and the French even coined a verb meaning "to Cartesianate" to express this mode of analysis that depended upon observation, experiment and reason. Explicit in this new intellectual methodology was the rejection of traditional authority unless that authority could bear the scrutiny of experimental analysis. In his *Discourse on Method,* Descartes specifically endorsed the value of skepticism, demanding that the researcher should doubt everything until he saw persuasive proof. Soon ethics, theology and politics also were adjusted to the new scientific and mechanical view of the world by Spinoza, Malebranche and Locke, and their followers were numerous. The eighteenth century English poet, Alexander Pope, summed up the universality of the impact of the new science in his couplet:

Nature and Nature's laws lay hid in night: God said,
Let Newton be! and all was light.

In a long perspective, the world view established by the scientific revolution, as distinct from the skepticism and the methodology that evolved from it, probably has been exaggerated in importance, for the twentieth century is overturning the conclusions of the seventeenth and eighteenth centuries with great rapidity, and acceptance for two or three hundred years is not nearly so good a record as Aristotle could claim. It is possible that relativity theory and investigations of sub-atomic structure, psychedelic drugs and genetic experiments with DNA and RNA, may leave Copernicus and Newton, Vesalius and Harvey, as antiquated as Aristotle and Ptolemy. But future investigators, however startling their discoveries, also should admit that they stand upon the shoulders of giants.

Chapter 16

The Rise of
the National State

When Philip II of Spain died in 1598, the Habsburg hegemony in Europe was far from ended. Despite the loss of the Great Armada and the rise of English naval strength, the reconsolidation of hostile royal authority in France and the *de facto* autonomy of Switzerland and the Dutch Netherlands, the two branches of the house of Habsburg still controlled vast territories. Spain remained the greatest military power in Europe, and though the Holy Roman Empire appeared still prostrate from the religious wars and the emperor weakened in relation to the princes, imperial claims to extensive authority throughout Germany never had been relinquished. Habsburg pretensions to universal monarchy still seemed a real threat, and England, France and the Netherlands were still very much on the defensive.

The beginning of the seventeenth century saw a few years of uneasy peace, but the situation remained far from stable. France was at peace officially after 1598, but King Henry IV continued to aid the Dutch in their war against Spain and to encourage the German Protestant princes in their political opposition to the emperor. In 1609 the Dutch signed a twelve years truce with Spain, but it seemed to be regarded by both sides as a pause to rearm and re-

equip rather than as an opportunity to negotiate a peaceful settlement. Imperial claims in a succession dispute over Cleves-Jülich, a
group of small territories on the lower Rhine, evoked the threat of
French intervention in 1609. Revived religious quarrels in Germany
led to the foundation of new armed alliances, the Protestant Union
in 1608 and the Catholic League in 1609, and there were comparable
difficulties in Bohemia. In 1606 the Austrians and the Ottoman
Turks signed an inconclusive peace, but the Danube frontier remained insecure. The war between England and Spain was ended
officially in 1604 by Queen Elizabeth's successor, James I, but beyond European waters, in the colonies and on the high seas, sporadic
hostilities hardly were diminished. In sum, about 1610 none of
Europe's major powers was at war officially, but old hostilities were
still powerful forces, and many issues from colonial rivalries to religious clashes had the potential of precipitating great conflict.

The massive war that dominated the first half of the seventeenth century was triggered finally by religious incidents in Bohemia and by Habsburg reactions to them. This struggle usually is
called the Thirty Years War (1618–1648) and often is designated
the last of the religious wars, but neither of these appellations
should be applied too rigorously. The Dutch long had talked of
the Eighty Years War, considering the fighting in the early seventeenth century as part of their long effort to break Habsburg power,
and a case can be made for considering the fighting of the whole
period from the 1530s to the 1640s a second Hundred Years War,
a struggle by non-Habsburg Europe to break the Habsburg encircle-
ment. The designation "last of the religious wars" also must be
considered carefully, for the implication that the war can be explained satisfactorily by religious motivation simply will not bear
scrutiny. Religious factors were an important though not exclusive
cause of the outbreak of the war, and they often complicated its
course, but the conflict between Catholic France and the Catholic
Habsburgs cannot be treated in terms of religious factors.

The Thirty Years War began with a Protestant revolt in
Bohemia in the spring of 1618, over a combination of religious
issues and a Habsburg succession question. Emperor Matthias
(1612–1619), who also was king of Bohemia, was childless, and
toward the end of his life he arranged to be succeeded by his cousin

Ferdinand of Styria. Ferdinand, however, was a strict Catholic and a leading exponent of the Counter-Reformation, so his accession was much feared in Bohemia, where Protestantism was well established, with roots going back to the fifteenth century Hussites. The Bohemian Protestants rose in revolt, and with help from German Protestants they drove Habsburg forces from Bohemia in 1619. At this juncture Emperor Matthias died.

The imperial electors awarded Ferdinand of Styria the crown of the Holy Roman Empire as Emperor Ferdinand II (1619–1637), which strengthened his position, but the Bohemian Protestants sought to prevent his accession to the Bohemian crown. Unfortunately the Bohemian estates once had elected Ferdinand successor to Matthias, but they reassembled, declared him deposed and offered the crown to Frederick Count Palatine; they hoped he could rally the Protestant forces of Europe to their defense, for he was one of the seven electors of the Holy Roman Empire, the leader of the Protestant Union and the son-in-law of King James I of England. Meanwhile, Emperor Ferdinand sought help from his Habsburg cousins in Spain and from Duke Maximillian of Bavaria, leader of the Catholic League.

The Protestant Union was divided internally by discord between Lutherans and Calvinists and by disagreement whether the Bohemian war was properly a religious or a political struggle, and in mid-1620 it abandoned Frederick. A few months later Bohemian forces were crushed by the army of the Catholic League at the Battle of White Mountain, and Frederick's Palatinate lands were invaded by troops from the Spanish Netherlands. By 1623 the Bohemian revolt was over, and Ferdinand's agents were eradicating Protestantism and political liberties.

The war that had begun in Bohemia spread quickly to Germany, however, largely as a result of Ferdinand's actions in the aftermath of the revolt. In addition to the repression in Bohemia, which frightened German Protestants by its display of the new emperor's fanaticism, Ferdinand also outlawed Count Frederick and other German princes who had supported the revolt and awarded part of Frederick's lands and his electoral vote to Maximillian of Bavaria. These actions raised a sort of constitutional issue, for traditionally, in the case of a prince, outlawry and confiscation could be decided only by the emperor and the other princes together, not by the emperor alone. Even those princes who had felt that

Ferdinand was justified in his policy in Bohemia had to fear the absolutist ambitions implicit in his unilateral action in Germany.

Christian IV, king of Denmark (1588–1648), was a prince of the Holy Roman Empire in his capacity as duke of Holstein. As a Lutheran he opposed the Counter-Reformation; as a German prince he opposed the emperor's political ambitions; as a dynast he aspired to secularized church lands as principalities for his sons. In 1625 he rallied some of the northern princes to oppose the emperor militarily, and in the summer of 1626 he marched south, opening what usually is called the Danish phase of the war. His campaign was supported by Bethlen Gabor, the Protestant prince of Transylvania (in Hungary) who attacked Austria from the east.

The emperor had new resources too, the army of Albrecht von Wallenstein. An adventurer who had made a fortune in land speculation in Bohemia during the repression, Wallenstein had offered to raise a force of twenty-five thousand men at his own expense if he might be allowed to command it. The emperor was delighted to accept the offer, for not only did it give him new resources in the spreading conflict but also a force which was not dependent upon the princes of the Catholic League, who were no more eager than Protestant princes to see a notable increase in the emperor's political strength. Wallenstein's army soon became infamous for living off the land, devastating any area it moved through like a swarm of locusts, but it was effective militarily. Part of this force turned back Bethlen Gabor, while the rest supported the armies of the Catholic League. Christian of Denmark was defeated at the Battle of Lütter am Barenberge in 1626.

Though Christian was forced to retreat, his army was still intact, and fighting continued for another two and a half years. Then Wallenstein thought he saw a new threat developing elsewhere and persuaded the emperor to make a moderate peace, the Treaty of Lübeck of 1629. By this treaty Christian got his lands back in return for a promise not to interfere further in German affairs; in addition, he abandoned his German allies, some of whom were outlawed and their lands given to Wallenstein.

The Treaty of Lübeck appeared to mark the collapse of opposition to the emperor's growing power. That Ferdinand II was determined to use this new power was made clear a few months before the treaty, when in March of 1629 he issued the Edict of Restitution. The Peace of Augsburg of 1555 had prohibited the confiscation of any more church lands, but this provision had proved unenforceable. During the succeeding three quarters of a century, Protestants had seized two archbishoprics, twelve bishoprics, and about one hundred and twenty monasteries. The Edict of Restitution proposed to restore all of these lands to the church and to break up all Protestant sects except Lutheranism, since only it had been given legal status with Catholicism by the Peace of Augsburg.

Concern over the emperor's growing power was not limited to German Protestants and princes, for a Germany firmly under the control of the Habsburgs also would have been a dangerous threat to France. During the 1620s the French crown was occupied with internal Protestant rebellions, but in 1629 the last of them was crushed, and the government at last could undertake a more aggressive foreign policy; having just concluded a costly civil war, it was not yet ready to send French armies across the Rhine, but French diplomacy and French gold were committed freely to persuade the king of Sweden, Gustavus Adolphus (1611–1632) to intervene in Germany. It was this threat which Wallenstein had seen when he advised the emperor to make a generous peace with Denmark.

Gustavus Adolphus was attracted by the role of Protestant champion, and he liked war and the command of armies; moreover, control of the German Baltic coast would have made the Baltic almost wholly a Swedish sea. He concluded a subsidy treaty with France, and in the summer of 1630 he landed an army in north Germany, beginning the Swedish phase of the war. The north German princes did not rally to Gustavus with enthusiasm, however, and a year was spent in negotiations to secure his base of operations and his supply line; but when his campaign began in the late summer of 1631, Gustavus Adolphus proved to be a military genius, and his army cut through Germany like a hot knife through butter. Wallenstein managed to cover the Danube Valley and protect Vienna, but for a year Gustavus Adolphus dominated the battlefields of the empire. Then at Lutzen, in November of 1632, the Swedish king was killed, and fighting was desultory for the next two years.

there was a national basis for the emerging new government remained uncertain, but it appeared to be developing rapidly the administrative and military components of a modern state.

Sweden also underwent an important transformation in the late seventeenth century. Domestic instability resulted from the abdication of Gustavus Adolphus' daughter Christina (1632–1654) and from the rivalry of aristocratic factions, while foreign policy was most notable for unsuccessful wars with Poland and Brandenburg. Toward the end of the seventeenth century, however, King Charles XI (1660–1697) succeeded in breaking the aristocracy's economic power by widespread confiscation of estates and its political power through limitation of the noble council's role. He established a strongly centralized royal government that was supported by highly developed popular national consciousness, and at his death in 1697, Sweden was a nascent modern national state. The royal victory was short-lived, however. Charles XII (1697–1718) had to fight to preserve Swedish control of the Baltic, but Sweden's resources were limited, and the series of wars he engaged in proved disastrous. Early in the eighteenth century Sweden's military power was broken, and an aristocratic resurgence undid the political achievements of Charles XI, so that Sweden declined to the level of a second rank power like the Dutch republic.

England experienced unique national development in the seventeenth century, moving from nascent absolutism through revolution and radical political experiment to restrained and responsible monarchy. When Elizabeth I died in 1603, she left a very delicate political balance to her Scottish cousin James I (1603–1625). The crown's frequent use of parliament had given that body the habit of regular assembly and a sense of institutional importance, especially in matters of money and religion. While it is certainly true that James I did not understand English political practice and that he lacked the Tudor's political skill, in all fairness it must be noted that England's peculiar interaction of king and parliament was without parallel anywhere and that the new king inherited difficult religious and financial problems from his predecessors. Further aggravating matters was the fact that James I, like most monarchs of his time, believed in the divine right of kings and sought to increase royal absolutism at the very time that the maturing parliament was seeking to increase the parliamentary role in government. Quarrels arose quickly, some over taxes and some over the demands of religious radicals called puritans, and these issues were aggravated by James's unpopular effort to achieve a Spanish alliance. In the early 1620s, tension reached a breaking point when parliament impeached some of the king's officers, criticized the proposed Spanish alliance and drafted the Great Protestation defending the parliament's right to debate any matter of government policy. In a rage, James destroyed the protestation and dismissed parliament.

Charles I (1625–1649) got on no better with parliament than had his father, and it presented him with the Petition of Right, a statement of parliamentary authority even more outspoken than the Great Protestation. Through the 1630s Charles attempted to govern without parliament, but severe religious troubles and shortage of money forced him to reconvene it in 1640, and the angry parliamentarians forced surrender after surrender upon him; he sacrificed counselors, agreed to summon parliament every three years, abolished unpopular courts and compromised on religious issues. Still the parliamentarians were not satisfied, and in 1641 when Charles refused further concessions, they raised troops and civil war broke out. After the war ended in victory for parliamentary forces in 1648, extremists wrested control from moderates, enacted radical religious reform and executed the king (January, 1649).

After the execution of Charles I, England attempted a Commonwealth (1649–1660), in theory a republic but in practice a military government run by Oliver Cromwell, a situation recognized in 1653 when Cromwell created a nominated parliament and adopted the title of Lord Protector. But despite almost dictatorial powers, even Cromwell had difficulties with parliamentary ambitions and continuing religious radicalism; when he died in 1658 English government was on no more stable basis than it had been in 1640, and a series of military *coups* led to the restoration of the Stuart monarchy in 1660.

The new king, Charles II (1660–1685), honestly sought compromise at first, but the old royal-parliamentary struggle soon flared again. The king tried financial expedients, including a subsidy treaty with Catholic France, to avoid dependence upon the parliament for money; he showed sympathy for Catholicism, and his brother and

Alleging rather obscure rights of inheritance called devolution, Louis tried to seize the Spanish Netherlands in his wife's name in 1667–1668, and Spain was too weakened to mount a very effective resistance. However, Europe had learned the effectiveness of cooperative resistance during the long struggle against the Habsburgs, and Louis soon found himself faced with a hostile coalition called the Triple Alliance: the Dutch, who feared to have France as a neighbor and commercial rival; the English, who feared the competition their trade might face if the port of Antwerp were in French hands; and the Swedes, whose commercial interests tied them to the Dutch and English. The French king was forced to content himself with a dozen fortified towns that strengthened France's northern borders.

Hardly was the War of Devolution ended when Louis XIV prepared an onslaught against the Dutch. He recognized them as the instigators of the alliance that had frustrated his first efforts and the chief opponents of French northern expansion; he resented their protection of French dissidents who published masses of hostile political tracts in the Netherlands; and he realized that Dutch commercial strength was one of the chief obstacles to French economic growth. By diplomacy and bribery he dismantled the Triple Alliance, concluding treaties with England in 1670 and Sweden in 1672, which drew them into co-operation with France. Then in the summer of 1672 he launched an army of 100,000 men against the Dutch while the English attacked them by sea. The Dutch war went well for France at first, and the southern Dutch provinces were overrun, but again Louis failed to achieve total success. The Dutch flooded their lands, stopping the progress of the French armies, and rallied around William III of Orange. Then France's allies abandoned her or were defeated. Again Louis XIV had to accept a negotiated peace. The Peace of Nimwegen of 1678 restored to the Dutch their conquered territories but allowed France some gains at the expense of Spain: border towns and the whole of the Franche-Comté.

In the 1660s and 1670s Louis XIV had aimed north and had met stiff opposition; about 1680 he began to aim eastward toward Germany. The Peace of Westphalia and subsequent treaties had given Alsace and other Rhineland positions to France, but the boundaries of these concessions were unclear. Louis established special courts, called chambers of reunion, to decide disputed cases and used his troops to enforce decisions. Naturally, French courts deciding

French claims on German lands tended to be prejudiced, and the result was a steady advance which the Germans called peaceful aggression. When the French seized Strasbourg in 1681, war seemed imminent, but the Empire was still weak, and negotiations resulted in a settlement in 1684. Louis kept most of what he had seized, and much of Germany was antagonized.

In the mid-1680s Louis XIV was at the height of his power. He had made significant territorial advances to the north and east, and he was respected and feared throughout Europe. But his neighbors were concerned to check his expansion, and the English and Dutch were fearful of the growth of French commercial power. Louis' policies were evoking general opposition such as had destroyed the Habsburgs. The hatred of Protestant Europe was increased further in 1685 when he revoked the Edict of Nantes; soon Protestant lands were flooded with Huguenot refugees who spread tales of the atrocities that had been committed in the king's name.

In 1686 the emperor, the kings of Spain and Sweden and some German princes concluded the League of Augsburg, aimed at containing Louis XIV. In 1687 the duke of Savoy joined. In 1688 William III of the Netherlands became king of England, and both the Dutch and the English joined the league, which then was called the Grand Alliance. Nine years of fighting resulted in a stalemate, however; Louis could not break the ring formed around him by his enemies, but neither could they crack his defenses and invade France. Peace was made finally at Ryswick in 1697, but it changed little except that France recognized William III as king of England, and the Dutch were permitted to garrison some towns in the Spanish Netherlands as a barrier against France.

The major powers agreed in 1697 to a settlement that settled almost nothing because of the growing crisis of the Spanish succession. The king of Spain was childless, and the Spanish branch of the house of Habsburg was about to die out. The French Bourbons and the Austrian Habsburgs had more or less equally good claims to the inheritance, though both faced legal complications. Because of the trade resources of Spain's colonies as well as possible effects upon the military situation in Europe, both the English and the Dutch felt their interests were involved and wished to prevent the union of Spain with either France or Austria. Thus, in the late 1690s all the powers sought to disengage so as to be free for whatever action their interests dictated when the king of Spain died.

The years immediately following the Peace of Ryswick saw a flurry of diplomatic activity in all the European courts, and the English and Dutch seem to have pursued the concept of a balance of power in which no one state could dominate Europe. Louis XIV understood this desire of the naval powers and was sympathetic to it; he was willing to forego the major inheritance, so long as it did not pass into Austrian hands, if that were the price of peace. For awhile it appeared that the issue might be settled peacefully, for though the Austrians were unwilling to accept a partial inheritance, they would have been helpless before a Franco-Anglo-Dutch agreement. Then a series of disasters befell the negotiators. In 1699 a Bavarian prince who had been chosen as a compromise candidate for the Spanish crown died, and hardly had new partition agreements been reached when the king of Spain died in 1700, leaving a will that prohibited partitions and left the entire inheritance to Louis XIV's grandson, Philip. When Louis XIV, as head of the Bourbon family, accepted the legacy, war with Austria was almost certain, but the English and Dutch were undecided at first. However, rapid French moves to exploit Philip's accession in Spain soon antagonized the naval powers, and in the autumn of 1701 the Grand Alliance was reestablished.

The War of the Spanish Succession was almost a replay of the War of the League of Augsburg except that Spain was allied with embattled France. Again France could not defeat her enemies and they could not invade France, though the brilliant English commander, Marlborough, won the Spanish Netherlands for the allies. Eventually the cost of the war forced the participants to the conference table, and the struggle ended in the Treaties of Utrecht in 1713 and Rastatt in 1714. The Spanish crown and its overseas colonies remained with the new Bourbon king, Philip V (1700–1746), but with the agreement that the Spanish and French crowns never would be joined. The Spanish Netherlands and most of Spain's possessions in Italy went to the Austrian Habsburgs. England made major gains: Newfoundland, Nova Scotia and the Hudsons Bay Territory from France and Gibraltar, Minorca and colonial trading privileges from Spain. The treaties also gave international recognition to the Protestant succession in England and to the royal crowns awarded to the duke of Savoy (Sicily, later exchanged with Spain for Sardinia) and the elector of Brandenburg (Prussia).

Most of all, the Treaties of Utrecht and Rastatt established the balance of power as the new pattern of European international relations. France remained the greatest power in Europe, but no longer could she threaten the security of the entire continent, for it had been proved that alliances could contain her. England had emerged as Europe's greatest naval power, but the Dutch, the French and the Spanish remained important in colonial affairs. Both Austria and Prussia had shown renewed vitality, and both had become significant politically and militarily. In the early eighteenth century western and central Europe counted England, France, Prussia and Austria as major powers with Spain and the Dutch Netherlands as secondary powers, but no one of them was strong enough to establish hegemony in Europe.

About the same time as the War of Spanish Succession, another struggle known as the Great Northern War was effecting equally significant changes in northern and eastern Europe. The basis of this war was the opposition of Russia, Saxony-Poland and Denmark to the Swedish hegemony in the Baltic area; the three powers allied in 1699 and attacked Sweden in 1700. However, the new Swedish king, Charles XII, proved to be a military genius, and he knocked Denmark out of the war, inflicted a humiliating defeat upon the Russians and then subjected the Poles and Saxons to a six-year struggle that ended in their defeat. But Peter the Great of Russia (1689–1725) was determined to continue the struggle until he held a secure harbor on the Baltic, giving access to the west, and during the half-dozen years that Charles was occupied in Poland the Russian armies were improved greatly. Thus, when Charles turned against Russia again, Peter was able to inflict a crushing defeat upon him in 1709, and the Swedish king had to flee southward into Turkey, where he spent several years in exile before returning to Sweden in 1714. Meanwhile, the Russians continued their conquests in the east, while in the west Denmark and Saxony-Poland revived and were joined by Hanover and Prussia. When Charles returned, he fought until his death in 1718, trying to restore the Swedish position, but without success. The war dragged on desultorily for a few more years until peace was made with the western allies in 1720 and with Russia in 1721. The Treaties of Stockholm and Nystadt dismembered the Swedish empire on the Baltic, giving Prussia and Hanover most of the north German lands formerly held by Sweden, while Russia secured most of the eastern Baltic coastal lands except Finland. Thereafter, Sweden was of secondary importance, while Russia became significant in Europe and a factor in the balance of power.

The first few decades of the eighteenth century were years of relative tranquillity, partly because the new balance of power brought international stability and partly because some of the major European powers were distracted by internal developments. In England, William and Mary died without children and were succeeded in 1702 by Mary's sister Anne (1702–1714). As Queen Anne also was without direct heirs, parliament passed a new Act of Settlement conferring the crown upon the related family of Hanover, excluding James Edward, the son of James II. Thus, when Queen Anne died, she was succeeded by the Hanoverian prince, George I (1714–1727), and England faced difficult adjustments. George I, who spoke little English and knew little of the laws and customs of England, was not a popular figure. Moreover, his succession caused a political reversal, for it was the Whigs who most strongly had favored transfer of the crown to him, while many of the Tories were Jacobites (from the Latin *Jacobus*, James) sympathetic to the claims of the Stuarts. Thus, in the new reign the Whigs formed the government instead of the Tories whom Queen Anne had favored. In addition, England was indebted heavily from the recent wars. Finally, the new government met serious crises at the very outset: in 1715 there was an armed rebellion in Scotland in support of the Stuarts, and in 1720 there was a financial crash and a scandal concerning illicit profiteering by members of the government. Out of this turmoil emerged a Whig government headed by Sir Robert Walpole, England's first real prime minister (who governed 1726–1742). Walpole concentrated upon pacification of the Tories and Jacobites, economic expansion, exploitation of colonial resources and retirement of war debts; the death of George I and the accession of George II (1727–1760) made little difference to these policies, so for many years foreign affairs held a subordinate place in English government.

At the same time France faced similar problems. Louis XIV died in 1715, at the age of seventy-seven, having outlived both his son and his grandson; he was succeeded by his five-year-old great-grandson, Louis XV (1715–1774), and France faced another long regency. Like England, the French government suffered financial strain from the wars, and a crash and scandal soon followed when a speculative financial scheme failed in 1720. As in England, the new government was insecure; young Louis XV's health was uncertain, and it was feared that if he should die Philip V of Spain might claim the French throne in defiance of the Peace of Utrecht and catapult Europe into another major war. Thus the regent, the duke of Orléans (governed 1715–1723), and after him Louis XV's first minister, Cardinal Fleury (governed 1726–1743), were inclined toward an unaggressive foreign policy and agreement with France's former enemies while encouraging economic development.

These programs of peace and economic growth also had their parallels in Prussia and Russia. In Prussia King Frederick William I (1713–1740) ran his state with what amounted to military discipline, rebuilt his treasury, and expanded his army to 83,000 men, an impressive force for a country with only two and a half million people. In Russia, Peter the Great launched a vast scheme of reforms that included breaking the power of the nobility in government and substituting a centralized and bureaucratized administration dependent upon the Czar, reduction of the independence of the Russian Church, and encouragement of commerce, manufacturing and education along western lines. Many of the Czar's reforms were superficial, and some proved impractical, but at his death in 1725 Russia had a modern army and navy, a revitalized economy, and a much stronger government than she had known previously. Peter's immediate successors were undistinguished rulers, but the effects of Peter's reforms and the influence of imported German advisors continued the modernization and strengthening of Russia as a great European power.

While the early eighteenth century was more tranquil than the seventeenth century, it was not unmarked by war. In 1717 and 1718 an attempt by Spain to seize Sardinia and Sicily resulted in joint military action by England, Holland, France and Austria to maintain the Treaties of Utrecht and Rastatt; but the affair was negotiated in 1720, and with a few territorial exchanges in Italy, peace was restored. Another conflict arose in the mid-1730s, the War of the Polish Succession, which set Austria and Russia against France, Spain and Sardinia. The war began in a conflict between French and Austro-Russian interests in Poland, but Russia quickly occupied Poland, and most of the later fighting took place in Italy between French and Austrian forces. Consequently, the treaty that ended the war not only left Austro-Russian influence dominant in Poland but also confirmed the Austrians in much of north Italy while recognizing a Spanish prince as king of the Two Sicilies (the island of Sicily and southern Italy up to Naples). But these struggles of the early eighteenth century did not spread to engulf all Europe as had earlier wars; the balance of power appeared to have established an equilibrium.

Toward the middle of the eighteenth century the issue of colonial supremacy emerged as one of the paramount questions in Europe. The Peace of Utrecht had given the English important trading privileges in Spain's American colonies, of which the most profitable was the *Asiento,* a thirty-year contract for the supply of slaves. In the late 1730s two factors made the situation explosive: as the *Asiento* neared expiration, a growing rapprochement between France and Spain seemed to threaten that France might replace England as a licensed supplier to the Spanish colonies, and the development of a more effective Spanish colonial coast guard threatened the illicit but very profitable smuggling that the English had built up around their legitimate trade. These threats evoked in England a faction within the Whig party that clamored for war with Spain and France, and in 1739 Walpole lost control of the situation. An English captain named Jenkins was caught smuggling by the colonial coast guard, and he and his crew were handled very roughly. At some point in the fray the Spaniards cut off Jenkins' ear, and he brought it back to England pickled. This atrocity story spread rapidly and provided the war party the issue it needed to overcome Walpole's objections. In 1739 parliament voted for war, and the ensuing struggle, which lasted until 1748, was known as the War of Jenkins' Ear.

About the same time, an equally serious issue was developing in central Europe around the question of the Austrian succession. Emperor Charles VI (1711–1740), who had no sons, hoped to see his lands pass intact to his daughter, Maria Theresa (1740–1780). This arrangement was set forth in a document called the Pragmatic Sanction, and the emperor succeeded in obtaining endorsement of it from several European governments. Despite the Pragmatic Sanction, however, there were many diverse legal traditions in the Habsburg lands, and a female succession was likely to be disputed in at least some areas. In fact, no sooner was the emperor dead than the king of Prussia, Frederick II (1740–1786), claimed and occupied the rich province of Silesia, triggering the War of the Austrian Succession.

The two wars became linked when France, already engaged against England at sea, joined Prussia against Austria in 1741, and a year later England allied with Austria. In central Europe the war raged for eight years, interrupted by numerous truces and short-lived treaties, but by 1745 a pattern was clear: Prussia held Silesia and could not be pried out, but Austria was able to fend off her other enemies; this was the basis of the Treaty of Aix-la-Chapelle of 1748. The colonial war went badly for England except in North America, where colonial forces took the great French fortress of Louisbourg at the mouth of the St. Lawrence, and military reverses forced Walpole's retirement in 1742. Then in 1745 another great rebellion broke out in Scotland in favor of the Stuart pretender, Charles Edward, son of James Edward, and for nearly a year badly needed English forces were tied down. At the Peace of Aix-la-Chapelle England had to give up even her small gains in North America to get back the important town of Madras that France had taken from her in India, so the war had accomplished nothing. Probably the only power satisfied with the Peace of Aix-la-Chapelle was Prussia, which retained Silesia. Both Austria and England were humiliated while France remained eager to rebuild the colonial position she had enjoyed before the Peace of Utrecht. Consequently, the years immediately following 1748 were not so much a time of peace as a time of preparation for renewed war.

The chief area of colonial rivalry had shifted to North America, where vigorous French expansion threatened the future of the English colonies. Solidly established on the St. Lawrence and the lower Mississippi, the French were moving into the Ohio and upper Mississippi valleys, building forts and trading posts. The chief routes of communication in North America were the river valleys, and west of the Appalachian Mountains everything drained toward the Mississippi; hence, a French line following the St. Lawrence, the Ohio and the Mississippi threatened to limit the English colonies to the narrow coastal plain between the mountains and the Atlantic. Clashes were frequent, and in 1755 war broke out between the French and the English in North America, providing a catalyst to the plans of Maria Theresa's brilliant chancellor, Count Kaunitz.

Having concluded that Austria was not strong enough to defeat Prussia alone, Kaunitz had proposed an encircling alliance, and agreements had been reached with Czarina Elizabeth of Russia (1741–1762) and some of the German princes. However, Kaunitz also desired to reverse traditional patterns and bring France into the coalition against Prussia, and this proved more difficult. Kaunitz knew the French court, and he succeeded in building a pro-Austrian party that included the king's mistress, Madame de Pompadour, but the French government was hesitant. However, the undeclared Anglo-French war that had begun in North America brought Kaunitz' plans to fruition. Fearful of a French attack upon Hanover, King George II signed a neutrality treaty with Frederick II of Prussia in January of 1756, and this apparent abandonment by Prussia caused great indignation at Versailles; in May France signed the alliance Kaunitz had been seeking, and a month later fighting between France and England broke out in Europe. Frederick II followed these moves carefully, and in 1756 he seized the initiative with a late summer campaign that occupied Saxony and defeated an Austrian army. Thus, in the mid-1750s a diplomatic revolution had taken place, and in an effort to break the stalemate of the old balance of power the Seven Years War was begun with changed partners: France, Austria and Russia against England and Prussia.

On the continent Frederick II again won brilliant victories, but he also suffered defeats, and in the long run his resources could not match those of his enemies. When the new king of England, George III (1760–1820), decided to stop English subsidies in 1760, Frederick was in serious trouble, and only luck saved him from disaster. In January of 1762 Czarina Elizabeth died, and her successor, Peter III (January to July, 1762), was a great admirer of Frederick. Though he was deposed a few months later, Peter reigned long enough to pull Russia out of the war, and freed of the Russian threat, Frederick again defeated the Austrians in the summer of 1762. As negotiations between the English and the French made it likely that France, too, soon would quit the war, Austria was forced to accept failure. By the Treaty of Hubertusburg (1763) Prussia kept Silesia, an area that increased her size and population between a third and a half.

In the colonial war the English, under the brilliant political leadership of William Pitt, soon established their superiority. English command of the sea left French colonial forces isolated, and in both North America and India they were defeated; the Battle of Quebec delivered all of French Canada to the English, and the capture of Pondichéry destroyed the French position in India. By the Treaty of Paris of 1763, France ceded to England all of Canada, the eastern side of the Mississippi basin and positions in the West Indies and Africa. Spain ceded Florida to England, in return for which she received Louisiana from France and the restoration of the positions in Cuba that the English had conquered. Almost wiped out of North America and Africa, France was in little better condition in India; she was allowed to retain only two unfortified trading stations. England took the rest.

Despite the mid-eighteenth century wars, the balance of power had survived. Although England and Prussia emerged somewhat strengthened, Austria and France somewhat weakened and Russia somewhat more involved in European affairs, after 1763 there appeared no greater danger than there had been in 1713 of the domination of the entire continent by a single power. That the value of the balance of power was recognized by the European governments was demonstrated in eastern Europe early in the 1770s. The once great monarchy of Poland had been in a state of decline for a century, a pawn in the schemes of its neighbors; after the Seven Years War the dominant influences were Russia and Prussia, alleging protection of Greek Orthodox and Protestant minorities against the Catholic majority. A fanatically Catholic anti-Russian group, the Confederation of Bar, soon emerged and won French support, and civil war broke out. The Turks, with French encouragement, chose this moment to attack Russia, and there appeared a real danger that the Polish-Turkish question might embroil the great powers in a new general war; this danger increased when Russian victories over the Turks threatened Russian occupation of the lower Danube to the detriment of Austrian interests, and Austria seemed about to intervene. At this point Frederick the Great, fearful that a general conflict would destroy Prussia, proposed a compromise to preserve the peace and maintain the balance of power. Russia would abandon her Turkish conquests and be compensated with Polish lands, gains not objectionable to Austria; to compensate for the increased Russian strength and westward advance, Austria and Prussia also would take slices of Poland. Thus, a sacrifice to the balance of power, Poland lost about a third of her territory and half her inhabitants. This unhappy solution to eastern European rivalries set a precedent; in 1792 Poland was partitioned a second time, and in a third partition in 1795 she disappeared altogether.

The late 1770s and early 1780s witnessed a sort of epilogue to the eighteenth century colonial struggles, the American War of Independence. Questions of political authority and powers of taxation that long had been irritants in Britain's relations with her North American colonies became serious issues after 1763. The territories that Britain had won in the Seven Years War had lengthened enormously the colonial frontiers that had to be defended against Indian attacks and the shipping lanes that had to be protected. Not unreasonably, the British government expected the colonies to bear some of the costs. The colonists, while happy to be relieved of the French menace, had economic problems of their own, for some of which they blamed crown policy, and they had seen enough blundering of the colonial administration that they were unwilling to accept further taxes without some voice in their expenditure. Ever more violent colonial protests and British attempts at compulsion grew into open fighting in 1775, which led a year later to a declaration of independence by the colonies. Almost immediately France took an interest in the affair.

France's position was delicate. Her resources strained by the costly mid-century wars, she could not afford to plunge recklessly into a new struggle with England. On the other hand, a colonial rebellion that might humiliate the British, weaken their Atlantic position and transfer important colonial trade to France could not fail to interest the government of Louis XVI (1774–1792). The French crown chose to remain neutral officially while giving the colonies large amounts of covert aid. A dummy company was set up, which sold arms to the rebels (the weapons actually financed by the French treasury), while the French government waited to see what the colonists could do against the British. It was not a long wait.

The British plan for 1777 called for dividing the colonies; General Burgoyne was to move down the Hudson Valley from Canada while Lord Howe was to ascend the valley from New York, a campaign that would have isolated New England. But inexplicably Howe turned aside for an attack upon Philadelphia and the Delaware Valley instead. Meanwhile, the colonial General Gates used his Indian allies to annihilate Burgoyne's scouts, and Burgoyne's army, alone and blinded, was left stumbling in near wilderness; after two engagements Burgoyne surrendered at Saratoga in October of 1777. That winter the colonies signed the Articles of Confederation creating the United States of America, and in February of 1778 France signed treaties of alliance and commerce with the new government. Of course this meant war between France and England, and the following year Spain joined in on the basis of a French promise to help retake Gibraltar and Florida.

Aside from such famous volunteers as Lafayette and de Kalb, Franco-Spanish overt assistance to the colonialists was chiefly in the form of naval support until Rochambeau arrived with six thousand French troops in 1780, but even the naval support was very significant. It helped assure the safe arrival of essential supplies, and it played a crucial role in the last campaign of the war. British strategy was founded upon command of the coasts, her fleets embarking and disembarking troops where they wished while colonial forces had to march great distances overland. After the disaster at Saratoga, the British attempted to overpower the southern states; Clinton took Charleston in 1780, and in 1781 Cornwallis fortified himself in Yorktown while awaiting support from the British fleet, preparing to hold off the forces of Washington, Lafayette and Rochambeau, which were concentrating around him. The arrival of Admiral de Grasse with a French fleet upset the British plans, for de Grasse blocked the seaward approaches to Yorktown, and Cornwallis was bottled up so that the British fleet could neither reinforce his army nor evacuate it. In October of 1781 Cornwallis surrendered with seven thousand men, and in the Treaty of Paris of 1783 Britain recognized the independence of the United States.

It is surprising how little immediate effect the success of the American War of Independence had upon the balance of power. The stability that had developed in Europe in the eighteenth century had spread around the shores of the Atlantic and was not upset by an armed conflict and a political readjustment. Trade with England, interrupted by the war, soon picked up again, and French hopes for a revival of French influence on the Atlantic came to nothing. The new nation, beset with economic and political problems in the aftermath of independence, exerted no great force on the international scene. Calm returned and the eighteenth century balance of power appeared secure for another decade until it was swept away by the new forces unleashed in the French revolution.

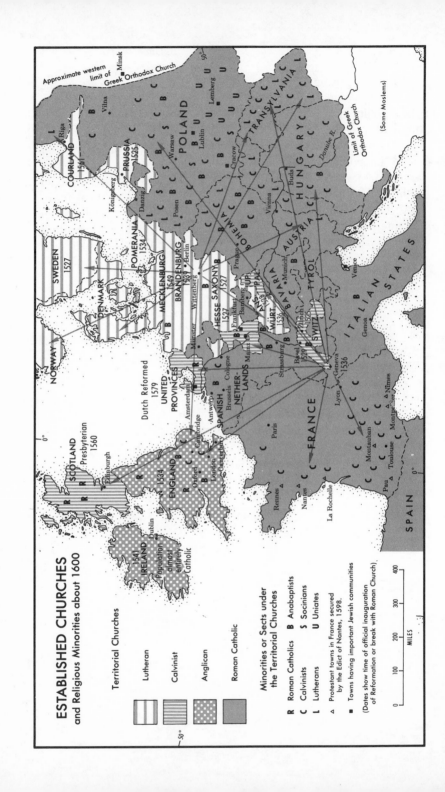

ESTABLISHED CHURCHES
and Religious Minorities about 1600

Territorial Churches

Lutheran

Calvinist

Anglican

Roman Catholic

Minorities or Sects under the Territorial Churches

R Roman Catholics   B Anabaptists
C Calvinists   S Socinians
L Lutherans   U Uniates

△ Protestant towns in France secured by the Edict of Nantes, 1598.

■ Towns having important Jewish communities

(Dates show time of official inauguration of Reformation or break with Roman Church).

Approximate western limit of Greek Orthodox Church

Limit of Greek Orthodox Church

(Some Moslems)

| 0 | 100 | 200 | 300 | 400 |

MILES

SWEDEN 1527

NORWAY

DENMARK

SCOTLAND Presbyterian 1560

Edinburgh

IRELAND 1541 Population almost entirely Catholic

Dublin

ENGLAND 1534

Oxford   Cambridge

London

Dutch Reformed 1579 **UNITED PROVINCES**

Amsterdam

SPANISH NETHER-LANDS

Antwerp   Brussels

Cologne   Münster

Paris

Rennes

Nantes

La Rochelle

FRANCE

Montauban

Pau   Toulouse

Nîmes

Montpellier

Lyon

SPAIN

COURLAND 1561

Riga

Vilna

Minsk

PRUSSIA 1525

Königsberg

POMERANIA 1534

Danzig

POLAND

Posen

Warsaw

Lublin

Cracow

Lemberg

TRANSYLVANIA

HUNGARY

Buda

Danube R.

Vienna

BOHEMIA

Prague

MECKLENBURG 1549

BRANDENBURG 1539

Berlin

Wittenberg

HESSE-SAXONY 1527

Frankfurt

Bamberg

BAVARIA

Munich

AUSTRIA

TYROL

SWITZ.

Zürich

Basel 1529

Geneva 1536

Strassburg

Mainz

WÜRT. 1536

ITALIAN STATES

Venice

Genoa

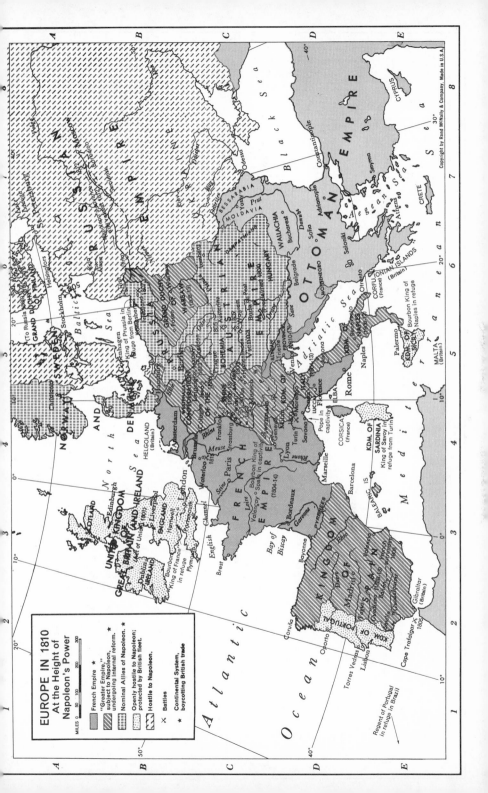

EUROPE IN 1810
At the Height of Napoleon's Power

MILES 0   50   100   200   300

French Empire ★

"Greater Empire," subject to Napoleon, undergoing internal reform. ★

Nominal Allies of Napoleon. ★

Openly hostile to Napoleon; protected by British fleet.

Hostile to Napoleon.

✕ Battles

* Continental System, boycotting British trade

Copyright by Rand McNally & Company. Made in U.S.A.

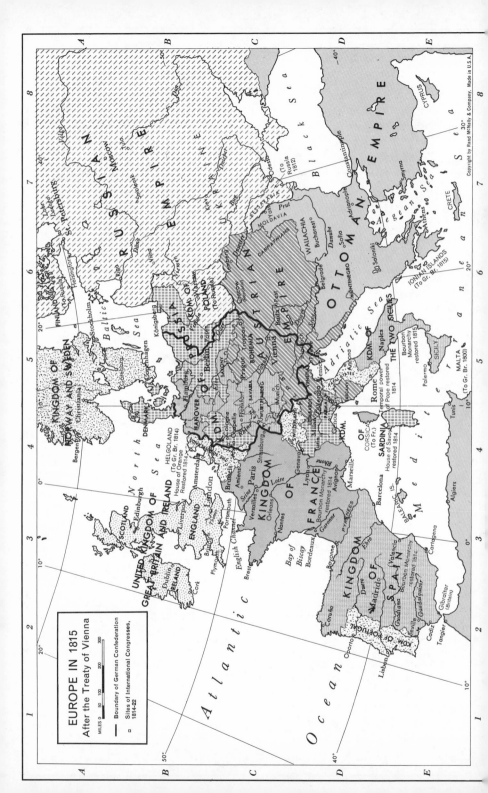

EUROPE IN 1815
After the Treaty of Vienna

MILES 0 50 100 200 300

——— Boundary of German Confederation

▫ Sites of International Congresses, 1814-22

Copyright by Rand McNally & Company. Made in U.S.A.

FRANCE
SWITZERLAND
AUSTRIAN EMPIRE
HUNGARY

Geneva

1859

TRENTINO

CARNIOLA

LOMBARDY
SAVOY
Legnano • Milan
Chambery
Novara • Magenta
Turin • Pavia Solferino
PIEDMONT
Genoa
Parma
PARMA
To France 1860
KINGDOM
1860
NICE
Nice • Monaco
To Tuscany 1847

VENETIA 1866
Verona
Villafranca
Mantua
Venice
Trieste • Fiume
CROATIA

Modena
Bologna Ravenna
MODENA
ROMAGNA
LUCCA
Florence San Marino
Pisa
Leghorn TUSCANY
1860 Siena
PAPAL
UMBRIA STATES
1860

Zara DALMATIA

OTTOMAN
EMPIRE

Ragusa

42°

CORSICA
Ajaccio To France
SARDINIA

ELBA

Adriatic Sea

ABRUZZI
PONTECORVO
KINGDOM
BENEVENTO
Bari
To Papal States Naples Salerno Brindisi
CAMPANIA APULIA
Otranto

Rome
1870

SARDINIA

Cagliari

Tyrrhenian
Sea

OF THE

CALABRIA

Mediterranean Sea

TWO

Messina Reggio
Palermo
SICILY
SICILIES
1860 Syracuse

PANTELLERIA

UNIFICATION OF ITALY

| 0 | 50 | 100 | 150 |
MILES

TUSCANY	Independent states in 1815
- - - - - - - -	Northern boundary of Kingdom of Italy, 1866-1919
1859	Joined by plebiscite with Sardinia
1860	Joined by revolution and plebiscite with Sardinia, to form Kingdom of Italy, proclaimed 1861
1866, 1870	Joined with Kingdom of Italy

12°

Chapter 18

Man, God, and Reason

During the eighteenth century, Europe experienced an intellectual revolution, the twin bases of which were skepticism toward accepted beliefs and a mechanical interpretation of both natural and human phenomena. Drawing heavily upon the discoveries and speculations of their immediate predecessors, eighteenth century intellectuals undertook to reexamine critically the very foundations of European society. Newton's description of a mechanistic universe was a major influence in this revolution, as was Descartes' skepticism, the doubting attitude which he advocated as essential to scientific inquiry; but in addition to the scientific revolution, eighteenth century Europe also had to assimilate the impact of foreign cultures and the discrediting of many of its beliefs concerning its own history.

Europeans traveled widely in the seventeenth century, often writing accounts of their travels which posed disturbing contradictions to Europe's ethnocentric confidence and sense of superiority, and after 1700 these were supplemented by fictitious voyages in which imaginary peoples and societies further challenged western values. Europeans tended to become self-critical, and eighteenth century literature became studded with idealized types, of which the simplest was the noble savage, derived from the American Indian; the idealizations exemplified the virtues of simplicity, honesty and loyalty which European writers found lacking in their own culture, and it was a short step from such idealized accounts of real people and societies to the invention of peoples and societies whose governments and morals made the Christian monarchies of Europe appear barbarous.

Religion also was challenged by the impact of foreign cultures and by European speculation stimulated by that impact. In the seventeenth century most Europeans were convinced, on the basis of Biblical chronology, that the world had been created about 4000 B.C., and it came as a shock to find that the Egyptians, the Babylonians and the Chinese traced their history back beyond that date; despite the tendency to discount the reliability of such "heathen" traditions, by 1700 confidence in Biblical chronology had weakened greatly. Moreover, study of Egyptian records revealed the striking similarity of Egyptian and Hebrew beliefs and raised the disturbing possibility that the Jewish prophets had derived many of their ideas from Egypt rather than from direct divine inspiration. Since early modern Christians of all varieties tended to take their Bible literally, the implications of derivative prophecy were distressing, and such problems were compounded by studies of fossils which made it clear that early life-forms had disappeared and new ones had appeared during the earth's history, neither phenomenon accounted for in the Bible.

Scholars as well as travelers and scientists contributed to the growing skepticism concerning the historical accuracy of Scripture. In the last years of the seventeenth century, Pierre Bayle's *Historical and Critical Dictionary* demonstrated the implausibility of some Biblical tales, ridiculed the moral examples in others and generally treated religious doctrine as ludicrous superstition. At the same time, Catholic scholars were preparing massive editions of the lives of the saints, trying to sift truth from myth and to establish the authenticity of texts; inevitably, the textual criticism of documents that they developed, summed up in Jean Mabilon's *De Re Diplomatica* (1681), soon were applied to Scripture itself. By 1679 Richard Simon, a Catholic priest and Biblical scholar, published *A Critical History of the Old Testament,* and this was followed in the 1680s and 1690s by his *Critical History of the Text of the New Testament* and comparable works on other versions of and commentaries upon the New Testament. With the best of intentions, a desire to establish a reliable text, he proved transpositions, interpolations and omissions, and skeptics used his work to deny the value of the Bible as revealed truth.

Under the impact of such challenges, large numbers of the European intelligentsia lost their belief in the traditional doctrines of Christianity, and many who tried to defend the old faith, such as John Locke in England and Malebranche and Fénélon in France, did so on the basis of the reasonableness of God as the architect of the Newtonian world-machine rather than on the basis of dogmatic theology; even Christianity's supporters were finding it difficult to accept their faith's revelation and miracles as more than superstitions or symbolic tales for the instruction of the ignorant and were trying to justify themselves on rational and secular grounds. This intellectual revolution had enormous implications, for rationalism and secularism left no possibility of justifying governments on religious grounds, and such attitudes set the intellectuals ever farther apart from the great mass of the population, which was reacting to the formality and coldness of the state churches with popular pietistic and revivalist movements.

Another basis for novel opinions developed out of seventeenth century England, where tumultuous political development inspired new reflections upon society and politics. In 1651 Thomas Hobbes' *Leviathan* sketched a purely secular and naturalistic basis for ethics and politics, proposing the theory that in a state of nature anarchy would prevail and life would be nasty, brutish and short. Hobbes suggested that government was originated by men seeking security of life and property. Hobbes' idea that government was initiated by men through a social contract rather than instituted by God was not as shocking as his conclusions that the state must have complete domination over churches and, with few exceptions, over all aspects of the subjects' lives if the society were not to revert to the anarchy of the state of nature. Obviously Hobbes' thought was conditioned by the political troubles of England in his day, but it remains notable for its purely secular postulates, and his conceptions of the state of nature and the social contract were very influential.

Secular and rational approaches to man and society were continued by John Locke, who was convinced that all understanding derives of experience. Rejecting theories of innate ideas, he asserted that a child was born with its mind blank and that experience wrote upon it, a conception that demanded new analyses of man as a social and moral animal. In considering politics Locke also posited the idea of a state of nature, but because of his concept of human psychology it was a different condition than that suggested by Hobbes. Locke felt that even in the state of nature man was bound by natural law interpreted by reason and experience and that men always established general principles for the safeguard of life and property, conventions that created society; this idea introduced an intermediate step in the agreement between subject and monarch, and repudiation of the monarch did not dissolve the social contract but only left society to make new arrangements for its governance. Because Locke's *Two Treatises on Government* appeared in 1690, because it was an easy step to interpret parliament as the voice of society and because he lauded William III, the author has been accused of acting as apologist for the Glorious Revolution, but his political ideas seem to have been worked out well before that event and to have proceeded from his basic philosophy.

Locke was read widely in the eighteenth century, and translations made both his *Two Treatises on Government* and his *Essay Concerning Human Understanding* accessible to continental readers; he became for psychology and philosophy what Newton was to physical science, a guide to fruitful areas of investigation and the architect of new conceptions. Though always moderate himself, he provided potent intellectual weapons to those who mounted an ever more aggressive attack upon tradition, and those who sought only security and stability were drawn into this attack. Locke's summation of the bases of social order as security of life, liberty and property is a fair outline of what many articulate men were concerned to protect in the early eighteenth century, and threats seemed to come less from a few intellectual innovators than from old institutions. For two centuries, sectarian quarrels and dynastic struggles had kept Europe immersed in civil conflict and international war; if life, liberty and property were to be protected by reasonable laws, it appeared that the claims of the theologians and the ambitions of dynastic monarchs would have to be restrained.

The leadership of England in the development of secular, rational and humane thought was founded on Newton and Locke, and it was reinforced by writers on both sides of the channel during the second quarter of the eighteenth century, but by the middle of the century intellectual supremacy had passed to France. The early writers of the French Enlightenment acknowledged their debt to the English, as in Voltaire's *Elements of the Philosophy of Newton*, but Paris quickly became the center of the new philosophy. The scope of the Enlightenment and the range of individual variation from one writer to another make generalizations difficult, but some common positions can be sketched briefly. At the foundation of most Enlightenment thought was a mechanistic view of a world governed by natural law that was discoverable by reason. Such as assumption implied that not only natural science but all aspects of life were integrated in a vast mechanical scheme such as Newton's laws of gravitation. Skepticism toward traditional beliefs and authorities was reinforced by the rapid advances in natural studies produced by the scientific method and by contemplation of exciting new possibilities in human and social studies; by comparison with the natural sciences, the social sciences were still primitive, but they had become empirical and inductive, and they had developed methods that could be used to judge traditional institutions and authorities by new standards.

Most writers of the Enlightenment shared the expectation that great discoveries would continue to be made, that reason would uncover further natural laws and that much that remained mysterious would become explicable. In this context, mysteries were but natural phenomena as yet unexplained, and miracles were fanciful explanations of natural phenomena, not only inaccurate but also an offense to human intelligence. The confidence in right reason and experience as tools leading ultimately to complete understanding was almost limitless. Few figures of the Enlightenment asserted atheism, however, for they still required a creator for their world-machine, an architect or engineer whose designs were the foundation of natural law, but their rejection of the miraculous generally meant a denial of concepts of an afterlife of salvation or damnation. Life no longer was a mere preparation, the world a vale of tears; life was reality, the world the place where fulfilment or frustration had to be found, and it began to be perceived that happiness in itself might be a valid goal in life.

Reluctant to affirm a thoroughgoing atheism, most eighteenth century intellectuals adopted a religious creed called deism, characterized as natural religion. Deists accepted a God, usually impersonal, who had fabricated the universe, and they accepted a set of morals that God had engraved on the hearts of all men. To some extent deism was a reaction against the arid arguments of Christian theologians and the horrors of persecution and religious wars that had resulted from Christian dissension; to some extent it was the outgrowth of the impact of foreign cultures which showed common religious tenets in many faiths and of the new science which stressed the orderliness of the physical universe and the unity of mankind. God was assumed to be rational, not capricious, so the deists had no patience with miracles, which would require the suspension of natural law, or with metaphysical revelation, which claimed knowledge of God other than through understanding His natural laws. Comparative religious studies convinced the deists that their tenets were the core of all the world's religions and that the varieties of religious belief were but superstitious error derived from false claims of particular revelation.

It was not angry Christian theologians but the Scotch skeptic, David Hume, who challenged these opinions most effectively; his *Natural History of Religion,* published in the late 1750s, attacked the fundamental assumption of the advocates of natural religion by denying that men allowed themselves to be guided by reason or that there was any universality of human motivation. Hume contended that reason was not and could not be a guide to principles but only a tool for devising the means of gratifying irrational impulses and desires which varied among individuals and societies; thus he negated, to his own satisfaction at least, the whole concept of rational natural religion and, incidentally, challenged the very basis of Enlightenment rationalism and its derivative structure of universal morality and self-evident truths.

Another common element of Enlightenment thought was optimism. This attitude was encouraged by the great scientific progress that had resulted from the new methodology, but its roots ran much deeper. On the one hand, the great German scientist, Leibnitz, was convinced of the existence of a beneficent deity, and his endorsement of optimism had some influence through his popularizer, Christian Wolff. But in a broader sense, the general optimism of eighteenth century intellectuals derived from their convictions about the nature of the universe. They believed firmly that all phenomena were explicable through natural law, and they were convinced that in reason they had found the key to understanding natural law; hence, they fully anticipated that further application of reason would make both the physical and social world more explicable and more predictable and that men would be able to plan their lives and their societies to avoid catastrophies. Some of the more superficial aspects of this optimism, especially the idea of a beneficent deity, were satirized brilliantly by Voltaire in his *Candide*, but general confidence in human progress continued to be characteristic of most eighteenth century intellectuals.

It was in specific applications to man and society that Enlightenment thought had its most far-reaching effects, in such concepts as the theory of natural rights. Grounded originally in principles of natural law, as time passed the theory of natural rights was justified more and more on the basis of empiricism, on the conviction that history showed that security of life, liberty and property was essential to the stability of society and the development of the potential of humanity. Fused with the older theories of the state of nature and the social contract, the doctrine of natural rights provided a standard against which to measure the performance of governments. To the extent that a government contributed to the greater security of life, liberty and property, it was fulfilling its function; when corruption of its purposes, as through subservience to dynastic ambition, for instance, weakened the security in which these basic rights were held, to that extent it failed to fulfill its purpose. Implicit, of course, was a notion of the right of revolution.

An important corollary of these ideas was the conception of society based on individuals who were born free and equal, in contrast to older notions of society based upon family units enmeshed in a web of divinely ordained social inequality and obligations to church and king. By born free and equal, the eighteenth century writers understood free to mean the individual's right to choose his own goals and equal to mean that all started life with minds the blank slate on which experience wrote; they quite accepted that qualitative differences of experience would produce human inequality, and they were not disturbed much by that so long as inequality was not institutionalized in law. Perhaps the best summation of the socio-political thought of the Enlightenment, natural rights and social contract with vague deistic overtones, is provided by the American Declaration of Independence of 1776:

> We hold these truths to be self-evident, that all men are created equal, that they are endowed by their Creator with certain unalienable Rights, that among these are Life, Liberty and the pursuit of Happiness.—That to secure these rights, Governments are instituted among Men, deriving their just powers from the consent of the governed,—That whenever any Form of Government becomes destructive of these ends, it is the Right of the People to alter or abolish it. . . .

The substitution of "pursuit of happiness" for Locke's "property" usually is attributed to the existence among the Americans of radical elements who were seeking to weaken property rights and would not agree to any endorsement of them in the declaration, but the idea that the "pursuit of happiness" was a natural right certainly was deep-rooted in Enlightenment philosophy and existed independent of the political maneuvers surrounding the framing of the Declaration of Independence.

Perhaps the most effective demonstration of the scope and variety of Enlightenment thought is provided by a brief survey of some of its leading advocates. In France, one of the earliest of these was Baron Montesquieu. As a young man, Montesquieu embarked upon the judicial career traditional in his family, but he soon turned to writing, and in 1721 he published his *Persian Letters;* the literary device of letters purporting to be written by two refined Persians traveling in Europe provided an opportunity for amusing but merciless satire of church, state and society in France, and the book became very popular. It was the first of the devastatingly witty works of social satire that were to typify the eighteenth century French rationalist critics who called themselves *philosophes.* In the 1730s he published some reflections upon Roman history, and then in 1748 appeared his greatest work, *The Spirit of the Laws;* a comparison of various constitutional patterns, this work demonstrated the sociological and anthropological relativism that was to transform the study of history and social science in the eighteenth century. The concepts of the separation of powers and checks and balances that Montesquieu presented in his idealized analysis of English practices proved very influential upon later writers of constitutions.

Of the same generation as Montesquieu was Voltaire, a notary's son who produced his first successful play in his mid-20s. A penchant for writing political satires resulted in occasional arrests and frequent exile from Paris; three years spent in England during his early 30s had a strong influence upon him, for he came to admire England's toleration of free thought and general absence of censorship. This influence showed itself in 1733, when he published his *Philosophical Letters on the English* and behind the pretense of comments on English society attacked the church and government of France. Official reaction to the *Philosophical Letters* was violent; the work was seized and burned, and the author escaped arrest only by another flight out of the country.

The continued development of Voltaire's critical spirit was marked in the late 1730s by the appearance of the *Elements of the Philosophy of Newton* and a *Treatise on Metaphysics,* which endorsed the value of experience and reason and renewed the attack upon religion. In 1751 he had to leave Paris again, and after sojourning for two years with Frederick the Great of Prussia, he settled near Geneva in a house that was in France but very near the Swiss border, in case escape should prove necessary. There he spent the last quarter century of his life, entertaining friends and writing voluminously, except for a final visit to Paris, where he died in 1778 at the age of eighty-four. During these last years he produced masses of letters, essays and lampoons attacking the establishment in church and state with bitter sarcasm, denouncing oppression and ridiculing the extremes of other rationalists. Some of the best of these efforts were his many contributions to the *Great Encyclopedia,* which involved him with the next generation of Enlightenment writers, who dominated the third quarter of the eighteenth century, and especially with the encyclopedia's general editor, Diderot.

Denis Diderot, a craftsman's son, first appeared on the literary scene in the mid-1740s with a translation of Shaftesbury's *Inquiry Concerning Virtue and Merit;* this was followed by his own *Philosophical Thoughts, The Promenade of a Sceptic* and a *Letter on the Blind,* the latter an assertion of man's total dependence upon his sense. The vigor of his skeptical criticism cost him three months in prison, but after his release he undertook a massive and even more daring work, the *Great Encyclopedia.* A Parisian publisher, André-François LeBreton, had conceived the idea of publishing a translation of the popular Chambers' *Cyclopedia,* but the project quickly grew into an original multivolume collection surveying the whole range of human knowledge, and as Diderot had some reputation as a translator and author, he was drawn into the venture, first as a staff writer and then as general editor. The series eventually comprised seventeen volumes of text and eleven volumes of illustrations, and most of France's great eighteenth century writers contributed to it. This encyclopedia reflected the unorthodox views of the *philosophes,* and it soon became a center of controversy; there were two attempts at governmental suppression in the 1750s, and in the 1760s Diderot discovered that the worried publisher, LeBreton, was censoring some of his more extreme articles. Nonetheless, the *Great Encyclopedia* emerged as a statement of faith of eighteenth century rationalism; more than a compendium of information, it was an arsenal of weapons and ammunition for the critics of eighteenth century society. Its explanations of science, its easy assumption of universally valid, simple mechanical laws of nature and its brilliant list of contributors offered reason, optimism and confidence to critics of the world as it was, and it became an enormous success. Published by subscription in advance, the work was issued first in fifteen hundred, then two thousand and finally four thousand copies, and hardly was it completed in 1772 than reissues and pirated editions began to appear; despite the protests of the establishment, the publisher and his associates made something in the range of four million dollars profit from the venture, for the spirit and the content of the *Great Encyclopedia* had caught the cosmopolitan and iconoclastic temper of the eighteenth century literate public.

One of the most direct influences of the Enlightenment was its impact upon progressive rulers who admired the *philosophes.* Few exponents of the Enlightenment had enough confidence in the common man to advocate a democratic society; most, like Voltaire, were supporters of enlightened despotism and aspired only to persuade the governing powers of Europe that rational law guaranteeing "natural rights" was the best basis of the state. They found some audience among Europe's crowned heads, and though enlightened despotism generally remained more theory than practice, it deserves notice. Most notable among governing powers who endorsed the idea were the sovereigns of Prussia, Russia and Austria, though there were others.

Frederick the Great of Prussia (1740–1788) was a cultured man as well as an able administrator and a distinguished soldier. Despite the mid-eighteenth century wars, he was the most effective of the enlightened despots, rationalizing and codifying Prussian law, adopting policies designed to improve the economic condition of his subjects and reforming the judicial system in an effort to assure equal justice; his attitude toward government was summed up best in his famous comment, "I am the first servant of the state." Catherine the Great of Russia (1762–1796) is more difficult to evaluate. She endorsed the *philosophes,* admired Voltaire greatly and entertained Diderot; but as she depended upon the conservative Russian nobility both for the maintenance of her domestic authority and for the support of her aggressive foreign policy, her avowed intention of governmental reform, such as codification of Russian law, produced no results. The most dramatic attempt to establish enlightened despotism was that of the Emperor Joseph II (1780–1790). When the death of his mother, Maria Theresa, delivered power into his hands, he plunged into rapid and radical legislative experimentation aimed at breaking the power of the church and the nobility and destroying provincial privileges. Joseph II achieved impressive results on paper, but in practice he aroused a storm of opposition that blocked the effective implementation of his intentions, and his brother and successor, Leopold II (1790–1792), had to revoke most of the radical decrees in order to undertake more moderate and more practical reforms. Probably even Louis XVI of France (1774–1792) thought of himself as an enlightened despot, at least in the early part of his reign, when he encouraged his minister Turgot to undertake reforms in justice, taxation and economic regulation; and other governments in Portugal, Italy and the German states were influenced by the principles of enlightened despotism.

Despite the Enlightenment, however, there were many people who supported different values and denied that the *philosophes* had discovered great new truths. Often their feelings were expressed through an emotional religious revival. In the late seventeenth century, France had the earliest experience of this movement, with a group called Quietists, whose faith was so mystical as to be dangerously close to a rejection of clerical authority, and another called Jansenists, who sought to introduce into Catholicism a puritanical and predestinarian doctrine reminiscent of Calvinism; the Quietists were suppressed quickly, and early in the eighteenth century the Jansenists were condemned, but the currents of emotional commitment to a more personal Christianity that they stirred flowed strongly among the common people in France while the intellectuals were debating reason and natural religion. The religious revival in Germany occurred in the middle of the eighteenth century, led by the Moravian Brethren who sought to find personal religious experience and preached a religion of the heart; genuinely tolerant on an individual basis, they condemned both rationalist deism and the dogmatic theology of the established Christian churches. The movement had a strong influence through many German states, encouraging the abandonment of an artificial French culture, and contributed importantly to the richness of the German language and the emotional sensitivity that marked Germany's late eighteenth century literary blossoming with Herder and Goethe.

Probably the most influential of the eighteenth century pietistic movements was English Methodism, organized by the devout and energetic John Wesley and inspired by the emotional evangelism of George Whitefield. Throughout England the Methodists preached and published the love of God, the assurance of salvation and the horror of sin; unfortunately, in their reaction against the cold rationalism of the elite they also were rather anti-intellectual, condemning science and critical study of Scripture as paths to atheism. Their meetings often aroused emotional hysteria repugnant to the fastidious upper classes, but whatever their shortcomings, the emotional preaching and the simple fundamentalism of the Methodists communicated to the horribly depressed masses of the eighteenth century and began their integration into modern English society.

Eventually distrust of the doctrine that reason and the senses were man's only reliable faculties penetrated even the intellectual elite. Dissenting voices were a minor counterpoint in the thundering acclamation of rational empiricism, but some of them spoke too forcefully to be ignored. As noted already, Hume, though no antirationalist, had challenged the psychological assumptions of his contemporaries in the 1750s, and another dissident of formidable reputation appeared in the person of Jean-Jacques Rousseau. A member for awhile of the Paris circle of *philosophes* and a contributor to the *Great Encyclopedia,* he broke with his associates in the mid-1750s over differences of principle, for the *philosophes* were reformers and Rousseau was a true radical who sought the overthrow and replacement of contemporary society. In his search for the nature of man, upon which a moral regeneration might be based, Rousseau reached conclusions radically different from those of Locke. He asserted that natural man was neither corrupted by original sin nor simply blank but filled with good impulses which society negated. Alienated from the world and the people he would have liked to have claimed as friends, Rousseau found himself committing actions he disapproved, and he concluded that he had been corrupted and degraded by society. With lashing invective, he damned the social order and pleaded for a return to nature, which he sought within himself; sweeping aside all of the sociological and anthropological inquiry of his contemporaries, he asserted the sole validity of his own experience and intuition. Proceeding from such tenuous foundations and susceptible to his own changing perceptions, Rousseau's philosophy often is contradictory, for at times he endorses unrestrained individualism, and at other times he projects a stringent collectivism. The unifying rationale is his passion for simple, unspoiled humanity at the same time exercising freedom and associating harmoniously, and these general ideas are more important than his specific theories. His love of nature and the beauty he discovered in it found a wide audience; his passion and his sensitivity offered a valuable counterpoise to the chill rationality of the *philosophes;* and his endorsement of human values provided a glow of warmth in the impersonal mechanistic universe of the Enlightenment.

The negation of the Enlightenment was a strong current by the late eighteenth century, revealed by English poets such as Gray and by a growing enthusiasm for things medieval, such as a revival of gothic styles and a fondness for old castles and abbeys in contrast to the classical enthusiasm of the mainstream of eighteenth century culture. A cult of sentimentality was growing that found the sterile intellectualism of the Enlightenment as much a prison for humanity as the metaphysical otherworldliness of the medieval churchmen.

Chapter 19

A Harvest of Violence

All over Europe the eighteenth century ended in a cataclysm of social upheaval and political innovation that began in France in the late 1780s. The French revolution developed from many factors: arbitrary government which, though not tyrannical, was unresponsive to important interests in the kingdom; the unpopularity of the royal family, which weakened traditional loyalty to the crown; the discredit of the government in consequence of military failures and its inability to relieve economic distress; and political awareness intensified by the critical literature of the Enlightenment. All of these problems were aggravated by inequitable taxation, which generated particular grievances as focal points for discontent and left the government tottering on the verge of bankruptcy in a prosperous nation. By the 1780s some sort of far-reaching reform probably was unavoidable, but there was nothing inevitable about the revolution that grew out of efforts at reform.

In the late eighteenth century France had a population of about twenty-six million and a complex social structure. At the top of the society stood the church and the aristocracy, both groups closely linked to the monarchy and both enjoying privileged positions with regard to taxation. The church depended heavily upon the king, for most of its high offices were filled by royal nomination, and it was exempt from direct royal taxes paid by commoners, for each year it

made a free gift to the government. While this sum was less proportionately than that paid by the peasantry, it should be remembered
that the church supported at its own expense most of the educational, charitable and hospital services of the society as well as
its religious obligations. The princes of the church, archbishops,
bishops and abbots, often were wealthy, powerful and urbane members of aristocratic families, active in politics, while parish priests
and simple monks were commoners, usually impoverished and often
ill-educated. Though all were considered together as the first
estate—the church—the social and economic gulf between the worldly
bishop at the king's court and the simple priest in a country parish
was enormous.

The aristocracy held a position comparable to that of the
church, both in its dependence upon the king and in its privileged
exemption from most direct taxation. Honorific and remunerative
positions at the court, commissions in the army, and offices in the
administration and the church depended upon the king's will, and
royal pensions formed an important part of aristocratic income. The
aristocracy was variegated, its common feudal and military character long lost. The distinction between nobility of the robe, with
titles earned in the royal administration, and nobility of the sword,
with older feudal origins, that had divided the aristocracy in the
seventeenth century had been blurred through marriage by the late
eighteenth century, but another equally divisive distinction had
grown up with the development of the court: the courtier nobility
that lived near the king and the country nobility that lived on its estates. Generally the courtiers depended heavily upon the king; they
drew rents from their lands as absentee landlords, but their chief income derived from royal appointments and royal pensions. They
lived in some luxury, and vast sums of money passed through their
hands to meet the high expenses of court life, but most were deeply
in debt and would have been ruined financially as well as socially by
loss of the king's favor. By contrast country noblemen lived upon
their estates and generally depended upon them for their income,
but even the country nobility was not homogeneous. Some were
modestly prosperous and lived as comfortable country gentlemen,
renting out their lands on relatively short-term leases that allowed
them to raise rents from time to time to keep pace with inflationary

costs. Most of these country gentlemen were important figures in the life of their districts, experimenting with new crops and livestock, adjudicating disputes among peasants, and articulating local grievances or needs to the government; generally they were regarded with respect and often with affection. By contrast, there was another class of country noblemen that was impoverished, frequently because family lands had been divided too often or because the lands were rented on perpetual or near-perpetual leases, leaving the owners defenseless against inflation. Often these impoverished noblemen, called *hoberaux*, were distinguishable from the peasantry only by their right to wear a sword and by the traditional dues they could collect from their tenants.

By the late eighteenth century the urban middle classes formed an important group in French society. At the top of the urban social structure was the *grande bourgeoisie*, wealthy bankers and large-scale merchants. Beneath them was the *petite bourgeoisie—*shopkeepers, artisans and small tradesmen, a class which had grown large with the urban and commercial development of the eighteenth century. And beneath these classes was the urban working force, not a vast modern proletariat, but a considerable group, nonetheless. These groups did not enjoy the general tax privileges of the clergy and the aristocracy, but many of them were privileged. Wealthy bourgeois often achieved exemption on a personal basis by buying royal offices which carried such privilege. Whole towns often enjoyed partial privilege, having negotiated special tax rates with the crown in return for extraordinary contributions or some other service. Thus, in the upper levels of the third estate the incidence of taxation was quite uneven.

At the base of the society were about twenty million peasant farmers, most of them free of any vestiges of personal servitude and many of them small landowners. The peasants paid rents, dues and tithes to landlords and to the church and heavy taxes to the government, but probably they were freer and economically better off than anywhere else in Europe; their participation in the revolution certainly was not a blind rebellion motivated by hopeless conditions. But upon the peasantry fell the major burden of taxation, and even at this level there were great differences in the burdens imposed. About two-thirds of the French provinces, the older ones, were called *pays d'élection;* there the crown's authority was great, and the *taille*, the major direct tax, depended largely upon the assessments of the tax collector. By contrast, the newer provinces, called *pays d'états*, had maintained local assemblies, and the *taille* was negotiated between royal and local officials.

Given this vast web of privilege—by class, by region and by person—it should not be surprising that the government faced bankruptcy in a prosperous country; the wealthy usually escaped taxation, and the government was left in the awkward position of taxing primarily the poor. Moreover, the mechanism of collection was costly and inefficient; the *taille* was collected by government personnel, but indirect taxes, such as the hated *gabelle* on salt, were contracted to private collectors called tax-farmers, and their charges often were exorbitant. Generally rising costs and the military expenses of the eighteenth century wars had forced the government to borrow heavily, and by the 1780s about fifty per cent of the crown's expenditure went to interest charges on the debt; another twenty-five per cent went to military expenditures, leaving only twenty-five per cent for all the costs of administration, public services and the court. Thus, the expenses of the court, while undeniably extravagant, were less significant than angry critics believed. The root of the fiscal difficulties was privilege, which protected France's wealth from governmental exactions; for political reasons it was not possible to reduce governmental expenditures significantly, and because of traditional privileges it was not possible to increase income to meet expenses without the consent of the groups that would have to pay. In the 1780s a number of finance ministers attempted various expedients to relieve the fiscal crisis, but the best of them always came to the same conclusion: those who were privileged would have to be persuaded to accept taxation. The question was how.

Early in 1787 the crown convened an assembly of notables, a hand-picked group of prominent people, and submitted new tax proposals to it, but this group refused to accept the responsibility and was dismissed without results. Then new tax edicts were submitted to the parlement of Paris, the high court that registered royal laws and provided the judicial machinery for their enforcement, but the parlement refused to accept them. Though a nonelective and nonrepresentative body, the parlement had become spokesman of the opposition to royal absolutism, and when the crown tried to put pressure upon the court, the parlementarians became public heroes for their resistance. They claimed that neither they nor the assembly of notables had the authority to approve what the crown asked and insisted that for such momentous decisions the estates general had to be revived.

France's privileged classes did not refuse adamantly to consider assuming some of the national burden, but they aspired to political power as the price of their support. The French admired England greatly, and though English government often was ill-understood, the French privileged classes understood clearly enough that in England royal power had been limited through parliamentary control of governmental finance; what they sought in the 1780s was to force the crown's officers to negotiate with a large and representative body dominated by the aristocracy and to concede some measure of political authority to that body in return for new taxes. They scored a victory when the crown agreed that an estates general should be convened in the spring of 1789, the first such assembly since 1614.

Unfortunately for the intentions of the aristocrats, they did not constitute the only politically ambitious group in France. The large middle class—prosperous, vocal and influenced by the *philosophes*—also desired a political voice as the price of their taxes, and their influence persuaded the government to authorize for the estates general as many representatives for the third estate as for the first two estates combined. The aristocracy quickly countered this maneuver by having the king declare that the estates would vote separately upon all resolutions. This was a desperately important issue, for if votes were taken by head the commoners could expect that with double representation and a little support from sympathetic lower clergy and country noblemen they could dominate the assembly; but if the estates voted separately, it could be anticipated that the two upper estates would stand together to evoke concessions from the crown in their own interest while blocking the ambitions of the third estate. Thus, when the estates general assembled in May of 1789 the commoners already were restless and angry, and there was an atmosphere of tension.

The royal financial position was worse than ever, and bad harvests had caused widespread economic distress. In the countryside there was violence, and rumors spread that the food shortages were the result of an aristocratic conspiracy to starve the commons into submission. The third estate was in an ugly mood. In June of 1789, in defiance of the king's order, it assumed the title of the National Assembly and invited the representatives of the other two estates to join it, and several of the clergy and some nobles did. Uncertain what to do, the king suspended the assembly and closed its meeting hall, but the delegates gathered in a nearby indoor tennis court and took an oath not to disband until they had given France a constitution; the king capitulated, ordering the remaining members of the upper estates to join the National Assembly, and the reform movement launched by the aristocracy had slipped from its control.

Despite this victory, the third estate remained distrustful of the vacillating king, for royal troops were concentrating around Versailles and Paris, and there were rumors that the government would break up the assembly; these rumors acquired more force early in July when the king dismissed the popular minister, Neckar, who had convened the estates general, and violence erupted in Paris. On July 14, 1789 a crowd stormed the Bastille, a royal fortress, massacred the garrison and seized the arms stored there, ready to fight if the king should try to use troops to suppress the National Assembly and its Parisian support. About the same time, peasant uprisings broke out all over France against the exactions of aristocratic landlords. In this revolutionary atmosphere a number of great nobles began to leave France, rioting spread, and popular militias and provisional governments were formed.

In August the pace of change accelerated. Liberal aristocrats began a voluntary surrender of feudal rights, and the National Assembly abolished titles and adopted a Declaration of the Rights of Man. Hunger and fear of repression caused more popular demonstrations in Paris, and a mob marched to Versailles and forced the royal family and the National Assembly to transfer to the city. A liberal monarchical constitution was adopted under which legislative power resided in a unicameral assembly, and the king's power was limited to a suspensory veto which could delay legislation for two terms of the assembly. Declarations of war and foreign treaties also required the consent of the assembly. In the summer of 1790 regional privileges were destroyed as the old provinces were abolished and France was redivided into eighty-three departments. The assembly then moved to the establishment of a new currency, a national reorganization of the clergy and the establishment of new political mechanisms (which included financial qualifications for voting). The revolution appeared to have been accomplished with the victory falling not to the aristocrats who had begun it but to the middle class.

There were groups that wanted the revolution to continue, however, most notably the radical political clubs of which the Jacobins, under the leadership of Robespierre, was most prominent. These groups tended to be republican and to favor abolition of the monarchy. Shortly before the elections that were to establish a legislative assembly under the new constitution, an attempted flight by the king and his family strengthened these radical groups by demonstrating the king's implicit hostility to the new limited monarchy, and the Legislative Assembly of 1791–1792, though still primarily representative of the bourgeoisie, had a republican majority. War with Austria and Prussia, which broke out in the spring of 1792, further stimulated republican and national extremism, and new elections in the fall of 1792 produced an assembly, called the National Convention, that was composed entirely of republicans elected by universal manhood suffrage. The new assembly was more radical than either of its predecessors; one of its first acts was to abolish the monarchy under mob pressure, and in July of 1793 Louis XVI was executed.

In the midst of foreign war, political activity in the capital became more and more radical, and by mid-summer of 1793 Robespierre and the Jacobins dominated the government through its Committee of Public Safety, backed by the revolutionary Commune of Paris. Alleging the dangers of counterrevolutionary activity, Robespierre inaugurated a reign of terror, with mass arrests, trials by revolutionary tribunals and summary executions, which lasted until his enemies overthrew and killed him in the summer of 1794.

The overthrow of the Jacobins and French victories in the foreign war brought more moderate policies, and in the summer of 1795 a new constitution provided for a two-house legislature with executive authority vested in a committee of five called the Directory. Radical Paris objected to the new arrangements, but in October a young Corsican general, Napoleon Bonaparte, protected the government by firing artillery into a mob, and the projected elections took place.

The foreign powers reacted with indifference to the first stages of the French Revolution, for they were distracted by other problems. Britain had just gone through a governmental crisis concerning her interests in India, she faced rising unrest in Ireland, and in 1788 King George suffered the first of his fits of insanity. English opinion generally was hostile to the rising tide of violence in France and shocked by the execution of Louis XVI, but the British held aloof until the French Republic declared war on them in 1793. Similarly the interests of the eastern monarchies (Austria, Prussia and Russia) were committed elsewhere, to traditional involvements in Poland and to new rivalries consequent upon the decline of the Turks. After 1789, however, refugee aristocrats from France began to pour into foreign capitals, particularly Vienna and Berlin, where they begged foreign intervention to restore their positions and the authority of Louis XVI. In August of 1791 the Austrian emperor and the king of Prussia met at Pillnitz to discuss various issues, and with reference to the French situation they announced that they would intervene only with the unanimous consent of all the great powers. Since such agreement was quite unlikely, the declaration of Pillnitz was not a very dangerous statement, but in France it appeared a serious threat, particularly as it came only two months after Louis XVI's attempted flight abroad.

Developments early in 1792 made war almost certain. In Austria the new Emperor Francis II (1792–1835) was sympathetic to the war party, and an Austro-Prussian alliance against France was signed in February. In France the republicans wanted a war which they anticipated would intensify national and revolutionary sentiment. Both sides were eager for the conflict when the French Republic began it in April of 1792.

At first the war went badly for the French, but about the same time that the Convention proclaimed the republic, they managed to stabilize the military situation by winning an artillery duel at Valmy, and then one French army swept the Prussians back over the Rhine while another conquered the Austrian Netherlands. These victories were followed by a French offer of assistance to any people that wished to overthrow its government, by the reopening of the Scheldt to commerce and by the execution of Louis XVI. This series of events brought Britain, Holland, Spain and the Holy Roman Empire into alliance against France, and in the summer of 1793 the republic was in real danger, for the allies overran the southern Netherlands (which France had annexed) and invaded northern France, while internally a number of revolts threatened political chaos. However, the war had the political effects that the republicans had sought. They were able to intensify the terror against their political enemies and to institute radical measures of price controls and rationing, and in August of 1793 they called to military service all males capable of bearing arms, putting fourteen armies into the field. In the autumn the French began achieving military success, and in 1794 and 1795 they were victorious everywhere. Both the Austrian and Dutch Netherlands were conquered and turned into a Batavian republic under French influence; Prussia and the lesser north German states were forced out of the war, and France annexed the left bank of the Rhine. In the summer of 1795 British troops and emigrant French royalists attempted a landing in Brittany, but they were defeated quickly. Thus, when the Directory took office the situation appeared quite favorable.

The successes of the rapidly levied and ill-trained French armies astonished their enemies. Part of the credit belongs to the splendid artillery and sound officer training of the eighteenth century royal army and part to Carnot, the brilliant member of the Committee of Public Safety who undertook the organization and logistical support of the armies of the republic, but the greatest credit belongs to the revolution itself. The abolition of privilege and the political reorganization of the country enabled the republic to mobilize the vast resources that had been beyond the reach of the royal government. Popular participation in political processes, the terror and a campaign of hatred against royalists and foreigners who would undo the revolution all contributed to a wave of unprecedented national and patriotic sentiment.

The crucial factor in the new armies was morale, which enabled them to survive reverses and withstand casualty rates that destroyed the professional forces of the eighteenth century, but though morale was crucial, it should not be overlooked that France rapidly developed new methods and tactics adapted to the large but raw armies she was putting into the field. The exodus of masses of aristocrats deprived the French army of many of its senior officers, some of them competent professionals but many of them titled bunglers who held their rank through favor; thus rapid promotion was open to talented junior officers, such as Bonaparte, and the battlefield quickly sorted the talented from the merely competent. New junior officers were chosen from among sergeants with experience in the old royal forces, and new recruits were organized around cadres of old professionals. The most startling innovation, however, was in tactics. The French lacked the time to train masses of new recruits in the complex drill of rapid fire musketry and swift field maneuver that was the basis of eighteenth century tactics, so they relied upon the bayonet charge after artillery bombardment had softened enemy ranks. In early encounters, casualties were very high, but in the new French forces casualties were replaced more easily than in the professional armies of Austria or Prussia, and as the new French armies acquired experience, their casualties decreased while their victories increased. Though a few precedents might be found in the Dutch forces that fought Spain in the sixteenth century, in Cromwell's army in the seventeenth century, or in the American colonial forces in the eighteenth century, Europe had never seen anything like the new French armies of the republic for sheer size and dedication. The revolution had mobilized both the economic and human resources of the wealthiest and most populous nation in Europe, and it soon reestablished French military domination of the continent.

The Directory, which lasted from 1795 to 1799, faced acute financial crises, and accusations of corruption swirled around its members, but it provided an effective war government. In 1795 the only great powers still in the field against France were Austria and Britain, with the support of the south German states. After some initial successes, two French armies invading Germany were checked by the Austrians in 1796, but a third army under Bonaparte swept the Austrians from north Italy and established two republics there under French domination; in 1797 Austria accepted a peace that recognized the new Italian states and ceded the Austrian Netherlands to France. The next year the French invaded both the Papal States and Switzerland, setting up two more republics. Thus, already by 1798 the French had altered the political organization of Europe greatly, and of all the great powers only Britain remained in the war.

Desirous of forcing Britain to terms and convinced that an invasion of England was not feasible, Bonaparte proposed the seizure of Egypt, from which position the French could threaten the British empire in India. Early in the summer of 1798, Egypt was occupied easily, but in August the British destroyed the French Mediterranean fleet, which negated the strategic value of the success. French forces remained in Egypt until 1801, but Bonaparte returned to France in the summer of 1799. The Directory never had won popular support, while military success had made a hero of Bonaparte, and in November of 1799 the general overthrew the constitution and seized control of the government. A consulate of three men was established (1799–1804) which was dominated by Napoleon Bonaparte as First Consul.

During the course of the fruitless Egyptian campaign, a second European coalition had been formed against France, this time including Russia. Early campaigns of Russian and Austrian forces drove the French out of south Germany, Switzerland and north Italy, but a British invasion of the Netherlands failed, co-operation among the allies broke down, and the Russians quit the war. The French then inflicted crushing defeats upon the Austrians in 1800, both in Germany and Italy, and in 1801 Austria had to sign the Treaty of Lunéville, which conceded to France everything west of the Rhine and recognized the client princes and the satellite republics that France had established. In the same year, long negotiations with the pope produced a concordat by which part of the Papal States was restored in return for papal acceptance of the situation of the church in France: high clergy appointed by the government, all clergy paid by the government, confiscated church lands in

France not to be restored and all education to be controlled by the state. Finally, in March of 1802, England also made peace with France by the Treaty of Amiens.

In 1804 Bonaparte abolished the Consulate, proclaimed the French empire with himself as Emperor Napoleon I and established a brilliant court with an aristocracy based on talent and service. The Corsican general had succeeded in establishing the absolute monarchy that the Bourbon kings had sought, and he appeared secure. War with England had broken out again in 1803, but the rest of Europe was at peace, and France was the strongest nation on the continent. The situation remained basically unstable, however, for the English felt that their security was threatened by French control of the southern Netherlands, and Austria was humiliated and determined upon vengeance.

In 1805 a third anti-French coalition was formed, including England, Austria, Russia and Sweden, and Europe plunged into war again. At sea the English victory at Trafalgar in October of 1805 broke French naval power definitively, but on land a series of French successes, culminating in the victory over the Austrians and Russians at Austerlitz in December, quickly knocked Austria out of the war again. In the aftermath, the greater part of west Germany was organized into a Confederation of the Rhine under French "protection," the Holy Roman Empire was dissolved, Austria confirmed earlier territorial concessions, and Napoleon made one of his brothers king of Naples while establishing another as king of Holland (the former Batavian republic). The war was far from over, however, for Russia was still in the field, and Napoleon's new arrangements in Germany brought Prussia into the war against him. In 1806 he broke the Prussians completely at Jena and Auerstädt, and in 1807 he defeated the Russians at the Battle of Friedland, which left the French in control of all of Europe to the Nieman River. By the Treaties of Tilsit, signed in July of 1807, Prussia was reduced to half of her former size, and Russia accepted the French reorganization of Europe. A few months later Russia joined France in the war against England.

Napoleon's policy at this time was dominated by the war with England and by new provisions for his family. In 1806 he had proclaimed the Continental Blockade, banning English goods from all the ports of Europe to break the economy of the nation of shopkeepers, and the desire to make the blockade effective led him to occupy Portugal and Spain, areas that he was never to succeed in pacifying. At the same time, he created a new kingdom of Westphalia in northwest Germany for another of his brothers and moved his elder brother from Naples to Spain, giving Naples to a brother-in-law. In 1809 Austria once again tried to raise Germany against Napoleon, but again she suffered defeat, at Wagram, and had to accept another humiliating peace that cost her much territory and three and a half million subjects.

About 1810 Napoleon was at the height of his power, but there were many signs of discontent. An English expeditionary force in Portugal received strong local support, and the French were unable to complete their conquest of that country; though the French occupied Spain, guerilla resistance never ceased, and large French forces were tied down; in Germany there were a number of uprisings against French domination; and in new quarrels with the pope, French armies reoccupied the Papal States in 1809, whereupon the pope excommunicated Napoleon and the pope himself was taken as a prisoner to France. All over Europe Napoleon's creation and dissolution of new states were resented, and all governments were strained by the large levies of men and money that Napoleon constantly demanded of them. But the greatest danger was the growing tension with Russia. Personal rivalry between Napoleon and Czar Alexander I (1801-1825) was reinforced by a conflict over a number of issues, such as the Continental Blockade, the future of Polish lands and Russian ambitions for expansion in the Balkans. As Franco-Russian relations deteriorated, Napoleon assembled the Grand Army, a multinational force of about six hundred thousand men, and in June of 1812 if advanced into Russia. The Russians fell back, forcing Napoleon to depend upon very long supply lines; then at Borodino they stood and fought a bloody engagement with heavy losses on both sides. After Borodino the Russians had to fall back again, and the road to Moscow was open, but the French could claim no great victory; the Russian army was still intact and dangerous. When Napoleon's army occupied Moscow, the Russians burned the city, leaving the French with neither shelter nor provisions, and Napoleon had no choice but to withdraw. He was caught by the Russian winter, while cold and hungry men and horses were harassed by Cossacks and armed peasants and sometimes had to fight the pursuing Russian army; only about one hundred thousand men of the Grand Army lived to recross the Nieman. Napoleon hurried back to Paris.

The disaster in Russia encouraged France's other enemies. In 1813 the Prussians allied with the Russians; England was already in the war, of course, with forces in Portugal and Spain. As Russian and Prussian forces gathered, Napoleon raised another army and prepared to defend his control of Germany, winning the first encounters in May of 1813. Then in August Austria once more declared war against France, and the ensuing conflict became a German war of liberation with strong Russian support. In October of 1813 the Battle of Leipzig, called the Battle of the Nations, was fought, and Napoleon was defeated decisively by the combined allied forces. The war in Germany had forced the recall of French troops from Spain, and the English army under Wellington soon crossed the Pyrenees and besieged Bayonne. The allies made steady progress in Germany, and in December of 1813 they crossed the Rhine into France; despite some brilliant defensive actions against superior numbers, Napoleon could not halt the allies, and on March 31, 1814 they entered Paris. The imperial senate declared that Napoleon had forfeited the throne, and on April 11 he abdicated, being granted by the allies the island of Elba and a pension. The victorious powers then settled to the task of shaping the peace, a major problem because the Europe of the 1790s had disappeared during two decades of the revolutionary and Napoleonic wars.

Chapter 20

Restoration and Reaction

Peace and stability were the dominant themes of the settlements made by the victorious powers in 1814 and 1815, and the first Treaty of Paris, signed in May of 1814, dealt fairly generously with their former enemy. France was restored to the rule of the Bourbon monarchy, and she had to recognize the independence of the European states that Napoleon had subjected and promise to abolish the French slave trade, but her frontiers were returned to those of 1792, allowing retention of the early revolutionary conquests, and England returned most of the French colonies she had captured.

In September of 1814 the Congress of Vienna assembled to expand this rudimentary treaty into a general European settlement. Strictly speaking, it was not a congress at all, for there were no plenary sessions, and representatives of Russia, Britain, Prussia and Austria made all the major decisions. Before negotiations had proceeded very far, however, the four great powers divided over an explosive issue, the future of Poland and Saxony. The Russian czar, Alexander I (1801–1825), wanted to reestablish Poland as a Russian dependency, while the Prussians wanted to annex Saxony. Austria and Britain opposed these ambitions, fearful that Prussian aggrandizement would threaten Austria's domination of Germany and that Russian expansion westward would upset the new balance of power that they hoped to create in Europe. This division among the former allies was exploited by the astute French diplomat, Talleyrand, to gain admission to the inner councils at Vienna, and in January of 1815 Britain, Austria and France signed a secret treaty committing them to fight if Russia and Prussia would not abandon at least part of their demands. At this point the whole effort to make a general settlement might have collapsed but for a new crisis that reunited the former allies.

The discord at Vienna was paralleled by the failure of France to rally to the restored Bourbon government, and Napoleon, well aware of both of these situations, determined to make an attempt to recover his throne. On March 1, 1815, he crossed from Elba to the south of France and began to march north; in the middle of the month the king fled abroad, and on March 20 Napoleon entered Paris. Since the allies refused even to negotiate with him, he realized that he would have to fight again, and he hastily gathered an army to oppose the English, who were first in the field. On June 18, however, he was defeated overwhelmingly at Waterloo and was exiled to the barren island of St. Helena in the south Atlantic.

While Napoleon was attempting to reestablish himself, the diplomats at Vienna continued their work, and early in June of 1815 the Act of the Congress of Vienna was signed, creating a new political framework for Europe. Czar Alexander's ambition was satisfied partially by the establishment of a kingdom of Poland (smaller than he had hoped) with himself as king, and Prussia got two fifths of Saxony as well as some other small territories, while Austria was compensated for the increased strength of Russia and Prussia by being given large parts of north Italy. No effort was made to reconstitute the eighteenth century maze of petty German states; instead, German lands were divided anew, in accordance with the wishes of Austria and Prussia. Thirty-nine states emerged, former petty princelings being compensated with titles and pensions, and a German confederation was created to replace the old Holy Roman Empire. The Dutch Netherlands, the former Austrian Netherlands (Belgium) and Luxemburg were combined into a kingdom of the Netherlands under Dutch rule, and a whole series of articles provided for the retention by England of some colonial conquests, the restoration of former dynasties in Spain and Sardinia and the reestablishment of an independent Switzerland.

After Napoleon's return from Elba, usually called the Hundred Days, a second Treaty of Paris was signed in November of 1815; this treaty reduced France to her boundaries of 1790, forced her to return the art treasures that Napoleon had stolen, and imposed an indemnity and an army of occupation. The regions that France lost through the adjustment of the frontiers were given to the Netherlands, Prussia and Sardinia in an effort to strengthen further the obstacles to any renewed French expansionism, and at the same time the major powers made arrangements for continuing enforcement of the settlements. In September they signed an idealistic document called the Holy Alliance, a mutual agreement to be guided by Christian principles, and concurrent with the second Treaty of Paris, they established a firmer basis for continuing cooperation; through the Quadruple Alliance they bound themselves to maintain the territorial arrangements and the exclusion of the Bonapartes for twenty years, and they agreed to hold further meetings to oversee the implementation of the treaties.

Meanwhile, with the Napoleonic adventure finally ended, the reconstituted European states groped for internal settlements that might produce stability and order, but the task was not easy, for during two decades of revolutionary warfare, legal and political changes had been inaugurated all over Europe. The lands of nobles and of churches had been confiscated, divided and sold; laws had been promulgated upon a basis of legal equality; and men had grown accustomed to the idea that in Napoleon's service advancement was open as far as their talents and energies could carry them. The violence and anarchy produced by the French revolution in large measure had discredited the idealistic liberalism of the Enlightenment, but with more cautious goals and more sharply defined principles, of which the most prominent was a doctrine of governmental noninterference, liberalism survived as a political creed with wide support.

The economic theorist Adam Smith had asserted in the 1770s in his *Wealth of Nations* that economic expansion would proceed most rapidly if governments would refrain from extensive regulation and would permit almost unrestricted private capitalism, and this opinion was endorsed on a broader basis in the late eighteenth and early nineteenth centuries. Liberals such as Jeremy Bentham maintained that government was a necessary evil, and that it ought to be restrained from interference with political and economic liberty so as to assure "the greatest good of the greatest number." Only a few radicals supported broadly democratic reform at the beginning of the nineteenth century, but many liberals desired constitutions which would set limits upon the scope of governmental activity, some form of representative political institutions and public education free of ecclesiastical control.

The other political conception that took root solidly in Europe during the Napoleonic era was nationalism. First stimulated in France by popular involvement in political and military affairs during the revolution, nationalism grew in other parts of Europe as both positive and negative responses to the French imperium. On the one hand the concept was transmitted positively by law codes and administrative and military structures based on French models and by geographical rearrangements such as Napoleon's creation of a kingdom of Italy; on the other, it developed spontaneously as a reaction against exploitative French domination, as exemplified by the stubborn resistance of the Spanish and by the national rising of the Germans.

The fortunes of war could transfer political power back to kings and aristocrats, but it could not undo the transformation of social and political consciousness that had taken place. Restoration could not mean the reestablishment of eighteenth century Europe, but most of the governing powers of the European states in the years just after 1815 were singularly incapable of comprehending this. Years of exile had put them out of touch with their own countries and had taught them nothing except to hate revolution and to be violently suspicious of all innovation.

The intellectual and cultural expression that characterized these dominant classes of early nineteenth century society is called Romanticism, a matrix of thought and attitudes composed of piety, emotional sensitivity, respect for authority and reverence for the past. To some extent Romanticism developed as a reaction against the rationalism, empiricism and anticlericalism of the Enlightenment, which were blamed for the chaos and bloodshed of the revolutionary and Napoleonic years, and to some extent it grew out of the dissenting subculture of the eighteenth century, the religious revival exemplified by pietists and Methodists and the admiration of nature and of simplicity voiced by Rousseau in France and by Robert Burns in Scotland. As well as affecting the arts, Romanticism also influenced political thought, its reverence for piety, tradition and authority encouraging conservatism. On the basis of ancient lineage, returning exiles were given responsibilities in the restoration governments for which they had no preparation at all; the anticlericalism of the revolutionary years was matched by the exaggerated piety of postrevolutionary governments, and the restorations were proclaimed as a victory of religion over atheism, most governments regarding organized religion as one of their most important defenders. In governmental circles, piety and caution replaced wit and boldness as the ideals of the courtier, and tradition replaced experiment as the foundation of policy. Most of the new rulers committed themselves mildly to reestablishing the aristocracy and the church, to trying to make history run backwards.

The only notable exception to the general incomprehension and inability of the restored monarchs was Louis XVIII of France (1814–1824). He showed clearly that he understood the need for a new fusion when he remarked that the problem was to nationalize the monarchy and to royalize the nation, but he found no support at all for this program, and his reign is one of the tragedies of the early nineteenth century. Shortly after returning to France he issued a declaration promising that he would grant a constitution, would honor the public debt and would uphold property rights and freedom of the press and of religion; it was obvious that he considered many of the revolutionary changes in France permanent and that he intended to rest his government upon the new society and not upon some idealized version of the old. However, the king's brother, the count of Artois, organized a reactionary party of ultraroyalists who hoped to restore the nobility and the church to their full prerevolutionary position; the extremism of these ultras, and the postwar reduction of the army, which scattered unemployed and dissatisfied officers all over the country, quickly eroded the king's position, and the necessity of flight during the Hundred Days diminished his prestige yet further. When he came back to Paris after Waterloo, it was said that he "returned in the baggage of the allies," but courageously he tried again to bridge the gulfs that separated Frenchmen from Frenchmen.

Despite Louis XVIII's desire that the past be forgotten, a White

Terror was launched by extremists who were, in an old French phrase, "more royalist than the king." All over France, men who had been active in the revolutionary or Napoleonic regimes were assaulted and sometimes killed by inflamed royalists, and in the midst of this hysteria, elections were held for the assembly created by the constitutional charter that the king had granted. A majority of those elected proved to be ultras, and the extremist measures that they enacted worsened the situation in a country already suffering the economic dislocation normal in the aftermath of great wars, but nonetheless this was an important experiment in representative government. Slowly the antagonists were learning the techniques of effective debate and party organization, while newspapers were stimulating a considerable public interest in the legislative quarrels. The king's moderation was winning respect, new elections produced a majority of moderate royalists and prosperity was returning. The prospect justified cautious optimism, but then disaster struck.

In 1820 the duke of Berri, Louis XVIII's nephew, was assassinated by a fanatic, and this event so inflamed the political situation that it ruined the king's hopes for a compromise policy that would merge liberalism and monarchy. The moderate center waned, and even the king himself no longer could resist the pressure of the ultras. A new ministry and new electoral laws marked the beginning of a more reactionary policy, intensified when Louis XVIII died in 1824 and was succeeded by his brother who reigned as Charles X (1824–1830). During the late 1820s the situation continued to deteriorate, for the liberals won a majority in the chamber, the business classes were antagonized by indemnification of the nobility at their expense and moderate royalists were driven into the opposition by reactionary legislation. In August of 1829 the king precipitated a crisis by appointing as head of a new ministry Prince Polignac, a dedicated ultra. Unable to obtain support in the chamber, in July of 1830 Charles X and Polignac issued five ordinances by royal prerogative, an action popularly interpreted as the beginning of government by decree. The Parisians revolted, throwing up barricades and rioting in the streets, and within a few days Charles X fled to England, leaving France committed to further political experiment.

In radical Paris there was a rather strong movement which sought to abolish the monarchy, proposing to create another republic with Lafayette as president. To many Frenchmen, however, republicanism recalled the Jacobins and the Terror, and liberal deputies in the chamber preferred constitutional monarchy under the duke of Orléans, the reputedly liberal head of the younger branch of the Bourbon family. To avoid a serious breach between the two groups, Lafayette accepted the duke of Orléans, and he was proclaimed Louis Philippe, king of the French (1830–1848). Revision of the charter of 1814 outlined a constitutional monarchy, and French liberalism appeared to have achieved an easy victory.

Disillusionment came quickly, however, when Louis Philippe proved to be no revolutionary king, refusing to aid the revolutions in Italy and Poland or to make concessions to the workers of Paris. Instead, he appointed cautious governments, and radical agitation continued, erupting into revolutionary violence in both Paris and Lyons. These insurrections were suppressed savagely, and in 1835 repressive laws were enacted censoring the press and providing for more severe treatment of insurgents, after which successive governments followed ever more conservative policies. Radical liberal and republican movements continued, however, and conditions consequent upon rapid industrial development soon added a socialist movement to the growing opposition. In 1846 and 1847 an economic depression worsened an already tense situation, and the opposition organized a series of protest meetings disguised as banquets. When the government tried to prohibit one of these banquets, in February of 1848, a street demonstration turned to rioting, and revolution was let loose again.

Nowhere else on the European continent in the years following 1815 were the good will and clear understanding of Louis XVIII found. The restored Bourbon king of Spain, Ferdinand VII (1814–1833), was greeted with wild enthusiasm upon his return, for he had become the symbol of national resistance to Napoleon, but this popularity waned quickly. The nation was impoverished from its long struggle against the French, but the king's sole interest was the restoration of ecclesiastical and aristocratic property and the reestablishment of the nobility's seigneurial rights. In 1820 dissatisfaction led to a mutiny of some of the army, and it required foreign help to suppress it, after which Ferdinand inaugurated a program of repression that lasted for the remainder of his reign; this policy failed to reestablish order, as also did his successors' programs of limited, controlled reform, and for the next fifty years Spain continued to be torn by revolutionary violence.

Elsewhere, comparable situations were developing. In the kingdom of Naples, reactionary policy evoked revolutionary ferment which broke into open violence in 1820, and the next year saw a rising in Piedmont-Sardinia. Again foreign intervention crushed the revolutions, but throughout the 1820s all of Italy remained restive, and the overthrow of Charles X in France in 1830 stimulated a new wave of revolutionary agitation. Secret societies espousing liberalism and nationalism recruited widely, and throughout the 1830s and 1840s only the strong Austrian presence in Italy maintained the reactionary governments that dominated the peninsula.

After the defeat of Napoleon German political development pivoted upon Austria's chancellor, Prince Clement von Metternich, one of the architects of the Vienna peace settlement and a firm conservative. Inevitably Metternich was concerned to repress any expression of the revolutionary movement, for Austria's subjects comprised half the races and religions of Europe, and national and liberal ideas threatened the very foundations of the Austrian empire. German resistance to Napoleon had been motivated largely by rising national feeling, and initially the Vienna settlement was not unsatisfactory to this still nascent sentiment; the more important units of German political life were reestablished, and the confederation appeared to provide loose unification. Liberals and nationalists were disturbed by the lack of constitutional guarantees, and they were distressed to see a conservative internationalist such as Metternich in control of Germany's political development; then their hopes for effective national and liberal leadership from Prussia, Austria's traditional rival, were disappointed when the king of Prussia proved unwilling to challenge Austrian predominance.

Finding no governmental support, liberal and national feeling was expressed through popular movements with no very clear goals. Almost immediately after Napoleon's defeat, German students began organizing nationalist societies, a movement highlighted in 1817 by a mass rally at Wartburg castle, Luther's famous sanctuary, and in 1819 by an assassination and another attempted one in the name of the liberal and nationalist cause. The chief result of this agitation, however, was a meeting of representatives of the foremost German states at Carlsbad in 1819 and the issuance by them of the Carlsbad Decrees, repressive measures aimed against student organizations and against the press. Despite some sporadic outbursts of revolutionary violence, Metternich and his sympathizers retained control until the late 1840s.

Although liberalism made no progress in Germany during the first half of the nineteenth century, one development was encouraging to nationalists. The existence of thirty-nine states, each with tariff barriers, was an obvious obstacle to the development of German economic life; in 1819 Prussia took the lead in the establishment of a customs union called the *zollverein,* and it grew steadily. By the late 1820s Prussia had established a large free trade area in north Germany, which was copied by some of the south German states, and in the mid-1840s the organizations were fused to create an economic unit comprising most of non-Austrian Germany. At the same time, steady administrative reform was establishing for Prussia a reputation for honest and efficient government. These developments prepared Germany for unity under Prussian leadership, excluding Austria, but the achievement of this political unification still lay many years in the future.

In Britain, the end of the war brought unexpected difficulties as governmental purchase of war supplies ceased, continental markets failed to open up rapidly, about 400,000 demobilized men were dumped into the job market and poor harvests drove food prices up. This situation was made worse by high tariffs enacted to protect the grain interests of large landowners and to compensate for the cancellation of a ten per cent wartime income tax. High prices and widespread unemployment caused serious popular unrest, but the conservative Tories governing Britain believed that victory over the French had demonstrated beyond challenge the merit of the existing social and political structure, and they were unwilling to change anything. The Whig opposition was moribund, and there appeared to be no parliamentary alternative to a government which, in the midst of widespread economic hardship, thought only of protecting vested interests and of begging the country to appreciate the blessings of peace and order. Consequently, the discontent tended to focus in private liberal clubs outside of parliament, and they organized mass rallies and open-air protest meetings. The government failed to distinguish between acts of violence and these controlled demonstrations demanding reform, and in 1817 it began a program of repression.

The repressive measures and the demonstrations disturbed the consciences of some members of the governing classes, and parliamentary elections returned more Whigs and some young Tories who were at odds with their own party on the issue of repression versus reform. Then in 1819 another economic slump sharpened the political crisis, and two issues rallied support through a broad political spectrum, parliamentary reform and repeal of the 1815 grain tariffs called the Corn Laws. Workers and factory owners alike were concerned with these matters; the unreformed parliament allowed no representation to the new industrial areas, and the grain tariffs appeared to the working man to keep his food costs high while to the employer they appeared to inflate his wage bills by forcing him to base wages upon an artificially maintained high cost of living. Thousands turned out for mass protest meetings in the north and in the midlands, and the government panicked.

In the summer of 1819 troops were sent to an open-air meeting at St. Peter's fields in Manchester with orders to disperse the crowd and to arrest the speaker. In the confrontation that ensued some people were killed and many were injured, and the affair became a national scandal. Satirists called it the battle of Peterloo, and many members of the establishment protested vehemently, but the government pressed on doggedly with a program of further repression. At the end of 1819 it passed the Six Acts, which facilitated the prosecution of agitators, restricted public meetings and limited the operations of radical journalists. England appeared to be drifting towards a serious confrontation between a reactionary government and a populace stirred to revolutionary agitation, but before any more serious crisis developed, economic revival and new men in the cabinet eased the tension and made possible evolutionary rather than revolutionary solutions.

In 1822 Castlereagh, the dominant figure of the old Tory

cabinet, committed suicide, and a reshuffle of the cabinet brought some young liberal Tories into it. These men were limited by what they could persuade their own party to accept, but through the 1820s they managed an important revision of the criminal code, abolishing the death penalty for many offenses; a revision of tariffs, lowering duties on many imports (but not on grain); and an easing of the laws concerning combinations and conspiracies which, in effect, made unions legal while forbidding strikes. A reaction on the part of the right wing of the Tory party forced the Tory liberals to resign, and from 1828 to 1830 the government was entrusted to the conservative duke of Wellington, Napoleon's conqueror. Reform had won such strong support, however, that even he was forced to amend the Corn Laws in an unsuccessful endeavor to bring about lower prices without abolishing protectionism entirely and to carry an emancipation bill allowing Catholics to sit in parliament. These partial measures further stimulated reformist sentiment without satisfying it, and in new elections in 1830 the Whigs, who had committed themselves to reform, won a majority.

The momentum of the legislation of the 1820s, the Whigs' electoral commitment and the stimulus of the 1830 revolution in France combined to press the English government into a decade and a half of far-reaching reforms. Despite the opposition of Tory peers in the House of Lords, in 1832 a bill was passed which redistributed many seats in the Commons and lowered the requirements for voting; this bill gave representation to new centers of population and increased the electorate by half. In 1833 one bill eliminated slavery in Britain's colonies and another began effective regulation of abuses of the industrial working force; 1834 brought a new poor law and 1835 an act reorganizing and democratizing local government. Minor reforms continued for another decade under both Whig and liberal Tory governments, and in 1846, under the pressure of famine in Ireland, Sir Robert Peel enacted the long-demanded repeal of the Corn Laws. Thus, by the late 1840s when continental Europe again was swept by revolution, England had moved far in the direction of the consolidation and democratization of a national society.

Concerned to preserve Europe's security, the members of the Quadruple Alliance had agreed to continue meeting from time to time after the war. The first of their conferences, at Aix-la-Chapelle in 1818, appeared innocuous; they rearranged some details of the peace with France and admitted France to their alliance. Later meetings dealt with much more sensitive issues, however, and the Quadruple Alliance and Holy Alliance soon became symbols of reaction and repression to liberals and nationalists.

When revolt broke out in Naples, Metternich felt that Austria's Italian interests were endangered, and he called a meeting at Troppau in 1820 to seek support from his allies. Although Britain and France refused to agree, the three eastern powers issued a statement announcing their intention to intervene wherever necessary to crush revolutions before they could spread, and after further consultation with his eastern allies at Laibach in 1821, Metternich sent Austrian troops to Naples. In 1822 a crucial meeting was held at Verona to consider a Greek revolt against the Turks and the revolutions raging in Spain and its colonies. Because of conflicting interests, the allies agreed to ignore the Greek revolt, but Spain became an issue on which congress diplomacy foundered. Castlereagh had died shortly before the conference, and his successor in office, Canning, had less commitment to the alliance and even greater determination to avoid the involvement of Britain in another country's internal affairs. Ultimately, to avoid the use of Russian troops in western Europe, it was agreed that France should send aid to Ferdinand VII of Spain, but western suspicion of Russia and England's intransigent refusal to be a party to the project marked the breakdown of the alliance. Equally as serious was Canning's determination that the repression should not extend to Spain's American colonies, where English trade was developing rapidly, and his discussions with the government of the United States were directly responsible for the proclamation of the Monroe Doctrine in 1823.

Despite the breakdown of congress diplomacy as a mechanism of the Quadruple Alliance, however, international cooperation continued to function, as in the Belgian revolution of 1830. The overthrow of Charles X in France stimulated the Belgians, who were dissatisfied with Dutch rule, to rise against the king of Holland. International reactions were uncertain at first, with Britain and France favorable to the revolution and the eastern powers opposed, but diplomacy avoided overt intervention and the possible clash of great power interests, so the independence of Belgium was achieved without escalation into a major international conflict. In retrospect, it may be said that the reactionary purposes that the eastern powers attempted to develop in the postwar alliance had little effect beyond a few specific interventions in Italy and Spain, but the principle of international cooperation in peacetime and the more sophisticated diplomatic mechanisms developed in the aftermath of the Vienna peace enjoyed moderate success and contributed importantly to the international stability of the nineteenth century.

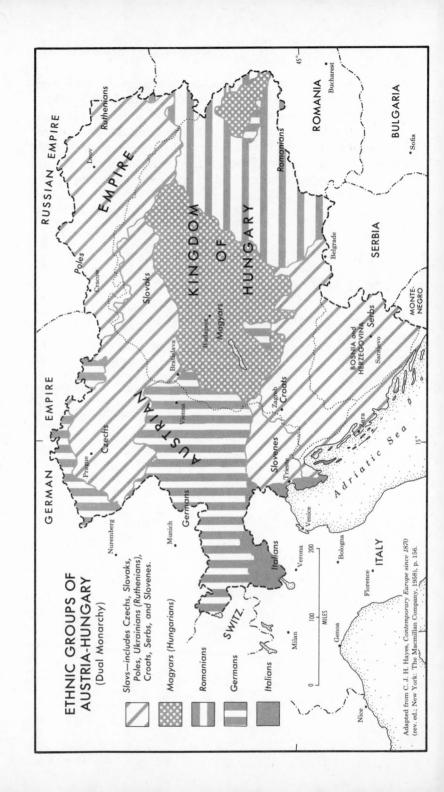

ETHNIC GROUPS OF
AUSTRIA-HUNGARY
(Dual Monarchy)

Slavs—includes Czechs, Slovaks,
Poles, Ukrainians (Ruthenians),
Croats, Serbs, and Slovenes.

Magyars (Hungarians)

Romanians

Germans

Italians

Adapted from C. J. H. Hayes, *Contemporary Europe since 1870*
(rev. ed.; New York: The Macmillan Company, 1958), p. 156.

MILES

0   100   200

RUSSIAN EMPIRE

GERMAN EMPIRE

AUSTRIAN EMPIRE

KINGDOM OF HUNGARY

ROMANIA

Bucharest

BULGARIA

Sofia

SERBIA

Belgrade

MONTE-
NEGRO

BOSNIA and
HERZEGOVINA

Sarajevo

Serbs

Zara

Adriatic Sea

ITALY

Bologna

Florence

Genoa

Nice

SWITZ.

Milan

Verona

Venice

Nuremberg

Munich

Prague

Czechs

Cracow

Poles

Lvov

Ruthenians

Slovaks

Bratislava

Vienna

Germans

Budapest

Magyars

Romanians

Croats

Zagreb

Slovenes

Trieste

Italians

45°

15°

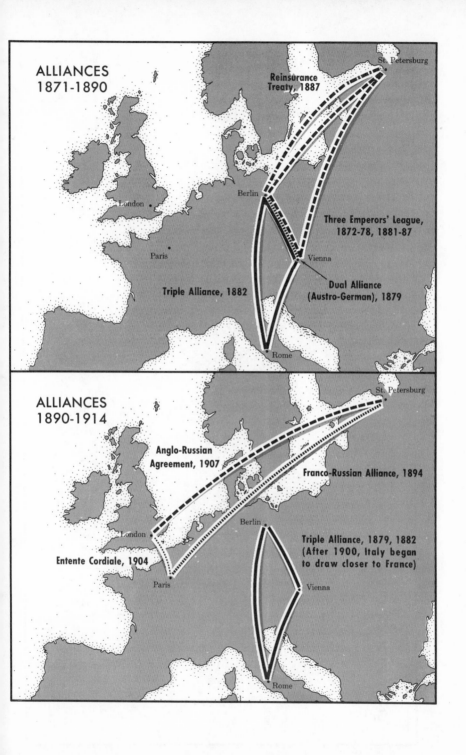

ALLIANCES
1871-1890

Reinsurance
Treaty, 1887

St. Petersburg

London

Berlin

Paris

Three Emperors' League,
1872-78, 1881-87

Vienna

Triple Alliance, 1882

Dual Alliance
(Austro-German), 1879

Rome

ALLIANCES
1890-1914

St. Petersburg

Anglo-Russian
Agreement, 1907

Franco-Russian Alliance, 1894

London

Berlin

Entente Cordiale, 1904

Paris

Vienna

Triple Alliance, 1879, 1882
(After 1900, Italy began
to draw closer to France)

Rome

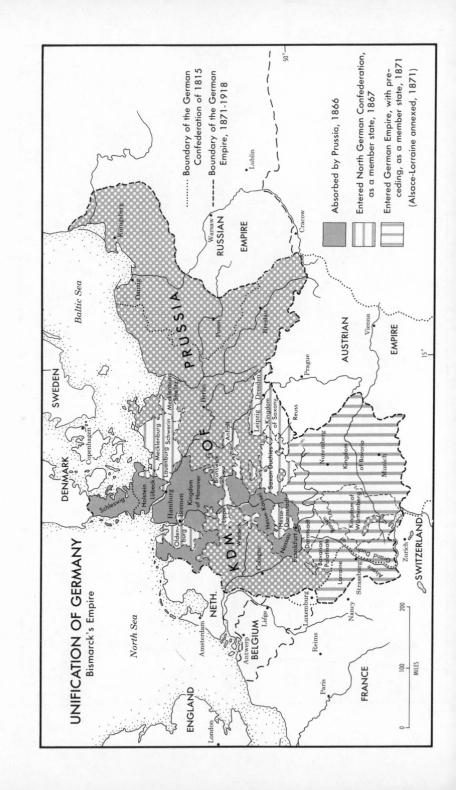

UNIFICATION OF GERMANY
Bismarck's Empire

Boundary of the German Confederation of 1815

Boundary of the German Empire, 1871-1918

Absorbed by Prussia, 1866

Entered North German Confederation, as a member state, 1867

Entered German Empire, with preceding, as a member state, 1871 (Alsace-Lorraine annexed, 1871)

ENGLAND

London

North Sea

Amsterdam

NETH.

Antwerp

BELGIUM

Liége

Luxemburg

Reims

Paris

FRANCE

Nancy

Strasburg

Lorraine

Alsace

Bavarian Palatinate

Darmstadt

Cologne

Nassau

Frankfurt

Hesse-Darmstadt

Waldeck

Oldenburg

Lippe

Hesse-Kassel

Grand Duchy

Kingdom of Württemberg

SWITZERLAND

Zurich

Bremen

Hamburg

Kingdom of Hanover

Brunswick

Anhalt

Saxon Duchies

Kingdom of Saxony

Nuremberg

Kingdom of Bavaria

Munich

Reuss

Prague

Dresden

Leipzig

Berlin

Mecklenburg Schwerin

Mecklenburg Strelitz

Lauenburg

Lübeck

Holstein

Schleswig

Copenhagen

DENMARK

SWEDEN

Baltic Sea

Königsberg

Danzig

PRUSSIA

Posen

Breslau

AUSTRIAN

EMPIRE

Vienna

RUSSIAN

EMPIRE

Warsaw

Lublin

Cracow

50°

15°

0   100   200

MILES

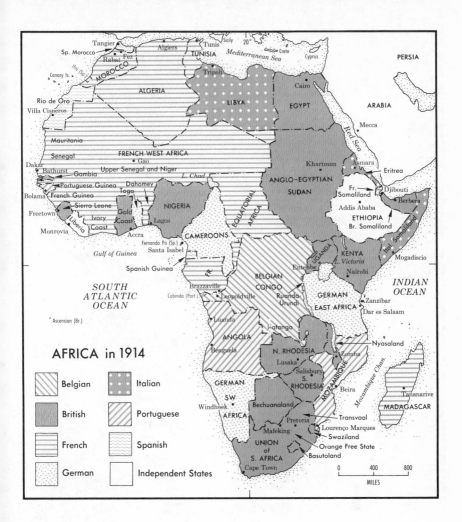

AFRICA in 1914

Legend	
Belgian	Italian
British	Portuguese
French	Spanish
German	Independent States

Map labels:

Tangier, Sp. Morocco, Algiers, Tunis, Sicily, 20°, Crete, Cyprus, PERSIA
Fez, Rabat, TUNISIA, Mediterranean Sea
Canary Is., Ifni (Sp.), MOROCCO, Tripoli, Cairo
Rio de Oro, ALGERIA, LIBYA, EGYPT, ARABIA
Villa Cisneros, Mecca
Mauritania, Red Sea
Senegal, FRENCH WEST AFRICA, Gao, Khartoum, Asmara, Eritrea
Dakar, Upper Senegal and Niger, L. Chad, ANGLO-EGYPTIAN, Fr. Somaliland, Djibouti
Bathurst, Gambia, SUDAN, Berbera
Portuguese Guinea, Dahomey, Addis Ababa
Bolama, French Guinea, Togo, NIGERIA, ETHIOPIA
Sierra Leone, Gold Coast, Br. Somaliland
Freetown, Ivory Coast, Lagos, CAMEROONS
Monrovia, Liberia, Accra, EQUATORIAL AFRICA, UGANDA, KENYA, Mogadiscio
Gulf of Guinea, Fernando Po (Sp.), Santa Isabel, L. Victoria, Nairobi
Spanish Guinea, Entebbe
SOUTH ATLANTIC OCEAN, BELGIAN CONGO, INDIAN OCEAN
Brazzaville, Leopoldville, Ruanda-Urundi, GERMAN EAST AFRICA, Zanzibar
Cabinda (Port.), Dar es Salaam
Ascension (Br.), Luanda, Katanga
ANGOLA, Nyasaland
Benguela, N. RHODESIA, Zomba
Lusaka, MOZAMBIQUE
GERMAN S.W. AFRICA, Salisbury, S. RHODESIA, Beira
Windhoek, Bechuanaland, Transvaal
Pretoria, Lourenço Marques, MADAGASCAR, Tananarive
Mafeking, Swaziland
UNION of S. AFRICA, Orange Free State
Cape Town, Basutoland

0   400   800
MILES

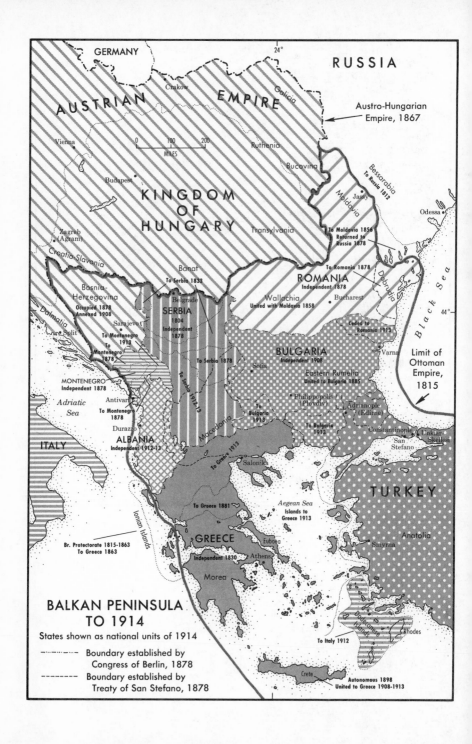

GERMANY

RUSSIA

AUSTRIAN EMPIRE

Crakow

Galicia

Austro-Hungarian
Empire, 1867

Vienna

Ruthenia

Bucovina

Bessarabia
To Russia 1812

Odessa

Budapest

KINGDOM
OF
HUNGARY

Jassy

To Moldavia 1856
Returned to
Russia 1878

Zagreb
(Agram)

Transylvania

Croatia-Slavonia

Dalmatia

Banat
To Serbia 1838

Bosnia-
Herzegovina
Occupied 1878
Annexed 1908

Belgrade

SERBIA
1804
Independent
1878

To Romania 1878

ROMANIA
Independent 1878

Black Sea

44°

Wallachia
United with Moldavia 1858

Bucharest

Dobrudja

Split

Sarajevo

To Montenegro
1913

To
Montenegro
1878

To Serbia 1878

To Serbia 1912-13

BULGARIA
Independent 1908

Ceded to
Romania 1913

Varna

MONTENEGRO
Independent 1878

Adriatic
Sea

Antivari
To Montenegro
1878

Sofia

Eastern Rumelia
United to Bulgaria 1885

Limit of
Ottoman
Empire,
1815

Durazzo

ALBANIA
Independent 1912-13

Macedonia

To
Bulgaria
1913

Philippopolis
(Plovdiv)

Adrianople
(Edirne)

To Bulgaria
1913

Constantinople
San
Stefano

Unkiar
Skelessi

ITALY

To Greece 1913

Salonika

TURKEY

Ionian Islands

To Greece 1881

Aegean Sea

Islands to
Greece 1913

Anatolia

Br. Protectorate 1815-1863
To Greece 1863

GREECE
Independent 1830

Euboea

Athens

Smyrna

Morea

Dodecanese
Islands

Rhodes

To Italy 1912

BALKAN PENINSULA
TO 1914

States shown as national units of 1914

—·—·—·— Boundary established by
Congress of Berlin, 1878

— — — — Boundary established by
Treaty of San Stefano, 1878

Crete

Autonomous 1898
United to Greece 1908-1913

24°

CENTRAL and EASTERN EUROPE in 1947

Chapter 21

Industrialization
and Its Consequences

The nineteenth century witnessed an economic transformation as fraught with consequences for European development as the political and social innovations of the revolutionary and Napoleonic experience. Beginning in Britain in the eighteenth century and spreading to the continent in the nineteenth century, heavy industrialization of manufacturing processes changed both the techniques and the capacities of European production and brought in its wake a whole series of new problems: urbanization, modern industrial labor forces, mass political movements united by economic interests, and reinvigorated international competition for markets and raw materials.

The beginnings of heavy industrialization in eighteenth century Britain turned on two major technological developments, a revolution in metallurgy and the successful application of steam power to manufacturing. The metallurgical improvement of such vast consequences was the discovery of the technique of smelting iron with coal purified by coking. By the eighteenth century, Britain, and indeed most of western Europe south of the Baltic, were experiencing severe shortages of the hardwoods traditionally made into charcoal for the smelting of iron. Early attempts to substitute coal, which

Britain had in quantity, were unsuccessful, as the impurities in the coal produced gases which caused bubbles in the iron, making it brittle and unreliable. It is uncertain exactly when the coking process to remove impurities was developed, but it was being used in the north of England in the early eighteenth century and had become rather widely known by the middle of the century. In the days of charcoal smelting, blast furnaces had to be small enough to be transported from one fuel source to another, whereas the utilization of coke allowed enormous facilities to be built over England's extensive coal fields; thus, in addition to solving a critical fuel problem, the use of coke increased productive efficiency and made much greater quantities of iron available at substantially reduced prices.

Besides its uses in construction, relatively cheap iron encouraged one of the most revolutionary developments of human inventiveness, the steam engine. Men long had dreamed of harnessing the power of steam, but only in the early years of the eighteenth century did such dreams become reality, when Thomas Newcomen built the first economically feasible steam engine. Its efficiency was so low that it was used only to pump water from coal mines, where cheap fuel was abundant, but it proved that steam could be put to work; James Watt began experimenting with improvements in the 1760s, found a partner to finance him, and by the 1780s was producing successful steam engines for general industrial use. It would be difficult to overestimate the significance of this invention, for until the eighteenth century, despite the development of some very sophisticated machinery, men depended for power upon wind, water and muscle; the steam engine was the first source of power that was independent of the vagaries of the elements and the fatigue of muscles, and despite the limited efficiency of the early engines, they represented an enormous technological advance.

Steam power first was applied widely in the production of cotton textiles, and study of this industry has prompted many historians to speak of an industrial revolution. It should be recognized, however, that cotton manufacture in many ways was an atypical industry, and one cannot generalize from it safely. The production of cotton cloth was a new industry in eighteenth century Europe, which previously had depended upon domestic wool and linen, so the industry was more susceptible to innovation than most, and it became centralized into factories or mills dependent upon steam power long before other industries were affected significantly. Moreover, traditional textile production was one of Europe's most decentralized industries, so the contrast was the more startling.

At the end of the middle ages and during the early modern period, the voyages of discovery had opened enormous new opportunities for trade, but the guild organizations that dominated Europe's manufacturing processes were oriented to ideas of stable markets and the security of the craft rather than to speculative production for expanding markets. Consequently, a number of entrepreneurs developed new sources of production outside the guild-dominated towns, particularly in textiles which were important trade goods. They instituted production through specialization of labor in villages; thus, their agents would deliver wool in one village for spinning into yarn, transport it to another village for weaving, to another for dyeing, and so on. Because this production was carried on in the workers' homes, it often was called the domestic system, and it was the most decentralized manufacturing to be found. By contrast, the new cotton industry soon came to depend upon cumbersome and costly machinery that necessitated centralized production. Even before the significant application of steam power, the development in the 1760s of the "water frame," a water-driven machine that spun yarn in quantity, established this pattern, and when it was converted to steam in the 1780s the process was accelerated by the cost of the new installations. The consequent availability of practically limitless supplies of yarn stimulated the invention of an economically feasible steam loom just after 1800, completing the centralization of cotton textiles into large factories and providing Britain the export product she needed for expanding nineteenth century markets.

The rapid development of some aspects of Britain's manufacturing industries was enormously costly, for construction of large blast furnaces and factories with steam engines required heavy investment. Moreover, the growth of large factories required a labor force, and this in turn depended upon a rather high degree of mobility of men able and willing to accept employment in the new enterprises. In both of these matters, eighteenth century England was singularly well equipped to take the lead in European industrialization. On the one hand, highly successful colonial expansion had built some great commercial fortunes in England; on the other, an accelerating transformation of English agriculture was producing both capital growth and a mobile work force.

At the end of the seventeenth century there began in England what sometimes is called an agricultural revolution. The foundation of this agrarian transformation was a process called enclosure, which created large consolidated farms from the common fields which had been characteristic of manorial practice. Enclosure negated the rights that many small farmers held under the common law, so it required an act of parliament, but as the large landowners dominated parliament, hundreds of enclosure acts were passed during the eighteenth century. On the resulting large farms production increased markedly through careful crop management and selective stock breeding, which often made the landowners wealthy, but traditionally small farmers had depended heavily upon their rights of usage of common lands, and when this usage was denied them many had to sell out. In addition, enclosure displaced cottagers, impoverished individuals with no actual ownership who built hovels on common land and eked out a meager existence. Small farmers and cottagers uprooted by enclosure often drifted toward the cities, where they formed a labor pool for the new factories.

The combination of export markets, risk capital, technological development and mobile labor catapulted Britain into the forefront of European manufacturing in the eighteenth century, and after the fall of Napoleon the new techniques and new patterns of industrial organization spread slowly to the continent. There, however, they were changed significantly. Mercantilist practices of the continental states in the eighteenth century had tended to make long-distance trade a government enterprise through colonial companies, so there were fewer private commercial fortunes. Moreover, continental Europe had not undergone an agricultural revolution; rather, the revolutionary and Napoleonic years had tended to confirm the organization of arable land into small peasant farms, so great agrarian fortunes were rare, too. Finally, heavy taxation to pay for two decades of massive war had diminished both capital and its owners' willingness to risk it. Inevitably, governments were much more involved in underwriting industrialization on the continent than was the case in England, for often it was only governments that had the necessary resources to take the risks involved and to await long-term return on heavy investment, whether direct— as when the Prussian government built railway lines, or indirect— as when Napoleon III's government provided subsidies and guaranteed loans to private developers.

The second stage of the economic transformation of Europe was the revolution in transportation that occurred because of steam power. As early as the eighteenth century horse-drawn railways were being used to move heavy loads such as coal, and the substitution of engines for horses was a natural step. During the 1820s and 1830s reasonably reliable locomotives were developed, and the next few decades saw a great era of railway construction, not only in Europe but also in its colonial dominions and in North America. About the same time, steam power and iron construction were being applied to problems of ocean transport. Ships were using a combination of steam and sails before 1820, and in 1826 a Dutch ship crossed the Atlantic wholly under steam power; in the 1830s the screw propeller replaced the paddlewheel, while the use of iron allowed construction of vessels large enough to utilize the power of steam efficiently. By 1840 regular steamship service had been established between England and Egypt and on a transatlantic route. The development of railways and steam-powered iron ships had enormous impact upon commerce, especially after the opening of the Suez Canal in 1869. Relatively cheap long-distance transport made it possible to gather raw materials from anywhere and to reexport finished goods to anywhere, and western Europe quickly became the industrial center of the world.

The most immediate social consequence of industrialization was rapid urbanization, as thousands of people poured into the burgeoning industrial cities seeking unskilled employment in the factories. Since labor was plentiful and unorganized, wages tended to be very low and hours very long. Moreover, many manufacturers hired women and children, who could be had more cheaply than adult males, and some factories were death traps with unshielded machinery and massive fire hazards. The inhumanity of early industrial society, discovered by governmental investigating committees and popularized in the novels of Dickens and Zola, defies belief. Since antiquated legislation encouraged orphanages to apprentice their charges in useful employment, children as young as six worked fourteen hours daily, and foremen beat them regularly to keep them awake at their work. Wages were far too low to allow an unskilled laborer to support a family, and factory owners assumed no responsibility for workers who fell ill or were injured in industrial accidents, so, typically, among industrial families husband, wife and children worked.

Industrial workers were housed in vast rapidly built slums where whole families lived in one room, and usually these slums lacked sanitary facilities, safe water supplies or any of the other amenities needed to protect life in crowded conditions. In these sprawling districts there were, of course, no schools, no nurseries and no medical services, so people of all ages who fell ill generally lay untended until they either died or recovered, while wasting diseases such as tuberculosis simply were accepted as normal to life. Compounding these horrors were the activities of unscrupulous and vicious individuals, typified in some of Dickens' novels: men who sired numerous children so as to live by the pittances they could earn in the mills and foster parents who collected unprotected children whom they destined to factories and mines or apprenticed to crime. The industrial slums became teeming jungles where humanity was reduced to the level of predatory animals.

The horrendous conditions that accompanied industrialization have tempted some historians to draw sharp contrasts between factory labor and earlier guild, domestic and agricultural employment, but the differences easily can be exaggerated. Producers under the guild and domestic systems worked equally long hours and were equally susceptible to unemployment due to market fluctuations, while agricultural labor always had been back-breaking drudgery. Industrialization even represented some improvement, for under the older form of production the workman usually had to buy or rent his tools, which left him to bear the cost of idle capital equipment during periods of unemployment. It is undeniable that early industrial conditions were frightful, but this does not mean that the previous condition of unskilled labor was much better. Rather, growing population meant that there were many more people experiencing this miserable existence, and urbanization meant that they were gathered together where their plight was more obvious to the rest of society. Certainly the health hazards and the degradation of life in the industrial slums represented a deterioration of the condition of the poor, but the long, grueling hours of underpaid work and the callous unconcern of the upper classes did not originate with industrialization.

The concentration of masses of the laboring poor in the new industrial cities made it impossible for the rest of society to ignore their plight. Many people called for government regulation, and this group included some industrialists who disapproved in principle of the practices to which they were forced in order to meet competition; they saw in regulation a device that would force the added cost of more humanitarian practices equally upon all producers, and it was a cotton magnate who pressed the first English factory legislation through parliament.

Economic regulation met serious resistance, however, not only in defense of profit but also on the basis of a relatively new economic doctrine called *laissez-faire,* a justification of unrestricted private enterprise that grew out of Adam Smith's *Wealth of Nations.* Generally the *laissez-faire* economists held that economics should be regulated only by natural laws, such as supply and demand, and that productivity and consequent national wealth would increase most rapidly in an environment of free trade and unrestricted competition. This school of thought also formulated the iron law of wages which held that the working force always must live at a level of bare subsistence because any increase in real wages only would encourage the poor to breed more children, who would eat up the increment.

As the nineteenth century developed, the massive contrast between the wealthy few and the numerous poor encouraged ever more fanciful rationalizations. Observing the immorality and lawlessness spawned by the industrial slums, the upper classes theorized that to allow leisure time to working people would be to encourage social instability and violence, and they concluded, therefore, that long hours of work were a good thing. In 1850 Herbert Spencer's *Social Statics* expounded the view that the lower classes were basically inferior, that the reason there *were* lower classes was because they were lazy and/or incapable of betterment, and this theory was reinforced in succeeding decades by pseudo-scientific analogies. In 1859 Charles Darwin's *Origin of Species* suggested that the explanation of evolution lay in the fact that the fittest examples of a species lived to breed and pass on their characteristics. This line of reasoning, and particularly the catch phrases "natural selection" and "survival of the fittest," soon were applied to social analysis, producing theories loosely termed "social Darwinism." According to this school of thought, not only were reformist movements doomed because the poor generally were incapable of betterment, but such reform would endanger the human race by encouraging the survival and procreation of the unfit. Both the classical liberals, as *laissez-faire* economists were called, and the later social Darwinists advocated the unhampered operation of private capitalism, holding that general welfare was achieved best through the unrestrained pursuit of self-interest.

These theories did not go unchallenged. In England those who wanted to use the power of government to pursue greater social justice, like their *laissez-faire* opponents, were inspired generally by Jeremy Bentham's "greatest good of the greatest number," while on the continent such aspirations usually derived of the French Revolution. On both sides of the channel, however, a number of men came to support a doctrine called radicalism. Though they often differed among themselves, most radicals sought extensive democratic reform, such as universal manhood suffrage; most tended to be republicans, at least until Queen Victoria made the monarchy popular in England, and most were anti-clerical. Under the impact of industrialism, some of the radicals extended their political thought to economics, developing doctrines called socialism.

Until the late 1840s socialism was rather amorphous, but all socialists agreed that the socioeconomic system as it existed was grossly unfair, for industrialization was making a few manufacturers unbelievably wealthy while workers continued to live in poverty. The socialists rejected the whole concept of private ownership and control of capital assets in favor of communal possession, with profits to be shared through the entire society, and they rejected the value of competition in favor of economic and social coordination through governmental planning. Early socialists tended to be utopian dreamers such as the English factory owner Robert Owen and the French theorists, the Count de Saint-Simon and Charles Fourier. More practical was Louis Blanc, who proposed the establishment of governmentally financed factories where workers might have the benefit of industrial employment without private owners taking all the profit; this idea was supported enthusiastically by Parisian workers whose disenfranchisement and isolation under the restored monarchy rekindled revolutionary ferment and hostility to the bourgeoisie, and despite England's industrial preeminence, it was in Paris that socialism found the strongest support during the 1830s and 1840s.

Industrialization and the problems it brought in its wake soon began to influence the political development of Europe. In Britain, working class unrest provoked the Peterloo massacre in 1819, but in the 1830s political and legal reforms and the beginning of protective legislation resolved some problems and seemed to promise early resolution of others, so the British labor movement did not develop a very deep radical and socialist commitment. By and large, such tendencies were subsumed in the chartist movement in the 1840s, and when this movement died, the aspirations of British labor began to reorient toward unionism.

The chartists derived their name from a People's Charter which was drafted in 1838 to draw together all those desirous of continuing reform; it incorporated six points, of which universal suffrage was the most important, and it rallied widespread working class support. In 1839 the charter was presented to parliament as a petition signed by one and a quarter million people, but parliament rejected it; it was presented again in 1842 with more than three and a quarter million signatures, and again it was rejected. These rejections sparked widespread rioting but when the immediate reaction had worn itself out, chartism went into a decline. Inspired by revolutions on the continent, there was a brief revival in 1848, and yet another petition was presented without effect; then chartism withered away, undermined by its failure to achieve results and by an improvement in the standard of living after repeal of the Corn Laws in 1846 lowered food prices.

On the continent industrialization had not yet progressed far enough nor socialist doctrine evolved sufficiently for the industrial labor force to have much effect upon the revolutions of 1830. In Paris workers formed a significant part of the republican movement, but they were unable to prevent Lafayette and the bourgeois leaders from accepting the Orléanist monarchy; in Belgium and in Piedmont-Sardinia the revolutions served national and liberal aims; and in the rest of Europe they were crushed. However, in the 1840s socialism became stronger and more self-conscious, and it formed an important element in the violence of 1848.

The political eruptions that shook Europe at the end of the 1840s varied widely both in causes and results from one area to another. In eastern and central Europe, where national feeling had not yet achieved institutional expression and where the liberal constitutionalism attained in the west had not yet developed, nationalism and liberalism were major forces, as they had been in the western upheavals of 1830–32. By contrast, in England, France and Belgium, where the bourgeoisie had achieved political power in the 1830s and industrialization had advanced markedly, the chartist movement and the revolutions of 1848 reflected a conflict of interest between the dominant bourgeoisie and the new industrial labor force. England escaped serious violence largely because socially conscious Tory landowners provided some counterbalance to bourgeois government and secured the passage of legislation that ameliorated laboring conditions somewhat, but in western continental Europe the more or less unrestrained domination of the capitalist classes led to a new confrontation. Since the upheavals that took place all over Europe in 1848 were sparked by a new outbreak of revolutionary violence in Paris, in which the working class played an important role, industrialization must be considered an important causative element even though only a small part of the continent was as yet industrialized.

The protests against Louis Philippe's government in France were organized by an opposition that was basically bourgeois-liberal and probably could have been contained within the constitutional monarchy by a few concessions, but when the king's minister, Guizot, proved intransigent and tried to repress even the protest banquets, the opposition broadened. The working class announced its adherence to the cause of change by raising barricades in the streets of Paris and rioting in front of Guizot's house, and it sought more than minor electoral reform. When Louis Philippe abdicated and fled abroad in February of 1848, radicals, including socialists, invaded the Chamber of Deputies and forced the proclamation of another republic; three of the ten members of the provisional government, most notably Louis Blanc, then formed favored socialism. Between February and April of 1848 they were able to obtain some concessions to their desire for broad economic and social reform, especially the creation of national workshops; these were public works projects rather than the collectivist factories that Blanc long had advocated, but at least they provided some relief from the high unemployment that had resulted from depressed economic conditions during 1847 and 1848. Socialist strength was limited to the Paris area, however, the rest of France being dominated by bourgeois and peasant conservatism, and the constituent assembly elected on a nationwide basis in May created a five-man executive that was intensely hostile to Blanc and his followers. A struggle soon developed between the Paris socialists and this cautious constituent government.

In May the Paris radicals revolted again, and the Constituent Assembly used troops to suppress them, but Paris continued to seethe with unrest, and when the government tried to abolish the national workshops in June, believing correctly that they were the centers of much of the sedition, it sparked an insurrection of the working classes. The government's solution was to entrust something near to dictatorial power to General Cavaignac, and toward the end of the month there occurred the Bloody June Days when class warfare raged through the streets of Paris. Cavaignac succeeded in restoring order, but thousands were killed, and in the aftermath thousands more were deported to the colonies. The events of June 1848 terrorized France, especially French property owners, and prepared the way for a revival of Bonapartism.

In December of 1848 elections were held for a president of the republic, based upon universal manhood suffrage, and the victor was not one of those who had been active in the revolutions of February and June but Louis Napoleon Bonaparte, nephew of Napoleon I. Louis Napoleon was not well known in France; he had written two books that indicated a strong sense of nationalism and a responsible concern for social welfare, but his chief strength in the election was the popularity of the Napoleonic legend. After three decades of monarchical experiment, bourgeois domination and lack of national purpose, the Napoleonic years were remembered not for their cost in blood and taxes but for the glory, the excitement and the temporary French hegemony that they had achieved. The general populace hoped the new Napoleon could restore some of these attributes to France; moderate republicans hoped he could control radicals; and conservatives, frightened of socialism and anticlericalism and divided between Bourbonists and Orléanists, hoped he could maintain order and protect the church. Thus, by early 1850 the radical revolution had evolved into a very conservative republic relying upon disparate groups held together only by nationalism and their desire for stability.

Once again revolution in Paris inspired uprisings in other European capitals. In March of 1848 an insurrection broke out in Vienna, whence rioting spread rapidly through Germany and Italy. Metternich resigned and fled; the king of Prussia was forced to promise the issuance of a constitution; and lesser governments collapsed one after another. In Hungary the diet adopted a constitution establishing autonomy within the empire; in Venice and Tuscany republics were proclaimed. The king of Piedmont-Sardinia issued a constitution before his government was overtaken by revolution and then tried to turn popular agitation in Italy to advantage by declaring war upon Austria, in which he was joined by volunteers from all over the peninsula. In March of 1848 the carefully balanced systems that Metternich had created collapsed, both within the Habsburg empire and beyond it in Italy and Germany, and everywhere governments yielded to nationalist and liberal demands for constitutions and political and legal reforms. Probably the most ambitious efforts of the nationalists were the convocation of an all-German assembly at Frankfort and a Pan-Slav Congress in Prague.

As in France, however, the force of revolution could not be sustained, and in the summer of 1848 conservatives in central Europe began to reassert themselves. In June Habsburg military forces succeeded in reoccupying Prague and broke up the Pan-Slav Congress; then in July they defeated the Sardinians in north Italy and reestablished Habsburg authority in Lombardy and the Venetia. In the autumn the non-Magyar population of Hungary rallied to the Habsburgs for protection against the excesses of Hungarian nationalism and by October the Hungarian insurrection was broken; at the same time, a last resort to violence in Vienna failed when Habsburg forces from Bohemia compelled the city to surrender. Conservatives were encouraged and forced the abdication of Emperor Ferdinand, who had made frightened promises of reform in March, and began to rebuild the Habsburg government around Emperor Francis Joseph, so 1848 ended with the Austrian empire shaken but intact.

In 1849 another wave of revolutionary violence swept central Europe, marked by widespread rioting in Germany, the proclamation of a republic in Rome and renewed Magyar insurrection in Hungary, but again the movement waned after initial successes, and by late summer traditional governments were in control again. At the same time, the all-German assembly at Frankfort, having failed to persuade the king of Prussia to lead a nationalist movement, began to disintegrate and a stubborn remnant finally was broken up by Prussian troops. In central Europe as in France, by 1850 the revolutions had run their course and had achieved little or nothing that the revolutionaries sought. Nationalism still lacked institutional expression in Germany and Italy, and in the few states where the constitutions extorted by the revolutions were maintained, they tended more to obstruct than to advance the cause of liberalism.

Chapter 22

The Nation Deified

Just as the cataclysm of the revolutionary and Napoleonic wars had discredited the Enlightenment's optimism and faith in reason, so the general failure of the revolutions of 1848 tended to discredit the Romantic's faith in popular nationalism and mass agitation. The new generation of nationalists was composed of hardheaded pragmatists who planned to further their ambitions through the manipulation of political machinery and the use of military force. In central Europe the major goal remained national unifications, while in Britain, France and Russia, where unified states already existed, nationalism tended to express itself in pressure for social consolidation and an aggressive international role.

In Britain the 1850s and 1860s were marked by increasing stability of government, a realignment of the party structure and a much more assertive foreign policy. During the quarter century following the Vienna peace, the prestige of the monarchy had eroded badly: George III (1760–1820) had suffered fits of insanity; George IV (1820–1830) had scandalized the nation by the debauchery of his private life and by inaugurating divorce proceedings against his wife; and William IV's reign (1830–1837) was too short and too much dominated by the great reform ministries to have much effect in reestablishing public respect for the crown. By contrast, Queen

Victoria (1837–1901) enjoyed a long reign and she showed dignity and strength of character that impressed her subjects very favorably; without attempting to intrude upon the rights of parliament she asserted herself forcefully to maintain her household's independence from politial questions, insisted on being consulted concerning foreign affairs and occasionally rebuked her ministers sufficiently to remind them that they were ministers of the crown and not republican officials. Queen Victoria refused to allow the crown to become either a political pawn or a meaningless anachronism, and the monarchy came to be a symbol of national unity.

The middle years of the nineteenth century also witnessed a transformation of the British party structure. Repeal of the Corn Laws in 1846 split the Tory party beyond repair, for Peel's conversion to free trade threatened the economic security of Tory landowners, while rifts appeared between the old Whig aristocrats and younger Whigs influenced by the sociopolitical theories of Bentham and his successors. Among the Tories, Benjamin Disraeli led a revolt against Peel, claiming he had betrayed the party and adopted the Whigs' principles, and traditionalist Whigs gravitated toward this conservative group, while the "Peelite" Tories and progressive Whigs began to cooperate with each other. By the end of the 1850s the Liberal and Conservative parties had evolved, but no great gulf separated them; both were committed fully to the constitutional monarchy and to further amelioration of the living conditions of the lower classes, and they differed chiefly on how these ends best might be served. Generally the Conservatives favored Tory democracy, with monarchy, aristocracy and church leading the nation and showing responsible concern for the physical improvement of living conditions, while Liberals were oriented more to the burgeoning industrial middle class and to continuing political reform, but in the 1850s and 1860s the new alignment was still a bit amorphous.

By 1840 Britain's increasingly nationalist foreign policy had been illustrated by the Opium War with China, when bombardments by British gunboats were used to settle a quarrel with the Chinese government, and this aggressiveness was shown again in 1850 against the Greeks. Don Pacifico was a Moorish Jew resident in Athens who held British citizenship; when the Greek government refused to settle claims he had against it and an anti-Semitic mob burned his house, a British naval squadron blockaded Athens and forced the Greeks to make restitution. While defending his action before the Commons, Foreign Secretary Palmerston compared British citizenship to classical Roman citizenship, and his bold appeal to nationalism won him an ovation. In the 1860s this aggressiveness was reaffirmed during the American civil war by Britain's friendly attitude toward the southern states, with whom she had important commerce in cotton, despite the risk of war with the United States.

These years of political growth and economic expansion in Britain were capped by another reform bill in 1867, more radical than its predecessor in 1832. Essentially a Liberal measure forced upon a Conservative government by popular pressure, it provided a redistribution of seats in the commons, and it reduced voting qualifications drastically, doubling the electorate and admitting most urban workers to the franchise. This extensive reform consolidated the nation thoroughly and prepared the way for the great imperial expansion of the late nineteenth century.

In France, the 1850s and 1860s were dominated by the efforts of Louis Napoleon to balance the contending factions of the French political scene. He attempted to rally various sorts of conservatives to his government, and since all that united these disparate groups was Catholicism and fear of radicalism, his early policy favored the church and repressed anticlericals and radical extremists. In the spring of 1849 French troops intervened in Rome to crush a revolutionary republic and restore the pope, and early in 1850 new laws extended considerably the role of the clergy in French education, limited the suffrage indirectly by establishing long residency requirements and prohibited political organizations and public meetings. But Louis Napoleon was no reactionary, and he had no intention of becoming a tool of conservative interests. He tried to inhibit the reestablishment of an absolutist papal government in Rome, and he agreed only with reluctance to extensive Catholic educational influence in France. His goal was the reestablishment of a popularly supported imperial government, and he wanted to encourage nationalism and economic growth and to practice moderate policies that would unite Frenchmen rather than divide them.

Unfortunately for Louis Napoleon, the issues of French politics were serious and the divisions bitter. Proclerical and anticlerical groups hated one another; property owners detested socialists, while socialists damned factory owners as exploiters; and monarchists despised the republic while republicans hated the monarchy. Moreover, these issues tended to align the nation in two great blocs; monarchists usually were proclerical property owners, while republicans usually were anticlerical and sympathetic to more moderate forms of socialism, so any policy threatened to evoke a massive political confrontation.

Louis Napoleon honestly believed strong leadership was needed in the maelstrom of French politics, but the constitution limited him to one four-year term, so at the end of 1851 he overthrew the constitution by a *coup d'état,* restored universal manhood suffrage, and went to the voters with a plebiscite asking for extraordinary powers to draft a new constitution. When the plebiscite was overwhelmingly successful, he proclaimed a constitution that put free and unfettered authority in the hands of the president and made him emperor in everything but title. Then, at the end of 1852 another plebiscite approved the reestablishment of the empire, and the president assumed the title of Napoleon III (out of respect for Napoleon I's son who had died without reigning).

In many ways Napoleon III's career exemplifies the first practice of modern popular dictatorship. He based his government upon nationalism and prosperity, using the plebiscite to affirm his personal popularity and offering a few material benefits to everyone: insurance and employment on public projects for workers, government contracts and subsidies for buisness interests. At the same time he employed all the awesome power of the modern state to repress opposition; newspapers were controlled rigidly, and thousands of political opponents were deported to Algeria (which France had conquered toward the end of Charles X's reign). The material success of Napoleon III's policies was impressive: during the 1850s railway trackage increased almost fivefold; Paris was rebuilt, and from a cluttered, jumbled town it became a beautiful modern capital of broad avenues and beautiful perspectives; and business and industry expanded rapidly.

Napoleon III pursued an aggressive foreign policy that he hoped would submerge domestic quarrels and promote nationalism as a unifying force, but in this he was singularly unsuccessful. When he intervened in Rome in 1849, his honest desire for a reformed papal government brought charges of interference with the church from

French Catholics, while the repression of the Roman Republic antagonized French liberals. The emperor enjoyed his only real success in foreign affairs in the mid-1850s, when a Russo-Turkish war broke out and he was able to persuade Britain to join him in intervention since both France and Britain were opposed to Russian expansion to the Mediterranean. The Crimean War succeeded in limiting Russian expansion, and it aroused considerable enthusiasm in the west, partly because war correspondents using the telegraph were able for the first time to provide fresh, vivid accounts to newspapers, but it did not heal the rifts in French domestic politics.

Napoleon III had particular sympathy for Italian national aspirations, for his family had an Italianate background and during his years in exile he had lived in Italy and had associated with Italian nationalists. He hoped to do something for the Italians, and his intentions were reinforced early in 1858 when an Italian terrorist, who thought his cause abandoned, threw a bomb at him. Napoleon III agreed to provide French help to the liberal monarchical government of Piedmont-Sardinia to expel the Austrians from Italy in return for the province of Savoy and the port of Nice, and in 1859 French and Italian forces quickly overran Lombardy. The Austrians withdrew to prepared positions in the Venetia, however, and it became evident that there could be no quick end to the war, while popular risings in Tuscany, Parma, Modena and the Papal States indicated that the unification movement was spreading farther than intended. French Catholics, fearful for the safety of the pope, became angry, and to avoid disaster Napoleon III quit the war, which led both the Italians and the French liberals to damn him.

In 1860 Napoleon III was criticized seriously both for the Italian fiasco and for an unpopular free trade policy, and in an effort to retrieve his position, he decided to liberalize the empire. Far from responding with gratitude, however, the emperor's enemies used the new freedoms to denounce him bitterly, and a strong opposition developed rapidly, so he determined to intervene in a Mexican revolution in hope that another foreign adventure might calm domestic disputes. The Mexican revolutionaries were violently anticlerical, so intervention that protected the church might mollify French Catholics; the French business community was antagonized by the emperor's free trade policy, but it might be appeased by investment opportunities in Mexico; relations with Austria, embittered by the French role in Italian unification, might be reestablished on a cordial basis by offering a Mexican throne to the Austrian emperor's brother, Maximillian; and the military glory of a successful campaign might revive flagging nationalist enthusiasm for the French emperor. Unfortunately, the adventure ended in another fiasco, for the French found themselves in a guerilla war that could not be won, the government of the United States demanded a French withdrawal, and because of growing political problems in Europe Napoleon III needed to recall his troops. In the aftermath of a Mexican total victory in 1867, Maximillian was shot, the church was expropriated and French investments were confiscated.

Another disaster further weakened the French emperor in 1866 when war between Prussia and Austria ended with a startlingly rapid Prussian victory. France received no compensations for the potential threat to her security, and as a result, Napoleon III's prestige suffered badly, while at the same time internal opposition to him was growing stronger and his health was failing. He liberalized the government further in an attempt at appeasement, but elections in 1869 showed a dangerous increase in monarchical and republican strength, while in a deteriorating international situation the French government was isolated. In 1870 the emperor staked everything on a final gamble and precipitated war with Prussia, but the French armies were defeated everywhere, and Napoleon III himself had to surrender at Sedan. Two days later, in Paris, the assembly proclaimed the dissolution of the empire and the establishment of yet another republic.

Though ultimately Napoleon III's government collapsed, his efforts cannot be judged futile. The French economy underwent tremendous expansion, his capital was rebuilt and became the most beautiful city in Europe, and even his foreign policy was not without important results, though it failed to preserve his government; the Crimean War undoubtedly kept the Russians off the Mediterranean, and French intervention launched the successful struggle for the unification of Italy. Napoleon III played a major role not only in the development of France but in the shaping of nineteenth century Europe.

Italian nationalism was the major issue of southern Europe in the middle of the nineteenth century, and when the failure of the widespread risings of 1848 discredited both republican nationalist groups and their terrorist tactics, the focus of the unification movement shifted to Piedmont-Sardinia, the only state in Italy that had maintained the constitution granted in 1848. This reorientation was encouraged both by King Victor Emmanuel II (1849–1878) and by his prime minister, Count Camillo di Cavour, the latter a moderate constitutional monarchist deeply influenced by English political practices and deeply committed to economic and particularly industrial expansion.

The first stages of the wars of unification already have been considered. By the spring of 1860, Austria was confined to the Venetia, and Piedmont-Sardinia had annexed Parma, Modena, Tuscany and some of the northern papal territories. At this point, the colorful adventurer, Garibaldi, secretly encouraged by Cavour, sailed from Genoa with a band of a thousand volunteers known as the Red Shirts to aid revolutionary ferment in Sicily; this band, supported by local uprisings, soon captured the whole of the Bourbon kingdom of Naples. Cavour then sent Piedmontese troops to the support of a revolution in the remaining papal states and secured central Italy while avoiding Rome, which was garrisoned by French troops. Plebiscites in Sicily and southern and central Italy produced overwhelming majorities for union with Piedmont-Sardinia, and in March of 1861, the kingdom of Italy was proclaimed. The new kingdom soon made an alliance with Prussia which proved advantageous in 1866, when one of the consequences of Austria's defeat by Prussia was that she was forced to cede the Venetia to Italy. Then, in 1870, when French troops had to be called home for the Franco-Prussian War, Italian forces crushed the papal garrison in Rome, and it became the Italian capital.

Even in conservative eastern Europe currents of nationalism ran strongly. A Polish national revolt in 1863–64 was repressed and cost Poland her autonomous administration as direct Russian control was reestablished; in 1867 Hungary succeeded in evoking massive concessions to nationalism, and the Austrian Empire was reformed as a dual monarchy with an autonomous government for Hungary; and in the Balkans there were many insurrections against Turkish rule all through the mid-nineteenth century. In Russia, Czar Nicholas I (1825–1855) suppressed any opposition movements successfully, while limited reforms and the national stimulus of foreign wars tended to reinforce his authority, and Czar Alexander II (1855–1881) freed Russia's serfs and made reforms of local government and the judiciary, which relieved some of Russia's most pressing problems and rallied considerable national support for expansion into central Asia and for development of the far eastern provinces.

Beyond a doubt, however, the most influential national movement in Europe was the unification of Germany. The failure in 1848–1850 of both a liberal parliamentary union and an appeal to Prussia left German nationalists stalemated for a decade, but the successes of the Italian nationalists in the early 1860s stimulated a new wave of German agitation, and about the same time Prussia became more sympathetic to German nationalism. In the face of Napoleon III's aggressive foreign policy, the Prussian king, William I (1861–1888), wanted to reform and modernize the Prussian army, but the Prussian parliament demanded further liberalization of the constitution as the price of voting the necessary funds, and the king was unwilling to make such extensive concessions. The resulting deadlock became serious, and in 1862 the king entrusted the government to his former ambassador to St. Petersburg and Paris, Otto von Bismarck, a man reputed for his boldness, his loyalty and his steady conservatism. Bismarck took up the struggle with the Prussian liberals, and for four years he governed extralegally, but meanwhile he so advanced the cause of German unity that nationalists rallied to him even if somewhat distrustfully.

In the 1860s there were two schools of thought concerning the form a unification movement should take. Austria and the governments of the smaller southern states tended to favor a big Germany to be established through closer integration of the German Confederation; this solution would have included the German parts of the

Austrian domains and would have offered some greater security for the independent traditions and Catholic religion of the south, which tended to orient toward Vienna. Bismarck, for nationalist reasons, and German liberals, because of distrust of Austria's extremely conservative and internationalist policies, tended to favor a little Germany solution, which would exclude Austria and create a unified state with a strong central government dominated by Prussia. Bismarck recognized that to achieve his aims it would be necessary to assert Prussian leadership in Germany aggressively and that it probably would be necessary to employ military action to force Austria to accept exclusion from a future union, and he adopted a policy of flexible opportunism, waiting to seize any occasion to strengthen Prussia's position.

The first opportunity that presented itself occurred in 1863 when the king of Denmark attempted to incorporate the duchy of Schleswig into his monarchy. This action inflamed German nationalism, for while Schleswig long had been an autonomous possession of the Danish kings, there also were strong traditions supporting its close association with the duchy of Holstein, which was a member of the German Confederation, and the inseparability of Schleswig-Holstein had been confirmed by recent international agreements. In the name of the German Confederation, Prussia protested strongly and provoked a war with Denmark, though she had to act in concert with Austria, for the Prussian government dared not commit its forces to the north while leaving Austria free to act in the south. Nonetheless, the Danish war affirmed Prussia's parity with Austria in national leadership, and its aftermath provided extended opportunities to further Prussian ambition. Austrian and Prussian troops quickly overran the disputed duchies, and arrangements for a joint occupation brought the two German powers into a close association in which friction was a distinct possibility.

Convinced that Austria would not accept exclusion from Germany willingly, Bismarck began to prepare for an Austro-Prussian war. Discussions with Napoleon III, which appear to have included hints of compensations for France, had assured French neutrality in the approaching conflict, and negotiations with Italy won its support in return for a promise that Austria would be forced to cede Venetia to the new Italian kingdom. Then, in the spring and summer of 1866, the Prussian government deliberately escalated disputes with Austria over both the reform of the German Confederation and the administration of Schleswig-Holstein, and in June war was declared. Contrary to the expectations of everyone, and especially of Napoleon III, who had anticipated a long war exhausting both belligerents, the Austrians were crushed in seven weeks, and Prussia was free to make peace on her own terms.

During the short war most of the smaller states had opposed Prussia, and after the defeat both they and Austria were totally vulnerable, but with a thought for future cooperation Bismarck imposed moderate terms. Austria was forced to accept exclusion from any German union, and she had to cede Venetia to Italy, but she suffered no other penalties; Prussia annexed some north German territory and forced the remaining northern states into a new North German Confederation under Prussian domination. The southern states, which remained quite fearful of Prussia, were allowed to maintain their independence, but playing upon their fears of French ambitions and the evidence of Prussian moderation, Bismarck managed to draw them into close military alliances.

The successful war with Austria also had important internal consequences for the Prussian government. Although they still found Bismarck's conservative policies distasteful, many liberals rallied to him because he was furthering their hopes for unification, and in September of 1866 the Prussian legislature passed an indemnity bill which approved retroactively the government's extra-legal action during the four year constitutional quarrel. Thus, by 1867, Prussia had returned to constitutional government, had asserted her leadership of Germany successfully, had excluded Austria from the national movement, and through annexations and a Prussian-dominated northern confederation had achieved the unification of the area north of the Main River. But there were serious obstacles to completing the unification and Prussification of Germany since both Catholicism and the traditional southern orientation toward Vienna separated the south from the Prussian north; the fear of France was the most potent force pushing the southern states into a Prussian orbit, and Bismarck played upon it cleverly.

The swift Prussian victory in the war with Austria and the subsequent consolidation of northern Germany discredited the already much-criticized foreign policy of Napoleon III, and the evolution of strong new political units on France's frontiers, the kingdom of Italy and the North German Confederation, caused many Frenchmen serious and justified concern for France's security. In a desperate attempt to redeem himself in the opinion of his subjects, the French emperor rather clumsily sought Bismarck's support for French aggrandizement at the expense of the Netherlands or the south German states, and Bismarck allowed these suggestions to leak to both foreign governments and the German public. The twin results were an intensification of French diplomatic isolation and a wave of nationalist concern and agitation in southern Germany. Circumstances favored Bismarck's ambitions when a Spanish revolution in 1868 expelled Queen Isabella II and the revolutionaries offered the crown of Spain to a relative of the king of Prussia.

The possibility of being caught between two Hohenzollern monarchies upset the French, and the Paris government tried to exert pressure upon the king of Prussia to reject the offer. Bismarck was able to represent the French efforts as an intrusion upon Prussian sovereignty and an affront to German national pride, and he escalated the issue into a major confrontation. In the summer of 1870, Napoleon III, who already was in political difficulty over a number of issues, declared war on Prussia, and both the collapse of the French empire and the fulfillment of German nationalist ambitions followed rapidly. The military alliances that Prussia had concluded with the south German states quickly made the conflict an all-German war against France, and the combination of united effort and decisive German victories stimulated unionist sentiment. One by one the southern states agreed to unification within the Prussian scheme, and in January of 1871 a federated German Empire was proclaimed with the king of Prussia taking the title of German Emperor. This union solved the German problem, one of the most disruptive issues of nineteenth century Europe, but it also upset the European balance of power and created new issues that were to plague European development for three-quarters of a century.

The failures of the revolutions of 1848 affected socialists as profoundly as nationalists in the sense of discrediting idealism in favor of pragmatism and persuasion in favor of force. That the conflict of interest between the impoverished working classes and the prosperous owning classes was potentially violent was illustrated indisputably by the Bloody June Days in Paris, and the hostility of established governments toward even moderate socialist measures seemed to suggest that socialist goals could be achieved only through violence. The most influential of the tougher socialist doctrines were those of Karl Marx and Friedrich Engels, but in 1848 they were only two members of a minor radical socialist group that was little more than a secret society of German emigrants in London, and at that time they were unknown beyond their own narrow circle. Early in 1848 they had published some of their ideas in a tract entitled *The Communist Manifesto,* however, and these ideas had a wider appeal after the events of 1848 and 1849.

At the root of Marxian socialism was a deep pessimism concerning the possibility of improving working class conditions within society as it existed. Marx and Engels accepted the iron law of wages with its implicit inevitability of bare subsistence pay for workers; they observed that political power was confined to the prosperous owning classes; and they concluded that improvement by evolutionary progress through existing political institutions was impossible. They were persuaded that the working man was exploited by his employers, who expropriated to themselves the fruits of his labor, used the power of the state to repress his protests and used the promises of religion to persuade him to passive acceptance of his condition. The situation might have appeared hopeless but for the example of the great French revolution of 1789 by which society had been forced to massive civil and legal changes. Marx and Engels believed that what the bourgeoisie had done, the working classes could do, that the proper application of violence could remold society.

To these concepts based upon industrialization and revolution, Marx added a philosophical element, dialectical materialism. Derived of the German philosopher Hegel, the dialectic was an explanation of change in terms of syntheses produced by conflicts; since a synthesis itself could evoke an opposition, a new conflict then would arise, producing a new synthesis, and so on. Marx applied this philosophical concept to an interpretation of history based upon the idea of classes, explaining social evolution in terms of class conflict, and this pseudo-scientific theory suggested that industrial society confronted the last stage of social evolution, bourgeois-working class conflict, and that revolution was inevitable. To socialists these theories were reassuring, for they confidently announced ultimate victory, and they were inspiring, for they gave direction to socialist efforts—encouragement of working class solidarity and education of workers to recognize how they were being exploited. Through most of the west, however, trade unionism and extension of voting rights provided an alternative to revolution in the struggle for emancipation of the working classes, and though Marxism retained an important influence in socialist thought, especially its concepts of solidarity and activism, its revolutionary character diminished greatly and might have disappeared altogether but for its revival by Lenin and its institutional establishment in Russia in 1917.

Chapter 23

The New Europe

Ever since the fall of the Roman Empire, the monarchy in France generally was the strongest power in Europe; sometimes it was weakened by internal divisions, as during the Hundred Years War, or overshadowed by external combinations, such as the great alliances that checked Louis XIV and defeated Napoleon; but it had human and natural resources that exceeded those of any other power, and those resources were organized by one of the most highly developed governments in Europe. During the nineteenth century this situation changed completely, for industrialization doubled and redoubled Britain's strength, and the unification of Germany created a state that was both larger and more populous than France. Thus, in the last quarter of the nineteenth century, in addition to confronting social problems consequent upon industrialization and political problems resulting from self-conscious and enfranchised working classes, the European states had to confront one another in an ill-defined international scene in which precedents had little value and the strength of allies and opponents only could be guessed.

Britain's major concerns, thanks to the stability of a highly consolidated national society, were to find raw materials and markets to serve her industrial economy. France was committed to another republican experiment while still experiencing the turbulence of rapid industrial development, and she had to grapple with the results of defeat in the Franco-Prussian War and the threat to her security implicit in the existence of a unified Germany. The new central European states, Italy and Germany, had to seek means of national development; and Austria had to struggle to maintain the stability of a multinational empire in an age of virulent nationalism while flanked by a reorganized Germany from which she was excluded and a hostile Italy whose government had further designs upon Habsburg lands. Finally, Russia, humiliated and isolated after the Crimean War, had to redefine her international position, settle and develop her territories in central and eastern Asia and build the industrial basis for a modern economy. Considerations of the late nineteenth century often are overshadowed by European imperial expansion, but this also was a period of internal European development that was fraught with consequences for the twentieth century.

During the 1870s and 1880s Britain's government was dominated by the towering personalities of William Gladstone and Benjamin Disraeli. During Gladstone's first ministry (1868–1874), liberal reform was continued, and many of the vestiges of an older and more authoritarian society were abolished. In an attempt to pacify Ireland, where violence was endemic, Gladstone ended the requirement that the Irish support an Anglican church to which few of them belonged and revised the legal structure of Irish land tenure to provide the Irish peasantry some protection against English absentee landlords. Within England, where there were educational facilities for only about half the children of school age, he established a system of public schools with government support and removed religious qualifications from access to higher education. In an attempt to open government service more broadly, he provided for competitive examinations in the civil service and ended purchase of military commissions. Finally, he provided for the use of the secret ballot in elections and reformed English courts to provide more rapid and more equitable judgments. In the spirit of Tory democracy, a Disraeli government (1874–1880) carried bills establishing minimal standards for public health and for workers' housing and providing safety regulations for merchant shipping. The second Gladstone ministry (1880–1885) returned to liberalization, further developing legislative protection of the Irish peasantry, extending voting rights in England again, enacting another parliamentary redistribution and attempting to limit corrupt practices in elections. During the last decade and a half of the nineteenth century Britain witnessed a notable expansion of trade unionism, culminating with the foundation in 1893 of the Independent Labour Party with an evolutionary socialist platform, but chiefly British politics after about 1885 were dominated by a fast-changing international situation.

Queen Victoria's death and the accession of Edward VI (1901–1910) brought no dramatic changes. Continuing prosperity maintained stability, and the government pursued a moderate program aimed at the gradual improvement of social conditions. A new Education Act in 1902 extended public education to secondary levels; a Trade Disputes Bill and a Workman's Compensation Act in 1906 improved the position of unions and provided further protection to laborers; and Old Age Pension Law in 1909 made provision for minimal support of every aged British subject; and a National Insurance Act in 1911 introduced both health and unemployment insurance. Britain experienced some political agitation—labor unrest over rising prices, conflict over the perennial question of home rule for Ireland and a movement to disestablish the Anglican church in Wales—but questions of foreign policy remained predominant, and most domestic quarrels were smothered by the outbreak of war in 1914.

In France, Napoleon III's defeat by German armies was followed by the proclamation of the Third Republic in Paris, and France entered the 1870s facing the twin problems of ending a losing war and launching a new government. After the surrender of Paris, the Germans permitted national elections to be held so that the peace would be made by a representative government and could not be repudiated easily; consequently, a new national assembly met in Bordeaux in February of 1871. The first task of this new government clearly was to make peace with the Germans, and in May it signed a treaty that provided for cession of Alsace and part of Lorraine, payment of a heavy indemnity and acceptance of an army of occupation; it was a harsh peace, but in the face of military collapse the government had no choice.

At the same time that it was dealing with the Germans, the new republic had to confront an insurrection, for Parisian radicals, recognizing that the national assembly was hostile to the radical republic that they demanded, formed a commune, seized the weapons available in the capital and prepared for conflict. Adolphe Thiers, whom the Bordeaux Assembly had elected as its chief executive, used regular troops to suppress the Parisian revolt, and the affair ended in bloody street fighting, but Thiers's action demonstrated to all of France that the government could maintain stability and that republicanism did not necessarily mean radicalism and the Jacobin terror of 1792.

The Bordeaux Assembly was divided quite seriously in its political aspirations; of the six hundred deputies, about four hundred were monarchists, but this majority was divided about equally between Bourbonists and Orléanists. Unable to resolve their differences, in February of 1871 they agreed to the Pact of Bordeaux, by which political quarrels were suspended temporarily so as to allow cooperation in the task of national recovery, and the monarchists left to the republicans the unpopular chores of signing a harsh peace with the Germans and crushing the Paris commune. Monarchical strength was shown, however, in a decision to settle the government at Versailles, the traditional royalist capital, rather than at Paris.

In 1873, fearful that Thiers's government was winning too much credit, the monarchists hurried him out of office as soon as he had finished paying the indemnity to the Germans and had secured the withdrawal of German occupation troops; then they chose the conservative monarchist, General MacMahon, as president of the Republic for a seven year term. Since the division between Bourbonists and Orléanists was still unresolved, and some sort of regular arrangements had to be made, in 1875 the monarchists enacted a rudimentary republican constitution that they hoped could be converted easily to monarchy. The new constitution simply provided for a strong president, with the powers of a constitutional monarch, and for a legislature consisting of a Senate and a Chamber of Deputies. In 1876 general elections were held under the new constitution, and monarchical fears that the republicans had been too successful proved justified. In the Senate, where the monarchists had tried to perpetuate themselves by providing for some members to be appointed and for the rest to be chosen indirectly, the elections left the republicans just two seats short of a plurality; in the Chamber, which was elected by direct universal manhood suffrage, republicans outnumbered monarchists more than two to one.

During the late 1870s, the government of the Third Republic was dominated by a legislative-executive struggle which ended with MacMahon's resignation and the Chamber's success in establishing the principle of ministerial responsibility. This republican triumph was followed in the early 1880s by amnesty for surviving communards, the legalization of trade unions and the enactment of a number of anticlerical measures designed to exclude religious influences from French education while making primary education compulsory. By the middle of the 1880s, however, the conservative republican government was being attacked from both the right and the left. Monarchists gained strength significantly in the elections of 1885, while radical republicans and socialists formed new parties committed to further social reform and the defense of the working classes.

Among supporters of the radical left, where the traditions of the French revolution of 1789 lived on, nationalism was very strong. They never had become resigned to the cession of Alsace-Lorraine, forced upon France in 1871, and their desire for a war of revenge against Germany precipitated a crisis in the late 1880s when they forced the government to appoint General Boulanger as Minister of War. Though favored by the radical left for reasons of foreign policy, Boulanger was rather authoritarian in his views on domestic affairs, and the monarchists, their divisions ended by the death of the last Bourbon, soon rallied to him, hoping that he would support a monarchical restoration. At the same time, the government was shaken by scandals which further increased Boulanger's popularity as a strong political figure who might clean out corruption. The climax of the Boulangist movement came in January of 1889, when having won an election in Paris he was expected to lead a march on the government buildings, demanding extraordinary powers to reform the government and to revise the constitution, but at the critical moment Boulanger proved indecisive, missed his chance for dictatorial power and quickly went into eclipse. The government considered trying him for treason, and he fled abroad, where he committed suicide two years later. The short-lived but powerful Boulangist movement appears to have been a sort of Bonapartist revival, a popular reaction against the constant bickering of the parties in favor of personal leadership by a strong, magnetic individual.

In the aftermath of the Boulanger affair the republic appeared much strengthened as general elections in 1889 produced large republican majorities, but new crises soon arose. Early in the 1890s the speculative company that was attempting to dig a canal across the Isthmus of Panama collapsed, wiping out massive investments, and subsequent investigations showed that a number of senators and deputies had accepted money from the company—had allowed their influence to be bought. And hardly had this scandal subsided when another crisis broke over charges of treason against a French army officer, Captain Alfred Dreyfus.

In 1894 French army intelligence obtained evidence indicating that someone on the general staff was selling information to the Germans, and though the evidence was very vague, a culprit had to be produced quickly since the story had reached the newspapers. Dreyfus had the misfortune to be a middle-class Alsatian Jew in an officer corps that was overwhelmingly aristocratic, Catholic and anti-Semitic, and he had had access to the documents in question; he was accused, tried quickly in a closed court martial, condemned and sent to Devil's Island. The case appeared to be closed, and the public was satisfied.

The Dreyfus case was hardly more than begun, however, for both the new head of French intelligence and Dreyfus' brother soon discovered the identity of the real culprit. The intelligence officer was transferred to a frontier post in Africa, for the army did not wish to reopen the question and perhaps have to admit that it had been wrong. In 1898 Dreyfus' brother finally obtained trial of the other suspect, Major Esterhazy, but a military tribunal found him not guilty, and again the army tried to close the case, and again it failed. The journalist and novelist Emile Zola lent his talent to Dreyfus' defense, and it was discovered that some of the evidence against Dreyfus had been forged by a member of the general staff, who admitted forgery and then committed suicide. By this time, however, the army considered itself committed, and in 1899 a retrial of Dreyfus by another military court again found him guilty, though he was spared further imprisonment by a presidential pardon.

What made the Dreyfus affair a great political issue was that the case crystallized opinion for and against the republic. Generally the left had rallied to Dreyfus' defense in the name of simple justice and the primacy of the individual in society, while under the cloak of patriotism the right had tried to insist that the army must be above criticism and immune to civilian review. A number of factors had complicated the affair. On the one hand, antagonism between France and Germany continued strong, while imperial rivalry in Africa almost led to war between France and Britain in 1898; many felt that in this situation the army, France's only shield, must not be questioned in any way, and they were willing to sacrifice one man to it. Moreover, the officer corps was the stronghold of the aristocratic Catholic families who hoped for a monarchical restoration, and if the conviction of Dreyfus could be upheld, it would help them to maintain the corps as a preserve for their own kind. On the other side, in addition to their commitment to the social principles of the great revolution, the radicals saw the case as an opportunity to bend the army to obedience to the civilian government of the republic and to break one of the important strongholds of the political opposition. Thus, to almost everyone except his family Dreyfus became a symbol of something: of the army embattled, of the republic threatened, of the church endangered, of monarchism resurgent. For a decade French politics were dominated almost wholly by what was called simply "the affair." It broke governments, caused suicides and destroyed careers. Ultimately, it affirmed the republic, ruined the monarchical party and reduced the church greatly. In the aftermath of Dreyfus' pardon, the left enjoyed a considerable electoral victory, and it consolidated its position by moving quickly to complete the disestablishment of the French church. Between 1901 and 1905 a number of laws were enacted dissolving Catholic orders, closing remaining church schools, guaranteeing absolute liberty of conscience and establishing complete separation of church and state. Appropriately, in 1906 the republic finally rendered justice to Dreyfus, who had been the instrument of its victory; the high court of appeals cleared his name, and he was reinstated in the army, promoted and decorated.

As the Dreyfus case faded into the past, France experienced a notable resurgence of aggressive nationalism, partly a reaction to imperial rivalries and partly a desire to reunite the nation in the face of a deteriorating international situation, but this movement had strong Catholic and monarchical sympathies and represented also the desire of authoritarian elements of the society to regain the position lost in the fight over Dreyfus. By contrast, there also was labor unrest as the socialists became more demanding, and after 1906 a whole series of strikes swept the country. Thus, France entered the first world war with many of the quarrels inherited from the revolution of 1789 still unresolved.

Hardly was the new German Empire proclaimed in 1871 than the government became involved in a serious struggle with the Catholic Church, known as the *Kulturkampf*. There were two major bases to the quarrel, the resurgence of papal power and the political activity of German Catholics. The reconsolidation of the papacy after the revolutions of 1848 culminated in the promulgation of the dogma of papal infallibility in 1870; to Bismarck, this appeared as preparation for papal support of the German church against the government, and he was antagonized. The tension was increased in March of 1871 by the organization of a Catholic Center Party to campaign in the first general elections of the German Empire; since the preponderance of German Catholic strength lay in the south, the Center Party tended to represent southern particularism as well as Catholicism, and on both grounds it was hostile to the imperial government dominated by Protestant Prussia. During the early 1870s these tensions developed rapidly into a serious struggle as the government expelled the Jesuits and extended governmental control of ecclesiastical education and discipline; then in 1875 it made civil marriage obligatory, suspended governmental financial aid to the church and dissolved all religious orders except those involved in nursing. The church in Germany suffered severely, and improvement came only at the end of the 1870s when Bismarck decided that the state was in no danger from the church and that the support of the Center Party would be useful to new tariff policies that he wished to adopt. After 1879 the repression was eased, and by the mid-1880s the *Kulturkampf* had died out, but the state's supremacy over the church in the new German Empire had been established clearly.

During the *Kulturkampf*, a new problem for the government developed with the considerable growth of German socialism and the foundation in 1875 of the Socialist Workingmen's Party. These early socialists were hampered at first by internal divisions between revolutionary Marxists and those who followed the evolutionary programs of Ferdinand Lassalle, a social-democratic thinker of the 1860s, but despite divisions they recruited very rapidly. At first Bismarck was inclined to repression, especially when two attempted assassinations of the emperor suggested a mood of violence in the country, and in 1878 an Anti-Socialist Law was passed prohibiting meetings, publication and fund-raising by socialists.

As German industry expanded, however, Bismarck appears to have recognized that socialist complaints about working conditions were well founded, and he undertook a series of state-sponsored reform measures which he hoped would undermine the socialists' appeal. Sickness insurance for workers in 1883 was followed a year later by accident insurance, and then in 1889 came old age and invalids' insurance. In the early 1890s, the Anti-Socialist Law was allowed to lapse, and the program of state socialism was extended by the establishment of industrial courts and a Department of Labor, which further protected workers against exploitation. These programs did not destroy socialism, but they improved greatly the condition of German workers, and they may have been an important factor in the development of revisionism in the early twentieth century—the weakening of Marxian revolutionary ideas in favor of parliamentary reforms and evolutionary betterment.

Bismarck's retirement in 1890 marked the end of an era politically and had significant repercussions on foreign policy, but economic development continued from foundations he had established. German industry expanded rapidly, for unification of the separate German states had brought together large reserves of coal and iron ore, the bases of heavy industrialization. To develop these resources, an Imperial Bank was founded in 1876 to provide capital, and protective tariffs were established in 1879 to shield infant industry from foreign competition. On the eve of the first world war Germany had passed both England and France in the production of iron and steel and was second only to the United States. The economic and military power of the new state kept it relatively stable internally, but under the personal direction of the emperor new foreign policies after 1890 took dangerous courses that led finally to disaster.

By contrast, the new kingdom of Italy failed to develop rapidly after unification. The mountainous spine of the Appenines divided it geographically; it lacked the vast natural resources of Germany; and no statesman of the first rank appeared to lead the government after Cavour's death in 1861. Moreover, Italy faced a critical and unique problem in its relations with the papacy.

Shortly after Rome was annexed by force, the Italian parliament passed the Law of Guarantees, which granted the pope royal dignities, free communications with Catholics all over the world, the right to receive foreign embassies, possession of the Vatican palace and other properties and a subsidy from the state treasury equivalent to his former income from his lands. The pope insisted he must retain some part of Rome, however, and when the government would not agree, he refused to accept the settlement and denied recognition to the new Italian state, forbidding Catholics to participate in its affairs. Thereafter, the pope styled himself, somewhat fancifully, the prisoner of the Vatican, and the issue remained unresolved as all attempts at compromise foundered on the Roman question. A major result of this quarrel was that many Italian Catholics refused to vote or stand for office, so that politics were left largely to the anticlerical parties that simply ignored the papal ban. In 1904 the papal position was modified somewhat by Pope Pius X who allowed Catholics to vote to preserve the social order, but relations between the papacy and the kingdom of Italy were not regularized until 1929, when the Mussolini government established the independent Vatican State (a bit more than one hundred acres) and a new indemnification.

Moderately conservative governments in the tradition of Cavour ruled the kingdom of Italy until 1876, when the first leftist ministry took office, but thereafter the government tended to nationalist ventures and doctrinaire radical measures that Italy could ill afford. A movement called *Irredentism*, agitation to secure from Austria the areas north and northeast of the Venetia, was encouraged, anticlerical policies were pursued without very specific goals and a haphazard imperialist venture was undertaken in Ethiopia.

Some economic expansion took place, particularly in shipping, but banking scandals inhibited the growth of confidence in the capital market, and just after the turn of the century growing socialist activism among workers led to a series of widespread strikes. On the eve of the first world war Italy still was basically a poor country, and she remained divided over the state-church issue and shaken by labor unrest.

The Habsburg empire, reorganized as the Dual Monarchy of Austria-Hungary in 1867, faced many serious problems in the late nineteenth century, but the most disruptive of them was Slavic pressure for some form of autonomy. Mostly the agitation took the form of a federalist movement seeking a position for Bohemia comparable to that granted to Hungary, but both Austrian Germans and Hungarian Magyars were opposed to this, and several governments fell without finding a compromise. Austria experienced some labor unrest, but the government that ruled all through the 1880s responded with a program much like Bismarck's, with the result that the issue did not become too serious. Toward the end of the nineteenth century Slavic agitation was intensified, as symbolized by the foundation of the radical Young Czechs, and again it toppled ministries and paralyzed parliamentary government. In the last half-dozen years before the first world war Austrian governments lacked parliamentary majorities and ruled by decree, so Austria entered the war amid political crisis.

Hungary faced problems quite as serious, for on the one hand there was a strong group that wanted full independence and objected to the compromise arrangements of the Dual Monarchy, while on the other, subject nationalities, especially Slavs, objected to education and language regulations designed to make Hungary wholly a Magyar state. Because the subject nationalities constituted more than half of the population, every Hungarian government refused to consider universal suffrage, and a Magyar aristocracy still ruled Hungary as a semi-feudal state when the first world war broke out.

The foundation of most of the troubles of Austria-Hungary was nationalism in one form or another, for the Dual Monarchy contained many peoples, and it was surrounded by states with which its minorities felt ties. Austrian Germans reluctantly had admitted the Magyars to equality with themselves, but both of these dominant peoples felt proudly superior to the other races of the empire. Slavs formed a major element in the population of the Dual Monarchy, but they had no institutions to express their national feeling, and inevitably they were attracted by the great Slavic state of Russia. Austria ruled Italian speaking peoples, and *Irredentists* from the kingdom of Italy constantly encouraged them to resent Austrian rule, while in Hungary's Transylvanian districts there was a large Rumanian population and a comparable *Irredentist* movement looking toward Rumania. The Italian and German achievements of unification inspired the nationalist ambitions of other peoples, and once the first world war weakened the central government, it is not surprising that the centrifugal forces of conflicting nationalities pulled the Dual Monarchy apart; what is astonishing is that the Habsburg empire managed to govern so long and generally so well over such a heterogeneous and often resentful collection of subjects.

In Russia the late nineteenth century saw growing opposition to czarist autocracy. Radicals and socalists advocated revolutionary overthrow of the whole social structure, claiming that the reforms of Czar Alexander II had not gone far enough. Liberals, influenced by western ideas, wanted a constitution, a demand that had been voiced in Russia as early as 1825. Secret societies developed a broad populist movement aimed at further agrarian reform; the emancipation of serfs, for instance, had included generous long-term compensation to landowners for lands transferred to peasants, which burdened the peasantry terribly. Advocates of the Pan-Slav movement blamed the government for not doing more to help Slavs under Turkish and Austrian rule. And, finally, a terrorist group known as Will of the People undertook a series of assassinations, culminating in the murder of the czar in 1881.

Czar Alexander II had been prepared to make some concessions just before his death, but his successor, Alexander III (1881–1894), reaffirmed the autocratic system and established a violent repression which included persecution of religious dissenters and subject nationalities. At the same time, however, he attempted a costly program of rapid industrialization, and while great progress was made in railway construction and iron production, an industrial working class was developed which lived in miserable conditions, and a staggering burden of taxation was imposed upon the peasantry. The end of Alexander III's reign was marked by growing unrest in the cities and famine in the countryside.

The new czar, Nicolas II (1894–1917) continued the policy of repression, but it failed to check the growing opposition. Socialists, though forced to live and write in exile, won a wide following among industrial workers, and shortly after the turn of the century one wing of the Social Democratic Party became frankly revolutionary. A Social Revolutionary Party, terrorist and peasant oriented, also developed. And liberal intellectuals formed a Union of Liberation to work for a constitution. All of these opposition groups were strengthened when crushing defeat in the Russo-Japanese War of 1904–1905 discredited the government utterly, and violence erupted all across the country.

At last the czar recognized the necessity of concessions, and he relaxed the efforts at Russification of minorities, eased the financial burdens on the peasants and announced the creation of a national assembly, the Duma, to have a consultative role in government. These measures were too little and too late, however, and in October of 1905 a great general strike occurred which quickly paralyzed the government. Czar Nicolas finally realized that real reforms were needed to pacify the country, and he dismissed his reactionary ministers and issued the October Manifesto which established a constitution, granted legislative powers to the Duma and protected civil liberties.

This program satisfied the more moderate liberals, but a progressive group established the Constitutional Democratic Party to press for further reforms, and the radicals and socialists continued to advocate revolutionary social change. The arrest of members of one of the more active socialist groups, the St. Petersburg Soviet (workers' council) led to a great workers' insurrection in December of 1905, but the government succeeded in suppressing it with regular troops, and 1906 opened with apparent stability. The violence had died down, a very large foreign loan had improved the financial outlook and the government appeared to have the situation firmly under control. Consequently, just before the meeting of the first Duma, new fundamental laws were promulgated which limited seriously the powers that the assembly had expected to exercise, and a year later a new electoral law weakened it further, with the result that the Duma did not develop into the effective parliamentary body that liberals had hoped it would become, and extremists were justified in their often-voiced distrust of the czar's reforms. Opposition continued widespread, terrorism remained endemic and the czarist government was far from secure in 1914 when it plunged into the war that was to destroy it.

Chapter 24

Competition and Collapse

During the late nineteenth and early twentieth centuries industrialization provided the power and nationalism the motive for the European states to impose themselves upon most of the rest of the
world. Earlier empires had consisted of little more than forts and
trading posts aimed at the control of precious metals and high
priced luxury goods such as tobacco, sugar and furs, but nineteenth
century imperialism sought possession of raw materials, domination
of sheltered markets and gratification of national pride. Prior to
the nineteenth century, India was the only highly developed old
culture over which the Europeans had established domination, but
the new imperialism with its colonial administrations, its protectorates and its spheres of influence tended to divide the whole world
among it.

About the middle of the nineteenth century both France and
Britain evinced new interest in imperialism. France long had held
trading posts in Senegal, on the west coast of Africa, and Charles X
had acquired a small position in Algeria, which Louis Philippe and
Napoleon III subsequently expanded. The west African holdings
remained little more than opportunities for commercial exploitation,
but in Algeria France made determined efforts to settle the country
with French colonists. Comparably, in the 1830s the British
launched planned settlement in Australia, which previously had

been regarded primarily as a convenient penal colony, and in the 1840s representative and ultimately responsible government was established in both Australia and Canada, which settled these colonial areas more securely into the British empire. Then in the 1850s a great mutiny in India led to the abolition of the private British East India Company and the reform of Indian administration under direct governmental control. Thus, by the 1860s both Britain and France had extensive commitments to growing empires.

Steamships also accelerated the growth of imperialism, for they made possible cheaper and more reliable long distance commerce, and it became economically feasible to ship coal from England to Italy, returning with cotton from Egypt or Indian goods brought up the Red Sea and transshipped via Egypt. Another stimulant to imperialism was the opening of the Suez Canal in 1869. The canal was built by a private company, but in 1875 the financially hard-pressed ruler of Egypt offered to sell his shares, and Disraeli bought them for the British government, which made it the major stockholder. The canal cut the passage from England to India from six months to three weeks, and voyages to the Far East were reduced comparably. One effect was to tighten Britain's control of India, and another was to expand tremendously Europe's trade with the Orient, increasing proportionately Europe's influence upon the non-European world.

In Egypt continued extravagance endangered large loans that had been contracted in England and France, with the result that the Egyptians were forced to accept a change of government and the appointment of English and French advisors. Resentment of this foreign intrusion led to a revolt of the army in 1881, in the course of which some Europeans were killed, and despite the fact that he was personally hostile to imperialism, Gladstone, then prime minister of Britain, had to send troops. The British soon controlled the whole country, and they reorganized it completely, governing through a British resident. Then, in the mid-1880s, a British force attempting to evacuate Egyptian garrisons from the rebellious Sudan, just south of Egypt, was massacred at Khartoum; a decade passed before Britain sent another expedition, but in the 1890s an army under General Lord Kitchener was totally successful, and the area became known as the Anglo-Egyptian Sudan. Government by British residents continued until the outbreak of the first world war, when British control was tightened through the establishment of a protectorate.

The situation in the extreme south of Africa was equally as complicated. Britain had captured the Cape during the Napoleonic wars, but most of the white inhabitants of the area were Boers, of Dutch extraction, and they resented British rule. In 1834 the abolition of slavery throughout the British empire created acute labor problems in south Africa, further antagonizing the Boers, and in the late 1830s several thousand of them trekked northward and resettled beyond British authority. As the British colony expanded, however, many of the Boers were absorbed again, despite resistance, and by the mid-1850s only the Transvaal and the Orange Free State remained independent; the rest of south Africa consisted either of the British colony or of native states under British protectorates.

In the mid-1880s, the discovery of gold brought a flood of people into the Boer territories—developers, miners and hangers-on, who aggravated further the political situation. The Boers were old-fashioned farmers, rural in their tastes, conservative in their social views and fundamentalist in their Christianity. The roaring boom towns that grew up around the mining industry negated most of their values, and they resisted stubbornly the influence of the new settlers, who soon outnumbered them. Led by Paul Kruger, the president of the Transvaal, they followed a policy that taxed mining interests heavily while excluding those interests from any voice in the government. Adding to the tension was the fact that the development companies were controlled largely by British financiers, most notably Cecil Rhodes, who became prime minister of the Cape Colony in 1890. Rhodes was an avid imperialist who wished to expand the British position in south Africa, and he was disturbed by mounting evidence of German interest in the area; to forestall such an intrusion, he launched privately the British South African Company to develop the large territory later called Rhodesia, northward of the south African settlements, which both extended British claims and hemmed in the Transvaal.

In 1895 Rhodes supported subversive projects intended to overthrow Kruger's government; the mining interests were to mount a revolution, and Dr. Jameson of the South Africa Company's forces was to invade the Transvaal in support of it. The revolt was postponed, but the "Jameson Raid" proceeded anyway and resulted in a fiasco. The invading forces were defeated and captured easily, Rhodes was forced to resign as prime minister of the Cape Colony, and the German emperor seized the opportunity to express solidarity with the Boers through a congratulatory telegram.

Convinced by the Jameson Raid that only war could save the Transvaal, Kruger triggered a conflict in the autumn of 1899. At first the Boers were notably successful, but ultimately the vastly superior resources of the British turned the tide. In the spring of 1900 the Orange Free State was overrun and annexed, and a few months later the Transvaal suffered the same fate. The Boers then went over to guerilla fighting, which prolonged the war until the spring of 1902, and Britain resorted to massive destruction property and the establishment of concentration camps for civilians; before the fighting was ended she employed 300,000 troops to crush fewer than 75,000 Boers and force them to accept British sovereignty. In 1906 and 1907 responsible government was granted in the Transvaal and the Orange River Colony, so workable compromises appeared to be developing, but these decisions were reversed in 1908 by the creation of the heavily centralized Union of South Africa. The struggle between British and Boer interests was still bitter in 1914 and produced considerable unrest and some violence in the new union while Britain was distracted by the war in Europe.

In the late nineteenth century France also expanded in Africa from Algeria and her positions on the west coast. The French followed the caravan routes across the Sahara, occupying key oases, and established claims to an enormous area by 1900. This growth almost led to war with England in 1898 over a conflict known as the Fashoda crisis, the basic issue of which was control of the upper Nile, but by the early twentieth century a French sphere of influence was delineated rather clearly and was accepted by most of the other powers. Britain held the upper Nile, and Italy was conceded primacy in Tripoli, but west of the Sudan France's position was recognized through most of the hinterland, and she had protectorates in Tunis and Morocco; meanwhile, this expansion in the north was supplemented by the growth of French control over the large island of Madagascar off the southeast coast, which became a French protectorate in 1890 and a colony in 1896.

Unique among the imperial efforts of the late nineteenth century was the development of the Congo Basin in central Africa. In the 1870s King Leopold of Belgium took an interest in the area and founded the International Association for the Exploration and Civilization of Central Africa, which was transformed rapidly into a company for development and exploitation. This activity galvanized the French into founding a protectorate on the north bank of the Congo River, but most of the great basin was claimed by King Leopold's association, and the Independent State of the Congo was recognized by the European powers at an international conference in Berlin in 1884–85, with the king assuming sovereignty over it as a personal possession.

This recognition left the Congo in the possession of a private development company unrestrained by the laws of any of the European states, and conditions soon deteriorated unbelievably. King Leopold had agreed at the Berlin conference to abolish slavery in the Congo, but the establishment of taxes in goods and labor in 1892 reintroduced it covertly as a government program; natural resources such as rubber and ivory were exploited ruthlessly; and frequent rebellions were crushed brutally. Congolese government was an international scandal until the Belgian government annexed the Congo State in 1908 and began a series of reforms.

The central European powers also tried to carve out bits of African territory. In the 1880s the new Italian kingdom secured an uncertain position in Ethiopia, but most of this was lost in an Ethiopian uprising in the mid-1890s. The Italians then turned their interests to Tripoli, just across the Mediterranean from south Italy, and shortly before the first world war they were recognized there in return for acceptance of the French position in Tunis. Generally Germany tried to stay out of the imperialist race so long as Bismarck dominated her policy, for he wanted to avoid the rivalries that imperialism produced, and he believed that imperial ventures would necessitate the construction of a large navy that unavoidably would lead to clashes with Britain. Even the old chancellor could not restrain the expansive enthusiasm of German merchants and missionaries, however, and in the middle and late 1880s protectorates were established in Togoland, the Cameroons, German Southwest Africa and German East Africa, positions over which German control was tightened after 1890, when Bismarck was dismissed.

While Africa was being parcelled out among the European powers, imperial rivalries also were developing in Asia. To guard India against growing Russian strength in Turkestan, the British fought two wars in Afghanistan in 1839–42 and 1878–81, which left Afghanistan a semidependent state. In southeast Asia a series of clashes between the Burmese and the British culminated in British occupation of the whole country by the mid-1880s, and during the late nineteenth and early twentieth centuries British rule was established throughout Malaya. Meanwhile, between the early 1860s and the middle 1890s the French acquired control of all of Indo-China, and Siam retained its independence, though it lost some territory, chiefly because Britain and France found it advantageous to maintain a buffer between their respective colonies. East and southeast of Malaya, Indonesia remained in Dutch hands, as it had been since the sixteenth century, while to the north the Americans, late starters in the imperial race, took advantage of a war with Spain in 1898 to establish a colonial position in the Philippines.

An exception to the general pattern of spreading European control occurred in Japan, where contact with imperialism stimulated an unparalleled national effort at modernization and industrialization that soon made Japan one of the imperial powers rather than one of their victims. In the mid-ninteenth century Japan was still a feudal and agrarian state little known to the west, for her government had followed an isolationist policy for over two hundred years; then the United States sought to break this isolationist policy so as to secure better treatment for shipwrecked American whalers and coaling stations for American ships engaged in the China trade. An American naval mission that attempted to open official contacts in the mid-1840s was rejected and some of its personnel were handled roughly, so in the early 1850s a second mission was sent in greater strength, and Commodore Perry, who commanded it, insisted on delivery of his letter to the emperor.

For more than two centuries the emperor's power in Japan had been exercised by an officer called the *shogun*, but delivery of Perry's letter brought the emperor back into governmental affairs, toppled the *shogun* and triggered a political revolution called the Meiji Restoration. Then followed social and economic revolutions of incredible rapidity. Feudalism was abolished, a program of industrialization was launched and modern military and naval forces were begun. Probably no nation that lacked Japan's long tradition of national unity and social cooperation could have achieved so much in so short a time; not only did Japan avoid partition by the western powers, but twenty-five years after the Meiji Restoration she was seeking for herself a share of the partition of China.

A major focus of imperialism in Asia was, of course, China. Europe had had some regular contact and trade with China since the sixteenth century, but the modern imperial experience began with the Opium War with Britain in the 1840s, which gave Britain Hong Kong and opened several ports to normal commerce. This forcible European intrusion discredited an already shaky government in Peking, and in 1850 a great insurrection known as the T'ai P'ing Rebellion broke out and soon engulfed the entire southern half of China. The overt revolution lasted for a decade and a half, but in fact the imperial government never reestablished effective control of the south before its demise in 1912, a major factor in China's impotence in the face of European pressure.

From the 1850s to the 1880s China slowly lost to the western powers more and more control of her own affairs, and while the westerners were pressing in from the ports the Russians advanced from the north, forced the cession in 1860 of the whole Manchurian coast and founded Vladivostok. The 1880s saw some attempts at modernization—a railway line, coal and iron mines and a steel plant—but the same decade witnessed the loss of two former client states, Indochina and Burma; and serious Japanese penetration into another, Korea. The Chinese government was weakened still further by the Sino-Japanese War of 1894–95, for the Japanese defeated Chinese forces easily, winning primacy in the development of Korea, a large cash indemnity and enormous prestige. After the war secret societies seeking the overthrow of the discredited regime in Peking became a problem which grew ever more severe as the imperialist powers wrested more and more concessions from that regime, including leases of large areas.

By the early twentieth century most of China had been divided into spheres of influence under foreign domination. The southwest was controlled by France, who had pushed northward out of Indochina; most of the coast and a large part of central China was in British hands; the Germans held an important position in the north; Korea was in Japanese hands; and Russia dominated northern Manchuria while Japan was expanding from Korea into southern Manchuria. Beset on every side, the tottering government collapsed. A revolution erupted in 1911, resulting in the abdication of the last emperor in 1912, and China fell into chaos and anarchy which remained still unresolved when the first world war altered drastically the relative positions of the imperialist powers.

While Europeans were competing all over the world for the prizes of successful imperialism, they also were involved in a search for security in Europe, where the most explosive issue immediately after the Franco-Prussian war was the bitter resentment in France. Since Bismarck feared that a new European conflict might rip apart the still fragile German state, the major purposes of his foreign policy during the next twenty years were to encourage France in any projects that might distract her from Alsace-Lorraine and to deny her the means of starting a war of revenge. Not only did he keep Germany out of the imperial scramble, as noted already, but also he made considerable efforts to support France's imperial ambitions and to help other powers find peaceful solutions to their conflicts. Thus, in the summer of 1878 he convened an international congress in Berlin, and patterns of development were worked out for the Balkans, where progressive disintegration of Turkish rule threatened to involve Austria and Russia; and he managed another on African affairs in 1884–85 which provided for recognition of imperial claims. Bismarck's role was that of mediator, or honest broker, as Germany's major interest at this time was maintenance of the peace rather than acquisition of new territory.

Beyond a doubt, Bismarck's greatest single effort to avoid a conflict was his development of a complicated alliance system that

isolated France diplomatically. The Franco-Prussian War had demonstrated that Germany was stronger than France, and rapid industrialization was increasing German strength, so France would not
dare to begin a new war unless she could find allies. Germany's complex alliances in the late nineteenth century are comprehensible only
if their underlying purpose is understood; they did not constitute a
power bloc to oppose France but a web of commitments and obligations to isolate the French government.

The first of the new German alliances, called the Three Emperors' League, was a loose association of the heads of state of Germany, Austria and Russia, negotiated in the early 1870s. In this pact,
the emperors agreed to cooperate to preserve monarchy, and the
two eastern rulers pledged support to Germany should trouble arise
with France. The German and Russian governments also negotiated
a reciprocal military defensive alliance in 1873, and in the same year
Italy associated herself loosely with the Three Emperors' League in
hopes of support if France should seek to intervene in the Roman
question on the pope's behalf. Then in 1876 Bismarck attempted to
interest Britain in an alliance that would have joined the greatest
land power and the greatest sea power in Europe, but the British rejected his advances; confident of her growing strength and secure
in her expanding empire, Britain preferred an isolationist policy at
this time, free of commitments to any other state.

During the mid-1870s the situation in the Balkans grew ever
more critical as the Russian government was supporting national
uprisings against the Turks. The threat of Russian influence extending more strongly across Austria's southern flank brought Russia and
Austria near to open hostilities, for by 1878 Russia had created a
satellite, Serbia. Since this advance threatened an early Russian
presence on the Mediterranean, British pressure forced the creation of an independent Bulgaria, too, as a counterpoise, but the
Russian achievement remained important. Desperately concerned
that Austria might precipitate a war and fearful of Russian aggressiveness, Bismarck then negotiated the Dual Alliance between Germany and Austria in 1879, a reciprocal agreement to full support in
the event of an attack by Russia; the alliance both checked Russia
and gave Germany the opportunity to impose some restraint upon
Austria. In mid-1881 a worried Russia secured renewal of the Three

Emperors' League, and while the Balkans remained turbulent, the likelihood of hostilities among the great powers diminished. Bismarck had achieved a system that held both Austria and Russia in alliance with his government despite conflicts between them, and to stabilize the situation further, in 1882 Italy was admitted to the Austro-German agreements, forming a Triple Alliance. In 1887 tension between Austria and Russia had become so great that the Three Emperors' League no longer could be maintained, but Bismarck renewed the Reinsurance Treaty, and in the same year France was isolated further by a Mediterranean agreement first arranged between England and Italy and then adhered to by Austria and Spain. Thus, Bismarck's system remained intact until his retirement in 1890, with France isolated and Austria and Russia restrained in their Balkan rivalries.

Even before 1890, however, serious dangers to Bismarck's Germany were becoming apparent. French resentment was intensifying, as evidenced by the Boulanger affair in the late 1880s, while in Russia there was violent objection to the German policy of restraint from nationalist groups that favored Russian solidarity with other Slavs and Russian expansion to the Mediterranean. These problems came to a crisis after 1890 when the aggressive German Emperor William II refused to renew the Reinsurance Treaty with Russia. Apparently he felt that the bitterness between Austria and Russia made it impossible to retain both as allies, and he hoped for some closer agreement with England, which opposed Russia's Mediterranean ambitions. This decision left Russia as isolated as France, and not surprisingly the two powers quickly gravitated toward one another, in 1893 signing a military convention that provided for joint action in the event that either were attacked by Germany or by another power with Germany's support. Thus, within three years of Bismarck's retirement the alliance system aimed at restraint had been transformed into two power blocs in confrontation.

During the 1890s Britain began to seek understandings with other powers, for splendid isolation appeared less attractive when she was embroiled in dangerous rivalries all over the world, and although she was not willing to commit herself to firm alliances, the Mediterranean Agreements of the 1880s constituted a precedent for loose accords. At first Britain seemed to incline toward the Triple

Alliance; on the one hand the Mediterranean Agreements had provided the basis for friendly relations with Italy and Austria, and the German emperor was seeking closer relations, while on the other, serious conflicts of interest in Africa and Asia divided Britain from both France and Russia. Through the late 1890s, however, a number of events, mostly related to the aggressiveness of Emperor William II, moved Britain toward the Franco-Russian orbit.

In January of 1896 the congratulatory telegram sent by the German emperor to President Kruger of the Transvaal, after the Jameson Raid, offended the British deeply and aggravated their fears of a close link between German Southwest Africa and the Boers. Then in the spring of 1898 Germany enacted a new naval law providing for the construction of a powerful high seas battle fleet, which was a challenge to what Britain felt to be her most vital interest. Growing Anglo-German tension was paralleled briefly by the Anglo-French clash at Fashoda late in 1898, but this was resolved by negotiation, and toward the end of 1899 another German project, a Berlin to Baghdad railway, threatened Near Eastern interests of Britain, France and Russia. Despite efforts by the Berlin government, Anglo-German relations continued to deteriorate at the turn of the century, for during the Boer War the press and public opinion in Germany were violently hostile to Britain, while the British resented Germany's overt sympathy for the Boers. Thus, in the early twentieth century, though Britain still was far from close understandings with France and Russia, Germany's belligerence and particularly Germany's naval construction program had cooled Anglo-German relations considerably. At the same time adverse international press reactions to Britain's war with the Boers made the British very conscious of the fact that they were friendless.

A major transformation of international patterns took place in 1902. In January Britain abandoned her isolationism definitively by signing an alliance with Japan. For Japan the agreement meant that in the very likely event of war with Russia, Britain would neutralize the fleet of Russia's ally, France; for Britain it meant that Japan would take over policing of some common interests in east Asian waters, allowing reassignment of British naval units so as to strengthen the home fleet against the rising threat of German naval power. Late in the same year France and Italy achieved an understanding over most of the issues dividing them, while Italy's participation in the Triple Alliance became almost meaningless due to new trouble with Austria over Italian irredentist ambitions for southern Austrian lands. Then a series of conversations in 1903 and 1904 resulted in an Anglo-French Entente, not a firm alliance but a settlement of outstanding colonial issues and the basis for joint action in the face of the common danger from Germany. The Entente was strengthened in 1905 by the first Moroccan crisis, a German attempt to intrude upon a French sphere of influence, and in 1906 Anglo-German naval rivalry was intensified by Britain's launching of the *Dreadnought*, a capital ship mounting only very heavy guns, and by Germany's decision to build ships of the same class.

In 1907 the reorientation of British policy was completed by the conclusion of an Anglo-Russian Entente. Ever since her humiliation in the Russo-Japanese War of 1904–5, Russia had been amenable to an agreement that would reduce the dangers she faced, and France had exercised her good offices in hopes of strengthening the anti-German bloc. As in the entente with France, Britain undertook no firm commitments, but outstanding imperial issues were resolved, especially in Persia and Afghanistan. By the end of 1907, Bismarck's diplomatic arrangements had been reversed; Germany had a firm alliance with Austria, but she faced a hostile Triple Entente of France, Russia and Britain, and Italy had moved so far toward agreement with the entente powers that she was a very dubious member of the Triple Alliance.

Continuing German ambitions sparked new Moroccan crises in 1909 and 1911, and though these were settled peaceably, like earlier colonial conflicts, in conjunction with the growing German naval challenge they contributed to rising animosity between Germany on the one hand and France and England on the other. Even more serious were clashes of interest in the Balkans as both Austria and Russia sought to expand into the vacuum created by the decline of Ottoman power. For Russia the issues had grown far beyond the simple question of access to the Mediterranean. Nationalist elements were too strong to be ignored after the 1905 revolution, and they rallied to the pan-Slav movement to such an extent that the government had little choice but to support Slav nationalism, and particularly Serbia, in the Balkans; thus, taking into account the humiliation of the Russo-Japanese War, the Russian government found both its international prestige and its domestic stability deeply involved in the

Balkan crises. To Austria Balkan affairs were no less critical. Since the creation of the Dual Monarchy in 1867, the greatest single problem of the Habsburg government had been Slavic aspirations for arrangements at least comparable to those achieved by the Magyars, and the emergence of the Slavic state of Serbia, with Russian support, had aggravated Slavic nationalism in the Habsburg domains seriously. Hence, to the Austrians as to the Russians, Balkan affairs seemed to involve not only territorial aspirations and international prestige but also questions of domestic security.

Russia had been forced to accept unfavorable settlements in the Balkans several times: in 1878 when an independent Serbia was created but with very limited frontiers, in 1908 when Austria annexed Bosnia-Herzegovina, and in 1913 when the state of Albania was created to deny the Serbs and their Russian backers an outlet to the sea. Thus, by 1914 Russia felt that she had been pushed to a point of no return; any further concessions to Austria likely would have meant further diminution of Russian prestige, total loss of Russian influence in the Balkans and charges of abandonment of pan-Slavism by domestic nationalists.

Unfortunately a new crisis was precipitated in June of 1914 when the Austrian Archduke Franz Ferdinand was assassinated by a Bosnian revolutionary who hoped by terrorism to promote Bosnian independence of Austria and incorporation with Serbia. Then the dangers of the interlocking alliances and inflexible military plans quickly became evident.

The assassination brought to a head the long-standing hostility between Austria and Serbia, for though the Serbian government had not supported the plot officially, it was demonstrated beyond reasonable doubt that high Serbian officials had known of it and had done nothing either to stop it or to warn Vienna. Consequently the Austrians resolved to act boldly, while they enjoyed the sympathy of world opinion, and to crush Serbia's aggressive ambitions definitively. In the first week of July Austrian inquiries elicited promises of German support, the first of the famous "blank cheques"; then the Vienna government, though unwilling to declare war immediately, decided to proceed strongly despite the risks.

Apparently the Austrians thought they could deal with the Serbs without Russian intervention, as in the past, but this time they were proved wrong. President Poincaré of France was visiting in St.

Petersburg, and he reaffirmed the Franco-Russian entente, which encouraged the Russians to take a firm stand. Thus both Germany and France failed to restrain their allies, and, confident of support, Austria demanded satisfaction of Serbia while Russia determined to uphold the Serbs at all costs. On July 23, the Vienna government sent to Belgrade an ultimatum so far-reaching that it would have compromised Serbian sovereignty, and the next day Russia warned Austria that the Serbs must not be attacked. Then, as the crisis deepened, France assured Russia of support, another blank check. In effect, both Germany and France had transferred control of policy to their allies.

When the predictable Serbian rejection of Austria's ultimatum was delivered on July 25, both Serbia and Austria mobilized; then on July 28, Austria declared war on Serbia, and all Europe teetered on the brink of war, though another week of frantic discussions took place before the great powers committed themselves. There was something almost pathetic about the last days of peace, as governments that had committed themselves too far tried to find a road back without sacrificing their alliances or their popular support; if peace could not be maintained, they sought at least to localize the impending conflict. Massive forces were working against them by this time, however, for military planning in most countries had not foreseen limited war, and everyone's plan anticipated full mobilization. The tragic element began to appear when it was discovered that the Russian army literally was incapable of mobilizing forces only against Austria and not against Germany, for the subsequent decision to order general mobilization on July 29 and 30 forced Germany's hand.

German war plans, which assumed Franco-Russian partnership, were equally inflexible and were based on rigid timetables. When last minute negotiations aimed at limiting Russian efforts, at neutralizing France or at finding a private Franco-German accommodation all failed, both France and Germany mobilized on August 1, and Germany began the invasion of Luxemburg. Then on August 3 Germany declared war on France, and within a few days all of the great powers had committed themselves to an attempt at a military solution of their rivalries. All were convinced of the justice of their causes, and all expected a short, victorious struggle; none suspected that they had embarked upon the first world war, four years of the most costly conflict Europe yet had experienced.

Chapter 25

The Retreat of
Liberal Democracy

Ever since the signature of the Franco-Russian alliance in the 1890s, German military planning had had to assume the likelihood of a war on two fronts, and in 1905 the general staff had produced a strategic project called the Schlieffen Plan to deal with this situation. This plan projected a massive invasion of France intended to encircle Paris and force a quick decision that would free Germany's forces for concentration against the Russians. In August of 1914 it appeared that the Schlieffen Plan might succeed, for the French focussed their efforts on an unsuccessful attempt to reoccupy Alsace-Lorraine, and German armies swept southward into France almost unchecked. Early in September, however, the French commander-in-chief, General Joffre, threw his forces into the path of the German advance and halted it at the Battle of the Marne. By mid-October a line of trenchworks extended six hundred miles from the Swiss border to the sea, and despite massive commitments by both armies, the lines hardly moved until the last year of the war.

On the eastern front a comparable situation developed. The Russians attempted to invade East Prussia almost immediately that war was declared, but in two battles at the end of August and beginning of September the Germans defeated them utterly. In the winter a Russian advance in Poland was halted, and in 1915 a combined Austro-German force occupied most of that country; then lines began to stabilize, developing into thirteen hundred miles of trenches from the Black Sea to the Baltic.

When war first broke out, Italy refused to join the Central Powers, and despite the Triple Alliance she declared her neutrality; then influenced by her territorial ambitions, she declared war on Austria-Hungary in the spring of 1915. The Austrians managed to contain the Italian attack, however, and late in the war they counterattacked with German reinforcements and broke the Italian army completely, so the Austro-Italian front never acquired major significance to the general course of the war.

At sea the British caught a small German fleet homeward bound from the Pacific in December of 1914 and destroyed it in the Battle of the Falkland Islands. More significant was the growth of German submarine warfare, which almost brought the United States into the war in the spring of 1915 when the passenger liner Lusitania was sunk with the loss of many American lives. The diplomats managed to smooth over this crisis, however, when the German government agreed to restrict attacks upon passenger vessels. Then in the spring of 1916 the major battle fleets of Germany and Britain met in the Battle of Jutland, and British superiority in capital ships forced the Germans to retire, though they inflicted more damage than they suffered. Thereafter, German naval effort concentrated upon commerce raiding, and in January of 1917 unrestricted submarine warfare was resumed. The submarine campaign destroyed eight million tons of shipping by the autumn of 1917, but eventually it was countered effectively by the development of the convoy system, and it proved costly, for it provoked a U.S. declaration of war against Germany in April of 1917.

The Russian Revolution of 1917 ended the fighting on the eastern front, but in the west casualties climbed rapidly as each side sought to break the stalemate. In July of 1918 the Germans made a final effort with a great offensive on the Marne, but it was repulsed, and as allied armies were reinforced by the daily arrival of ten thousand fresh American troops, they turned the German retreat into a rout. On November 11, a general armistice was signed, and at last the war ended, having killed about ten million men and wounded twice that number.

In Austria-Hungary and Germany as well as in Russia the war triggered political revolutions. Subject nationalities in the Habsburg lands staged several uprisings during the summer of 1918, and in late October both Czechoslovakia and Yugoslavia declared their independence. A few days later naval crews in the north German ports mutinied, and revolution broke out in Munich; in the face of these disturbances, the German chancellor announced the abdication of the Kaiser on November 9, and the leader of the German socialists promptly proclaimed a republic. Then on November 12, the Habsburg emperor abdicated, and republics were proclaimed in both Austria and Hungary.

In January of 1919 a peace conference convened in Paris, the city where animosities toward Germany were most inflamed. The Germans thought they had surrendered on the basis of President Wilson's Fourteen Points, an idealistic program aimed at justice and stability, but it quickly became obvious that Britain and France sought indemnification and retribution above all else. Under the terms of the harsh Treaty of Versailles submitted to the Germans in May of 1919, Germany accepted full responsibility for the war and agreed to pay reparations, the amount to be decided later (eventually the impossible sum of thirty-two billion dollars); she agreed to cede territory to France, Belgium and Poland to give up her colonies; she accepted international administration of the Saar coal region for fifteen years; the German army, navy and merchant marine were to be reduced sharply; and the Rhineland was to be demilitarized. Having no choice, the German government ratified the treaty on July 7, 1919. Austria signed the comparable Treaty of St. Germain and Hungary the Treaty of Neuilly, which provided territorial cessions to Italy, Yugoslavia, Rumania, Czechoslovakia and Poland, reparations payments and limitations of armed forces; in addition the union of Austria and Germany was forbidden. Subsequent treaties then arranged settlements in the Balkans.

The Paris peace settlements were full of contradictions, for once the pressure of the war ended, President Wilson's idealistic influence waned rapidly, especially when his own government refused to participate in the League of Nations. After proclaiming "open covenants openly arrived at," the major allied powers wrote the settlements in closed sessions. After endorsing national self-determination, the victors transferred large blocs of Germans to foreign governments and drew arbitrary boundaries in the Balkans, where the mix of nationalities made minority problems inevitable. After offering France international guarantees of her security so as to dissuade her from even harsher demands upon Germany, the United States and Britain proved unable to fulfil their undertaking; the United States Senate refused to ratify the alliances, and France was left to confront a still united Germany with no firm commitments from her erstwhile allies. And a major European power, Russia, was excluded from the conference entirely although the question of Russia's western borders was critical to an eastern European settlement.

In the early twentieth century intellectuals generally considered the nineteenth century a period of peace. In fact it was far from that if one considers the Greek revolt, the Crimean War and the Austro-Prussian and Franco-Prussian Wars or if one counts domestic strife, the revolutions of 1830 and 1848 and the bloody Commune of 1871; moreover, through much of the latter part of the century Europeans were fighting in Egypt, South Africa, India and China. But though the century of peace was an illusion, it is true that Europe had been spared great holocausts such as the Napoleonic Wars during the century between 1815 and 1914, and intellectuals had begun to assume that European nations had outgrown war, had passed to a higher stage of civilization where war was anachronistic. Thus, the outbreak of a new general war in 1914 shook them badly.

It also had been believed widely that social change generally resulted in progress, some desirable transformation, despite occasional setbacks. Human society was assumed to pass through natural stages from tribal life to aristocratic feudalism to royal absolutism to some sort of participatory democracy governed by the liberal-democratic compromise, majority will restrained by constitutional guarantees for the rights of individuals and minorities. In the early twentieth century there were grounds to believe that this liberal-democratic compromise was a natural result of social evolution. Democratic systems based on the British model had developed in Canada, Australia and the Union of South Africa, and the American system of congressional federalism showed every likelihood of proving both flexible and strong. The unifications of Italy and Germany had resulted in the establishment of parliamentary monarchies in central Europe, and something comparable had developed in Japan by the 1880s. Austria-Hungary appeared to be moving toward responsible parliamentary government; the establishment of a duma in Russia in 1905 was interpreted as a first step in the same direction; and even in China the revolution that broke out in 1911 seemed to be fumbling toward parliamentarianism.

Obviously World War I was a bewildering shock to western intellectuals. Convinced that war was barbaric, and hence unwilling to believe that it remained an important tool of statecraft for European governments, they ignored the chauvinistic and bellicose clamor of the decades that preceded the war and decided that it had been a great mistake, that because of some sort of failure of diplomacy Europe had fallen into a war that no responsible person had wanted. This self-deception, which distorted facts to fit a theory, spawned a number of studies which sought to identify the great mistake or mistakes that had brought on this conflict, but while the intellectuals thus were explaining away the great war, new challenges to their theories of inevitable liberal-democratic progress appeared in the postwar era, most especially the depression of the 1930s.

An analysis of the origin and spread of the great depression belongs to later considerations of international developments in post-war Europe, but the experience of the separate European states cannot be set in proper perspective without some estimate of the general impact of the economic collapse. The late 1920s were characterized by prosperity and optimism, but between 1929 and 1931 financial crises and bank failures all over the world restricted the availability of investment capital, limited market opportunities and brought on industrial failures. Through the greater part of the 1930s there was massive unemployment, and the hardship and despair that resulted must be counted one of the major sociopolitical forces of the two decades following the end of the first world war. Men who were jobless, hungry and hopeless were vulnerable to arguments of social and racial exploitation and were attracted by proposals for extremist solutions, which undermined the liberal-democratic development that the peacemakers had hoped to see. As early as the relatively prosperous 1920s, there were signs that the liberal democrats had been too optimistic, and the profound socioeconomic impact of the depression of the 1930s completed the ruin of their hopes.

Among the least stable areas of post-war Europe were the new states recognized by the peace treaties of 1919—Austria, Poland, Hungary, Czechoslovakia and Yugoslavia. In the new republic of Austria about twenty-five per cent of the population was in Vienna, an industrial city cut off from its former resources and markets by high tariff walls. Some of the other new states were in a better economic position but faced serious minority problems: Slovaks, Ruthenians and Sudeten Germans in Czechoslovakia; Ukrainians, Germans and Jews in Poland; Slavs and Jews in Hungary; and Croats and Slovenes in Yugoslavia. In addition, there was almost constant fighting over the new borders, and these varied troubles produced political chaos, especially when they were aggravated by the depression. In the 1930s Austria experienced suspension of parliamentary government, bloody repression of socialist dissent, dictatorship and finally union with Nazi Germany. Czech government foundered on the problems of minorities, especially the three million Sudeten Germans, and in 1938 Germany seized a third of Czechoslovakia, occupying the remaining fragment the following year. In Poland a military coup established an authoritarian government in the mid-1920s, and the regime became a dictatorship through constitutional revisions in 1935. Hungary remained a semifeudal state of great seigneurs and peasants with a very restricted parliamentary assembly, and it was drawn more and more into the German orbit. And Yugoslavia's parliamentary monarchy collapsed in 1929 when the king proclaimed a dictatorship. Thus the new states did not evolve along the lines expected by western liberal democrats.

Developments farther east, in Russia, were still more discouraging. Except in her western cities, Russia had entered the twentieth century a land of backward and illiterate peasants and equally backward country nobility, and except for some state-owned factories, mostly in St. Petersburg and Moscow, society was still preindustrial. The Russian army, which had been a decisive factor in the defeat of Napoleon, had been humiliated later in the nineteenth century, and its position had worsened by the twentieth century. After the revolution of 1905 Russia's situation appeared to be improving as industrial expansion strengthened the economy and the convocation of four dumas seemed to promise development of peaceful channels of protest. At the same time, however, terrorism continued, industrial growth swelled the urban proletariat and national minorities, especially Poles and Finns, grew more restive. The czar attempted limited conciliation, but he refused to concede ministerial responsibility to the duma, and in the autumn of 1915 he compounded his unpopularity by dismissing a highly regarded commander-in-chief and assuming command of the armies himself, an ill-advised move that linked him directly with Russia's military fortunes in the war. Military priorities and repeated mobilizations resulted in labor shortages, the breakdown of the transportation system and serious shortages of food and fuel in the cities, and violence erupted in March of 1917. Strikes and riots turned to revolution when troops in the capital mutinied, and the duma resolved to form a provisional government. In mid-March the czar abdicated, and the first step of the revolution had been accomplished.

The moderate liberals who dominated the provisional government were prowestern, however, and while they announced better treatment for minorities and eventual land reform, they were committed to the alliance with the western powers. The leaders of the workers' soviets disagreed, and they were strengthened when a number of exiled radicals led by Lenin returned to Russia. Lenin advocated the supremacy of the soviets over the provisional government, immediate peace without regard for western war aims, unconditional transfer of land to the peasants and control of industry by the workers. With slogans such as "all power to the soviets" and "peace, land and bread," Lenin's group, called Bolsheviks, found considerable support from a war-weary and deprived population. A premature coup failed in July of 1917, but another succeeded in the autumn, and control passed to the Bolshevik wing of the socialist movement, soon called the Communist Party.

Czarists, liberals, moderate socialists and minority independence movements resisted for three years, and the Bolsheviks quickly resorted to authoritarian measures. A secret police was organized, land and industry were nationalized, foreign debts were repudiated, private bank accounts were confiscated, and forced labor and requisitions of food were inaugurated. In March of 1918 the Bolshevik government concluded the Treaty of Brest-Litovsk with Germany, giving up Poland, the Ukraine and several western border regions, and partly because St. Petersburg (renamed Leningrad) thus became dangerously exposed, the new government then moved the capital to Moscow.

The western powers, regarding the Bolsheviks as pro-German as well as radically socialist after the Treaty of Brest-Litovsk, put troops into Russia to support counter-revolutionary movements, and though ultimately all such opposition was defeated, devastating civil wars raged from 1918 to 1920. In March of 1921, to stimulate national recovery, the government was forced to accept a temporary retreat from communism, the New Economic Policy, which permitted some revival of private ownership and profit incentive. This proved largely successful, and toward the end of 1922 the victory of the revolution was consolidated by the organization of the Union of Soviet Socialist Republics. This victory was a great disillusionment to western liberal intellectuals, for the Bolshevik government's birth in revolutionary violence, its authoritarian suppression of dissent with secret police and political executions and its one-party political system set the U.S.S.R. well outside the liberal-democratic tradition.

In 1924 Lenin died, and in the ensuing struggle for power victory fell to Josef Stalin, who added a decidedly nationalistic note to a revived socialist drive. Proclaiming a New Socialist Offensive, Stalin's government undertook rapid industrialization and renewed collectivization of agriculture in a series of five-year plans, turning ever more industrial output to armaments and consolidating control of the party through purges of rivals. Russia had moved from the absolutism of the czar to the dictatorship of Stalin, and whatever the material benefits, the new authoritarianism was more frightening than the old because it was so much more efficient.

In east Asia as in Europe, liberal democrats were disillusioned in the 1920s and 1930s. China fell into chaos after the revolution of 1911; despotic warlords controlled several provinces, civil war was endemic and the government in Peking was paralyzed by personal rivalries. The leader of the revolutionary Kuomintang Party, Dr. Sun Yat-sen, was influenced profoundly by western liberal and democratic ideas, expressed in his Three Peoples' Principles of nationalism, democracy and social progress, but he died early in 1925, and the promise implicit in his program died with him as rightist and leftist elements in the Kuomintang engaged in a struggle for power. On the left was the Chinese Communist Party, supported by Russian advisors; on the right was the creator of the Kuomintang's military organization, Chiang Kai-shek, a conservative reformer from an old gentry family. By the spring of 1927 Chiang's forces, known as the Nationalists, controlled the Kuomintang, and the Communists had been driven into the desolate north. By late 1928 some warlords had been suppressed, and others had adhered to the Nationalist movement, but under the pressure of civil conflict and new foreign problems, Chiang's thought had drifted farther to the right. The Kuomintang assumed absolute control of the new government, explaining that "political tutelage" was a necessary forerunner of constitutional democracy, and when a crisis developed in 1931 over Japan's seizure of Manchuria, discipline gained ascendency over democracy.

In 1937 the Japanese seized Shanghai, then followed up with the occupation of much of the Chinese coast, and Chiang had to move the capital to Chungking, deep inland. This cut the Kuomintang off from the revenues of the coastal cities, making it dependent upon the conservative country gentry and upon foreign aid, and resistance to the Japanese became almost the only policy of the government. Political tutelage, social welfare programs, industrialization and land reform had to be suspended, and the Kuomintang, which had raised hopes of liberal democratic evolution in the mid-1920s, evolved into just another military government.

Japan's experience was even more tragic, for by the 1920s a viable parliamentary system had been functioning for three decades, but unfortunately for liberal democracy in Japan, the civilian elements of the government had proved far less effective than the military in advancing the nation's interests. In the mid-1890s, after the new Japanese army defeated China, the European powers refused to allow Japan to impose upon China the sorts of terms that they had been imposing for years, and the generals said that what they had won on the battlefield was lost at the conference table. A decade later, when Japan fought Russia, her successes were astonishing, and again her gains seemed to slip through the fingers of her diplomats.

Russia was humiliated, but Japan did not gain a clear sphere of influence in Manchuria, and she did not obtain an indemnity to relieve the economic strain resulting from the war. In truth, these disappointments resulted largely from the fact that the army lacked the resources to pursue the enemy and impose terms, but once again the diplomats were criticized. The end of World War I saw the same sorry pattern repeated; although Japan stood firmly with the victorious allies, the Versailles Peace Conference refused to grant her Germany's Asian possessions and failed to recognize Japan's special position in Asia, further discrediting the civilian elements of Japanese government.

The result of these disappointments was considerable instability: in 1921 a premier was assassinated; in 1922 there were riots; in 1923 there was an attempt on the life of the prince regent. Natural catastrophes and foreign governments aggravated the difficulties. A great earthquake hit Tokyo in 1923, followed by fires and tidal waves, with losses estimated at nearly a quarter of a million lives and a billion dollars worth of property. In 1924 a new U.S. immigration act excluded all Japanese, and resentment was widespread. The situation worsened with a bank crisis, labor troubles, the depression and a rash of assassinations. Finally, in the spring of 1932, affirming the triumph of authoritarian influences over earlier liberal democratic trends, a military cabinet took office and inaugurated a policy of aggressive military imperialism that was to lead to total war and disaster.

One of the most serious failures of liberal democracy occurred in Italy in the 1920s. The end of the great war left Italy resentful, disillusioned and loaded with debt. Though part of the victorious alliance, her armies had performed with no great distinction, and at the peace conference she failed to acquire either control of the Adriatic Sea or possession of German colonies, her two prime goals. Moreover, an already strained labor market was flooded with two million demobilized troops. The strongest popular force in Italian politics was the violently anti-clerical Socialist Party, for Catholics generally held themselves aloof because of the Roman question, and after the war the socialists were influenced strongly by the revolutionary tactics that had succeeded in Russia. In the face of massive unemployment and economic stagnation, they secured the largest single bloc of seats in the parliamentary elections of 1919, about one third of the total, as well as control of many local governments.

The conservative reaction focussed around Benito Mussolini, a former socialist turned vehement nationalist. In postwar Italy demobilized soldiers were jeered instead of cheered, and there were no jobs for them. Mussolini organized them for self-protection and political action into bands called *fasci,* and his followers soon were called fascists. The Fascist Party never developed very coherent doctrines, but a few basic principles emerged. Mussolini was an unquestioning supporter of nationalism and imperialism, and he believed that war had great moral values, bringing out the best of courage and dedication in men. Though convinced that Italy could not afford the economic wastage implicit in competitive enterprise, he had no use for the socialists who wanted to control industry for the benefit of the workers; his goal was national strength, not individual welfare, so he advocated great corporations or cartels under government supervision. This combination of pragmatic programs and romantic idealism exercised a sort of magnetism upon Italian veterans who were humiliated, impoverished and angry.

At first the Fascist Party did not do well politically, winning no parliamentary seats in 1919 and only thirty-five in 1921, so the fascists turned to intimidation and violence. Fearful of turning popular discontent into revolution, the national government normally stood aloof from local disorders, and Mussolini's fascist squads were able to take over local governments through intimidation of voters or simply by seizing government buildings. The patronage jobs thus secured won some popular support, and the ouster of the normally socialist local governments won covert financial aid from wealthy conservatives. Then at a party congress in 1922, Mussolini endorsed limited monarchy and an appeal for army support, and the fascists marched on Rome. As the king refused to declare martial law, the government resigned.

Mussolini, though leader of only a splinter party in the parliament, was asked to form a new cabinet, and the parliament gave him dictatorial powers for a year in order that he might reestablish order and introduce reforms. He used this authority to tighten his control of the apparatus of government, appointing fascists to key posts and enacting a new electoral law. Elections in the spring of 1924 left the parliamentary opposition impotent, and during the next two years political arrests, laws censoring newspapers and decrees suspending local elections assured that the opposition would find no extra-parliamentary support such as had raised the fascists to power. Absolute fascist control was achieved in January of 1926 when parliament authorized the prime minister to govern by decree, and the last potentially dangerous opposition was neutralized early in 1929 when a concordat won papal recognition of the fascist government at the price of independence for the Vatican City. Thus in the 1920s, a troubled but operative parliamentary system passed under the control of an authoritarian party, and Italy became a dictatorship.

There also was great discontent in Germany following World War I, for many Germans refused to believe that their nation had been defeated. They asserted that the new government had made a shameful peace in order to win recognition from the western powers, and had stabbed the army in the back. This stab in the back theory, which the Nazis later exploited profitably, was wholly wishful thinking, for in the summer of 1918 the German commander-in-chief, Ludendorff, had informed Berlin that he no longer could hold back the enemy. But German discontent also had more solid foundations, for the Versailles Peace Treaties had held Germany solely responsible for the war, and consequently Germany had had to agree to pay enormous indemnities and reparations, to give up the territory won from Russia at Brest-Litovsk and to allow Germans to fall under the rule of France, Czechoslovakia, Poland and Belgium. Moreover, she had to accept the isolation of Austria and agree to maintain an army of no more than one-hundred thousand men and to equip them with no heavy weapons. The new German government had signed such a treaty not so much from ambition as from resignation; the alternative was allied occupation.

Violence erupted in Germany almost immediately the war was over as coups were attempted from both the communist left and the monarchical right, but the army's tradition of obedience to the government kept the military loyal, and the center moderates managed to restore order. In 1922 and 1923 the currency began to collapse due to the weight of reparations payments, and then the French, fearful of German recovery, seized a pretext of default on reparations to occupy the industrial Ruhr area, triggering a first grasp for power by Adolph Hitler and the Nazi Party.

Hitler, an Austrian by birth, had settled in Bavaria after the war and involved himself in the shadowy world of ultranationalist politics and paramilitary societies, becoming the leading figure of the minor group named the National Socialist Democratic Workers Party, usually called the Nazis. Largely a hate group that preached antibolshevism, anticapitalism, anti-Semitism and national power, the Nazis nonetheless attracted both a popular following and the support of some army officers and ex-officers whose careers had been blighted by the military limitations of the peace treaty, including Ludendorff, the immensely prestigious former commander-in-chief.

In the confusion following the French intervention and the financial collapse of 1923, the Nazis tried to seize the Bavarian state government, in emulation of the tactics of the Italian fascists, but the German authorities were willing to use police and military forces to maintain order; the *putsch* was broken easily, and Hitler and his colleagues served short jail terms. After their release, they turned to legal tactics as a political party seeking parliamentary seats, but during the economic recovery of the late 1920s, the situation was unfavorable to extremist parties, and neither the Nazis nor the Communists enjoyed much electoral success. Nonetheless, Hitler kept the party intact, developing a paramilitary troop, the S.A. or brownshirts, and a personal bodyguard, the S.S., and when the beginnings of the depression shook Germany, the Nazis were ready to profit from the public impulse to seek extremist solutions. In the elections of 1930 the party's parliamentry bloc jumped from a dozen to over a hundred seats, though in the same elections the Communists increased their strength from twenty-three to seventy-seven seats, and all the moderate parties lost heavily.

In 1931, as the depression settled fully upon central Europe, unemployment figures in Germany rose to six million, and disorders multiplied, with numerous clashes between Nazi and communist street gangs. In 1932 Hitler ran for the presidency and lost to old general von Hindenburg, but in parliamentary elections in the same year the Nazis secured about half the seats, not a working majority but enough to paralyze Germany's political machinery for the next several months, and in January of 1933 von Hindenburg was forced to offer Hitler the chancellorship. The Nazis secured a majority in new elections in March, and the Reichstag then passed the momentous Enabling Act, which gave Hitler's government dictatorial power for five years.

While the Nazis by no means enjoyed the unqualified confidence of the whole country, it is clear that their support was broad. The brownshirts both intimidated opposition and evoked emotional chauvinistic responses; the party's anticommunism appealed to conservative and business interests; anti-Semitism appealed to middle classes ruined by the depression and eager for the elimination of Jewish competition; and Hitler's denunciation of the Versailles Treaties and his promises to restore Germany's self-sufficiency and self-respect exercised a broad appeal that cut across class lines. Party strife and a depression had destroyed another liberal democracy.

A whole structure of western intellectual assumptions was collapsing like a house of cards. In the Austrian domains, in Russia and in China bright promises proved illusory and melted in the heat of material problems. In Italy, Japan and Germany, established parliamentary systems proved unable to survive the strains of the post-war era. Even the west appeared endangered, for the post-war period saw the growth of leftist radical parties in France, while a comparable popular awakening in England resulted in the growth of the Labour Party. In both countries conservatives overreacted, and there was talk of Bolshevism and wildly exaggerated fears of imminent communist revolution, which the depression heightened. A sort of paralysis developed in which both left and right watched one another suspiciously and neither dared attempt more than a caretaker government. The dangers of this irresolution were shown during a Spanish civil war in the mid-1930s.

By 1931 the many opposition groups in Spain had developed into a strong republican movement, and the king fled abroad. A republic was proclaimed, but the new government was unable to achieve stability because of internal rivalries between moderates and radicals, and by 1936 the situation had degenerated into civil war between a leftist republican government and a large part of the army led by General Francisco Franco. Italy and Germany quickly recognized Franco and sent aid, seeing the civil war as an opportunity to test their new military forces and a fascist Spain as a potentially valuable ally. At the same time, Russia sent help and advisors to the republican forces, hoping thus to strengthen the republic's leftist elements and to turn the civil war into a communist revolution. Meanwhile, England and France were paralyzed by their internal political situations and their reluctance to undertake foreign spending during the depression. The result was that the republican moderates were boycotted by their friends while the authoritarian extremists of both right and left got foreign aid.

By early 1939 Franco's forces controlled so much of the country, and the republican forces were so deeply influenced by the Russians, that Britain and France recognized the Franco government, and the United States followed suit a few months later; Madrid surrendered to Franco in March, and the civil war was over. The first direct confrontation between the new authoritarian governments and the old liberal democracies showed the contrast between the ruthless pragmatism of the former and the hesitancy and paralysis of the latter. Given the aggressive ambitions of Mussolini and Hitler, the implications were chilling.

Chapter 26

The End of
the European Hegemony

Despite the shortcomings of the Versailles Peace and the wide-spread dissatisfaction with it, especially in Germany, Italy and Japan, for a brief time it appeared that the settlement might endure and be strengthened. The many disputes immediately consequent upon the peace tapered off in the mid-1920s, and new developments held forth some hope of stability.

Recognizing that the original reparations schedules were un-realistic, especially after the German economic collapse that fol-lowed French occupation of the Ruhr, in 1924 the allies accepted a committee report called the Dawes Plan; this plan revised pay-ment schedules and provided for massive loans to Germany to re-stabilize her economy. Then in 1925 international discussions re-sulted in the Locarno Treaties; the most important aspect of these was Franco-Belgian-German acceptance of existing borders, with Great Britain and Italy serving as guarantors, but there also were a number of arbitration agreements, chiefly concerning Germany and her neighbors, and a Franco-Czech mutual assistance pact. For several years the "spirit of Locarno" suggested growing security and the reacceptance of Germany into the European community.

In 1926 Germany was admitted to the League of Nations; the next year saw the first of several disarmament conferences; in 1928 most of the major powers signed the Kellogg-Briand Pact renouncing aggressive war; and in 1929 diminishing hostility toward Germany led to another revision and reduction of reparations under the Young Plan.

The progress toward international stability that seemed so apparent in the late 1920s evaporated rapidly under the pressure of the international depression of the 1930s, but actually economic affairs long had been the weak point in international cooperation. Nationalism, one of the prime causes of World War I, had emerged from the war stronger than ever, and many governments were striving for national self-sufficiency. This desire and the drive for rapid industrialization by most of the new states resulted in high tariff barriers and other artificial impediments to the redevelopment of international commerce in Europe. Moreover, much prewar trade could not be recovered, for while Europe had been locked in a grim struggle, industrialization had proceeded rapidly in the United States, Canada and Japan, and these nations had secured a large share of the world's non-European markets. Ironically, however, behind the facade of national effort, the economies of all nations were linked closely in a great web of international finance to which the United States and Germany were the keys. During the war, Britain and France had contracted enormous debts for munitions bought in the United States, and the Washington government insisted on repayment, but the only way the western European powers could manage this was to collect reparations. Since a major source of the funds with which Germany and Austria paid reparations was loans from the United States, the cumulative effect was that dislocations in any one economy, but especially that of the United States, would have repercussions all through the loans-reparations-war debts cycle.

Such a dislocation of major proportions occurred in October of 1929 when the American stock market collapsed as a result of unrestrained speculation, limiting the flow of funds to Germany. Compounding the problem was the American government's shortsighted response to its own crisis, the Smoot-Hawley Tariff Act, which raised import duties fifty to one hundred per cent in an effort to protect the American economy from foreign competition. Thus, at the same time that the flow of American money to central Europe diminished, impeding the collection of reparations, increased American tariffs made it impossible for Britain and France to repay war debts through expanded trade with the United States. Moreover, by late 1931 some two dozen other nations had retaliated by increasing their tariffs, further impeding international trade.

As the problems multiplied, the pressure on international credit increased enormously. In the spring of 1931 the Austrian State Bank failed, and though guarantees from the Austrian government and from other large European central banks staved off disaster, a panic ensued, and quantities of foreign funds were withdrawn from central Europe. In the face of the spreading crisis, President Hoover arranged a moratorium on all intergovernmental debts in the summer of 1931, but the panic continued. A few months later the Bank of England was forced to abandon the gold standard, a covert form of devaluation which lowered the price of British goods on the world market in an attempt to salvage British trade. All over Europe and North America industrial enterprises failed and unemployment soared. Overall European production fell to less than seventy-five per cent of 1929 levels by 1932, and the value of world trade fell to less than half of 1929 levels during the 1930s. To ease the economic crisis a few nations turned to government spending—public works in the United States and a combination of public works and military projects in Germany and Italy—but most governments simply tried to balance budgets, to protect the national economy against further shocks from abroad and to maintain order while hordes of the unemployed roamed around in search of work.

In Germany the depression of the early 1930s finished what the inflation of the mid-1920s had begun, the ruin of the middle class, and in such troubled conditions Nazi support continued to grow. Hitler had promised that he would secure revision of the clauses of the Versailles Treaty which were humiliating and economically ruinous, and he began quite early to dissolve Germany's international commitments. Late in 1933 he announced withdrawal from both the disarmament conferences and the League of Nations; early in 1935 he denounced the arms limitations provisions of the treaty and reintroduced universal military training in Germany; early in 1936 he reoccupied the demilitarized Rhineland. These last moves were clear violations of the World War I peace settlements, and undoubtedly Hitler was testing the willingness of the allies to defend those settlements. The answer was clear; confronted by determined action, none of Germany's former enemies was willing to act.

Meanwhile, other governments had been making the same discovery. Late in 1931, acting on very dubious provocation, the Japanese had occupied Manchuria, and while a League of Nations report a year later generally condemned the action, it accepted the result. Then, in 1935, Italy began a full scale occupation of Ethiopia, which was completed successfully in 1936. This time the League was harsher in its condemnation, and it applied partial commercial sanctions, but again it proved unable to affect the course of events. Then came the Spanish civil war, already considered, which made the paralysis of the western governments and the impotence of the League of Nations glaringly apparent. Further emboldened, late in 1936 Italy and Germany signed a pact establishing the Rome-Berlin Axis, which again divided Europe into two hostile blocs, and very shortly Japan began to move toward the Axis.

There were many reasons why the western powers and the League of Nations did so little to check the aggressive policies of Italy, Japan and Germany. Two great powers did not participate in the League of Nations, the U.S.A. and the U.S.S.R., and without them any burden of enforcement clearly would fall upon France and Britain; but in France and Britain governments were paralyzed by the clash between increasing socialist strength and fearful conservatism, and both countries were reluctant to undertake expensive foreign policies during the depression. France had a special problem in that she had no firm military alliance with Britain, and the first world war had broken her morale to such an extent that she could not contemplate facing Germany alone; in Britain a considerable sympathy for Germany had grown up with a more sophisticated understanding of the world war for which Germany had been the scapegoat, and also there was a tendency to regard a revived Germany as a bulwark against the westward spread of Bolshevism. All in all, during the 1930s the post-war peace settlements had few supporters against moderate revisionism, and those few supporters were handicapped seriously by the effects of the depression.

By the middle of the 1930s the combination of Stalinist nationalism and the menace of Nazi Germany had led to some regularization of the Soviet Union's international position, but this came too late and was too uncertain to exercise any restraining influence upon Hitler. In 1932 France and a number of east European states with which she had close ties signed non-aggression pacts with the Stalin government; in 1933 the United States extended formal recognition; in the autumn of 1934 the Soviet Union joined the League of Nations; and in the spring of 1935 a Franco-Soviet alliance provided for joint action if either were the victim of unprovoked aggression. But underlying all of these developments was continued hostility. The Soviet government had not forgiven the other powers their counter-revolutionary interventions in Russia's domestic affairs in 1918–1920, and the westerners tended to regard international communist activity, which the Soviet Union supported, as a threat at least as dangerous as a rearmed Germany.

The lack of any fundamental agreement between the Soviet Union and the western powers was demonstrated clearly during negotiations aimed at an international agreement to oppose German aggression. The British and French governments were eager for Russian participation, but they were unwilling to make any territorial concessions at Poland's expense, while Russia desired to reclaim territory lost by the Treaty of Brest-Litovsk. Soviet demands were received more cordially by the Germans, and in the summer of 1939 first a trade treaty and then a non-aggression pact were concluded between the Soviet and German governments.

Growing bolder as they met no opposition, Japan and Germany intensified their aggressive revisionism. Still endeavoring to win recognition of her special position in Asia, Japan launched an undeclared war upon China in the summer of 1937, and in a little over a year she conquered a large part of the Chinese coast. The League of Nations condemned the action but did nothing more. Meanwhile Hitler was developing a propaganda campaign based upon aggressive German nationalism, aimed at the Austrians and at the German minorities that existed in several countries. Austria was a Germanic state in an unrealistic economic position because of the peace settlements; and given the virulence of nationalism at the time, it is undeniable that German minorities often were the victims of discrimination, as Hitler claimed. But Hitler's government was not concerned primarily with the welfare of these Germanic peoples outside of Germany; rather, the propaganda campaign sought to develop support for aggressive Nazi intervention in the affairs of neighboring states and for German expansion through annexations.

There is no doubt that union with Germany was attractive to Austrians and to German minorities in other countries, for the national mobilization and remilitarization undertaken by Hitler had a tremendous economic impact. By 1938, when most countries still faced serious problems of idle industry and high unemployment, both agriculture and industry in Germany were operating at levels of peak production, and there actually was a shortage of labor. Much of this was an artificial prosperity, for a large proportion of the production was directed to military purposes and paid for by high taxation, so there was no general improvement of standards of living, but in the 1930s full production and full employment anywhere were impressive to the uncritical observer.

Early in 1938 Hitler precipitated a governmental crisis in Austria through a speech promising protection to Germans outside of Germany, and unable to control the agitation of the Austrian Nazi Party without provoking German intervention, the Vienna government resigned. Then the Austrian Nazis took office demanding annexation to Germany, German troops poured across the border and Hitler proceeded to Vienna to proclaim the union of the two countries, another successful violation of the Versailles Peace.

Having achieved the incorporation of Austria, Hitler turned his attention to the Sudeten Germans in Czechoslovakia, three million people in a population of fifteen million. Nazi influence spread rapidly, and there were outbreaks of violence against the Czech government; then in September of 1938, Hitler demanded that the Sudeten Germans be given the right of national self-determination, a clear threat of German intervention if the Czechs tried to move forcefully to control public disorder in the Sudetenland. As this situation clearly was dangerous to international peace, Britain's Prime Minister Chamberlain travelled to Germany for personal discussions with Hitler in mid-September, and a larger international conference was held in Munich later in the month. On the basis of Hitler's assurances that his ambitions did not extend beyond the Sudetenland, Britain and France abandoned the Prague government, and the Czechs then had no choice but to surrender to Hitler's demands, losing a third of their territory and population and giving up their defensible frontiers.

The Munich agreements of 1938 have been damned as cowardly surrender, but it is difficult to conceive what alternatives the western powers might have adopted at that point. Germany was rearmed, and Hitler made it clear that he was willing to risk war. In both Britain and France pacifism was widespread, economies were just beginning to recover from the depression and there was great political confusion in the wake of the Spanish civil war and of growing socialist strength. Britain's armed forces were ill-equipped and under strength, and though French forces appeared in better condition, they were trained and equipped wholly for defensive action. Hitler may have been bluffing, but neither Britain nor France was in any position to call his bluff, and they had to seek accommodation. That his assurances were totally unreliable was demonstrated a few months later, in March of 1939, when German troops occupied the rest of Czechoslovakia, but the Czech crisis had stimulated rearmament in Britain and France, and the western powers hoped to negotiate from strength in any future clashes.

Hardly was the dismemberment of Czechoslovakia completed when Hitler launched a comparable campaign based upon the German minorities in Poland. Understandably, he believed on the basis of past record that Britain and France would object but would acquiesce, and when the matter developed into a crisis, he did not hesitate to invade Poland on September 1, 1939. This time, however, Britain and France did not acquiesce, and two days later they declared war on Germany.

Polish resistance to the German attack was crushed in eighteen days as Hitler's armies employed a new type of campaign called the *blitzkrieg* (lightning war), a combination of air strikes at vital communication centers and deep penetration through enemy lines by armored columns; most strategists still thought in terms of the static operations of World War I, but the Germans had developed fast-moving mobile warfare. Under the terms of the nonaggression pact, Germany and the Soviet Union divided Poland between them, but otherwise nothing much happened during the winter of 1939–1940;

probably Hitler hoped, that confronted with his rapid victory in Poland and denied Russian support, Britain and France would negotiate. But no accommodation was achieved during the winter, and in April of 1940 Hitler's forces occupied Denmark and Norway, an important move that protected Germany's northern flank and assured access to Scandinavian iron ores. Then, in May, German armies crossed into Belgium, the Netherlands and Luxemburg and began the invasion of France.

In the face of German successes, Prime Minister Chamberlain resigned, and a British war cabinet was formed by Winston Churchill, while French resistance crumpled. German mechanized units slashed to the sea, dividing French forces and almost trapping the British expeditionary force at Dunkirk. Italy joined the war against France and Britain, and in late June, France surrendered. For all practical purposes, by mid-1940 fascist governments controlled the European continent from Russia to the English Channel and from Scandinavia to the Mediterranean. Given the acquiescence of Russia, based upon the nonaggression pact, and the nonintervention of the United States, based upon strong American isolationist sentiment, Britain was left to face the German onslaught alone. In the late summer the Battle of Britain began, a fierce struggle for control of the air on which hinged the feasibility of a German invasion, but the British air force maintained its superiority, and Britain survived.

The new hostilities in Europe were paralleled by rising tensions in east Asia and the Pacific. Fearing Japanese aggression, in the summer of 1940 the American government undertook a considerable expansion of naval strength aimed at creating a two ocean navy, and a few months later it inaugurated military conscription. Confirming the American concern, in September Japan occupied French Indo-China and concluded a Three Power Pact with Germany and Italy. Although the government of the United States still was not prepared to intervene militarily, its sympathies were obvious, and in March of 1941 it passed a Lend Lease Act that provided for the supply of arms and war materiel to Britain on credit. Japan's desire to be free for action in the Pacific and Stalin's concern that his agreements with Hitler would not endure resulted in a Russo-Japanese neutrality treaty in April, and by the summer of 1941 the stage was set for a vast expansion of hostilities.

Having failed to crush Britain, Hitler was eager for a successful campaign, and he distrusted Stalin; at the same time, Japan was controlled by a military government and was aggressively resentful of years of discrimination and humiliation by the west. The war exploded to a global scale when the Germans invaded Russia on June 22, the Japanese attacked American and British positions in southeast Asia and the Pacific on December 7, and Germany and Italy declared war upon the United States on December 8. The fury of the onslaught, combined with growing evidence of German atrocities against captured westerners and German genocidal policies against the Poles, Russians and especially Jews, added an ugly racist note to the struggle, and popular commitment to total war developed rapidly.

In early 1942 the British-French-American-Russian position was grim. German armies had penetrated deeply into Russia and were threatening to take her most important western cities, while another German force had slashed through north Africa and seemed about to overrun the British position in Egypt, which would open the way to the middle eastern oil fields. The Japanese had swept into southeast Asia, taking the Philippines, Indonesia, Malaya and Burma, and they appeared to threaten Australia and India, while at the same time their seizure of Pacific islands caused concern for Hawaii. During 1942, however, the allied position stabilized. Two American fleet actions in May and June, the Battle of the Coral Sea and the Battle of Midway, halted the Japanese advances toward Australia and Hawaii; in late summer the British stopped the German drive in north Africa at El Alamein and began a counteroffensive; and in the winter Russian defenses stiffened, and the Germans were held before Stalingrad. From early 1943 onward, the allied position continued to improve as the enormous productive capacities of the allies, particularly the United States, began to outstrip the capabilities of the Axis countries. The Russians launched a winter counteroffensive that pushed the Germans back on all fronts, and in the first three months of 1943 the Germans lost a half million men. In February of the same year the Battle of Guadalcanal broke Japanese naval air power, securing allied possession of the Solomon Islands and beginning the Japanese retreat. In May Axis resistance in north Africa ended, and in July allied forces invaded Sicily. The direction of the war was becoming clear, though there were still two years of hard fighting ahead before the Germans surrendered in May of 1945 and the Japanese followed suit in August.

The nature of the peace settlement intended by the allied powers, assuming they were victorious, was outlined at several wartime conferences. As early as August of 1941, before the United States was even in the war officially, President Roosevelt and Prime Minister Churchill had conferred and had issued a statement of peace aims called the Atlantic Charter, essentially a repudiation of territorial ambitions by the great powers, an endorsement of freely chosen self-government everywhere and an expression of hope for international cooperation. Early in 1943 at another meeting in Casablanca, they determined to prosecute the war until their enemies were forced to unconditional surrender. Then, through 1943 and 1944 representatives of the allied powers created a Relief and Rehabilitation Administration, an Organization for Educational and Cultural Reconstruction, an International Monetary Fund and an International Bank for Reconstruction and Development, all agencies intended to promote postwar recovery. The Big Three— Churchill, Roosevelt and Stalin—met at Tehran in the winter of 1943–1944, at Yalta early in 1945 and at Potsdam in July of 1945 (at the latter conference President Truman replaced Roosevelt who had died in April); at these meetings they coordinated their military operations, endorsed the idea of a new postwar international organization to maintain the peace and determined upon occupation and close control of their enemies to assure demilitarization, denazification and trial of war criminals. A formal organization to achieve these aims was founded officially in October of 1945, when a draft charter for a United Nations Organization was accepted by more than two dozen participating nations.

To some extent these peace aims represented an understanding of basic weaknesses in the treaties of 1919, and to some extent they were reactions to immediate problems. The principles of the Atlantic Charter illustrated a desire to avoid repetition of the imperial ambitions and the minority problems that the Versailles Peace had left unresolved. The decision to demand unconditional surrender probably reflected reaction to the stab in the back legend as much as contemporary wartime hatreds. The intention to try war criminals likely was a response to mounting evidence of shocking atrocities, but provisions for occupation, reeducation and restructuring of social institutions showed some understanding of the contradictory nature of the 1919 treaties which had removed weapons from the defeated but left them the kind of leadership and economic organization that made remilitarization relatively easy. Finally, the creation of agencies to aid reconstruction indicated recognition of the fact that political stability depended in large part upon economic recovery.

On the other hand the victors of 1945 proved no more successful than their predecessors of 1815 or 1918 in grappling with significant new problems resulting from the war, and they showed equal reluctance to accept the fact that serious issues could divide the coalition quickly once the common goal of victory had been attained. Among the many problems of the postwar world, three in particular were difficult for the peacemakers to recognize and accept: the diminished importance of the European great powers due to the military maturation of the two superpowers, the U.S. and the U.S.S.R.; the development of non-European peoples to a point where they no longer would accept peacefully European imperial domination; and rapid emergence of fundamental conflicts of interest between the U.S.S.R. and the west.

The French armies had been crushed early in the war, and the only thing that saved France from depending totally upon the allies for liberation was that two groups of Frenchmen refused to accept defeat, a resistance movement within France largely led by the Communist Party and a determined band of exiles called the Free French led by General Charles De Gaulle. At the end of the war, France's economy was chaotic, her industry and communications had been damaged badly by military operations and these two rival groups struggled for political control, each claiming to have been the major French element in the allied victory. In such condition, France was unable to resume her former international role smoothly.

Britain had escaped defeat and occupation, but she had suffered German bombing, her economy was staggering under the load of wartime expenditure and her domestic politics were rather turbulent as postwar elections swept the Labour Party to power and it embarked upon rapid nationalization of industry. Germany was a defeated and bombed-out ruin, divided into allied occupation zones; and though Italy had escaped harsh terms by repudiating Mussolini in the summer of 1943, it was war-torn, economically ruined and politically impotent. Behind the facade of the wartime alliance and the United Nations Organization, the old global preponderance of Europe had been broken, and at the end of the war there were two great powers economically and militarily, the U.S. and the U.S.S.R.

Moreover, the war had transformed fundamentally the nature of Europe's relationship to non-European peoples. Hard-pressed by the Axis, the western Europeans had appealed for support and help from their colonial peoples as never before, making them active partners rather than subject populations. The Free French in particular had relied upon France's African colonies, though to a greater or lesser degree the British, Dutch, Belgians and Americans had done the same thing. In Africa, the Pacific and southeast Asia the colonial powers had proved unable to defend their colonies during the early years of the war, undercutting their former prestige. Perhaps most significant of all, the Japanese had demonstrated the capacity of an Asian people to defeat westerners, and while they were unable to rally other Asian peoples to their own war aims, they had stimulated enormous national pride and confidence among non-European populations all over the world through the spectacle of western armies in retreat and western soldiers as prisoners. For both of these reasons, when the war ended many colonial peoples were unwilling to accept passively the reestablishment of their former colonial status.

Finally, the attempt to work out the details of the peace settlements outlined at wartime conferences quickly illustrated that the distrust and latent hostility between the U.S.S.R. and the west had not disappeared during the war. Even while they were fighting as allies there had been serious misunderstandings between them, as when Stalin wanted the westerners to open a second front in Europe long before the actual invasion of Normandy, to draw some of the pressure off Russia's armies, but the western governments felt that the estimated casualties would be higher than they could bear; and if the westerners underestimated the severity of Russia's suffering, so also the Russians, working in a different social and political context, misunderstood western hesitation and thought the western powers wanted the U.S.S.R. to be exhausted before the ultimate victory. Thus, the specter of the old struggle between socialist and capitalist never disappeared entirely, even when they were fighting in a common cause, and after the war it became more pronounced.

The Soviets, like their imperial predecessors, were very conscious of their long and indefensible frontiers and were eager to maintain a buffer of friendly or subservient states along them. Consequently, after the collapse of Germany, a divisive issue arose quickly between Russia and her western allies concerning the governments to be recognized in Poland, Czechoslovakia, Hungary and other east European areas liberated by the repulse of Axis forces. On the one hand, there were governments in exile in London, generally procapitalist and prowestern, claiming authority over liberated areas; on the other, people's governments, generally communist dominated and pro-Russian, arose out of resistance movements. Where Russian armies were responsible for the German retreat, the Russians tended to hand authority to people's governments, while in areas liberated by the west, governments in exile were restored. Since Russia had declared war on Japan in August of 1945, a comparable situation existed in east Asia with regard to Manchuria. And where the surrender agreements provided for joint occupation, as in Germany, Austria and Korea, or left an unstable political situation with the competing influence of the victorious powers undetermined, as in Greece, Turkey, China and the colonial areas of southeast Asia, conflict arose almost immediately. Despite wartime conferences and the establishment of the United Nations, allied cooperation broke down, and a new polarization quickly became apparent, a polarization in which the once dominant European powers played only a secondary role.

Epilogue

Brave New Worlds

The superpower rivalry that emerged from World War II soon divided the world into armed camps again, and when civil wars broke out in Greece and Turkey in 1947, the United States supported conservative postwar governments while the U.S.S.R. supported communist insurgents. To organize this support several western governments agreed to a European Recovery Program financed by the U.S. (the Marshall Plan), and the Soviet Union and a number of east European states set up the Communist Information Bureau (Cominform). Generally the western powers made some progress: the communist rebellions were crushed in Greece and Turkey; nationalist and anti-Russian elements were so encouraged in Yugoslavia that in 1948 that country was expelled from the Cominform, though its government remained nominally communist; and in Italy and France liberal-democratic governments were reinforced against the threat of communist electoral victories.

In subsequent years the dichotomy between east and west was institutionalized further. In April of 1949 the North Atlantic Treaty was signed, a defensive arrangement within the Atlantic community (later extended) which provided for mutual assistance, especially American support against aggression, and for military integration in an American dominated alliance; on the other side of the earth a comparable arrangement was attempted in 1954 by a Southeast Asia

Treaty, but most Asian nations refused to participate, so the treaty's chief effect was to rally colonial powers around the United States. At the same time, the Soviet Union was tightening its ties with supporters and client states; in 1950 it signed an alliance with the new communist government of China, and in 1955 the Warsaw Pact provided for military bases and the integration of east European forces under the U.S.S.R. in much the same manner as the North Atlantic Treaty had integrated western European forces under the U.S. Thus, the Soviet Union and the United States divided over the shaping of the postwar world, and each rapidly developed a galaxy of satellite states.

The dispute between the superpowers slowly intruded itself upon the independence struggle of colonial peoples. Agitation in the Indian subcontinent, mostly in the guise of nonviolent demonstrations led by Mahatma Ghandi, led to a British concession of independence to both India and Pakistan so quickly (August of 1947) that the movement did not become an issue in the superpower rivalry, though there was much bloodshed between Hindus and Moslems. Burma followed the same course and was granted independence in January of 1948, but in this case a communist rebellion contested the authority of the newly established government, and fighting on a large scale continued into 1950, never dying out altogether. By contrast, when Indonesian leaders proclaimed a republic two days after Japan's surrender in August of 1945, the Dutch government refused to accept this declaration of independence, and with British support it soon found itself engaged in open hostilities against a people's army. A full-scale civil war then ensued until the end of 1949, despite U.N. efforts at mediation; finally the Netherlands had to accept Indonesian independence, and in the course of the war the independence movement showed more and more communist influence while the western powers showed themselves committed to the colonial status quo.

By 1948 a comparable situation had developed in Malaya where the communists had espoused the nationalist cause, and the British found themselves in the unfortunate position of apparently defending continued colonial domination; in this instance, however, effective British military action combined with political concessions and astute manipulation of local racial tensions managed to achieve compromise leading to eventual friendly independence rather than surrender of the country to pro-communist insurgents.

In Indochina another nationalist movement proclaimed independence immediately after the Japanese surrender in 1945, and again there was conflict. The French were willing to grant the new government limited autonomy, but fighting broke out as the Indochinese sought more extensive independence, and again the communists adopted the nationalist cause while the west rallied to France. In 1950 the west recognized the pro-French states of Viet Nam, Laos and Cambodia, while communist states recognized the insurgent Viet Minh, and with foreign aid the fighting intensified. The Viet Minh's capture of the French position at Dien Bien Phu in 1954 finally forced the French to admit defeat in Viet Nam, and the north was surrendered to the Viet Minh while a prowestern independent government was established in the south of the divided country.

Indisputably, however, the great event in Asia was the revolution in China. As far back as the 1920s the Chinese Communists had made a serious bid to dominate the government, and though Chiang Kai-shek had defeated them, they had not been destroyed. During World War II they won considerable prestige in China for their vigorous resistance to the Japanese, and after the war they were strengthened when the Russians made certain that large supplies of captured Japanese weapons fell to them rather than to the Nationalist government. Chiang Kai-shek and his Kuomintang Party were in a difficult position. Nationalist forces had achieved no great success in the struggle with the Japanese; the Nationalist government had become riddled with corruption, and, confined to inland areas where it was dependent upon the conservative country gentry, it had found no solution to China's single most pressing problem, land reform. Thus, in the postwar era the communists made rapid progress, for they enjoyed a good war record, were well armed with captured Japanese equipment and were willing to tackle the land redistribution problem by shooting landlords. In the latter part of 1949 surviving Nationalists withdrew from the mainland to the island of

Taiwan, and in the now clearly established division between Soviet and American blocs, China passed under the control of a government sympathetic to the Soviet bloc.

By the end of 1949 the Soviet Union was surrounded by a band of satellite or sympathetic states on most of its frontiers, ironically proclaiming itself anti-imperialist while building a more extensive empire than ever the czars had managed, and it had caused serious problems for the westerners elsewhere. On the other hand, the western powers had checked the growth of Soviet influence in western Europe and had defeated Soviet supported communist uprisings in the Balkans and in parts of southeast Asia, though they had shown themselves curiously ineffective in the propaganda war. Both powers practiced the same policies, and both experienced limited successes and some failures, but in the non-European world the Soviet Union managed to present itself as opposing colonialism and favoring national independence while the United States appeared as the supporter of colonialism and the defender of dictators.

In this growing superpower rivalry there had been many small clashes as the U.S. and the U.S.S.R. supported opposing forces in revolutions and colonial wars, and finally a major confrontation occurred in Korea in mid-1950. Since the end of the nineteenth century Korea had been dominated by Japan, so at the end of World War II it was regarded as a liberated nation; in 1945 the allies arranged that the U.S. should occupy the south and the U.S.S.R. should occupy the north until elections could be held to establish a unified democratic government. Deteriorating relations between the superpowers in the late 1940s precluded agreement on the conditions for such elections, and two separate regimes developed on a *de facto* basis, each committed to the policy of its superpower patron.

After the Japanese surrender in 1945 the U.S. army had been demobilized so quickly that American military potential practically was destroyed except for the massive retaliation implicit in the possession of the atom bomb, but extensive American economic aid had proved effective in countering Soviet probes except in China, where special conditions prevailed. By about 1950, however, the U.S. bloc clearly was on the defensive all around the world, with the U.S.S.R. probing for weaknesses in the defense, and in mid-1950, seeking to exploit this initiative and American military weakness, the Soviets' North Korean client state attacked South Korea. The

U.S. promptly committed troops to the defense of its client, and since the occupation zones were part of a United Nations arrangement, the U.N. Security Council endorsed this action and called for support from member states.

After serious reverses early in the war, by October of 1950 U.N. forces were approaching the Manchurian border, and at this point occurred one of the most significant developments of the early post-World War II period. Whether because the Russians were unwilling to risk further commitment or because the Chinese felt their security jeopardized is unknown, but for whatever reasons, Chinese forces intervened, indicating the emergence of a second force within the communist world. Chinese intervention forced a retreat of U.N. forces, and by late November the conflict had stabilized along the old line of demarcation between north and south, where the war finally ended after another two and a half years of desultory fighting.

The Korean War showed that the U.S. was willing to undertake military as well as economic action to defend its sphere of influence and enforce its policy of containment of the Soviet Union. It also showed that the U.S.S.R. set limits to its expansive ambitions and would stop short of superpower war that might involve atomic weapons. And it demonstrated that China was not willing to accept Russian tutelage but intended to assert a great power role herself.

The 1950s and 1960s showed three main themes. First, colonial independence movements, such as had broken out in south Asia in the 1940s, intensified and spread, and comparable racial conflict developed beyond colonial areas as nonwhite peoples became more self-conscious. Secondly, while the U.S. and the U.S.S.R. remained the prime movers of international affairs, schismatic movements appeared within both blocs and many new nations refused alignment with either of the superpowers. Finally, while the U.S. and the U.S.S.R. continued to support opposing sides in many conflicts, peaceful coexistence became the keynote of their direct competition, channeling some of their rivalry into nonmilitary ventures.

In the Middle East as well as in south Asia, World War II diminished the stature of the colonial powers and stimulated nationalistic aspirations. One of the most bitter problems of the postwar world arose in Palestine, where Jewish nationalists were seeking to reestablish a Jewish homeland in an area claimed by Arab nationalists. The British, who had held the area in trust since the first world war, were regarded with intense hostility by extremists on both sides and were subjected to terrorist attacks, with the result that in 1948 they withdrew from Palestine, leaving the Jews and Arabs to fight it out. The Jews maintained themselves and succeeded in establishing the small state of Israel, while Arab forces tended to consolidate behind Egypt, led by Gamal Abdel Nasser, the foremost exponent of surging Arab nationalism. No compromise could be achieved, and irregular skirmishing has continued ever since, occasionally erupting into full-scale military operations which the Jews have dominated consistently. Inevitably such a quarrel, casting a shadow over the whole eastern Mediterranean and the Middle Eastern oil fields, has attracted superpower interest, and while both the U.S. and the U.S.S.R. have seemed eager to prevent the conflict from spreading, both have supplied economic aid and military equipment, the U.S. to Israel and the U.S.S.R. to the Arab states.

In Africa anticolonial and nationalist sentiment showed itself at first in the formation of secret societies and in outbreaks of terrorism, but it was not until the mid-1950s that nationalist forces became strong enough to force the colonial powers to withdraw. Then in a decade almost all of the continent was freed. The experience of these newly independent states has not been tranquil, for frequently the withdrawal of European authority has been followed by economic chaos and tribal warfare, but former colonial peoples appear willing to pay this price for independence. At the southern end of the continent, the new black nationalism created special problems as South Africa was independent and Rhodesia was moving toward independence, but both states were dominated by longsettled white minorities. Generally the reaction of these white governments has been repression, and while explosive tensions build, no solutions have appeared.

After the French withdrawal from Indochina in the mid-1950s, the government of South Viet Nam continued to be insecure as it was threatened by the expansionist ambitions of its northern neighbor and was unable to win broad popular support within its own borders, while at the same time insurgent activities intensified in Laos and Cambodia. To counter the potent combination of nationalist aspirations and communist promises of radical social and economic reform, in the early 1960s the United States and its Southeast Asia Treaty allies began to give more and more military aid to the noncommunist governments of the area, finally making the fateful decision to commit American ground forces. An unfortunate pattern was developing in which nationalist independence movements could find support among the communist powers, while the western nations appeared willing to support any anticommunist element, however authoritarian and unpopular.

Anticolonial agitation had strong repercussions in the western hemisphere, too, for many Latin Americans felt that though nominally independent, their governments really were only clients of the United States; and, in any case, obvious American domination of economies in which the gulf between rich and poor was enormous encouraged anti-Americanism. A whole series of coups and insurgent movements developed, forcing some autocratic governments to programs of social reform and toppling others, but the only one of these movements that actually accomplished a far-reaching revolution was that of Fidel Castro in Cuba. Shortly after he succeeded in establishing a revolutionary government in the late 1950s, Castro confiscated foreign investments, inaugurated confiscatory taxation of Cuban fortunes and appealed to the communist bloc for support. As in the African anticolonial experience, the price was high in economic recession and extralegal repression of opposition, but Castro's anti-Americanism and his support of nationalism seem to have found broad popular support. This restiveness in the western hemisphere has been terribly disturbing to the United States, which has considered the Americas its special preserve since the promulgation of the Monroe Doctrine in 1823, the more so as most of the insurgent movements are strongly anti-American and some are avowedly communist, hoping to fight American influence through close ties with Russia or China as did Castro.

While worldwide patterns of economic exploitation and white domination have been breaking before the strength of anticolonial-ism, comparable quarrels between dominant and dominated peoples, often including virulent racial animosities, have disrupted the domestic tranquility of many nations old and new. Thus, there are riots against economically dominant minorities, such as Indians in Africa and Chinese in Indonesia; and the United States experiences ever more militant protest movements by economically dominated minorities seeking the elimination of poverty and the establishment of black equality, protests challenging the traditional domination of the American white protestant middle class so forcefully that violence threatens to shred the very fabric of American society.

But if the 1950s and 1960s witnessed a grim parade of colonial wars and racial violence, these two decades also saw an encouraging redevelopment of pluralism on the international scene, agitation for greater independence on the part of nations within the superpower blocs and the growth of a third world, mostly new nations, which have refused commitment in the superpower rivalry. Where the grasp for greater independence is too radical and causes superpower concern for basic defense, the result sometimes has been military intervention, such as the Soviet Union practiced in Hungary in 1956 and in Czechoslovakia in 1968 and the United States attempted in Cuba in the famous Bay of Pigs incident in 1961. But that the world no longer can be described in terms of two monolithic blocs is attested not only by the startlingly virulent Sino-Soviet dispute but also by the increasingly independent policies of Rumania and Albania within the communist orbit and of France and Japan within the American orbit, while the growing strength of former colonial nations offers grounds for hope that an increasingly pluralistic international society will continue to ameliorate the dangerous rivalry of the superpowers.

It is in this frame of reference that Europe's role seems to be cast for the immediate future. In 1945 a shattered western Europe was almost totally dependent upon the United States for military guarantees against Russian expansionism and for economic aid for reconstruction. After two decades of recovery, however, Europe appears unwilling to continue docilely to allow the U.S. to direct western policy and is demanding more equal partnership. Germany, dominated by aspirations for reunification, has been more willing than the other European powers to accept American leadership, and Britain, beset by continuing economic crises, has been in no position to protest very strongly. But France quickly recovered economic stability and national assertiveness, and under the conservative Gaullist regime her rejection of American domination was quite forceful during the decade subsequent to 1958.

Moreover, western Europe has grown ever more integrated through the common market, developing combined economic strength that approaches the level of "superpower." Thus far the common market has provided a strong popular sense of European internationalism by providing for the free movement of goods and people among member states without making much progress toward political union; but progress toward integrated economic and social development has been considerable, and on a much more friendly basis it carries the same implications for the western bloc nations as does the growth of Chinese assertiveness for eastern bloc nations—a diffusion of leadership and a reduction of the dangers implicit in domination of international affairs by only two intensely competitive superpowers.

Finally, there appears to be an encouraging tendency for the superpowers to subsume their rivalry into economic, scientific and diplomatic competition designed to win prestige and attract the support of the uncommitted nations. Thus in Africa, in India and in many other parts of the world the United States and the Soviet Union both offer economic and technical aid, each eager to demonstrate the superiority of her own sociopolitical system in meeting the rising levels of expectancy in developing nations. In space technology, the exploration of the moon and unmanned probes to Venus and Mars replace military confrontations. And in diplomacy the attempt to win popular approval has made the U.N., whatever its shortcomings as a supranational government, a forum of international debate, the focus of a war of words that is infinitely preferable to a war of atomic weapons.

No one can afford to be too optimistic, for the fearsome arsenals of the superpowers continue to grow, and nuclear technology is spreading. Brutal wars continue in Viet Nam, the Middle East and Africa, and cities burn in the United States, but in the past man has shown an encouraging capacity to survive his own follies. Whatever may be the future, however, it is certain that the European political hegemony has ended; and while European ideas such as nationalism, capitalism and communism continue to exercise global influence, the future rests largely in the hands of non-European peoples.

Suggestions for Further Reading

The following lists comprise paperback volumes, generally inexpensive, which amplify the brief sketches contained in this text. Naturally some works are applicable to more than one chapter, but they have been listed only once, with the chapters to which they seem most appropriate.

Chapter 1. **Preliminary Considerations**

Caesar, J. *The Conquest of Gaul,* trans. S. A. Handford. Harmondsworth, 1951.

Collingwood, R. G. *The Idea of History.* Oxford, 1946.

Geyl, P. *Debates with Historians.* New York, 1958.

Gooch, G. P. *History and Historians in the Nineteenth Century.* Boston, 1959.

Laistner, M. L. W. *The Greater Roman Historians.* Berkeley, 1947.

Muller, H. J. *The Uses of the Past.* New York, 1954.

Tacitus. *On Britain and Germany,* trans. H. Mattingly. Harmondsworth, 1960.

Tarn, W. W., and Griffith, C. T. *Hellenistic Civilization*, 3rd ed. London, 1952.

Tierney, B., et al., eds. *What Is History, Fact or Fancy?* New York, 1967.

Toynbee, A. *Greek Historical Thought.* New York, 1952.

Chapter 2. The Twilight of the Roman Empire

Chambers, M. *The Fall of Rome: Can It Be Explained?* New York, 1963.

Cowell, F. R. *Cicero and the Roman Republic.* Harmondsworth, 1956.

Dill, S. *Roman Society in the Last Century of the Western Empire*, 2nd rev. ed. New York, 1958.

Gibbon, E. *The Portable Gibbon: The Decline and Fall of the Roman Empire*, ed. D.A. Saunders. New York, 1952.

Havighurst, A. F., ed. *The Pirenne Thesis: Analysis, Criticism and Revision.* Boston, 1958.

Lot, F. *The End of the Ancient World and the Beginnings of the Middle Ages.* London, 1931.

Mattingly, H. *Roman Imperial Civilization.* London, 1957.

Pirenne, H. *Mohammed and Charlemagne.* New York, 1939.

Taylor, L. R. *Party Politics in the Age of Caesar.* Berkeley, 1949.

Wheeler, M. *Rome Beyond the Imperial Frontiers.* Harmondsworth, 1955.

Chapter 3. The Heirs of Rome

Cochrane, C. N. *Christianity and Classical Culture.* New York, 1944.

Dawson, C. *The Making of Europe.* London, 1932.

Dill, S. *Roman Society in Gaul in the Merovingian Age.* London, 1926.

Gregory of Tours, *The History of the Franks,* trans. E. Bréhaut. New York, 1968.

Lewis, A. R. *Emerging Medieval Europe, A.D. 400–1000.* New York, 1967.

Runciman, S. *Byzantine Civilization.* London, 1933.
Van der Meer, F. *Augustine the Bishop: Church and Society at the Dawn of the Middle Ages.* London, 1961.
Vryonis, S. *Byzantium and Europe.* New York, 1967.
Wallace-Hadrill, M. *The Barbarian West, 400–1000.* London, 1952.
———. *The Long-Haired Kings.* New York, 1962.

Chapter 4. Early Carolingian Europe

Andrae, Tor J. E. *Mohammed, the Man and His Faith.* London, 1936.
Brentano, R. *The Early Middle Ages, 500–1000.* New York, 1964.
Easton, S. C. and H. Wieruszowski. *The Era of Charlemagne.* New York, 1961.
Einhard. *The Life of Charlemagne.* Ann Arbor, 1960.
Fichtenau, H. *The Carolingian Empire.* Oxford, 1957.
Ganshof, F. L. *Feudalism.* London, 1952.
Latouche, R. *Birth of Western Economy.* New York, 1960.
Rand, E. K. *Founders of the Middle Ages.* Cambridge, 1928.
Stephenson, C. *Medieval Feudalism.* Ithaca, 1942.
Strayer, J. R., ed. *Feudalism.* Princeton, 1965.

Chapter 5. A Time of Trial

Bede. *A History of the English Church and People,* trans. J. Sherley-Price. Harmondsworth, 1955.
Brøndsted, J. *The Vikings.* Harmondsworth, 1960.
Daniel-Rops, H. *The Church and the Dark Ages,* 2 vols. New York, 1960.
Duckett, E. *The Wandering Saints of the Early Middle Ages.* New York, 1959.
Hoyt, R. S., ed. *Feudal Institutions: Cause or Consequence of Decentralization?* New York, 1961.
Lewis, B., *The Arabs in History,* 4th ed. London, 1958.
Lopez, R. S., ed. *The Tenth Century: How Dark the Dark Ages?* New York, 1965.

Magnusson, M., and Palsson, H., eds. *The Vinland Sagas.* Harmondsworth, 1965.

Whitelock, D. *The Beginnings of English Society.* Harmondsworth, 1952.

———, et al. *The Norman Conquest: Its Setting and Impact.* London, 1966.

Chapter 6. The Birth of Feudal Monarchy

Barraclough, G. *The Origins of Modern Germany.* New York, 1948.

Fawtier, R. *The Capetian Kings of France.* London, 1960.

Haskins, C. H. *The Normans in European History.* Boston, 1915.

Herzstein, R. E. *The Holy Roman Empire in the Middle Ages: Universal State or German Catastrophe?* Boston, 1966.

Kelley, A. *Eleanor of Aquitaine.* Cambridge, 1950.

Lyon, B. *The Middle Ages in Recent Historical Thought, Selected Topics,* 2nd ed. Washington, 1965.

Painter, S. *The Rise of the Feudal Monarchies.* Ithaca, 1951.

Petit-Dutaillis, C. *The Feudal Monarchy in France and England.* London, 1936.

Stenton, D. M. *English Society in the Early Middle Ages.* Harmondsworth, 1952.

Tellenbach, G. *Church, State and Christian Society at the Time of the Investiture Controversy.* New York, 1970.

Chapter 7. Merchants, Money and Social Changes

Adelson, H. L. *Medieval Commerce.* Princeton, 1962.

Bennett, H. S. *Life on the English Manor: A Study of Peasant Conditions, 1150–1400.* Cambridge, 1948.

Homans, G. C. *English Villagers of the Thirteenth Century.* Cambridge, Mass., 1941.

Luchaire, A. *Social France at the Time of Philip Augustus.* New York, 1912.

Mundy, J. H., and P. Riesenberg, *The Medieval Town.* Princeton, 1958.

Pirenne, H. *Economic and Social History of Medieval Europe.* New York, 1937.

———. *Medieval Cities.* Princeton, 1925.

Power, E. *Medieval People.* London, 1924.

Saalman, H. *Medieval Cities.* New York, 1970.

Schevill, F. *Siena, the History of a Medieval Commune.* New York, 1909.

Chapter 8. The Apogee of Medieval Christianity

Adams, H. *Mont-Saint-Michel and Chartres.* Boston, 1933.

Brundage, J. A. *The Crusades, Motives and Achievements.* Boston, 1964.

Copleston, F. C. *Medieval Philosophy.* London, 1952.

Haskins, C. H. *The Renaissance of the Twelfth Century.* Cambridge, Mass., 1927.

———. *The Rise of the Universities.* New York, 1923.

Joinville, J. de, and Villehardouin, G. de. *Memoirs of the Crusades,* trans. Sir F. T. Marzials. New York, 1958.

Kern, F. *Kingship and Law in the Middle Ages.* New York, 1970.

Leff, G. *Medieval Thought.* Harmondsworth, 1958.

Southern, R. W. *The Making of the Middle Ages.* New Haven, 1953.

Williams, S. *The Gregorian Epoch: Reformation, Revolution, Reaction?* Boston, 1964.

Chapter 9. Challenges and Conflict in Later Medieval Society

Bryce, J. *The Holy Roman Empire.* London, 1904.

Cheyney, E. P. *The Dawn of a New Era, 1250–1453.* New York, 1956.

Huizinga, J. *The Waning of the Middle Ages.* New York, 1956.

Lea, H. C. *A History of the Inquisition of the Middle Ages,* 3 vols. New York, 1922.

Myers, A. R. *England in the Late Middle Ages.* Harmondsworth, 1952.

Otto of Freising. *Deeds of Frederick Barbarossa*. New York, 1953.

Powell, J. M. *Innocent III: Vicar of Christ or Lord of the World?* Boston, 1963.

Runciman, S. *The Medieval Manichee*. New York, 1961.

———. *The Sicilian Vespers: A History of the Mediterranean World in the Later Thirteenth Century*. Cambridge, 1958.

Tierney, B. *The Crisis of Church and State, 1050–1300*. New York, 1964.

Chapter 10. The Hundred Years War

Coulton, G. G. *Medieval Panorama: The English Scene from Conquest to Reformation*. New York, 1955.

Figgis, J. *Studies in Political Thought from Gerson to Grotius*. Cambridge, 1931.

Froissart, J. *Chronicles of England, France, Spain and the Adjoining Countries*. New York, 1961.

Jacob, E. F. *Henry V and the Invasion of France*. London, 1947.

Jewkes, W., and J. B. Landfield, *Joan of Arc*. New York, 1964.

Michelet, J. *Joan of Arc*. Ann Arbor, 1957.

Oman, C. *The Art of War in the Middle Ages*. Utica, 1953.

Painter, S. *French Chivalry*. Ithaca, 1957.

Perroy, E. *The Hundred Years War*. New York, 1951.

Pollard, A. F. *The Evolution of Parliament*, 2nd ed. London, 1926.

Chapter 11. The Disintegration of Medieval Europe

Cipolla, C. M. *Guns, Sails and Empires*. London, 1965.

Elton, G. R. *The Tudor Revolution in Government*. Cambridge, 1953.

Gilmore, M. P. *The World of Humanism, 1453–1517*. New York, 1952.

Kendall, P. M. *The Yorkist Age: Daily Life During the War of Roses*. New York, 1962.

Machiavelli, N. *The History of Florence.* New York, 1960.

Morison, S. E. *Christopher Columbus: Mariner.* New York, 1955.

Parry, J. H. *The Establishment of the European Hegemony, 1415–1715.* London, 1949.

Penrose, Boies, *Travel and Discovery in the Renaissance, 1420–1620.* New York, 1962.

Runciman, S. *The Fall of Constantinople, 1453.* Cambridge, 1969.

Wood, C. T., ed. *Philip the Fair and Boniface VIII.* New York, 1967.

Chapter 12.   The Renaissance

Ady, C. M. *Lorenzo de' Medici and Renaissance Italy.* London, 1955.

Burckhardt, J. *The Civilization of the Renaissance in Italy.* New York, 1958.

Ferguson, W. K., et al. *The Renaissance, Six Essays.* New York, 1953.

Hay, D. *The Italian Renaissance in Its Historical Background.* Cambridge, 1961.

Helton, T., ed. *The Renaissance: A Reconsideration of the Theories and Interpretations of the Age.* Madison, 1961.

Kristeller, P. *Renaissance Thought.* New York, 1961.

Mattingly, G. *Renaissance Diplomacy.* Boston, 1955.

Schevill, F. *The Medici.* New York, 1949.

Sypher, W. *Four Stages of Renaissance Style.* Garden City, 1955.

Von Martin, A. *Sociology of the Renaissance.* New York, 1945.

Chapter 13.   Religious Reaction and Reform

Bainton, R. *Here I Stand: a Life of Martin Luther.* New York, 1955.

Bindoff, S. T. *Tudor England.* Harmondsworth, 1950.

Brandi, K. *Emperor Charles V.* New York, 1940.

Dickens, A. G. *Reformation and Society in Sixteenth Century Europe.* London, 1966.

Elton, G. R. *Reformation Europe, 1517–1559.* Cleveland, 1963.

Hillerbrand, H. J. *Men and Ideas in the Sixteenth Century.* Chicago, 1969.

Hughes, P. *A Popular History of the Reformation.* Garden City, 1957.

Mattingly, G. *Catherine of Aragon.* Boston, 1941.

Tawney, R. H. *Religion and the Rise of Capitalism.* New York, 1955.

Weber, M. *The Protestant Ethic and the Spirit of Capitalism.* New York, 1948.

Chapter 14.   Habsburg Hegemony

Brodrick, J. *The Origin of the Jesuits.* London, 1940.

Davis, J. C., ed. *Pursuit of Power: Venetian Ambassadors' Reports on Turkey, France and Spain in the Age of Philip II, 1560–1600.* New York, 1970.

Elliott, J. H. *Imperial Spain, 1469–1716.* London, 1963.

Franklin, J. H., ed. *Constitutionalism and Resistance in the Sixteenth Century: Three Treatises by Hotman, Beza and Mornay.* New York, 1969.

Mattingly, G. *The Armada.* Boston, 1959.

Neale, J. E. *The Age of Catherine de Medici.* London, 1943.

———. *Queen Elizabeth I.* London, 1957.

Roth, C. *The Spanish Inquisition.* New York, 1964.

Trevor-Davies, R. *The Golden Century of Spain, 1501–1621.* London, 1937.

Williamson, J. A. *Sir Francis Drake.* London, 1951.

Chapter 15.   The Scientific Revolution

Andrade, E. N. *Isaac Newton.* London, 1954.

Butterfield, H. *The Origins of Modern Science,* rev. ed. New York, 1957.

Caspar, M. *Kepler.* London, 1959.

Farrington, B. *Francis Bacon: Philosopher of the New Science.* New York, 1961.

Fermi, L. *Galileo and the Scientific Revolution.* New York, 1961.

Hall, A. R. *From Galileo to Newton, 1630–1730.* New York, 1963.

———. *The Scientific Revolution, 1500–1800,* 2nd ed. Boston, 1962.

Koyré, A. *From the Closed World to the Infinite Universe.* New York, 1957.

Kuhn, T. S. *The Copernican Revolution.* Cambridge, Mass., 1956.

Tillyard, E. M. W. *The Elizabethan World Picture.* London, 1961.

Chapter 16.   The Rise of the National State

Aston, T., ed. *Crisis in Europe, 1560–1660.* London, 1965.

Barbour, V. *Capitalism in Amsterdam in the Seventeenth Century.* Baltimore, 1950.

Cronin, V. *Louis XIV.* London, 1969.

Friedrich, C. J. *The Age of the Baroque, 1610–1660.* New York, 1952.

Jones, J. R. *Britain and Europe in the Seventeenth Century.* London, 1966.

Nussbaum, F. L. *The Triumph of Science and Reason, 1660–1685.* New York, 1953.

Steinberg, S. H. *The Thirty Years' War.* London, 1966.

Wedgwood, C. V. *Richelieu and the French Monarchy.* New York, 1949.

———. *The Thirty Years' War.* London, 1938.

Willson, D. H. *King James VI and I.* London, 1956.

Chapter 17.   The Birth of the Balance of Power

Bruford, W. H. *Germany in the Eighteenth Century.* Cambridge, 1935.

Cobban, A. *History of Modern France,* 2nd ed., vol. 1. Baltimore, 1962.

Dorn, W. L. *Competition for Empire, 1740–1763.* New York, 1940.

Fay, S. B., and K. Epstein, *The Rise of Brandenburg-Prussia to 1786.* New York, 1964.

Klyuchevsky, V. *Peter the Great.* New York, 1959.

Moote, A. L. *The Seventeenth Century.* Lexington, Mass., 1970.

Plumb, J. H. *England in the Eighteenth Century.* Harmondsworth, 1950.

Roberts, P. *The Quest for Security, 1715–1740.* New York, 1947.

Wolf, J. B. *The Emergence of the Great Powers, 1685–1715.* New York, 1951.

Wolf, J. B. *Toward a European Balance of Power.* Chicago, 1970.

Chapter 18. Man, God and Reason

Barber, E. *The Bourgeoisie in Eighteenth Century France.* Princeton, 1955.

Becker, C. *The Heavenly City of the Eighteenth Century Philosophers.* New Haven, 1932.

Cassirer, E. *The Philosophy of the Enlightenment.* Boston, 1951.

Figgis, J. *The Divine Right of Kings,* 2nd ed. Cambridge, 1922.

Ford, F. *Robe and Sword: the Regrouping of the French Aristocracy after Louis XIV.* Cambridge, Mass., 1953.

Hazard, P. *The European Mind, 1680–1715.* London, 1953.

———. *European Thought in the Eighteenth Century.* New Haven, 1954.

Lanson, G. *Voltaire.* New York, 1966.

Martin, K. *French Liberal Thought in the Eighteenth Century,* 2nd ed. London, 1954.

Talmon, J. L. *The Origins of Totalitarian Democracy.* New York, 1961.

Chapter 19. A Harvest of Violence

Beik, P. H., ed. *The French Revolution.* New York, 1970.

Brinton, C. *A Decade of Revolution, 1789–1799.* New York, 1934.

Brunn, G. *Europe and the French Imperium, 1799–1814.* New York, 1938.

Gershoy, L. *From Despotism to Revolution, 1763–1789.* New York, 1944.

Geyl, P. *Napoleon: For and Against.* New Haven, 1949.

Lefebvre, G. *The Coming of the French Revolution, 1789.* Princeton, 1947.

Palmer, R. R. *Twelve Who Ruled.* Princeton, 1941.

Rudé, G. *The Crowd in History, 1730–1848.* New York, 1964.

Rudé, G. *Revolutionary Europe, 1783–1815.* Cleveland, 1964.

Tocqueville, A. de. *The Old Regime and the French Revolution.* Garden City, 1955.

Chapter 20.   **Restoration and Reaction**

Artz, F. B. *Reaction and Revolution, 1815–1832.* New York, 1932.

De Ruggiero, G. *The History of European Liberalism.* New York, 1927.

Jelavich, B. *The Habsburg Empire in European Affairs, 1814–1918.* Chicago, 1969.

Kissinger, H. *A World Restored: Metternich, Castlereagh and the Problem of Peace, 1812–1822.* London, 1957.

Mael, W. H., ed. *The Reform Bill of 1832.* New York, 1967.

May, A. J. *The Age of Metternich, 1814–1848.* New York, 1966.

Mazour, A. G. *The First Russian Revolution, 1825.* Berkeley, 1937.

Nicolson, H. *The Congress of Vienna: a Study in Allied Unity.* New York, 1946.

Webster, C. K. *The Congress of Vienna, 1814–1815.* London, 1950.

Wolf, J. B. *France, 1815–1919.* New York, 1940.

Chapter 21.   **Industrialization and Its Consequences**

Ashton, T. S. *The Industrial Revolution, 1760–1830.* London, 1948.

Berlin, I. *Karl Marx*. New York, 1948.

Clapham, J. J. *The Economic Development of France and Germany, 1815–1914*. Cambridge, 1936.

Fasel, G. *Europe in Upheaval: the Revolutions of 1848*. Chicago, 1969.

George, M. D. *London Life in the Eighteenth Century*. New York, 1964.

Langer, W. L. *Political and Social Upheaval, 1832–1852*. New York, 1969.

Marcuse, H. *Reason and Revolution: Hegel and the Rise of Social Theory*. New York, 1941.

Mayo, E. *The Human Problems of an Industrial Civilization*. New York, 1933.

Robertson, P. *The Revolutions of 1848*. Princeton, 1952.

Young, G. M. *Victorian England*. Garden City, 1954.

Chapter 22. The Nation Deified

Delzell, C., ed. *The Unification of Italy, 1859–1861*. New York, 1964.

Gooch, B. D. *The Reign of Napoleon III*. Chicago, 1969.

Mosse, W. E. *Alexander II and the Modernization of Russia*. New York, 1958.

Shafer, B. C. *Nationalism: Myth and Reality*. New York, 1955.

Strachey, L. *Eminent Victorians*. Cape Town, 1947.

———. *Queen Victoria*. New York, 1921.

Taylor, A. J. P. *Bismarck: the Man and the Statesman*. New York, 1955.

Taylor, A. J. P. *The Habsburg Monarchy*. Harmondsworth, 1948.

Thompson, J. M. *Louis Napoleon and the Second Empire*. Oxford, 1954.

Williams, R. *Gaslight and Shadow: the World of Napoleon III*. New York, 1957.

Chapter 23. The New Europe

Barzun, J. *Darwin, Marx, Wagner*. Garden City, 1958.

Gay, P. *The Dilemma of Democratic Socialism: Eduard Bernstein's Challenge to Marx*. New York, 1952.

Hayes, C. J. H. *A Generation of Materialism, 1871–1900.* New York, 1941.

Himmelfarb, G. *Victorian Minds.* New York, 1970.

Irwin, W. *Apes, Angels and Victorians.* New York, 1955.

Schorske, C. E. *German Social Democracy, 1905–1917.* Cambridge, Mass., 1955.

Seton-Watson, H. *The Decline of Imperial Russia, 1855–1914.* London, 1952.

Thompson, D. *Democracy in France Since 1870.* New York, 1952.

Tuchman, B. W. *The Proud Tower.* New York, 1966.

Williams, R., ed. *The Commune of Paris, 1871.* New York, 1969

Chapter 24. Competition and Collapse

Fay, S. B. *The Origins of the World War,* 2 vols. New York, 1928.

Langer, W. L. *European Alliances and Alignments, 1871–1890.* New York, 1950.

Lenin, V. I. *Imperialism: the Highest Stage of Capitalism.* New York, 1939.

Massie, R. K. *Nicholas and Alexandra.* New York, 1967.

Northrop, F. S. C. *The Meeting of East and West.* New York, 1946.

Remak, J. *The Origins of World War I, 1871–1914.* New York, 1967.

Schumpeter, J. A. *Imperialism and Social Classes.* New York, 1955.

Tuchman, B. W. *The Guns of August.* New York, 1962.

Winks, R. W. *British Imperialism.* New York, 1963.

Wolfe, B. D. *Three Who Made a Revolution.* Boston, 1955.

Chapter 25. The Retreat of Liberal Democracy

Abel, T. F. *Why Hitler Came into Power.* New York, 1938.

Chamberlain, W. H. *The Russian Revolution, 1917–1921,* 2 vols. New York, 1935.

Deutscher, I. *Stalin.* New York, 1949.

Fischer, L. *The Life of Lenin.* New York, 1964.

Graves, R., and A. Hodge, *The Long Weekend: a Social History of Great Britain, 1918–1939.* New York, 1941.

Jaszi, O. *The Dissolution of the Habsburg Monarchy.* Chicago, 1929.

Seton-Watson, H. *Eastern Europe Between the Wars, 1918–1941.* New York, 1945.

Thomas, H. *The Spanish Civil War.* New York, 1961.

Wheeler-Bennett, J. W. *Brest-Litovsk, the Forgotten Peace, March 1918.* London, 1939.

Wolfers, A. *Britain and France between Two Wars.* New York, 1940.

Chapter 26. The End of the European Hegemony

Bullock, A. L. C. *Hitler, a Study in Tyranny.* New York, 1958.

Carr, E. H. *The Twenty Years' Crisis, 1919–1939.* London, 1939.

Churchill, Sir W. S. *The Second World War,* 6 vols. Boston, 1948–53.

Gilbert, F., and G. A. Craig, eds. *The Diplomats, 1919–1938.* Princeton, 1953.

Shirer, W. L. *The Rise and Fall of the Third Reich.* New York, 1959.

Snell, J. L. *Illusion and Necessity: the Diplomacy of Global War, 1939–1945.* Boston, 1963.

Taylor, A. J. P. *The Origins of the Second World War.* New York, 1961.

Waite, R. G. L., ed. *Hitler and Nazi Germany.* New York, 1965.

Wheeler-Bennett, J. W. *Munich: Prologue to Tragedy.* New York, 1948.

Wilmot, C. *The Struggle for Europe.* New York, 1952.

Epilogue Brave New Worlds

Feis, H. *The China Tangle.* Princeton, 1953.

Gatzke, H. *The Present in Perspective.* Chicago, 1965.

Kennan, G. F. *Realities of American Foreign Policy.* Princeton, 1954.

Luethy, H. *France Against Herself.* New York, 1955.

Roberts, H. L. *Russia and America.* New York, 1956.

Seton-Watson, H. *The East European Revolution.* London, 1956.

Snell, J. L., ed. *The Meaning of Yalta.* Baton Rouge, 1956.

Spear, T. G. P. *India, Pakistan and the West.* New York, 1952.

Staley, E. *The Future of Underdeveloped Countries.* London, 1954.

Werth, A. *France, 1940–1955.* New York, 1956.

Index

369

PRINTED IN U.S.A.

1806 Schoolcraft Mount F & B